# HANDICAPPED CHILDREN

# HANDICAPPED CHILDREN

by

## JOHN D. KERSHAW
M.D., M.R.C.P., F.F.C.M., D.P.H.

*Consultant, World Health Organisation.*
*Formerly M.O.H., Colchester, Divisional School M.O., North-East*
*Essex, Consultant Physician, Myland Hospital, Colchester, Chief,*
*Rehabilitation Unit, United Nations Secretariat.*

**THIRD EDITION**

WILLIAM HEINEMANN · MEDICAL BOOKS · LTD
LONDON

First published 1961
Second Edition 1966
Reprinted 1968
Third Edition 1973

by the same author
AN APPROACH TO SOCIAL MEDICINE

ISBN
0   433   18381   0

*To the memory of William Kershaw, 1872-1955,*
*and Christopher Kershaw, 1936-60, who, in their different ways,*
*served the handicapped with the true concern.*

PRINTED BY
WILLMER BROTHERS LIMITED
BIRKENHEAD

# Contents

# Preface to the Third Edition

The field of work for the handicapped is one of exceptional, perhaps even unique, rapidity of change and development. In some countries, happily, some disabilities which were common a decade ago are becoming rare, though none has vanished from the scene. No completely new ones have appeared to take their place, though the process by which medical science makes possible the survival of handicapped children who would formerly have died at or soon after birth continues to ensure that the total number of the handicapped shows little diminution. Advancing knowledge and the dissemination of that knowledge ensure that handicapping conditions are recognized more effectively and earlier. As the pressure on workers which was exercised by some of the more spectacular disabilities lessens it is becoming possible to give more attention to conditions which, though less grossly disabling, are none the less severely handicapping to their unfortunate victims.

Widening of outlook and better understanding are leading to new tactics and new techniques in approach to identifying the handicapped, in defining their disabilities and in providing better treatment, education and general care. No less important, experience is helping us to profit by our past errors. Perhaps the greatest advance of all is that the interdependence of all the disciplines involved is being increasingly appreciated and that the concept of team work is changing from a pious hope into an accepted reality.

So rapid is progress that most workers are suffering embarrassment when they re-read or hear quoted something which they may have written or said even five years ago. That is why this third edition differs considerably from the second, with more than a few radical alterations and many changes of emphasis. It has three new chapters. 'Living with Handicap' takes a more detailed look at the long-term social and emotional problems of the handicapped. 'Doctor and Parent' may be of use to the medical reader but I would hope that it would also help the non-medical reader to understand some of the doctor's particular problems and to help him in solving them. 'Specific Learning Disabilities' offers some comment on an aspect of the work which is still too little explored and understood but is now beginning to receive the serious attention it deserves. The chapter on 'Deafness' has been virtually re-written in the light of recent developments in knowledge and understanding.

For convenience of presentation I have, as in the previous editions, discussed the more important disabilities in separate chapters. This is not to be taken as an endorsement of the present administrative categorization of disabilities. Obviously, there must be some categorization and, no less obviously, the present one has considerable shortcomings, but no-one has yet been able to produce an ideal one and the devil one knows is better than the devil one does not know. One of the most important recent advances in approach has been the general realization that multiple disabilities are becoming the rule rather than the exception over most parts of the field and it is most improbable that the use of certain headings for chapters in one book will set its readers thinking again in terms of single disability. To quote from the last edition, 'while handicaps may be categorized, children must not!'

This edition appears at a critical time. In 1974 the structure of the health services is to be unified. We can hope at last for an integrated 'Child and Youth Health Service' with opportunities for better understanding and collaboration between the various branches of medicine which are concerned with handicapped children. On the other hand, the social services have already been separated from the medical services within the local authorities and 1974 will take the medical services into an entirely different administrative system from that which is responsible for education and social service provision. Is this to bring chaos or challenge? Whether people work together is determined in the last resort less by administrative structures than by the people themselves. I have seen enough of work for the handicapped in a diversity of countries to convince me that it provides a cause which can bring together as wide range of people of goodwill in spite of administrative barriers. Indeed—and especially where children are concerned—I believe that the presence of those barriers can actually provide an extra incentive to cooperation. It is with these considerations in mind that I have, in this edition, stressed even more than in its predecessors the importance of looking at the handicapped child as a person living in his family and in the community, with the right to live as full a life as his potential allows as a full member of mankind.

JANUARY 1973                                                    J.D.K.

## CHAPTER 1

# The Problem in Outline

The term 'handicapped child' is becoming established as standard usage and is probably the best for practical purposes. 'Disabled' as an adjective still clings tenaciously to its old place, especially where the adult is concerned, but its connotation of major, general or total impairment is regrettable and it would be better eliminated or at least restricted to the limited number of cases in which the victim cannot reasonably expect to lead a substantially normal life. The French term 'diminué' has its value in that it expresses literally the fact that the child's powers and abilities are reduced or restricted, but its meaning is too easily extended to the assumption that the child himself is a diminished person.

The Anglo-Saxon peoples have a natural habit of taking their metaphors and similes from sport but this does not impair the validity of the terms they use. A handicap is something which essentially encumbers the participant in a race. Life is a competitive business and, like the weight carried by a horse, the time penalty of the motor racer or the stroke penalty of the expert golfer, the motor, sensory, emotional or intellectual impairment of the handicapped person is something which holds him back in competition with other people. The handicap of the 'plus' golfer is significant only when he is playing golf against less skilled players. It ceases to operate when he is playing against equally skilled opponents—competing with his equals—and it is of no importance when he is playing bridge or engaging in his ordinary daily business. Precisely the same is true of the handicapped person. The blind man is at no disadvantage as compared with the blind or the cripple as compared with other cripples; their disabilities impede them only when they compete with the sighted in activities involving sight or with the physically sound in physical pursuits.

How, then, does handicap affect the handicapped?

It affects them in obtaining and carrying on gainful employment. Only rarely does it make them totally unemployable, but it restricts the range of employments open to them. The vast majority of handicapped people are capable of doing competent work in certain fields, so that the problem which faces those who would help them is to find the field which is open to them and to train them to make full use of their powers in that field.

It impedes them in the necessary activities of ordinary daily life. Again its effect is to restrict their range of competent activity, but while in employment these is a great deal of scope for making a selection from the things one can do best, there are some activities of daily living which are essential. One must do them—or have them done for one—and accept the discomfort, fatigue or embarrassment which may follow. One must work out one's own way of living, deciding what limitations to accept and what sacrifices to make, what daily routine is the least stressful, physically or emotionally. Helping the handicapped includes defining the range of the individual's powers, modifying his environment so that it does not overtax him, providing him with such appliances and apparatus as may be available to compensate for his defects and developing the power which he does possess so that they may in some degree compensate for those which he lacks.

It affects their relationships with other people. To possess a handicap is to be different from the majority. There is a deep need in human beings to be one with and of the community and anything which prevents one from doing the things which others do tends to isolate one. It may isolate in actual fact, as deafness cuts one off from that conversation which is the basic stuff of human intercourse, or it may isolate only indirectly by making the handicapped person shy of exposing his inadequacies in the company of normal people, by destroying confidence or by exaggerating self-consciousness.

It affects other people's relationships with them. Few people are entirely at ease in the presence of the handicapped. Some feel an acute revulsion, a natural, if exaggerated, manifestation of the herd instinct which rejects the imperfect as something unsocial. As is only to be expected, the revulsion is greater if the disability is accompanied by disfigurement or obvious deformity, but it can exist even if there is no evident deformity. No doubt this reaction is stimulated by the tradition in folk-lore and up-to date fiction that warped body and warped mind go together. Those who do not feel revulsion may feel aversion, or lesser manifestations down to perhaps a moderate degree of embarrassment, this last made more acute by doubt as to whether one should offer to help the handicapped person or should try to ignore the fact that he is otherwise than normal.

These consequences of handicap rarely occur singly and commonly combine to produce enhanced effects, for life is a whole and its parts cannot be arbitrarily separated. Perhaps this may be made clearer by the description of an actual individual case.

James was referred to the school medical officer at the age of thirteen as probably mentally subnormal, because of his failure to make any progress at school. An intelligence test showed that he was actually above average, with an intelligence quotient of 115. He had, however, had poliomyelitis at the age of six and had missed two years of schooling at a stage when he ought to have been learning the fundamentals of reading and arithmetic; when he went back to school he was two years behind his contemporaries and having missed essential steps in education he not only failed to catch up but was beginning to fall even further behind. Physically his recovery was good, but his right leg was permanently impaired and he wore a caliper. He was therefore unable to join other boys in normal play and when he reached the age at which boys begin organized cricket and football he was very definitely isolated.

Unable to compete either in work or in play, he became more and more withdrawn into himself and made no effort in school. His teachers lost patience with him and he retaliated by showing even less interest, and becoming surly and moody. At thirteen he hated his school, his teachers and his fellow-pupils and they, not unnaturally, hated him. He was already a confirmed misanthrope, and likely to grow worse rather than better. His home, though his parents and his brother and sister were well-intentioned enough, was not helping him. The brother and sister were both intelligent, both much older than he and both settling into careers after completing college courses. The parents, working-class with only elementary education, lacked the knowledge to appreciate what was happening. To the whole family he was, in fact, the crippled baby, to be protected and sympathized with, and the unintelligent, ineffectual one from whom nothing was to be expected.

It seemed obvious that three things were needed, a school where he could have individual attention, a change from the overprotective home and a period of life in competition with his equals—other cripples—rather than with normal children, so arrangements were made for him to go to a first-class boarding special school. Already at this stage the school medical officer appreciated that James needed education for a career and he visited the school to discuss the prospects. Like most such schools at that time it had four or five vocational training workshops. The nature of James's disability ruled out certain types of occupation but his intelligence was obviously worth cultivating and using, and it was decided to train him in the printing workshop for a career which offered good prospects for an intelligent boy.

He spent his Christmas and Easter holidays at school and came home for the first time after three terms away, transformed from a maladjusted, shrinking misanthrope into a charming, self-assured young man—it seemed as if a miracle had happened. School, school medical officer and parents were hugely delighted and their delight continued as James forged ahead. He entered his last year at school and the parents began to look for a post for him in the trade for which he was being trained. The school medical officer had tried to look ahead but had not been far-sighted enough. He had failed to realize that in those days—1939—printing was very much a 'closed shop' and that a youngster with no relatives in the trade and no influence was unlikely to find an opening. To retrieve his error he used his personal influence and eventually found the promise of a place for his protégé. The head of the firm was ready to help and all seemed well, but the workers themselves were the stumbling-block; the father of the printers' chapel announced that they were not prepared to accept a cripple into the shop and was unshakeable in his decision.

The field of search was expanded. James's father was prepared to give up his present work and move to another town if only a job for James could be found with any printer within a hundred miles, but the wider search was as fruitless as the narrow one. At sixteen James left school, trained for work in which he would undoubtedly do well but unemployable. He had been shown the promised land but was held back at the frontier.

The parents were still not defeated. They realized all their life's savings and bought a fish-and-chip business—a lucrative prospect in pre-war Lancashire—in which to install their son. The boy, whose courage was equal to the challenge, settled down to work in the shop and for a few weeks all looked well. But then Hitler invaded Poland, war began and there was a shortage of fish, a rationing of frying fats and, to complete the disaster, a potato famine. The shop closed down and James was again unemployed and the family without resources and with little hope. The school medical officer looked round again. Among his friends was the managing director of a local engineering works which was beginning to expand to meet the flow of government contracts. He told the managing director James's story, making it as eloquently pathetic as he could. The prospects for a cripple in engineering were limited, especially for a lad with no training in engineering work, but he was offered a post as assistant to a storekeeper, and James made his start. The good storekeeper needs intelligence, tact and personality. James had them, in the right measure, and in a surprisingly short time was a storekeeper in his own right. From then on he never looked back and by the time the war ended he was permanently established in work, a happy young man with a charming wife and the proud father of a thriving son.

James's story has been worth telling at some length because it brings out so many facets of the problem of the handicapped boy. It emphasizes the effects of the interruption of education which so often occurs when a disability requires prolonged hospital care. It shows how physical disability can have emotional repercussions and lead even to lasting emotional crippling. It underlines the risks which exist when parental good intentions are not accompanied by enlightened understanding. Had that school medical officer been in office when James first came back to school after his poliomyelitis the story might have been different, for active interest and, if necessary, intervention five years sooner might have prevented the initial troubles from arising; the boy should have been under observation from the start.

It was sound policy to look ahead to a future career for James when he started at the special school, but if the school medical officer had been wiser and more experienced he would have known that it was not enough to make a decision on the basis of the boy's abilities and the school's facilities. He should have considered at that stage the possible employments which would be open to the boy in his own town in three years' time and the youth employment officer should have been brought into consultation then instead of later.

Even so, James might have found a career in printing had it not been for the prejudice or ignorance of his prospective fellow-workers. What motivated their decision is uncertain. It might have been simple prejudice against cripples or it might have been a feeling that a cripple would not be able to pull his full weight in the workshop so that he would need help and slow down the pace of the work and thus reduce the earnings of his fellow-workers. It might also have been craft solidarity—the tradition that the entrance to a craft must be through full orthodox apprenticeship and not by special training. (This last is a feeling not confined to the printing trade and by no means unknown at the present time.) Probably all three factors operated simultaneously as they still operate today.

That the story had a happy ending instead of an unhappy one was quite fortuitous, and largely due to James's own inherent qualities. It has a moral which is as pointed in the nineteen-seventies as it was in the nineteen-thirties. The handicapped person is a person, a whole person who needs to live a whole life. His care is a matter of team work in which he and his family are as much members of the team as the professional workers who are paid to look after him. And that care must start early and must be planned ahead from the very beginning.

Certain principles must underlie all work for the handicapped and cannot be lost sight of for a moment. Three are axioms which are of fundamental importance.

### 1. The effect of a disability must always be judged in relation to the present and probable future circumstances of the person concerned

The extent to which any disability handicaps its possessor always depends on circumstances; indeed there are disabilities which may not be handicaps in certain circumstances. It is easy to draw a few examples from the important sphere of work. Colour-blindness is a disability and is for obvious reasons an absolute bar to employment in such occupations as those of navigating officer at sea and locomotive driver on shore. Outside those limited fields the colour-blind worker is at little disadvantage in employment and many colour-blind people live right through their lives without ever discovering that they are not as others. A stammer may matter little to a watch-maker or a laboratory worker but is disastrous in a salesman or a university lecturer. Arthritis will disable a postman at a much earlier stage than a director of a large industrial company.

It is a truism that money cannot buy health but it can certainly buy the means of health. Most disabled people find that it is valuable to be able to have people or machines to supply what they lack—the deaf person needs a hearing-aid, the paraplegic a self-propelled chair, the blind person an amanuensis—and, in fact, every person with a major physical disability finds that other people must do for him some of the things which normal people do for themselves. Other things being equal, the handicapped child who is poor will suffer from his handicap more than the child whose parents are comfortably off and not all the benefits of a welfare state can correct this disparity. It is also true to say that in most parts of the world the chance of the handicapped child to get adequate care and treatment varies directly with the parents' income.

Money, of course, is not the only factor in deciding whether a home is good or bad. The intelligence of the parents, their social competence and their ability to understand the child and his problems are all vitally important. So is the house in which the child lives, the number, ages and characters of his brothers and sisters and the locality of the home.

This last, indeed, may sometimes be critical. Some areas are well provided with services for the handicapped, while others have very little to offer. Whether a child with a moderate physical disability can attend an ordinary school or must go to a special school may depend on whether he lives in a town or in a country hamlet; geography very often determines whether he should go to a day school or a boarding school. The town offers a wide range of employments to the physically handicapped, has more public facilities to enable them to get on with the business of daily living and usually has more and more easily available social services for their help. On the other hand, it may present the mentally handicapped with complex social problems of living which may be beyond their capacity. The country village offers less chance of the skilled technical employment which may be the best hope for the physically handicapped, but still has unskilled employments available for the mentally handicapped and its community life may be more tolerant of and less taxing for the 'simpleton'.

On the wider, national scale the whole social and economic structure of a country may alter the whole perspective of handicap. The primitive agricultural country puts a premium on physical strength; physical disability, even of a moderate degree, may be a gross and permanent handicap, while the simpleton may be at no disadvantage. Life in an industrialized country makes demands on intelligence and skill rather than on strength, while emotional handicap—maladjustment—is most serious in its effects in the civilized and sophisticated West.

Not only is it important to take circumstances into account in the initial assessment of handicap but they have their importance in long-term treatment and prognosis. It cannot be too strongly stressed that one of the first things to be done in helping each handicapped child is to look into his future and try to forecast how far circumstances will permanently hamper or help him. And this should be no passive consideration; it is important to estimate how far the circumstances can be modified and how far the child's life can be planned so that the winds of circumstance will blow favourably rather than adversely.

### 2. Disability is as a rule only partial, the individual being otherwise normal

This ought to be obvious, but practical experience shows that it is not. The doctor, who is commonly the initiator of care and treatment for the handicapped person, has been trained in the detection and treatment of the abnormal and instinctively focuses his attention on what is wrong. The medical auxiliaries, whose work is to give treatment for the disabling condition, are similarly biased. Even teachers sometimes fall into the same error, so that school reports on handicapped children begin with detailed consideration of the handicap and only later speak of the child. The ordinary man or woman in the street, therefore, can hardly be blamed for noticing first and attaching importance to the thing that makes the handicapped person different and even the parent can be obsessed by the blemish in his child to the detriment of his appreciation of what is right with him.

In actual fact, the number of cases in which the handicap must dominate its victim is very small. Total handicap would be present only in a blind, deaf and mentally defective quadriplegic—an exceedingly rare combination of disabilities. Formerly, those with a single handicap were very much more common than those with multiple handicaps. Nowadays, except for the purely mentally handicapped—and even these can have secondary emotional difficulties—multiple disability is becoming much more the rule than the exception. However, even so, it is probable that some of the multiple disabilities will be comparatively minor and that some organs, senses or systems will be unimpaired or even better than the average, so that handicap rarely restricts all the powers and capacities of its victims but merely restricts their range.

The restrictions can be complex in their operation. A mentally handicapped person may have a perfect body but be unable to use it with maximum skill and purpose. A blind person's legs may be sound and strong but he still has difficulty in walking about in unfamiliar places. Injury to the part of the brain responsible for controlling movement may, as in some spastics, prevent high intelligence from being used to the full. The fact remains, however, that the great majority of handicapped people possess useful and usable powers and faculties and the art of helping them consists very largely in developing those faculties and finding opportunities for their use.

It must also be remembered that one disability can produce secondary handicaps. The most obvious of these, which is considered fully later, is the occurrence of speech defect or the absence of speech in a child whose speech organs are normal but who has a severe hearing defect and has thus been prevented from hearing speech. In the physical field, disabilities of the legs may be a cause of spinal deformities or spinal deformities favour the development of respiratory troubles. One cannot too strongly emphasise that any kind of disability, by causing physical, social or emotional stresses, may bring about some degree of maladjustment. The prevention of secondary disability is in fact one of our most important aims in the whole field of treatment, management and education.

The assessment of handicapped persons really needs to be carried out in terms of function rather than of anatomy and physiology and to do it as accurately as it should be done requires much closer analysis of the activities of work and daily living in functional terms. There is a great field here for research and it is to be hoped that greater efforts will soon be made in this direction.

### 3. To be handicapped is not an unmitigated disadvantage; it may bring real and positive compensations

This dictum may sound at first like a mere consoling platitude, but experience in work with the handicapped shows that it is an important truth. History has plenty of examples in which handicapped people appear to have achieved great successes in spite of their handicaps, but a closer study of such cases suggests that some part of the achievement at least has been made possible by the handicap itself.

To a normal person with a full range of faculties and physical powers the world is full of attractive activities and it is only human to seek to live as fully as possible by engaging in a multitude of those activities. But the day has only twenty-four hours and the mind and body only a limited amount of energy; the greater the number of outlets for the energy and the greater the number of demands on one's time the more likely one is to become a dilettante and achieve only a little in each of many directions. Because handicap reduces the possible range of one's activities it therefore follows that more time and more energy can be given to the remaining activities within one's range. The handicapped person, in fact, may sometimes find it easy to attain a concentration of effort and purpose which comes with difficulty if at all to many normal people.

Psychologically, a physical handicap may have the effect of a challenge. To fight against one's handicap in an effort to pretend that it is not there can lead to disaster, but to accept it and still try to conquer it may be a very different matter. A great deal of invaluable work for the handicapped has been done by handicapped people who have seen this personal challenge in wider terms and have helped their fellows the more effectively because of their subjective knowledge of what handicap means. But in any field of life there is a fascination in the use of one's skill and ingenuity to overcome obstacles and in work and in play it has led more than a few handicapped people to successes comparable with and even greater than those of normal people.

Even sensory handicap has compensations. The senses are the gateways by which stimuli reach the central nervous system and so many crowd in so constantly that the mind may be hard put to it to select those to which it should respond and to suppress or reject the others. Loss of sight or of hearing limits perception of many useful and important things, but it also limits the number of distracting stimuli and thus makes concentration easier. The blind are commonly believed to have exceptional powers of concentration and memory and even to possess senses denied to sighted people. It is at least probable that concentration is made easier for them by the lack of visual distractions and that their 'sixth sense' is no more than a general development of hearing, touch and smell which the sighted person never takes the trouble to acquire because there is no need for him to do so.

For the child whose disability is congenital or arises in very early life these compensations may come easily, almost automatically, as he learns the only way of life open to him, though he will need skilled help if he is to develop them to the full. When the disability is acquired, later, the situation is different. Its immediate effect is to impede or destroy a way of life already learned, often so suddenly and severely that the very idea of there being compensations is inconceivable. The later in life that the disability is acquired the more this is true, but given skilled management during the stage of despair and bewilderment which succeeds the onset of disability and the right sort of training and support afterwards, the end-result, though it may take longer to reach, can be equally satisfactory.

Various aspects of this matter of compensations are discussed in more detail in other chapters. It is specially mentioned here because it has axiomatic importance as one of the basic principles on which care for the handicapped should be founded. It should never be forgotten, either in the original assessment of the potentialities of a patient or in the continuing help, education and advice which are given to him during his early and even his later life.

## FURTHER READING

*General*
Bowley, A.H.   The Young Handicapped Child.   Livingstone, Edinburgh.
Clarke, J. S.   Disabled Citizens.   Allen and Unwin.
Ferguson, T. and Kerr, A. W.   Handicapped Youth.   Oxford University Press.
McMichael, J. K.   Handicap.   Staples, London.
Ministry of Education.   The Education of the Handicapped Pupil.   H.M. Stationery Office.
Moncrieff, A. (Ed.).   Child Health.   Eyre and Spottiswoode.
Spock, B.   Caring for Your Disabled Child.   Collier-Macmillan.
Taylor, W. W. and Taylor, I. W.   Services for Handicapped Youth in England and Wales.   Int. Soc. for Rehabilitation of the Disabled.
Wallis, J. H.   Counselling and Social Welfare.   Kegan Paul.
World Health Organization.   First Report of the Expert Committee on Medical Rehabilitation.   H.M. Stationery Office.
Younghusband, E., Birchall, D., Davie, R. and Kellmer Pringle, M. L.   Living with Handicap.   National Children's Bureau, London.

# CHAPTER 2

# Public Attitudes

The handicapped, whether children or adults, have to live in a world of normal people and to live and work in close association with those people. All human relationships are two-way—A's attitude to B is in part determined by B's attitude to A—and the handicapped person more than the non-handicapped is sensitive to the manner in which other people treat him. At home, at work and at play the life of the handicapped is made harder or easier by the attitudes of those among whom they move and when the community considers the making of provision for the handicapped out of community resources the climate of public opinion determines whether that provision shall be generous or not.

Though public attitudes toward the handicapped are steadily becoming more enlightened, the immediate reaction of most people is unfavourable rather than favourable. This goes back to the earliest times, when those who sought an explanation as to why some should be afflicted and others left untouched decided that at any rate those disabilities which were congenital or arose from some imperfectly understood process were the expression of divine disapproval. A child was born afflicted because of the sins of his parents; an adult was suddenly smitten with blindness or paralysis because of his own offences. Even disabilities which arose less suddenly as the sequelae of disease were manifestations of the wrath of the Gods. Only those handicaps caused by obvious physical injury or accident were accepted in a matter-of-fact way, with always the proviso that disability from war wounds was a more or less honourable thing which might, in certain circumstances, entitle its victim to special respect from the community.

To these exceptions there could be added, in certain societies at certain periods, two other types of disability, madness (and, perhaps, mental handicap) and epilepsy. While other handicaps were marks of divine displeasure these were occasionally considered to be marks of divine favour which set their wearers apart as a class to be treated with special respect and reverence or, at any rate, with tolerance. So ambivalent can be the unreasoning mind that even a Society which believed in demoniac possession as a cause of insanity and treated its lunatics with fantastic brutality to drive out the demons could combine that brutality with a strange reverence and awe. But on the whole history teaches that a community which was beginning to treat the afflicted with deliberate brutality was beginning to leave its primitive phase and become more civilized; only to the primitive were the insane holy.

As civilization developed the patterns of behaviour became more complex and less predictable. One community might regard a humped back as an infallible mark of a witch while another would have its members touch the hump for luck. A whole religious system might allow a special holiness to attach to all deformed and disfigured beggars, irrespective of the origin of the defect, and let some reflection of that holiness rest on those who helped them or gave them alms. There was certainly a progressive broadening of community tolerance and the expression of pity and sympathy, at least in public, was considered good social behaviour. This last has spread so widely that at the present day it is universally accepted as a formal pattern. The unfortunate thing is that its public acceptance by overt community attitudes obscures the fact that it is not by any means accepted by individuals in their private capacities.

Western folklore and its descendant, the popular stories of modern fiction, consistently find something sinister in handicap. In nineteenth and twentieth century story-writing in England a multitude of blind master-criminals have only one blind detective to oppose them. The cripple and the hunchback tend to be cast in the role of villain, if the piece is to have a villain. For it must also be acknowledged that there is another popular superstition that a slight limp is 'distinguished' and may make a man attractive to the opposite sex; it is even believed in some places that the cripple is endowed with exceptional sexual skill and potency! And fiction inevitably reflects popular belief, as it must do if it is to be acceptable to the populace.

More or less deep in everyone is a belief that a warped body holds a warped nature. Within the personal experience of everyone there have been instances which would support this belief. It is inevitable that some people should fail to adjust to life with a handicap and should show this in unsocial or even anti-social behaviour. It is equally inevitable that their failure should make a more marked

impression than other people's success and should help to perpetuate the legend. The tragedy is that so often their failure should
have been produced or at any rate precipitated by this very lack of
understanding on the part of those who condemn them.

The herd instinct and the herd tradition automatically produce
a prejudice in favour of those who conform and against those who
do not conform. Anyone who is 'different' can be accepted only by
a special effort. It follows that there must be some automatic
rejection by the normal of the abnormal and perhaps this can
never be entirely eliminated so long as men live in herds. It may
be that some of the more elaborate myths, superstitions and tradi-
tions are simply rationalizations of this rejection, but that does not
alter the basic trouble, which is worsened by the fact that those
whose disability makes them depart from the physical norm will
also, because of their disability, find it hard to conform to the day-
by-day pattern of activity and behaviour which the herd requires
of its members.

It is interesting to consider briefly the different ways in which
different handicaps are regarded in the typical Western community today.

The war disabled, as a class, are still specially privileged because
of their disability and its origin. It is almost universally accepted
that they have 'given' their sight, their hearing or their limbs to
save their fellow-countrymen from nameless horrors, and whether
they were volunteers or conscripts, brave men or cowards, the
sacrifice sanctifies them. Whatever may be one's attitude toward
war, whether one believes that they have made a voluntary
sacrifice or that their country has wantonly swindled them,
the fact remains that they would not have been disabled unless
their country had required them to risk disability. Whenever,
therefore, a country is considering the making of provision for the
handicapped and their rehabilitation, the veterans come first. In
most countries the best and in some the only provision for rehabilitation is that made for the veteran. In even very advanced
countries it is possible for the State's resources to provide only for
the veteran and for the handicapped child and adults disabled in
civil life to be left to the more or less generous mercy of private or
semi-private charity. In all countries the disabled veteran receives
a measure of special personal respect because he is a disabled
veteran, while the disabled civilian must be content with such
respect as he can earn for himself, often against great odds.

Of special disabilities, irrespective of their origin, blindness stands by itself in the public's regard. This may very well be because of all disabilities it is outstandingly the one which can be most easily appreciated by the ordinary unimaginative man or woman. It is the 'supreme' handicap; because sighted people depend on sight for so many of their daily activities they feel that the loss of their sight would be almost tantamount to the loss of life itself. By a simple extension of this they regard it as bordering on the miraculous that a blind person should be able to do *any* of the things which they do in a normal day, even though, in actual fact, those things come as easily—or even more easily—to the blind than to the sighted. Literally everyone is sorry for the blind and no-one will refuse to contribute a little to an appeal on their behalf. Voluntary funds for the blind are always wealthier than those for the other classes of disabled and state aid is more readily given in cash or in kind. No-one baits or ridicules them. A play which tried to raise laughs by depicting a comic blind man would be hissed off the stage. Taking advantage of the blind—stealing a penny from a blind man's cup—is the standard expression for the ultimate in meanness. Apart from the inevitable reluctance of the hard-headed business man to employ any handicapped person—and here sympathy for the blind has made exceptional progress in recent years—it might be said that the public's attitude toward blindness errs principally in being too kind in that both individuals and groups may be so insistent on helping the blind in their way that they actually impede the efforts of the blind to help themselves.

Very different is the public attitude toward the deaf. Here is intolerance rampant. The deaf are stock figures of stage, screen and radio comedy and in real life they provoke laughter and irritation in almost equal proportions. Of course everyone knows that deaf people are funny and are irritating, yet the very actions which provoke these reactions are counterparts of things which in the blind serve only to enhance sympathy. Probably the main source of this difference in attitude is precisely that factor which makes deafness such a tragedy to the deaf—the impediment in communication by speech. It is much easier to be kind, sympathetic and understanding to a person if one can talk to him. The blind can show their good humour, their patience, their philosophy, their adjustment to their disability, in speech; the deaf have no means of showing it except by a mirth-provoking sign language which no-one understands or by writing—a slow and tedious business. And so the deaf are likely to be shunned or, at best, tactfully avoided and allowed to shrink still further into introversion. It is true that the deaf child, with the special claims to sympathy of all children, is better tolerated in theory, but in practice even the most generous offer of tolerance is impeded by the curtain of silence.

The mentally handicapped are tolerated or not in the light of highly irrelevant considerations. If they do not obviously 'look like defectives' and have learned elementary social behaviour they are quite readily accepted up to the point at which intellectual contact is attempted and fails. But most ordinary routine social contacts stop short of that point. Unless he is so socially incompetent that it is essential for him to be placed in an institution—when, of course, individual social attitudes in general life cease to have any significance for him—it is probable that the mentally handicapped person will find and settle down among those who will accept him as he is. The worst social difficulties are likely to be encountered by the mentally subnormal person who is the child of intelligent, upper-class parents. In his normal class environment he is unacceptable because he is incapable of sharing the interests and the conversation of the majority and reveals his defect whenever he is brought into the conversation. In an environment of semi-literate or illiterate manual workers, the environment for which he is best suited, he will be a misfit not because of his lack of intelligence but because he is distrusted as an interloper from another social world.

Social acceptance of the epileptic depends mainly upon the degree of his disability. Occasional petit mal attacks can easily pass unnoticed and are even, under the euphemistic title of 'black-outs', accepted as inconsiderable. The epileptic who suffers from major attacks, however, will meet a great deal of social rejection. There is reason in this. A major fit can be a most alarming and distressing spectacle and a considerable embarrassment to bystanders who feel that they ought to do something, who fear unmentionable disaster but have to remain helpless witnesses. Habituation sometimes works wonders. Villagers in the neighbourhood of epileptic colonies accept fits in colonists taking an afternoon stroll as something quite normal. But in general the epileptic still has considerable difficulty in finding friends or employers once it is known that he is liable to major fits.

The general social attitude toward physical defect or deformity varies as widely as do physical disabilities themselves. Aesthetic considerations cannot be ignored. There are people who, though kind, rational and in most other ways model members of society are repelled by the sight of a physical malformation and the gross and obvious congenital deformity or acquired mutilation is intolerable to them. This apart, the general tendency is to allow the physically handicapped person to try to find a place in the social group and to accept him on his merits. The exceptional success of many disabled persons in performing 'normal' physical activities has been a considerable help in this way. Obstacles to acceptance arise, however, if the disability is manifestly such as to suggest that the handicapped person cannot easily approach normality. A wheel-chair or a double caliper will fence its possessor off from quite a considerable number of potential human contacts.

The spastic has a particularly difficult time. His disability is manifest and unpleasant to look upon. His speech is hesitant and often hard to understand. He may 'look mentally defective'. He has difficulty in performing a whole host of the little activities of daily life which go to make up social life. He is quite certain to embarrass his would-be friends in the presence of others. Carlson's autobiographical 'Born That Way', though it was published a quarter of a century ago, remains a classic in its illuminating treatment of this point. The hardest thing of all is that precisely this embarrassment and fear of doing the wrong thing add to the psycho-physical tension and make the disability worse.

This briefly outlines the broad general patterns of public attitude to the adult handicapped person. Naturally it is considerably modified in favour of the handicapped child. Most people have a soft spot for children and even those who have only limited fondness for their own offspring may be kind to the children of strangers—possible because they can do so without incurring any responsibility. To the handicapped child they bring a feeling rather akin to the feeling which the English have about injured animals, a rather irrational and not very constructive sort of protective pity.

Because of its contrast with the attitude of adult to adult this makes things very difficult for the handicapped child when he leaves school. A world which has been sympathetic, indulgent and over-protective suddenly and for no apparent reason turns into a world of non-committal and evasive strangers. This is one of the reasons why it is so important for the handicapped child to be shielded during his childhood from the worse effects of too much sympathy and to be taught that in spite of appearances he is really going to have to rely very largely upon his own efforts when he grows up.

Fortunately the attitude of the normal child to the handicapped child does not usually follow the adult pattern. Child can be heartlessly cruel to child without intending cruelty, but this is not more wounding than the clumsy attempt of the adult to avoid contact with the handicapped. Children are realists and accept each other at face value. A child who has a major epileptic fit in the middle of a tedious lesson in school may well frighten the teacher, but his schoolfellows may be grateful to him for the diversion. What the handicapped child cannot do will inevitably isolate him from his comrades but what he can do may be esteemed perhaps even higher than its intrinsic worth. The only major exception is the stammerer, for his disability is, unfortunately, one which produces grounds for laughter with distressing frequency. Even so, he may be less embarrassed in conversation with his fellows than when he is called upon to speak or read in class and he will learn to tolerate attempts to imitate his stammer when they come from children whom he has proved to be his friends in other ways.

Some authorities have stressed as an important reason for leaving the handicapped child in an ordinary school the probability that this will help to educate normal children in how they should behave toward the handicapped, and thus lead to the education of adults. That adults need such education is quite certain, but it is doubtful how far patterns of behaviour of this kind which have been learned in childhood will persist into adult life. It is notorious that Gentile children who have been to a school which had a minority of Jewish pupils and white children who have been to a school with a minority of coloured children can be victims of race or colour prejudice when they grow up, even though they may have seemed unconscious of race or colour in their schooldays. Perhaps it might be sufficient to say that the unthinking tolerance of childhood is a good basis on which to build a more stable reasoned tolerance in adult life.

At the same time, what happens in school may point the way to one road to better understanding. The normal child accepts the handicapped child in shared activities and the best way for the normal adult to learn to understand the handicapped adult is similarly to share activities with him—particularly work. Shared recreation is also good, but for many and obvious reasons the handicapped cannot easily share the favourite recreations of the normal adult. There is nothing like sharing the same work-bench or office room to make the normal adult realize what the handicapped can do and how to steer that difficult middle way between helping him and refraining from helping him. The tragedy is that initial prejudice or lack of understanding so often denies the handicapped person the chance of getting into employment to start the process of bridging the gap.

# CHAPTER 3

## Living with Handicap

Most handicapped children grow up; the childhood years are but a quarter of their life-span. Some fortunate ones can hope for their disability to be cured, some for its effects to be alleviated; for others the outlook is one of deterioration. The majority, however, will have a disability more or less constant in both nature and degree which remains with them for a life-time of more or less the life span which ordinary people can expect. They will spend thirty, forty or fifty years living in a world which is shaped for the convenience of non-handicapped people, mixing with that public whose attitudes I have just been discussing and, indeed, making up part of that public. Our essential task in helping them in childhood is to use all possible means to make life worth living for them after childhood has ended.

Not long ago, I was discussing with a little group of young severely handicapped adults some of the problems which they met and how far the work which had been done for them had prepared them for those problems. In the course of discussion I asked them whether they had been conscious of a gap between 'us'—the handicapped—and 'them'—the non-handicapped. All agreed that they had. The next question was, obviously, 'Who is to blame for this, 'us' or 'them'? They were unanimous—the blame was to be equally shared! In the face of this, it seems worth while to remember that most of the people who are responsible for treating, educating and generally caring for the handicapped are not themselves handicapped and to try to be subjective for a few pages and think what handicap means to the handicapped themselves.

However lightly or severely one is handicapped and whatever is the nature of the disability, certain facts have to be realized.

There will be some things which, because of one's disability, one cannot possibly do. There will be some things which, in spite of one's disability, one can do just as well as any non-handicapped person. There are other things—let us call them the conditional things—

which one can do reasonably competently but more slowly than other people or with pain or emotional or physical strain or stress.

Some of the activities which go to make up living are essential; others are desirable or agreeable but not essential. If some essential activity falls into the totally impossible class—if one cannot feed oneself, wash oneself or get into and out of bed by oneself—there is no choice in the matter. One must be dependent on other people for such purposes. However there are not many activities which are absolutely essential and not many handicapped people who find them totally impossible. For the majority of the handicapped, living demands the working out of a complex of compromises.

If there is any choice in the matter, most handicapped people prefer that the essential things should be done by themselves. They are intimate and personal things. To have them done by others has an element of indignity and can be inconvenient in the sense that one is no longer free to decide when they shall be done; one must function to the helper's timetable. When the essential things are among those which one can do quite normally all is well. When they fall within the conditional range, then the price has to be paid. Perhaps a price in moderate pain is the easiest to pay. To pay the price in time or stress is harder, for it restricts the time and energy available for the non-essential things and it is the non-essentials which make the difference between mere existence and worth-while living. Some of these non-essentials must be sacrificed and it is particularly unpleasant to find, as too often happens, that there is no time or energy available for some of the desirable non-essentials which one could do perfectly normally if only one had those precious commodities.

Handicap, as I have said, depends upon circumstances. If it were possible to provide for the handicapped a special environment, so that they lived as equal members of a community in which there were minimal impediments to their activities and in which all had reached the appropriate compromises which I have just discussed, living with handicap would be a much easier business. This is undoubtedly done in special schools and, to a limited extent, can be done within the ordinary school for the less severely handicapped. It can also be done in special hostels and homes for the older handicapped.

It is, however, unthinkable that this could or should be done for all the handicapped. It follows that one's compromises must have a considerable bearing on one's total life. What, then, are the problems of living when one has to restrict one's range of activities or accept an appreciable measure of dependance upon others—or, most probably, both?

To be unable to do things which are regarded by most people as normal and natural integral parts of living is to be inferior in some degree to ordinary people. Some 'inferiorities' arise out of sheer lack of community understanding of the needs of the handicapped. It is particularly galling to be unable to go to concerts or to the theatre, to be unable to use public libraries—or public lavatories—or to travel by public transport because the people who design buildings or transport vehicles have not deigned to consider the probability that handicapped people have ordinary wishes to do ordinary things. Something is now being done about these difficulties and the situation is improving, albeit slowly.

Everybody has a dash of the Walter Mitty in his life—he wishes, according to his tastes, that he could be a footballer of the calibre of a Charlton or a Pele, that he could play the violin like an Oistrakh, that he could be a famous surgeon or barrister. He envies those who excel, but he accepts that kind of inferiority. What he finds it difficult to accept is that he cannot, if he is handicapped, do some of the quite ordinary things that 'ordinary people like himself' do daily as a matter of course. Some can never completely reconcile themselves to this but most, with the right sort of help, learn to find satisfaction in doing well what they can do. However, there is one aspect of living within one's capacity that has been less fully considered than it might have been. If one is to use one's abilities to the full, one must plan one's living to ensure maximum performance with minimum stress and pain. This means, to a considerable extent, working out a daily routine and keeping to it. It also means that many routine things and all non-routine things need to be worked out in detail in advance. A short shopping round may need to be programmed with as much care as a normal person might have to give to a day's excursion, a fifty-mile journey to visit friends need as much forethought as a normal person might give to a week's touring. Missing a 'bus, the late arrival of a train, a misunderstanding over a hotel booking, all minor inconveniences which the normal person can shrug off with a smile, can be something of a disaster to the handicapped.

If one cannot cope with minor emergencies, one is under pressure to avoid any activities which might conceivably involve emergencies; the handicapped not infrequently tend to circumscribe their activities unduly just for this reason. And even short of that, the general necessity for planning takes the spontaneity out of living and adds another aspect of inferiority. Part of the pleasure in being able to do a thing lies in being able to do it when one wants to.

It is, then, difficult enough to live for oneself when one is handicapped. But the world contains other people and one has to live with them. As a minimum one must try to get on with those in one's immediate circle, or life is intolerable. If life is to be better than tolerable and any of its richness is to be realized, then it is not enough merely to accept the existence of others; it is essential that with some of those others one should have deeper relationships. True relationships with others are based on many things, but those which are lasting and satisfying need a basis of shared interests and, also, of shared expression of those interests in activity. This is not to say that there must be complete coincidence of interests between two people; indeed, many relationships are the better and the stronger because outside the area of shared interests each partner has a sort of private garden of interest which the other understands but into which he does not intrude.

Because the handicapped are essentially restricted in their interests and activities they have fewer potential points of contact in the formation of relationships with others. The consequence of this, is that while they may have plenty of acquaintances there will be fewer people with whom there is a probability of close friendship, and this is particularly so in relationships with the non-handicapped, whose range of interests and activities is potentially so much wider. A friendship need not necessarily suffer because one partner has interests which are totally outside the range of the other or because one is more learned or more accomplished or can be more active in the pursuit of a shared interest. But between friends there must be some equality of demand and an understanding of the need for give and take. The great risk in a relationship between the handicapped and the non-handicapped is that the handicapped partner may be so eager to share fully the interests and activities which can be pursued in common that he begins to restrict unduly these activities of the non-handicapped one which he cannot share. When this happens, the relationship may be in serious jeopardy.

This risk is inherent to some extent in any relationship between a handicapped person and one who is not handicapped. It is

B

probably recognized, though perhaps unconsciously, more often than is suspected. It certainly has something to do with the way in which some normal people are ill at ease with the handicapped and probably accounts for some of the hesitation which many handicapped people have over becoming involved too deeply with the non-handicapped.

The other great impediment to relationships is dependence. Equality has an active as well as a passive aspect; each partner in a relationship is usually expected to give as well as to take. Unless the handicapped partner restricts all his activities to those in which he can be entirely independent, which is possible only for the lightly or moderately handicapped and can be somewhat cramping even for them, he will to some extent be dependent on the normal partner. Though a balance of give and take is usual in relationships between normal people, there is no reason why the handicapped and the non-handicapped should not be able to establish a perfectly satisfactory relationship in which the handicapped one is the giver rather than the taker, but this is difficult to achieve and failure to achieve it is probably the most important single factor in producing and perpetuating the 'us and them' division. It is consequently worth discussing in some detail.

Childhood is essentially a period of dependence, whether one is handicapped or not. It is the period during which one is beginning to grow out of a self-centred—and selfish—approach to life into a more social outlook. Though personal relationships may at the time be felt deeply, they necessarily lack the depth of relationships between adults. Though a child's time-scale is shorter and a month may feel like a year or a year seem to be an eternity, most relationships which are formed during childhood with one's peers are transient. To have to be dependent during childhood because of a disability is certainly an affront to one's dignity, in that it tends to equate one with one's juniors and emphasizes feelings of inferiority, but it is by no means intolerable. Indeed, there is a considerable temptation to accept the easier life which dependence offers, which is why I have stressed elsewhere the desirability of education toward independence. It is not until schooldays are over and one has to mix with adults and live in a world in which adult standards are the rule that one's troubles really begin.

Let us consider a few cases. Peter acquired a painful crippling disability during his later school years, a disability which was permanent and became somewhat worse as he grew older. He had been active and enthusiastic in several sports during his early adolescence. He knew himself as normal and had mixed with normal people as equals. He was prepared to pay a price in pain for continuing normal activities; it is possible, though not certain, that he paid a hidden deferred price in that his insistence on doing normal things may well have worsened his disability. Only when he became incapable of keeping up to the level of performance of his contemporaries, did he relinquish, one by one, the physical activities which meant so much to him.

He stubbornly refused any help or concessions from his companions. When he became dependent on their goodwill for continuing an activity he gave up that activity and, in consequence, he excluded himself from their group. Nevertheless, he had the common sense to try to find other activities which would give him new chances of mixing. His range of contacts was considerably reduced, but he certainly contrived to keep some satisfying relationships. What he has never fully achieved has been to accept help gracefully in the ordinary simple things which make up so much of living. In middle age he still tends to prefer pain to accepting the offer of a seat in a crowded train, or to contract out of a trip which involves walking rather than to have his companions modify their programme or put themselves to any trouble or inconvenience to help him along.

Erica was struck down by severe poliomyelitis. Her legs and arms are useless and she is dependent on mechanical aids for breathing. Most of the things which normal people enjoy are barred to her and she has to rely on others for help with almost everything she does—even the most intimate and personal things. Of course, she has professional paid help for the essential things, but for the non-essential things she has to rely on friends. She has given up the 'impossibles', but has plenty of determination and has a very elastic definition of the word 'impossible.' Her family has broken up, so that she can put little reliance on help from those who are bound to her by family obligations. Yet she goes to parties and concerts, gets away for holidays and even achieved a transatlantic trip.

She makes plenty of use of her friends and I have waited for years to see them dropping out, as they found themselves unable to continue to cope with her demands. So far I have waited in vain. She has nothing to offer them in return for their aid except the feeling that they are making life fuller for her and her own personality.

The glow of self-satisfaction usually wears itself out in the course of time, but Erica's personality and the privilege of her friendship seem to provide a continuing reward independent of time.

Hubert is crippled by cerebral palsy. He cannot walk, his speech is exceedingly poor, he cannot use a typewriter and his only effective means of communication is by laboriously spelling out words by pointing to letters on a board. He is highly intelligent; had he been physically normal he would undoubtedly have made a distinguished career for himself and even with his disability he has achieved a high level of education over a limited field. Naturally, he feels that life has given him very much of a raw deal. He is determined to get his own back on life, so to speak, and has turned himself into a passionate crusader on behalf of the underprivileged and the handicapped. He has money enough to pay for some help in addition to what is provided by the social services, but for the self-realization and self-fulfilment which he naturally seeks he has to depend on freely given help. To those who give that help he can offer nothing but involvement in his crusade and because it is his own crusade they are less his partners than his servants, who help him for a while but inevitably find him too demanding and desert him.

I have constantly found that a shared interest in work for the handicapped has been a most potent influence in bringing together a diversity of people, handicapped and non-handicapped and that usually it has not merely brought them together but kept them together. Even their rivalries—pride in their professional disciplines or special consideration for people with different disabilities—have been tempered by tolerance in a common cause. As Peter, who has done some most useful work for the handicapped, put it 'I'd work with the Devil himself if it were going to benefit the handicapped.' But Hubert, alas, seems to be one of the exceptions. With a first-class brain imprisoned in a fourth-class body it may be that he is driven to make the cause serve him as much as he serves the cause. It is forgiveable but nevertheless tragic.

Most of the handicapped have only moderate disability. They are much nearer to Peter than to Erica or Hubert. On the whole it is easier for the more severely handicapped to accept dependence, because it is an obvious fact of life. If one has to depend on others for the sheer mechanics of living, then dependence is, so to speak, built in. And because severe physical disability is obvious—

crutches or a wheel chair can be detected at sight—there is no temptation to try to conceal the disability and pass for normal. As a rule, those who have been handicapped from birth learn to live with their disability better, because they have never known what it is to be independent, but there are still Huberts. Those who acquire their disability after early childhood have to unlearn one way of life and learn another. For the victims of severe disability, needs must when the Devil drives; not every one of these is an Erica but most of them make good after an initial period of storm and stress.

There is a fundamental decency in most people. They are ready to make allowances for the handicapped and to accept a relationship in which they have to give more than they receive, provided that their handicapped friend accepts their gifts gracefully and is in his turn willing to give whatever he can whenever he can. A theoretically unequal relationship can thus become one of practical equality if its terms are defined and understood by both partners. As it becomes closer with increasing understanding it becomes deeper and more lasting.

I have referred to education for maximum independence, but it has an important corollary, namely education for planned dependence. Peter may well feel that the pain and other inconveniences which he has suffered have been worth while for his stubborn rejection of dependence, but I cannot help wondering whether he may not have done other handicapped people a disservice by that rejection, whether those whom he has rebuffed may have been diffident about offering help to others who might have needed it more and have been much readier to accept it.

It is undoubtedly necessary to make a realistic assessment during childhood of the probable extent to which a handicapped youngster is going to need help and to explore also the best means by which it can be provided in the circumstances in which he is likely to have to live his life. In this context, 'circumstances' includes people. Obviously the special ties of family life lead one to expect with reason that the family will be prepared to offer more help for less tangible return than would strangers, but this is no excuse for demanding of the family that it should accept stresses which would damage or restrict unduly the lives of its other members. The neighbourhood environment has to be considered; in the small town or the village neighbourliness still exists and the handicapped individual and the family can rely on the support of those who live near them, but in the city or the city suburb a family may be in effect as isolated as if it were walled round or there were no other habitation within miles.

Mechanical aids are important. They can reduce the physical effort which is needed for the handicapped person's living. It is quite inexcusable that friends and relations should have to do by hand what can be done by other means. They can reduce, too, the non-physical stresses. Here the classical example is, perhaps, the hearing aid. Too many hard of hearing people make life unnecessarily difficult for all who have contact with them by refusing to wear an aid 'because it makes them conspicuous'—usually rationalized as 'because it is inconvenient.' The late Bernard Baruch, severely deaf himself, had a rule that any of his employees who had an aid but did not wear it was liable to dismissal. This was perhaps drastic, but it is a good principle that anyone who has a handicap and refuses to use any device which might help him on the grounds that it advertises his disability should be firmly pressed to use it whenever it is appropriate to do so.

Poverty hinders, having money helps. The British services for the handicapped provide a wide range of aids, but provision tends to be geared toward meeting essential needs. The cripple's individual travel for and from work and for other essential purposes is tolerably well catered for; the cripple who wants to travel for pleasure or to have a companion on the journey must usually rely on a friend with a car, when the friend is available, unless he or she can afford to own a car. To be able to hire a taxi or to pay first class fare on a crowded train may also reduce dependence on the friend with the car. There are people who find non-standard—and more expensive—aids more acceptable, people who find that specially-made clothes are easier to put off and take on, housewives whose cooking and other household chores are more easily done—and thus need not be delegated to others—if they can afford to buy labour-saving equipment.

Basic help in the home is usually provided for those with low incomes, but it is provided at the times when it is available and by no means always at the times when it is most convenient to the handicapped person. If one can afford to hire additional help, well and good; if one cannot, one must depend on members of the family or on neighbours for help of the right quality and one must temper one's demands accordingly for fear of imposing on the family and friends. Until the well-justified claims for an income as of right for the disabled have been met, in assessing and planning dependence it is necessary to take into account whether and how far one can rely on being able to afford these extras.

The making of the assessment may be far from easy and there are many risks of error. For the handicapped child in a special school, this is particularly so. The environment favours him, in that as many impediments as possible have been removed from it. True, much can be done to make the house in which he is going to live easier for him to live in, but there are limits to the possibility of making the streets less hazardous, improving the local bus service or even making the buses easier to get into or alight from. Again, the range of activities is necessarily restricted in the special school. He may be able to take part fully in everything which there is to be done in the school, but how far will he be able to do independently, or with minimal dependence, those things which he may want to select from the far wider range which life outside the school has to offer him? It is easy to under-estimate dependence by basing the assessment on what he can accomplish for himself in the school surroundings. It is also possible to make an over-estimate of his dependence, for the favoured environment may not have tested his potential. It is by no means uncommon that when he is challenged by some new and desirable activity he may find powers that he has never thought of using.

This is why I have stressed in other chapters the desirability of, whenever possible, giving the special school child a period in the environment of an ordinary school before he finally quits school altogether. Not only does it offer him a chance to put his independence and dependence to the practical test in an environment which is more challenging than that of the special school and yet not quite so brutal or inconsiderate as that of the workaday world, but it gives him also the opportunity of finding what it feels like to be dependent on ordinary people who lack the special skills, the special understanding and the dedication of those who have helped him so far.

Every handicapped person has to find his own personal way of living with people. His inborn traits of character, the personality which he has developed and the nature and degree of his disability must all be taken into account. In a number of chapters I have offered practical guidance; the aim of this chapter has been to suggest some principles which have to be borne in mind in the following of that guidance.

CHAPTER 4

# Parent and Child

Every parent wants to have perfect children. There is no need to go too deeply into the motives which produce this wish. Part of it is undoubtedly due to the fact that the child is a possession of which the parent likes to be proud; that his or her baby should be taller, prettier, cleverer, more graceful or more successful than the children of other people is material for pride and it is not surprising that parents find it where others are unable to discern it. Part of it is equally certainly due to the fact that the child is the parent's means of immortality. Most middle-aged men and women are secretly disappointed by the way in which life has failed to come up to their highest hopes and they yearn to see their children having the joys and the triumphs which have eluded them. Every imperfection in the child is a blow to proper parental pride or to vicarious ambition and makes for some kind of difficulty in the parent-child relationship.

It is common experience for doctors and midwives that the first question that a mother aks after her baby is delivered is 'Is he all right?' Of course this means 'Is he alive and breathing?' but it also means 'Is he or is he not deformed or disfigured?' She knows that some children are born handicapped and the fear that hers might be one of them has been lurking at the back of her mind all through her pregancy; sometimes popular superstitions, the horror stories she has heard from other mothers or the unintelligent reading of some of the would-be informative books and magazines which are on the market may have brought the fear much nearer to the front of her mind.

How does one expect her to react if, in fact, the baby has some manifest congenital disability? In recent years much play has been made of the 'guilt reaction'; it has become so much a standard part of the expected pattern that I have met mothers who felt that there might be something wrong with them because they did not feel guilty.

In the first place, it is perfectly ordinary, in every aspect of life, whenever something goes amiss to wonder why it went amiss. This applies to anything from the over-cooking of the Sunday joint to the death of a close relative. Usually the first reaction is to try to find a way of putting the blame on to another person and more than a few parents do succeed in convincing themselves that their child's disability is due to the negligence or incompetence of the doctor or the midwife. This, however, is comparatively uncommon, possibly because of the popular belief that doctors are infallible but probably because of something which applies uniquely to the business of having a baby.

Conception is a very private matter shared by husband and wife alone. Pregnancy is even more private. For nine months the baby has been inside the mother and she knows that no harmful agent can have reached the child except through her. Even, therefore, if whatever damaged the infant was the result of accident or intention originating with someone else, *she* ought to have interposed a shield. Consequently, she is going to analyse her pregnancy in retrospect, asking herself the question 'Is this deformity or defect caused by anything I have done or could it have been prevented by something I have neglected to do?' Few mothers, looking back critically, especially during the first days after delivery when it is natural for a woman to feel depressed, can fail to find something which either fact or fable regards as improper during pregnancy.

The imagined 'crime' may have been little more than a minor dietary indiscretion or having been rather energetic during the spring cleaning. Often there is more on which her imagination can feed. Most couples use some method of contraception and, entirely apart from the fact that for some people there is still a smell of guilt about contraception in general, a woman may be forgiven for fearing that the prolonged taking of the 'pill' or the use of some intra-uterine device may have had some adverse influence. (This is especially so if the pregnancy has been the result of a failure of contraception.) At the present time it is still fairly common—no-one quite knows how common—for women who find themselves unintentionally pregnant to try to produce a miscarriage. In sober fact, most of the means which an expectant mother is likely to use, unless she has the help of someone who is locally regarded as knowledgeable in these matters, are most unlikely to affect the child at all, but that is to her unimportant;

abortion is a 'crime' and the child's defect is God's punishment.

Taking all these into account, it is obvious that many mothers of handicapped children will have some degree of feeling of guilt, but this is not necessarily or invariably so. Some wonder seriously about 'a taint in the family', but this is usually a quite acceptable 'act of God' and helps the mother to be fatalistic. It does, however, occasionally happen that a mother may lay the blame on a 'taint' on her husband's side of the family and that this can impair her relationship with him.

It is obvious to the parents that the bringing up of the handicapped child is going to present difficulties. Not only will it involve more work and more strain than the care of a normal child but that work and that strain will have specialized elements which are quite outside ordinary parental experience and expectations. It follows that the mother particularly will be likely to feel unequal to the task. Probably a good deal of what is often ascribed to guilt feelings is basically a feeling of inadequacy. The two are interlinked. A mother *ought* to be able to cope with her child and if she cannot do so there is something wrong with her. While it is almost impossible to reason parents out of the primary guilt feelings mentioned above, because they are largely irrational, feelings of inadequacy can be assuaged by reason and it is important to reassure the parents that the task before them is in fact something outside and beyond that which parents of normal children have to face and that help will be available to them.

The reassurance is not always easily accepted. If there is a strong basic guilt feeling, then the parents may well take the line that the extra burden is part of the punishment for the offence and that it must be borne by them and by them alone. In such a case it is quite probable that the acceptance of the penalty helps to lessen, in the course of time, the feeling of guilt and that it is indeed good emotional therapy not to take the whole of the extra load off the parents' shoulders but rather to follow a policy of making that load more tolerable. Certainly it is important to insist that those parts of the child's care which require expertise beyond the parents' capacity should be undertaken by the appropriate experts.

Parental rejection of a handicapped child can produce exceedingly difficult problems. That feeling of depression after childbirth which makes it easy for a mother to feel guilty can cause a woman who is quite normally endowed with maternal feelings to 'take against' a perfectly normal child in the first days. Few people except those who have had long experience with the handicapped can resist a feeling of unease, embarrassment or downright revulsion when brought face to face with a handicapped child. Taking these together, it is no matter for surprise that a mother whose baby has a disability at birth should sometimes react by rejecting the child; the wonder is rather that rejection is uncommon.

Obviously this is most likely to happen in cases of congenital deformity. If the child looks normal there is no reason to do anything but accept him. But rejection can and does sometimes happen when a child who has at first seemed normal comes to show signs of disability later. Once he has been accepted and normal feelings of love and affection have developed the odds must be against these feelings being reversed, but especially in cases of severe cerebral palsy and severe mental handicap the change from hope and expectation to disappointment and despair is very hard indeed to face.

If the deformity is severe and obvious, the feeling of rejection may be insuperable, so that the child can never look for more than an outward show of parental affection. More commonly, however, normal sentiment begins to conquer rejection and in this process it is possible that guilt may play a part. 'If anything which I have done or omitted to do can have caused this, then I must devote myself to atonement' is the unspoken and even the unconscious feeling in the background. In any event, it is hard to carry rejection to its full expression while the child is small and completely dependent; it is just not a practical proposition to get rid of the infant until he is older. So reluctant acceptance and a sense of extraordinary obligation mingle in variable proportions and condition the atmosphere in which the infant has to live.

There are cases in which rejection is never modified. The parents are prepared to tolerate the child until, and only until, he can be placed in an institution of some kind. This is most likely to happen where the disability is considerable and obvious so that the parents cannot for a moment forget it, cannot conceal it from their friends and neighbours and cannot visualize any useful future for the child. If it is associated with disfigurement, so much the worse. And it must be remembered that the child has not just been born to parents but has been born into a family. He may produce tensions and dissensions in what has previously been a harmonious family group. He may be so helpless as to prevent the parents giving proper care to their other children; this sort of situation can be accepted for the short period of infant helplessness of an ordinary baby but is far less acceptable if it seems likely to go on indefinitely and become even worse with the passage of time.

If the handicapped child is the first born, then it is the obvious reaction of the parents to want to have a normal child as soon as possible. The reaction is a healthy one and to be encouraged, but it is hard to expect a mother to embark on the adventure of having and bringing up another baby if the first one is going to be a continuing and increasing burden to her, as may happen if the first child is very grossly mentally defective.

Irreconcilable rejection has to be met realistically. It is not enough blandly to assure the parents that they will learn to love the child in the end. There has to be a careful assessment of the prospects and it may well be best for both child and parents to effect a complete separation as soon as practicable. There are, however, cases in which the disability appears worse than it really is or in which there is some prospect of improving the child's condition by surgery or otherwise when he is three or four years old. The clear and frank explanation of the position to the parents may bring them to reluctant tolerance and if the optimistic forecast proves to be right all may turn out well in the end.

These cases are, however, a minority. In the great majority of instances a considerable degree of acceptance comes quickly. All babies are helpless for the first few months of life and the usual clothes of a baby or the blankets of a cot conceal everything but the extremities. It is not difficult for a mother to convince herself that the child is really normal and for the father to develop something of the customary degree of proprietorial pride. Trouble begins only when the baby reaches the age at which he ought to be making use of the impaired faculties or members. It is then that the neighbours begin to notice that something is amiss and few things are harder for parents to bear than neighbourly commiseration on their child's shortcomings, whether it be expressed in clumsy frankness, in exaggerated tact or in a conspicuous absence of reference to the subject. From this springs an important danger for the child, in that the mother may hesitate to take him out as she would a normal baby so that from the earliest months he is robbed of the social contacts and social experience which are such an important part of a normal baby's informal education.

In the meantime, another important force is at work. Both

psychological theory and common observation tell us that most mothers like their babies as babies and have some pangs of regret as they grow up and become independent. Because the handicapped infant is impeded in doing things for himself his period of baby-helplessness is prolonged and the mother has to do more for him for a longer period than for his normal brothers and sisters. Because he is less nimble, less skillful or slower in his reactions than a normal child he is more liable to accident or injury and the mother has more need and more incentive to protect him. Out of this develops a pattern of over-protectiveness and over-possessiveness which, from the long-term point of view of the child's later success in life, can be more damaging than the handicap itself.

If there is one thing which is more important than others in the upbringing of the handicapped child it is that he should start to learn from the earliest possible time the art and science of living with his handicap—of using the sound limbs and faculties to the full in such a way as to compensate for what is lacking. Protectiveness and possessiveness rob him of this chance and the longer he remains dependent the more difficult will he find it and the more reluctant will he be to adventure toward independence.

There is another thing which can operate to limit him in this way, that unique blessing of man's life, hope. If a limb be missing, then it is obvious to any parent that no-one can replace it by a new natural limb, but the majority of disabilities do not proclaim themselves so plainly and finally. It is possible for parents to convince themselves that somewhere there must be some wonderful drug or some genius of a surgeon who can make the blind see, the deaf hear and the paralysed walk or that by some 'brain operation' the 'imbecile' can be made normal. One should not be too superior or too intolerant toward the credulous parent. New advances in surgery in the past quarter of a century have made a few of the blind see and a few of the deaf hear. Spastic children who would a mere twenty years ago have been written off as hopelessly crippled and mentally defective can now be offered prospects of a useful and happy life. Just round the corner of the years there may be something to bring the chance of fulfilment to any group of the handicapped.

These advances, however, are not spectacular in the sense of offering splendid prospects to large numbers of the handicapped. They have even had unhappy consequences in that they have encouraged parents who had no grounds for hope to go on searching and to postpone the moment of truth in which they accepted their child as he was and began to set his feet purposefully on the right, though stony and uphill, track. For most handicapped children that moment does finally come. It is a difficult but essential part of the duty of those who have to advise the parents to cut as short as possible the wearying and delaying round of visits to this hospital after that, to doctor after doctor and then down the ranks of the quacks and charlatans and even to country after country in search of the miracle; the longer the journey in search of the miraculous light the deeper the plunge into the final abyss of darkness.

These things happen when the disability is one which openly proclaims itself in the first days or, at any rate, weeks of life. The position is similar yet different in the case of those disabilities which, though congenital, are not obvious early in life. A moderate degree of mental subnormality may not be suspected even by the family doctor or the health visitor until the child is five or six months old and even then they may be sufficiently uncertain to be reluctant to call the parents' attention to the possibility. Such a child *looks* perfectly normal and it is probable that not until he is reaching the end of his first year will the mother admit to herself that he is in any way backward. She, too, is likely to start on the weary round of the hospitals and consulting rooms, hoping to find someone who will tell her that all is well, and she may not be ready to face the facts until the child is nearing school age or even until his first weeks in school produce the practical proof that something is wrong. By this time, again, a pattern of over-protectiveness has been set and the future has been made a little more difficult.

That in cases of this sort an original feeling of rejection has been overcome or outgrown does not necessarily mean that it has permanently disappeared. It may merely be latent and show itself again when, as he grows older, the child loses his baby attractiveness and his abnormality becomes more obvious. At this stage, however, the possibility of a boarding special school can be considered and may offer a happy compromise. The British tradition that the 'best people' send their children to boarding schools, still acceptable in the juvenile literature of all social classes, goes a long way to make a British child who is sent away to school for any reason feel that he is being well done by, rather than deposited in a sort of social left luggage office.

Where the handicap is an acquired one, parental rejection or revulsion is likely to appear only where the previously existing parent-child relationship is unsatisfactory. Excessive protectiveness and possessiveness remain dangerous possibilities; to the mother inclined in that direction the fact that her baby who had grown out of babyhood has suddenly returned to dependence can offer an irresistible opportunity. The special danger of this is that the child has already developed a way of living and is suddenly faced with the necessity of starting all over again to learn a new one. He is not only helpless and bewildered but acutely conscious of his own helplessness and his whole future may hinge on the way in which he is helped or hindered in the first critical months of readjustment, when the emphasis should be placed on the positive qualities he retains rather than on what he has lost.

There is no golden rule for helping parents manage these problems, except, perhaps, that the would-be helper should realize that every parent of a handicapped child is emotionally vulnerable, if not actually emotionally unbalanced, in everything pertaining to his or her relationship to the child. Both advice and help must be related to the particular problem and given in the realization that the shape and the nature of the problem change with the passage of time and, also, with the family's circumstances. The arrival of a new baby in the family may alter the perspective and upset a balance which was just reaching stability. An older sister who has been tolerant of the handicapped one may change her attitude completely when, in her teens, she wants to bring boy friends home. As a mentally defective child grows older and more physically vigorous the task of keeping an eye on him to make sure that he is not getting into danger or up to mischief can become almost impossible to a mother who was formerly quite able to cope with him.

There is no doubt that the sooner the problem of the child's handicap and all its implications is frankly faced, the better for all concerned. On the family doctor lies the first responsibility for this. If he suspects a handicapping disability it is his duty to make certain as quickly as possible whether his suspicion is well-founded. The temptation to procrastinate may be considerable; no-one likes to be the first to tell a mother that there is something seriously and irrevocably wrong with her child. But the temptation must be overcome. If there is any doubt, then it is important to get a good second opinion as quickly as possible and when it has been obtained the parents must be told the truth. It is not always necessary to tell the whole truth at once with uncurbed frankness. A spade is a spade; there is no need to call it a 'bloody shovel' but it is dishonest and useless to pretend that it is a silver spoon.

If the child is mentally subnormal, then polite fictions about 'late developers' are to be avoided. The parent must at least be told that the child has some brain damage which will cause him to be always backward—time can be left to show how backward he will be. If he has cerebral palsy, then it is important to let the parents know that whatever has damaged the motor parts of the brain may also prove to have damaged the 'thinking part'.

The principal obstacle in the way of enlightening the parents is that in the very young child it can be exceedingly difficult to assess the amount of disability and thus to give an answer to the parents' inevitable question 'How bad is it going to be?' The nature and degree of the difficulty vary from case to case and from one disability to another; these problems of assessment are discussed in more detail in the chapters which deal with the specific conditions. Total blindness is one of the very few 'absolutes' in this respect. There is a good probability of its being diagnosed while the child is very young and between seeing and not seeing it is possible to draw a sharp line of demarcation. Partial sight is a very different matter; if the child has perception of light it will be many months before any decision can be made as to how far he is above the minimal perception level and whether he has or has not useful sight.

Deafness is much more difficult to deal with. Even total deafness cannot be diagnosed with certainty in infancy and partial deafness, whether it be an overall impairment of hearing or a defect on certain frequencies, may have to wait until the child is four or five years old before anything approaching an accurate assessment can be made. Physical deformities, birth pareses and the like may or may not be susceptible to surgical treatment and their effect cannot be forecast until surgery has been carefully considered and in the suitable cases, actually tried.

Acquired disabilities are in some cases easier to assess, especially where sight and hearing are concerned, because the older the child at the time he acquires the disability the more he will be able to co-operate actively in the assessment tests. This does not apply, of course, in such matters as paralysis or paresis following poliomyelitis, where it may be impossible for a matter of months to decide whether the residual disability will be serious or not and the final picture may not be seen for as long as two years.

Prognosis, then, should always be guarded and optimism regarding the results of treatment should be desirably restricted to somewhat less than the actual probabilities would justify. There is, however, one perfectly legitimate way of giving parents encouragement and that is by pointing out the child's positive assets and showing just what can be achieved by children handicapped in that particular sort of way. Nothing can be more encouraging to the parents of almost any handicapped child to visit a good nursery or school for children of the appropriate class and to see how 'normal' is their behaviour and what they are able to do.

The encouragement and reassurance of experts is of enormous value, but there are times when, faced with the recurrent difficulties of daily life and seeing little apparent progress in their child, parents will inevitably wonder whether the experts really understand the detailed problems which come from actually having a handicapped child in the home. When this happens the best tonic may well be to meet other parents who have successfully coped with the same difficulties or even greater ones. One of the most valuable developments in recent years has been the growth of parents' organisations which can provide just this sort of contact. Such organisations have often been criticised for unrealistic activities as 'pressure groups', and indeed the criticism has at times been well founded, but as they mature these bodies meet an important need which cannot be easily provided for in any other way. Parents must be left under no illusions about the hardness of the road which they will have to travel but they will journey more successfully if they are given a reasonable hope that at the journey's end they will find that there is some reward for their effort—and if they have the company of other travellers on the way.

## FURTHER READING
*Parent and Child*
Bowley, A. H. and Gardner, L. The Handicapped Child. Churchill, London.
Sheridan, M. The Handicapped Child and his Home. National Children's Home, London.
Carnegie U. K. Trust. Handicapped Children and their Families.

CHAPTER 5

# Doctor and Parent

Every parent of every handicapped child will be regularly and frequently in touch with doctors. Every doctor—general practitioner, paediatrician, orthopædic surgeon, neurologist, psychiatrist, child health clinic doctor, school medical officer—will come into contact with handicapped children and their parents. For some of them this will be a regular part of their daily round; for others it will be an uncommon experience. It is, therefore, desirable to make some comment on the doctor-parent relationship.

It usually falls to a doctor to have the unpleasant task of breaking to the parents the news that their child has a disability. I have referred to this in general terms in Chapter 4, stressing the importance of honesty as well as compassion and the need to tincture the bad news with whatever hope it is possible to offer.

Which of the many doctors who may be involved should undertake the task? None of them likes it and all of them would gladly leave it to another. The choice is something which they will have to work out between them, deciding in accordance with the circumstances and their assessment of the parents' personalities and emotional state. The family doctor may often have an excellent rapport with the parents, built up over the years, or they may have been so robustly healthy that they are no more than names on his list. It is possible that he may have had comparatively little contact with parents of handicapped children and may, indeed, never have encountered a child with that particular disability.

The paediatrician will certainly have the experience of contact with handicapped children and their parents but he will probably never have seen these parents and their child until they were referred to his clinic because a disability was suspected or provisionally diagnosed. To them he is the ultimate authority for the time being and often they have come to him hoping that he was going to tell them that their fears were groundless or that at least the outlook was less bleak than they were afraid it might be.

Other consultant physicians and surgeons are less often involved in news-breaking. The child is generally referred to them when a fairly firm diagnosis has been made; almost invariably his task is less to establish the fact that a disability exists than to give an opinion on its precise nature and degree and on the possibility of its being cured or alleviated by treatment. The parents know that they would not have been sent to him unless something was wrong and they are, in a sense, already prepared for the worst. Equally, unless they are very uncommon parents, they have come to him hoping for a miracle of some kind and, no less than any of the other doctors in the case, he must remember that the happiness not only of one child but of a whole family may hinge on his patience and understanding.

The clinic doctor may know the parents well: quite possibly they have been regular clinic attenders with their older children. At the present time, when screening for disability is the regular practice of many child health clinics, it is not infrequently the clinic doctor who has actually initiated the child's referral for special investigation and in doing so he has in some degree prepared the parents for the possibility that something might be wrong.

It is essential that there should be clear, understanding communication between the doctors who are involved and that from the start each of them should have an idea of what has passed between the others and the parents. The initial referring letter from clinic doctor to family doctor, from family doctor to clinic doctor or from either to a consultant or to a special assessment centre will certainly say 'I suspect that Johnny Jones may have such and such a disability' but it should also go on to indicate to what extent and in what way the doctor who writes it may have explained to Mr or Mrs Jones why he is referring the child.

The return letter, from the paediatrician or other consultant or from the general or special clinic must be equally explicit on the same point. Parents who are being told for the first time that there is definitely something substantially—and probably permanently —wrong with their child, even if this is only a confirmation of their suspicions, are inevitably disturbed and unable to think as clearly as they normally would and however adept the doctor who has told them may be in explaining medical matters to lay people it is highly probable that they have not grasped quite the whole of his meaning.

They will have asked him those questions which occurred to them on the spot but there will undoubtedly be other and possibly more important questions which will occur to them after the consultation has ended. Unfortunately, the consultant's hospital or the special clinic may be miles away from their home and they cannot go back there a day or two later to ask these supplementary questions. They will consequently take them to the doctor who is most easily accessible, the family doctor or the local clinic doctor. This necessitates that the consultant or the special clinic must send on the detailed report with an absolute minimum of delay. If the consultant knows that there may be some delay for reasons beyond his control, then he must warn the parents on the spot that he knows that they will want to have a talk with doctor so-and-so but that it may be a week or so before his report gets through.

While considering this question of communications it is worth while to make some more general comment. They must not only be good initially but they must continue to be good. Family doctor and clinic doctor must be in regular touch and keep each other posted with any developments of any kind. There are still consultants who have inhibitions about communicating with local clinic doctors, a most unfortunate matter, since it is almost certain that action in the child's interests will have to be taken through the child health clinic or the school health service. There is, however, a converse and complementary obligation, not always fulfilled, for the clinic doctor or school M.O. to tell the family doctor or consultant as soon as possible that Johnny Jones has been provided with a hearing aid, admitted to a nursery or offered a place in a special school. Perhaps, in Britain, reorganization of the National Health Service in 1974 may make this communication easier, but it is axiomatic that though co-operation may be facilitated by the right sort of administrative structure it depends in the last resort on understanding between individuals.

At the moment of the breaking of the news, should both parents be present or should it be broken to one of the two? Ideally both should be present; it is better that both should hear it from the original source than that one should merely have it relayed through the other. But this is not always physically possible, as when the father's work takes him away from home for long periods or makes it impossible for him to travel to a distant hospital or clinic on the consultant's clinic days. There are also occasions on which the relationship between the parents or the emotional state of one of them makes it positively desirable that one should be told before the other; it is the task of the referring doctor to warn the consultant or clinic of such possibilities.

It is worth while to underline what I have mentioned elsewhere, namely that many parents will inevitably 'shop around' for further medical opinions or even seek the help of various non-medical practitioners of unorthodox techniques. It is only natural for the doctor already involved to feel a little resentment at this; he has given his best opinion and may be absolutely certain that he is right; he may feel that his judgement is being called into question and that the parents have no confidence in him. He must do every-thing he possibly can to avoid a breach with the parents. He should certainly warn them that they are, in his view, wasting money and time and may be delaying the start of treatment which ought to be started soon, but he should not put any obstacles in their way and should be willing and ready to write to the person or place from which the parents are seeking another opinion telling them what has happened up to date and how matters stand. If he should turn out to have been wrong in the beginning, then he has not 'lost face.' If the parents search for a miracle in vain, then they will come back to him in the end with even greater confidence in his judgement than they had before their troubles began.

Parents of handicapped children worry. It is natural, right and even desirable that they should do so. And they can be expected to bring their worries and anxieties to any doctor who is trying to help them and with whom they have a reasonably good rapport.

There is no standard pattern of anxieties but in the majority of cases, as might be expected, there is an initial stage of continual and considerable anxiety which begins to wear off as the parents get used to the child, his problems and the problems he produces for the family as a whole and begin, also to develop confidence in their capacity to cope with the situation. After this stage has been reached, they can be expected to be understanding and realistic and to detect crises as they occur, asking for help or guidance when they do so.

Some parents appear never, or only seldom, to worry. A few of these are people of the stable and quietly competent type, whose way of living is to get on with whatever job faces them without fuss. There are, however, two other kinds of parents who are more numerous and must be carefully watched. The first are those who are stolid, unimaginative and perhaps lacking in that quality of intelligence which expresses itself in forethought. More than a few of these can do a competent, routine job of caring for their child, but because they cannot foresee crises they may well blunder into them. If the child's problems are at all complicated or subtle— this probably applies most often when the child is deaf or has multiple disabilities—they may fail to notice early signs that things are not going as well with the child as they should and thus bring him for further investigation undesirably late. The remaining group are those who, for a variety of reasons, decide to keep their anxieties to themselves, however much they feel those anxieties; these are the ones who are likely to crack under the strain, with disastrous consequences for the whole family. The doctor, working in concert with the whole team, must be on the alert for both these groups. If he feels that he is dealing with the former kind of parent he will either arrange to see parents and child regularly himself or will make sure that the other members of the team keep a regular unobtrusive watch on how things are going.

If it is suspected that the parents belong to the latter group, it is not enough to be passively watchful. Someone, somehow, has to break through the shell which the parents have created for themselves and make some kind of meaningful contact. The word 'meaningful' is used quite deliberately and not in the loose, vague sense which is too fashionable nowadays. These parents are not going to come to the doctor spontaneously about their child but it may be that one of the non-medical members of the team or even someone who is in touch with them about matters entirely unconnected with the child's disability may succeed in getting their confidence. The doctor—especially the family doctor—may be able to use the contact which he makes with them over an episode of physical illness in either parent or in one of the other children to get them to unburden themselves. But even what some people would consider a 'bad' contact may pave the way to something better. I have more than once found that by casting myself in the role of the harsh, unfeeling, bureaucratic villain I have been able to get such parents to seek the help and sympathy of a colleague whom they regarded as by contrast an angel of light and understanding. (Needless to say, all the actors in such a charade must each know what the others are doing and what roles they themselves are expected to play.)

The pouring out of worries is a healthy cathartic in itself and in modern society the doctor is becoming recognized as taking the place which the priest held in earlier times. Where the parent has guilt feelings he can offer explanation, reassurance and, sometimes, even absolution. He must be a good listener and not only have time to listen but make the parents feel that he has that time. This is why the experienced clinic doctor may sometimes be more effective than the G.P. or the Consultant; the majority of lay people automatically assume that doctors doing clinical work are always and inevitably pressed for time but have an image of the clinic doctor as a person to whom one can go for talk rather than medicine.

On the whole, more parents are driven into the stage of chronic worry by a sense of inadequacy rather than one of guilt. They feel that they cannot cope and though they may follow advice meticulously they still need to be reassured that they are doing it well enough. This sort of reassurance is in fact an essential element in support and in building up confidence. In time it usually becomes less necessary but one has to accept that there will always be some parents who will, if they are to succeed in bringing up their handicapped child, continue to need injections of reassurance as genuinely as the diabetic needs his injections of insulin.

It is the experience of most doctors in the field that mothers appear to worry more than fathers. There is, of course, a special tie of concern between mother and child and the mother, being with the handicapped child during most of his waking life and being the provider of the most intimate care, is likely to observe his behaviour and progress in detail. For obvious reasons she most commonly accompanies the child on visits to the doctor. Fathers, less closely preoccupied with the child, may well have less stimulus to worry but it must not be assumed that in fact they usually do not do so. One must remember the social convention that men must show themselves as the tougher sex and that 'fussing' over a child is essentially a feminine trait. The truth is probably that men are less prepared to admit that they worry and that often the father who says to the doctor 'I wouldn't have brought him to you but my wife is terribly worried'—often with the postscript 'You know what women are!'—is at heart substantially anxious himself.

It is easy to say to oneself 'Mothers are poor witnesses' when a mother complains that she suspects that there is some disability which has not been suspected before or that the child is not progressing as expected. It must be remembered that the witness who is untutored, intimately concerned and inarticulate, though unable to tell 'the whole truth and nothing but the truth' may nevertheless have in her testimony some important grain of the essential truth. Because of her intimate and close involvement she may well pick up some clue to a latent or incipient disability which could be overlooked by even a professional observer who sees the child comparatively briefly and, perhaps, at fairly long intervals. The mother who has previously had children has one advantage which the doctor does not enjoy, in that she is comparing this child with his siblings and thus has a standard of comparison which is by no means unimportant. There is thus an important duty on the doctor not to dismiss a mother's suspicions without making absolutely sure that they are unfounded. What is more, he must manifestly show the mother that he has taken pains to be sure; otherwise his reassurances are not likely to carry conviction. If she believes that her child has a disability, then to her he has one until she can be finally convinced to the contrary.

# CHAPTER 6

# Handicap and Work

To most students of the subject, the word 'rehabilitation' connotes very largely fitting the patient for employment. Training for work is the main feature of most rehabilitation schemes in every country which possesses such schemes. One of the aims of the present book is to try to put all the aims of care for the handicapped in perspective and to emphasize that work is only a part of life and is far indeed from being the whole of the picture.

It must, however, occupy a prominent place in the foreground for several reasons. Not the least of these is that human society is founded on a principle which can be crudely expressed as 'those who do not work have no right to eat'. The principle has, in most countries, lost its original strictness and it is rarely indeed that the disabled person must starve. Even in the highly civilized West, however, it is not unknown for the disabled to have to fall back on the primitive expedient of their fellows in less enlightened lands and beg for their daily bread. Not all begging is obvious. There is little difference between the outright mendicant and the mendicant who holds a tray of bootlaces or matches ostensibly for sale. But is it not also begging for a man to get his charity through a large organization which collects from the public and pays him a dole? And what is the essential difference in principle between these and asking the public to pay considerably more than the market price for an article—sometimes an inferior article—on the grounds that it has been made by disabled people?

There are three good reasons why the disabled should work. One is that brains and hands which are unnecessarily idle are a waste of the community's resources. The second is that no community can afford to provide its disabled with the means to a really full life through state pensions or open or disguised charity; it may give them their bread and butter but if they want the jam which other people enjoy they will have to work for it. The third, and by no means the least important, is that to be idle in a world in which

47

others work is something which is bad for the body, bad for the mind and bad for the spirit. There is a dignity in work and a fellowship in working with others. To be unable to share that dignity and that fellowship is to be diminished as a person and isolated from the main stream of life.

There are four types of work which may be provided for the handicapped, normal employment under standard conditions, normal employment under modified conditions, employment in a sheltered workshop and home employment.

## a. Normal employment under standard conditions

By this we mean that the worker is employed in an ordinary factory, workshop, workplace or office, working side by side with non-handicapped persons at similar tasks and for similar hours and earning a similar rate of pay. This is obviously the ideal type of employment for the handicapped, bringing them, as it does, a maximum income, a maximum share in the communal life of the place of work and a maximum degree of satisfaction and fulfilment. Many people with minor handicaps find and keep this sort of employment by themselves, without external help, but the idea that gravely handicapped people can make good in normal work is being accepted only slowly. One of its chief enemies is the tradition that there are certain crafts which are particularly suitable for the handicapped, such as basket-weaving, hand-loom textile weaving and mat- and brush-making. These crafts were provided in the first sheltered workshops simply because they were convenient to introduce and did not require any elaborate or expensive machinery and their association with handicap is purely fortuitous. A second enemy of normal employment is that public and private prejudice against the handicapped which is discussed at length in Chapter 2. The third is the simple and hard-headed logic of the employer who reasons that since a particular job has always been done by workers in full possession of all their faculties, limbs and senses and since even some of those workers have failed to do it well, it is obvious that someone who is only part of a normal person has a lower-than-average chance of doing the job even tolerably well.

The answer to all these is the one which we met at the beginning of this book and which must be repeated and stressed almost *ad nauseam*, that in the majority of cases handicap simply restricts the range of activities possible to its victim. If it is possible to find work which requires only activities which are within that restricted range, there is no reason why any individual handicapped person should not be as good as, or even better than, a normal worker.

This was demonstrated in a most spectacular way during the 1939–45 war, when a shortage of man-power made it important to employ the handicapped as fully as possible. Before 1939 it had been generally accepted that most jobs could not be done by blind people; the statutory definition of blindness as involving 'inability to do work for which sight is essential' had endorsed this principle, with consequences which have since become embarrassing. A reappraisal of work needs showed that a considerable number of tasks formerly regarded as needing sight could be done by the blind and that modifications in equipment and apparatus could allow of their being used by the blind. Before long, people with little or no sight became a commonplace in engineering and other factories and many of them more than justified themselves. (See Chapter 8).

It might have been expected that such spectacular demonstration that even the blind could work side by side with normal people in factories would have prepared the way for a much more liberal acceptance of the handicapped in industry, but this has not yet happened. Though it is now common to see a few blind workers in any large industrial concern, the battle for acceptance seems to have to be fought anew for each separate group of the handicapped. I have no doubt that the problem would be easier to solve if the analysis of both handicap and work in functional terms, to which I have already referred, were thoroughly undertaken; a great many of the powers and abilities of the normal person are strictly unnecessary for many types of industrial work and a considerable number of machines which are designed for operation by normal people could be simply modified to suit handicapped workers. It is only necessary to look at the ingenious devices which are used to adapt motor cars for the use of disabled drivers to see what could be done, with a little thought, to other machinery.

The initial placement of the handicapped youngster is important. A substantial number of normal young people find their career employment by a process of trial and error; it seems to do them no harm to spend a year or two moving from job to job. The handicapped youth cannot do this so easily. He meets with some measure of employer-resistance every time he applies for a new post and to an employer who is sceptical about the handicapped the fact that an applicant has tried and abandoned one type of work is apparent evidence that his disability makes him a poor worker. Every rebuff is a blow to the young person's confidence and he is discouraged if he has to admit failure at a job that he has tried. He must find the right niche as quickly as possible and it is therefore desirable that before he leaves school there should have been some attempt at practical assessment of his abilities. This can best be done if he has had an opportunity to spend some time in workshops which bear some relation to the real thing and which allow him to try his aptitudes with a variety of tools and machines.

As I indicate in the chapter on Education, there is still scope for argument about vocational training as such. At its best it can end with the youth mated to an appropriate type of work and already possessing enough knowledge for him to go straight into industry and convince the most stubborn employer that he is a good business proposition. At the least it can still provide what has been aptly called 'vocational exposure'; the youth has, by experiment, shown that certain types of work are beyond his powers but that others are likely to be suitable, so that whoever is helping him to find work has some guidance.

### b. Normal employment under modified conditions

The minor modifications of machinery and routine to which reference has been made above will go a long way toward bringing normal work within the reach of many handicapped people. There are, however, some types of handicap which are more general in character and demand some more drastic adjustment of circumstances. The obvious case is that of the person who, because of some cardiac or respiratory disability or some chronic disease tires easily and cannot therefore work at full pressure for a working day of normal length. Many industries are organized on a team or sequence basis. In the former a group of workers carry out a set of more or less simultaneous operations while in the latter a series of operations have to be performed in succession, each operative or machine depending on a constant flow of material from the preceding one. If one worker cannot keep up the same pace as his fellows, fails to turn up on time or is unexpectedly absent, output and efficiency fall and so do the earnings of the others in the group or on the production line.

It is obviously difficult to employ in either team or sequence work a person who cannot work at an adequate speed for the whole working day, or one who is subject to exacerbations of his disability which may cause him to be absent from work frequently and without warning. If, therefore, a firm wants to employ a person suffering from this kind of disability, it must place him in a department which does not depend on team or sequence work or must employ him part-time, for the number of hours for which he can be certain of working at normal speed and standard, with possibly another part-timer to cover the remainder of the working day. A large factory may be able to establish a special department for disabled workers, assigning to it tasks which can be handled on a part-time or intermittent basis and in which a set speed is not essential. Alternatively, special employment may be devised for the handicapped individual; it is not unknown for a firm which is having difficulty in accepting its quota of disabled persons to create some sort of miscellaneous or 'odd-job' post for this sort of purpose. (See Appendix 2.)

An increasingly common problem is presented by the worker who has difficulty in getting about from place to place. Even if a sedentary job within his powers is available, this is of no use to him unless he can be present to do it. The morning and evening rush hours in the larger towns and cities congest public transport to a point at which handicapped people cannot use it without strain or even actual risk of injury, while traffic congestion at those same times presents difficulties for those of the handicapped who try to use private transport. When an adjustment of hours is possible, to allow the handicapped worker to start half an hour later and finish half an hour earlier than the standard time may well make the necessary difference to him. If the journey to and from suitable work is a long one and the worker's circumstances permit, suitable lodgings or hostel accommodation near his workplace during the working week may be the answer.

### c. Employment in a Sheltered Workshop

The sheltered workshop is essentially one so organized that it can accept the handicapped person who is unable to attempt normal employment, who is likely to be frequently absent from work or who is incapable of keeping up the pace of ordinary industrial work in a factory. It frankly faces the fact that it is never likely to be self-supporting and is subsidized out of public funds, organized charitable appeals, charitable endowment or a combination of these. Since it is the only type of establishment which can employ many severely handicapped people it is a manifestly necessary institution, but it has certain disadvantages which must be mentioned.

In the first place, by its very existence it is an obstacle in the way of those handicapped people who seek and could do normal work in an ordinary factory. So long as there are sheltered workshops there will continue to be employers who will feel that the sheltered workshop is the proper place for all handicapped people. In the second place, it fails to provide an adequate incentive for those who need incentives. Most handicapped people are tempted at times to take the line of least resistance and it is easy to succumb to the attractions of a place which offers one a safe, slow, part-time job at a wage higher than the actual work output would justify, rather than to go out into the competitive world. Thirdly, it is very easy for low standards to creep in and for second-rate or outright shoddy work to be accepted. Fourthly, because of the difficulty of organizing work on the necessarily rather small scale of a sheltered workshop there is a tendency to rely on the outmoded handcrafts mentioned above. This can easily produce among the workers a feeling that they are not able to do what the world recognizes as 'proper work' and feelings of inferiority and frustration can readily arise. Finally, we must mention a quite understandable tendency to retain in the workshop handicapped workers whose physical condition or whose skill have developed to a point at which they could go out into normal competitive employment; as star workers they help to reduce the working deficit of the establishment.

The first two of these are in some degree inevitable, though good management will reduce the effect of the second. Good management will also reduce the effects of the third and the last, provided that in the latter case it is clearly recognized that the object of the workshop is to subsidize the severely handicapped rather than to show a profit on the work of the best employees. The fourth disadvantage is now being partly overcome by taking into sheltered workshops on sub-contract suitable work from ordinary industry such as small-part assembly and the sorting of nuts and bolts.

Economically, the sheltered workshop makes good sense. It is better to pay a worker a full wage for half a week's output, making up the deficiency by subsidy, than to pay him two-thirds of a week's wage for doing nothing at all—better for the worker and for the community. In spite of all its disadvantages, for some of the disabled it remains the most practical solution for the employment problem. What matters is that it shall be used only for those for whom it is manifestly most suitable.

## d. Home employment

A very few fortunate people among the handicapped, those whose career lies in such creative arts as writing and painting, will be home-employed as a matter of course. For the remainder, however, home employment is a last resort. It is, in general, badly paid; the earnings of able-bodied home workers are small and those of handicapped home workers smaller still and far below the level of self-support. At least equally important, it tends not merely to leave a person in isolation but to confirm him in that isolation, since even if he wishes to go out he must spend a sufficient time at home to do his daily stint of work.

It is probable that the first of these defects could be remedied in some degree, for most traditional home employments are routine unskilled or semi-skilled ones. Some of the skilled work now placed on sub-contract with sheltered workshops could be done as home work, at least in places near enough to the factory to make transport of the material and finished work practicable. (The Swiss watch and instrument industries have probably done more in this direction than any other concern in the world, being prepared to lend out precision machinery to workshops and even individuals who are capable of using it.)

The evil of isolation, however, remains. It has already been mentioned that some handicapped people may be confined to their homes simply because they cannot make or endure the journey to the place where suitable work is available for them and that an adjustment of working hours or the provision of hostel accommodation can overcome the difficulty. If an ordinary factory cannot adjust its hours, there may be a sheltered workshop with flexible hours within reasonable travelling distance and the present tendency for sheltered workshops to provide their own transport to collect workers and, in strategic centres in the more rural areas, to have their own hostels is strongly to be encouraged.

While mass production techniques are driving out the individual skilled crafts there are still a few villages and small towns where a skilled watch-mender or shoe repairer can earn a living independently. In some of the less-developed countries it has proved a practical proposition to equip disabled people for work of this kind on a considerable scale and the opportunities in Britain, while fewer, are none the less worth looking for. It is also possible to train handicapped people and provide them with transport so that they can undertake service activities. The blind piano tuner has long been established in this field, and while the domestic piano is becoming rarer there is no valid reason why suitable sighted handicapped people should not engage in the servicing of radio and television sets and other domestic appliances. Given transport— an invalid car or a van with adapted controls—and provided that he can get into and out of houses, a handicapped person in a rural or suburban area can make a satisfying and remunerative career in this field, with the advantage that he is within limits his own master and can adjust his time-table and work-load to his daily capacity.

Summing up, we may say that employment in ordinary industry is the best thing for the handicapped and that the field of such employment has been so far cultivated only on its fringe. Its full exploitation requires more education of factory managements and trade unions and also a fuller exploration of the powers of handi-capped individuals and their specific and intensive training. It is vitally important, as will be shown in other chapters, that assess-ment of potential employability should be made early and care-fully and that this should always be related to the possible range of employments actually available to the individual in the neigh-bourhood of his home. It is also essential that the search for actual employment should begin well before the young man or woman finishes education, so that whatever the type of work may be there is no long, depressing wait before entering it.

# CHAPTER 7

# Handicap and Recreation

It would be foolish to minimize the importance to the handicapped of finding and doing useful work, but it is no less foolish to allow the importance of work to blind one to the equal importance of certain other things. This often happens and it is worth stressing once again that work is not the thing that matters most but is at most the first among a number of equals. Even for the normal person, troubles and shortcomings in the other parts of his life may interfere with his work and even make him unemployable; for the handicapped person, whose life is inevitably lived under strains which others do not feel and may not appreciate, this is even more true.

The life of the modern Western world has given recreation a significance which it has never previously had. The individual has a multitude of physical and mental faculties and an deal life would be one in which all these were being regularly exericised so that there should be no risk of disuse atrophy, no over-fatigue of some in relation to others and no frustrations from lack of opportunity. With every decade that passes, Western civilization makes it more and more difficult for such a balance to be achieved. In a peasant economy most people have to make use of their arms and legs as well as their eyes and ears in most of their daily activities. Their intelligences may not be constantly strained on the rack but they have to use common sense fairly consistently and there is a fair proportion of employments which demand the balance of physical and mental skill and activity which is the essence of craftsmanship.

The new tendency is for mental work and physical work to be separated. The physical worker is likely to have a routine repetitive job which needs little if any thought, while the brain-worker may often have nothing more physically strenuous in his work than the lifting of a telephone receiver. He may not even need to use his legs to go from his home to his work or to climb stairs to his office.

C

And there is an increasing degree of the breaking down of work into specialized activities so that the physical worker spends his seven or eight hours each day not so much exercising his body as in exercising a few groups of muscles and the sedentary worker in thinking, if indeed he needs to think, along and about a limited number of predetermined patterns.

What happens in work can easily happen outside it, with life settling down into a system of minimal routines of laziness in which not merely food for the body but even food for the mind comes ready-processed from the machine. It is therefore necessary to make purposeful use of leisure in order to correct imbalance. In its crudest expression—but correct as well as crude—the office worker needs to get fresh air and exercise at the week-ends and in the evening in order to be a healthy animal as well as an active intelligence, while the manual worker needs recreation which will give his brain some activity in order that he may not degenerate into a healthy animal and nothing else. We have been told *ad nauseam* that recreation means a 're-creation'; it is a little disturbing to find that such a well-worn platitude does in fact hold a momentous truth.

Though important, this is not the whole of the story. For social and human beings need 'interests'. There must be some things in their lives which compel them to an activity in which they find pleasure. Without this, life is merely a tedious waiting for death. A few lucky people find this in their work and achieve a notable fulfilment but the majority, in the world as it is today, can find it only in their recreations. The ways of doing it are legion— organizing the local Boy Scout movement, painting scenery for the amateur dramatic society, collecting matchboxes, playing in a string quartet or 'following the United'—but it would be a foolish man who tried to say which are better than others for any particular person.

It is also to be remembered that recreation has a social value, in that it brings an important and satisfying feeling of fellowship and 'belonging'. It matters considerably to the individual that he shares his recreation with others. Some get almost orgasmic satisfaction from being one of the cheering fifty thousand on a football ground while others have an equal satisfaction in a milder way in the knowledge that they are members of the exclusive and even esoteric hundred who specialize in collecting match-boxes from the South American Republics. A last, but important aspect of the subject is that community in recreation can transcend class barriers and come nearer to true social values than almost anything else in a class society. The bank manager is quite ready to let the barber give him a few hints and tips at the model engineering club and if the grocer captains the village cricket team, those who give him orders in the shop will accept orders from him in the field.

It is worth while setting out these general considerations in some detail, because they apply with special force to the handicapped, who have at least the normal need for as full a life as possible and who, because of their handicap, have often considerable difficulty in obtaining it. It is dangerously easy for them to concentrate so much on work that they have little time and energy left for recreation and to dismiss recreation as comparatively trivial may have repercussions which are almost disastrous.

## 1. Physical recreation

Physical recreation, though desirable for both sexes, has special importance for the male. Boys—and grown-up boys—make much of the playing of games and in most boys' schools or out-of-school groups prowess in games is a major factor in social acceptance. The boy who is good at school work may be popular with his teachers but unless he plays games with at least average competence his fellows are likely to dismiss him as a mere 'swot'. There is no doubt at all that in the case of James (Chapter I) his inability to join in cricket and football did much to start the process which led to his general maladjustment and his failure in school work. In short, to 'belong' to the community one has to be a tolerable performer in some activity which the community regards highly. Up to the age of fourteen or fifteen custom and convention in Britain give top rating to football and cricket, a lower rating to tennis, swimming and athletics, a lower one still to chess, debating, amateur dramatics and the other non-physical out-of-school pursuits and the lowest of all to academic work. During the next five years values tend to shift and the absolute priority of cricket and football is reduced, but a good deal of irreparable damage may have been already done.

It is obviously impossible for the physically handicapped boy to compete in the more strenuous physical activities and, therefore, two things must be done. There must first be an attempt to alter his own scale of values, so that he sees his own lack of competence in this field in proper perspective. This in itself, however, is not enough. He must be encouraged and helped to reach competence in some socially acceptable recreation. Because of its importance in maintaining physical fitness it is desirable that he should do this in one of the secondary physical sports.

Where the handicap is present from an early age this orientation of outlook is easier to achieve, and tuition can be started much sooner so that competence may be reached during schooldays. For the boy with a leg lesion, swimming offers considerable possibilities, the more so since many competent cricketers and footballers never learn to swim; it is very satisfying to know that one can do something of this kind better than the captain of the first eleven! For the boy with damage to one hand or arm but unimpaired legs, tennis and badminton offer considerable possibilities.

The most difficult cases are those in which a lad of ten or twelve, already games-oriented, is suddenly handicapped in a manner which involves a radical alteration in his habits. I know of no more instructive case than that of Paul, who, an intelligent boy, passionately fond of cricket and football, had a severe attack of poliomyelitis at the age of twelve and had to face the fact that he would never walk again without crutches and calipers. His initial adjustment was excellent and during a year in an orthopaedic hospital he seemed to be doing very well indeed. On his return to school, however, his new status as the school cripple, dependent on others for help and able only to watch where he had once taken part, produced rapid emotional deterioration and a falling-off even in his work.

It was obvious that something had to be done and desirable to give that something a dramatic touch. I therefore advised that Paul should have swimming lessons in a neighbouring swimming pool during the winter season, but that his lessons should be kept strictly secret. He persevered and when the next summer came round he joined his class at the baths. Carried by his friends to the dressing cubicle and from there to the water, he suddenly and spectacularly shocked them by proving himself the best swimmer of the class! This was the turning point; Paul had plenty of difficulties still to come, but the boost to his morale gave him new impetus to face them and he is now a happy young married man, well launched on a satisfying career.

The range of physical recreations is such that quite a large proportion of handicapped people can find one that suits them if the effort is made to give them opportunities and training. I have met first-class fencers and competent 'middle-handicap' golfers who were lame enough to have to wear calipers. Neubauer and others in Austria have taught disabled people—even people wearing artificial legs—to reach high standards in ski-ing. Guttmann's paraplegic patients at Stoke Mandeville, though confined to wheel-chairs, have become better than average archers.

There are, of course, two standards in every sport, the competitive standard which produces the satisfaction of being as good as or better than other people and the rather lower standard at which one practices the sport for one's own satisfaction and the sheer physical pleasure which is inherent in it. The majority of handicapped people will have to be content with the second standard, which means that they will be largely excluded from team sports and will have to concentrate on individual ones. This has its disappointing side, because playing as one of a team, even if it be only neighbourhood 'back-patch' football, is a preparation for later working and living as one of a team. For this reason it is important for the handicapped to find other recreational activities in which co-operation is a regular feature.

A final word may be said about 'spectator sport'. It is the fashion among intellectuals to look down upon those who spend their spare time watching cricket, football and baseball matches and the like, instead of actually playing the games. Curiously enough, those very intellectuals spend their own spare time watching and listening to expert musicians or walking through art galleries, though they themselves have never handled a violin bow or an artist's brush or pencil. I have already mentioned the satisfaction of the herd instinct which comes from being one of a partisan crowd of spectators; the connoisseur can also find artistic satisfaction in watching a game being superbly played. The handicapped person who can never hope to play well, or even to play at all, can still get a good deal of happiness from learning the finer points of a sport and watching experts in action and there is much to be said for encouraging him to do so.

## 2. Non-physical recreation

Youth passes, children grow up and assume adult responsibilities, and the tide of life, though no less strong, runs more gently and smoothly. A sense of perspective and an appreciation of adult

values replace the prodigal enthusiasm of childhood and adolescence. The most eager and assiduous of games players becomes a
spectator and as his reactions slow and his waist-line expands is
content to sit in the club-room and talk of giants long ago. The
enduring recreations are not competitive physical games but the
less strenuous, if equally keen, contests at the chess-board and the
bridge-table and the co-operation and friendly rivalry of hobbies.
In fact, we all come in the end to enjoy the pursuits which have
been possible to the majority of handicapped people from the
beginning.

This is poor consolation for the young handicapped person in
his youth, because, in the world which his normal contemporaries
inhabit, these activities are followed only by 'sissies' or by ancients
who have already one foot in the grave. It is virtually impossible to
save a handicapped boy from the pains which he suffers from
knowing that he is outclassed by all his friends in physical sport.
Not infrequently those pains are such that he refuses to consider
any alternative to physical activities and, he may prefer to try his
hand at any physical recreation before admitting that he must look
for fulfilment elsewhere. Games are much less important to girls
and though she has troubles enough ahead of her the handicapped
girl may be fairly content with making progress in her school work
and becoming good at knitting or sewing.

Somewhere in the early 'teens, however, most boys and many
girls normally pass into a phase of interest in hobbies. The interest
may be desultory and transient, but the idea is there and someone
should be on the watch to detect, cultivate and strengthen interests
which seem to have potentialities. This cultivation of interests is
referred to in more detail in the chapter on Education. At the
moment it is enough to give some indication of what the handicapped person can gain from following the interest when it is
fully aroused.

Even the single-handed pursuit of a hobby does good. It
provides an outlet for energies, mental and physical, which are,
because of the handicap, being denied expression through certain
other channels. One of the unfortunate consequences of handicap
is that its victim tends to become withdrawn and shut-in; a hobby
which really appeals to him will not only provide intrinsic interest
but will stimulate extensions of that interest. It is no means uncommon for the desire to know more about his hobby subject to
lead a youngster into wide reading and the study of geography,

history, mathematics or other subjects which have offered no attraction to him in school.

The incentive value extends into a great many useful fields. Frederick, for instance, was quite severely physically handicapped and found it difficult to get about. He surrendered to his handicap and was reluctant to make use of what powers he had. He would leave the house only for essential journeys and was well on the way to becoming home-bound. A voracious reader, he was content to let his fancy travel for him. An ingenious adult friend of the family lent him books on natural history, which Frederick read at first mainly for their travel interest. He began, however, to develop some curiosity about birds and their habits and was eventually persuaded to allow the friend to take him on a few bird-watching expeditions in his car. Before long the boy began to acquire enthusiasm and was prepared to turn out in all weathers and cover, with crutches and calipers, country footpaths which were trying enough for normal pedestrians. Once he had been thus enticed into discovering his true powers of mobility he never looked back and his physical development and the growth of his total personality matched his waxing enthusiasm for his hobby.

Because so many handicapped people have difficulty in moving about, are reluctant to display their disability in public or are embarrassed by casual contacts outside the home, this tendency to stay at home is one which is quite commonly met with and it is of some importance to try to encourage recreations which take one out of doors. Any form of active interest in nature is useful; so is an interest in archaeology or architecture in that it compels one to travel in its pursuit. Even the present of a camera will provide an incentive to go out of doors to find subjects, and for the minority who have real artistic ability outdoor sketching and painting are admirable outlets.

In the long run, of course, it is the personal contacts which provide the greatest satisfaction and fill the greatest need. The invisible barrier between the handicapped person and the normal person is often one which they have both helped to build and is made up, as I have indicated, of many things which may include genuine difficulty in communication (as in the case of the deaf or those who have a speech disability), inability to share normal living activities on an equal basis, feelings of inferiority or its opposite, aggression, in the handicapped person and the very common prejudice—or fear of seeming prejudiced—and embarrassment which the normal can feel in the presence of the handicapped. Quite often, this embarrassment has as one of its roots the feeling in the mind of the normal person 'What have he, with his maimed life, and I in common to talk about? If I talk about my normal life I shall only pain him.'

Interest in a hobby, recreation or indoor sedentary game can provide precisely that common point of contact. The range of possibilities is vast and except in the most isolated of rural areas there will always be, close at hand, groups of enthusiasts in several different recreations. Every recreational club and every group too small to be a formal club has among its members some who are eager to infect youth with their enthusiasm and to give the young recruit advice, tuition, and practical help and even to lend him equipment. Those who are interested in the welfare of a handicapped boy or girl will rarely ask in vain for such help.

Ideally—and the ideal is often fulfilled in practice—the handicapped person should become so competent in one or more of his recreations as to be the equal or the superior of some of his normal associates. The confidence which this engenders will spread to other aspects of life. To reach this point will require some experiment and the handicapped young person's first hobby may not prove to be the one which eventually gives him this fulfilment. But even if the hobby of first choice is superseded by another it will have served the important purpose of showing that he can meet normal people on a basis of equality and thus of making him more ready for future contacts.

It is probably worth while to make some special comment on music as a recreation. It has little to offer to the severely deaf, but within its wide range of the popular, the 'light' and the classical there is something to interest virtually everyone else. It can be enjoyed communally in the concert-hall or in solitude by the radio and the gramophone. The latter is a mixed blessing; it may help to confirm in their isolation those who, like Frederick, ought to be trying to move out of it. For those who are physically able to do so, the ability to make their own music on some instrument or other is worth encouraging and developing. It *can* lead to the delight of joining with others. But whether this can be done or not, there is much to be said for offering all handicapped young people some training in musical appreciation. The enthusiast who gives that training may be disappointed when his proteges, in their late 'teens, succumb to the blandishments of 'pop' or 'folk', but however much he may despise popular music it gives something to its devotee and as the youngster grows older his liking for any sort of music may develop into a taste for the more enduring values.

I have mixed feelings about social organizations for the handicapped, especially when they are clubs exclusively for those with one particular disability. In any event, one needs to put as much emphasis as possible on what is normal in them and to encourage mixing with normal people; to segregate them can too easily make them think of themselves as people apart and discourage them from joining with normal people in those activities in which they can cooperate or even compete on the same level.

There is a tendency in the 'one-disability' club for activities to be geared to the more severely disabled and their capacities. It has the advantage that the members have some important problems in common and that help can be practically provided on that basis. For the more severely disabled it can be a good introduction to community life in that most of those concerned will have had a common basis of experience at the time when they join. For the blind and the deaf, the provision of specialized facilities which they need may make some degree of exclusiveness appropriate.

But for the physically handicapped in particular, any kind of grouping must be based on what one is interested in and what one can do rather than on whether one has been disabled by cerebral palsy, by spina bifida or by poliomyelitis. Organizations like the 'Invalid Tricycle Association', on a national scale, or the 'St. Raphael Clubs' on a local scale, offer enough diversity of company and interest to provide variety and challenge. They may be a useful way of introducing the more severely disabled to community life, and even some of the more diffident lightly handicapped may find them of help in bridging the gap between the sheltered life of school and the more vigorous life of the adult community. On the whole, however, the club for the handicapped is best regarded as a supplement to ordinary recreational groups rather than as a substitute for them.

Summing up, non-physical games and sports, hobbies and recreational interests have value as 'diversional therapy' but this is only the lesser part of their importance. They are primarily the occupational therapy of the mind and the spirit and can do much to build a whole personality in a maimed body.

## CHAPTER 8

# The Education of the Handicapped Child

There are many prejudices and preconceived ideas which exist in connection with particular handicaps and the techniques for helping children in particular groups and categories; these are dealt with severally as they arise in the various parts of this book. In the field of education there are some such preconceived ideas which are so fundamental that they are well worth special consideration before the reader begins to consider educational details. It is possible, in any context, to make certain general statements which are broadly true and, within reasonable limits, generalizations may be made about the education of the handicapped. Unfortunately there has been a tendency to make generalizations which are too broad altogether and the consequences have proved anything but happy.

Taken as a whole, the British provision of special school education is the best in the world. Its standards are high and the scale of provision is liberal. There is no other country in which the average handicapped child, irrespective of where he lives or what his parents' income may be, has quite such a good prospect of getting into a suitable special school. It still falls substantially short of the demand in the case of educationally subnormal children and some small categories of children, whose problems have only recently been fully recognised—'non-communicating children' and children with two or three substantial disabilities are examples— are as yet not very well provided for. Otherwise, waiting lists are now comparatively short and it is not difficult to place children suitably.

There are, however, certain disadvantages in having a well-established service with adequate accommodation. It encourages people to become special school minded; school medical officers are tempted to refer handicapped children to special schools as a matter of course and when public opinion begins to organise itself on behalf of any section of the handicapped its first action is to clamour for more schools. The apparent success of the system makes visitors from less highly developed countries concentrate their attention on these schools and the countries from which they come press ardently for help from various international bodies in the establishment of a special school system.

Recently, however, there has been a good deal of new thinking on the subject. One school of thought, strong in the U.S.A., regards the special school as the place of last resort for a handicapped child. Perhaps the opinions of psychiatrists on the importance of home life for the child have been taken too literally and interpreted too widely; part of the process of growing up, even for the normal child, must be growing out of the home and into the world. The theory that the handicapped child who goes to an ordinary school is less conscious of his handicap and feels his 'difference' from ordinary children less acutely may be true of the child who is only lightly handicapped, but for the more heavily disabled constant competition with his normal contemporaries is much more likely to emphasize his inferiority.

Two other generalizations, that the handicapped child's need of home life is so much greater than that of the normal child that he should never be sent away and, on the contrary, that parents are the least suitable people to prepare him for life in the world at large, are equally foolish. It is also important to remember that the presence of a handicapped child in a family may cause such a physical burden or may produce such social and emotional strains and stresses that the family can become a positive dangerous place for the child himself and for his brothers and sisters. The special school, in short, is a uniquely valuable instrument when it is used with intelligence and discrimination. A well-judged placement can be the making of a child but an ill-judged one a calamity and good judgement involves not only the selection of the right school but the selection of the right time for the child to go there and the right time for him to leave. Dogma and generalization are, then, to be sedulously avoided. Nor should one generalize about the age at which children should start to attend special schools or the need of the handicapped for an extra year's schooling after the normal leaving age.

Not the least important part of the recent self-questioning has been to ask whether it is necessary to see the education of the handicapped child as demanding a choice between ordinary education in an ordinary school and special education in a special school. Is it possible to think in terms of special education in an ordinary school? The answer is undoubtedly 'Yes, sometimes'. Already ordinary schools are accepting far more moderately handicapped children than they did ten years ago, but their capacity for this is restricted by the fact that few teachers in ordinary schools have had any appreciable amount of training in the management of handicapped children and their special problems. This deficiency is being remedied by progressive education authorities arranging for their teaching staff to have some basic training.

I have referred in Chapter 14 to the success of special units for partially hearing children which have been set up within ordinary schools. Not all of these have fulfilled the initial promise of the pioneer ones—possibly some of them were established too enthusiastically, before the organizational and educational problems which they posed were fully understood—but the idea has certainly justified itself and experiments are now going on in which similar integrated units for children with other types of handicap are being tried. The possibilities are considerable, though there are obvious limitations. In particular, the smaller schools may well not have within their catchment areas a sufficient number of children with certain handicaps to justify the setting up of a special unit. Where that is so, an alternative may be the provision of a remedial unit to serve a group of schools, the children attending their ordinary schools part-time and going to the remedial unit part-time.

Every handicapped child is essentially a new and separate problem in education and must be individually considered and studied as such. The school medical officer, the educational administrator and the teacher, whether they are considering what education should be given to one individual handicapped child, or what special educational provision should be made in a city or a country, must if they are to plan wisely, be neither for nor against special schools, and must beware of supporting home against school or vice versa. The first essential is a clear understanding of fundamental educational needs; when and only when this is established is it possible to begin to judge how those needs may be best supplied for the handicapped individual or group.

There are five basic components of the education of the handicapped. These are:

General education, formal and informal.
Therapeutic education.
Education in special living techniques.
Vocational preparation.
Education in living with a handicap.

Some handicapped children will need all of these in a greater or a lesser degree. Others—the majority—will need only three or four out of the five. Some of them will require highly specialized provision of several of these components, while others may be able to acquire some of the five incidentally and without special aid.

## General Education

It is not possible to live in any society, even the most primitive, without some general education. The range of that education, however, varies widely. At the one extreme the child may acquire in the home, from the other members of the family, all the instruction which he will ever really need to live in the community of which he is a member; while at the other extreme he will need ten or twelve years of formal schooling by trained pedagogues together with all the training in practical living which can be given over twenty years or more by wise and widely-experienced parents. The English child needs at least the whole of what is comprised in the curriculum of the Secondary Modern School, together with training in the techniques of living in a highly complex society. Unless he has all these he is inevitably socially handicapped and will find it hard to lead a happy and successful life. If, therefore, his physical or mental handicap prevents him from acquiring this general education he faces adult life with a double handicap.

The mentally handicapped child is essentially unable to obtain such a full education and is, in consequence, faced with an inevitable social handicap. The best that can be done for him is to minimize his difficulties by giving him as much general education as he is able to receive and use, making up for the deficiencies by giving him some kind of social protection in later life against the hazards to which his lack of education will expose him.

Physical handicap, however, need not be essentially disastrous in the same way. It may affect education by closing one of the sensory gateways by which education enters the mind—sight or hearing. In this case, fuller use must be made of the other gateways.

The blind or deaf child can receive as full a formal and academic education as the child in full possession of his senses. He will, in later life, be unable to engage in as wide a range of activities as the normal child, but he can and should be educated for the fullest possible living within that limited range.

Other physical handicaps present appropriately different problems of general education. The crippled child, for instance, or the child with some chronic organic defect such as diabetes or a heart disability, is virtually certain to have his education interrupted by periods of acute illness or long stays in hospital for operative treatment. Fortunately for him, the essentials of school education require ten years of schooling only when that schooling is provided through a mass educational system. With special individual attention it is possible to cover the curriculum in a substantially shorter period. A child who spends three years in hospital between the ages of five and fifteen has still seven years in which to get his schooling and can get it in that time, *but not within the ordinary educational system*. Every gap in his school attendance will involve his missing certain steps in the ordinary educational ladder and, therefore, being unprepared to take the next steps when his class comes to them. The hospital school or special coaching to make up for lost time, or both together, will be necessary if he is to be up to standard when his schooldays end. With these he may be able to fit into the school system in a general way during his physically fit years, but the character and duration of the interruptions may be such that only a special school can give him the education he needs in the time he has available.

Sometimes a physical handicap is such as to prevent the child from getting from his home to a school. Special transport may meet his need, but it is in this kind of case that the boarding special school may come into its own. The home teacher, not easy to find and expensive to provide, is an alternative, but the 'intangibles' of life in the school community, an important part of informal as well as formal education, are lost. A more serious, though less appreciated, consequence of physical handicap lies in the way in which it restricts the social experience of the child; going to places and meeting people is essential education, the provision of which for the handicapped is at least as important as for the normal.

Summing up, it is fair to say that for the handicapped child, as for any other child, the ideal is that he should live in a good ordinary home and go from there daily to a good ordinary school.

It is justifiable to send him to a special school or to take him away from his home for either or both of two reasons. The first is that his home or his ordinary school, for some reason and in some way, are hampering his physical, mental or social progress. The second is that for proper progress or development he needs something which is essential and cannot be provided in any other way. Such need may lie not only in the general educational field but in the other aspects of education which we are now going to consider.

## Therapeutic Education

Therapeutic education is needed only by a minority of the handicapped, but for that minority it is essential. Its most obvious expression is to be found in the treatment of speech defects, where it may be the only type of special education which is required and the only therapy which is needed. Most children whose only disability is a defect of speech attend ordinary schools and take part in all their activities, going to a speech clinic for their therapeutic education. Where the speech defect is incidental to another handicap, speech therapy must be combined with whatever special education is appropriate for that handicap.

The child with cerebral palsy needs one or more types of therapeutic education in addition to other special education. Just how and why modern techniques help these children is still uncertain. They may educate or re-educate damaged nerve-muscle mechanisms or, as others suggest, bring into action unused 'spare' parts of the brain to replace those which have been damaged, but whatever the reason they produce results. The child crippled by poliomyelitis may also require therapeutic education but with the more clearly defined aim of re-developing groups of muscles which have become weak and wasted after the acute stage of the disease.

For the deaf child, speech education and auditory training, which are dealt with in the appropriate chapter, are therapeutic education, as are some parts of the general and social education of the maladjusted child.

Generally speaking, the ordinary curriculum of the ordinary school does not provide therapeutic education in a sufficiently intensive form to help a seriously handicapped child. Where handicap is moderate or where the main therapeutic education has already been given and the child needs chiefly 'follow-up' care it is possible and indeed desirable to consider letting him attend an ordinary school and have his therapeutic education in a neighbouring clinic, but really intensive therapeutic education of the types indicated above is usually available only in a special school.

## Education in Special Living Techniques

This is outstandingly necessary in the case of the blind. The need to learn Braille reading and writing is obvious but there are many other ways, major or minor, in which the blind child's other senses can be trained to make up for the missing one. The traditional white walking stick can be a most sensitive antenna and hearing an accurate means of judging direction. Even smell and sensitivity to heat and cold can be turned to useful purpose. The totally deaf need to learn lip-reading and the partially deaf how to use a hearing aid. The child with cerebral palsy may have to learn to use a typewriter instead of pen and pencil, the lame child how to walk with crutch or caliper and the amputee how to use an artificial limb. There are a multitude of little tricks and shifts which come in useful in the activities of life, from tying a tie to writing a book or managing a household.

For the blind child, the task is so special and complex that he needs special facilities over a very long period and will almost certainly make the most hopeful beginning in an environment specially adapted to his needs. For most of the other groups of handicapped children this teaching may be given in short, full-time intensive courses, in longer part-time courses, by tuition in the home, by incidental tuition in an ordinary or special school or by a combination of these methods. But though it may need less in the way of special institutional provision it must never be left to chance. True, many children pick up the essentials of some of these little arts in the course of their ordinary home life, but with skilled guidance they will learn the right techniques quickly instead of wasting time learning wrong techniques which may have to be unlearned before anything positive can be done. Deplorably often one finds handicapped people who have received general education and have been taught a trade but who have virtually given up the struggle because the constant harassment of the little tasks of daily living has been too much for them, and every activity a little more difficult or tiring than it need have been if they had only, at the plastic age, learned to make the best use of what they have.

## Vocational Preparation

To ensure that a handicapped child shall make a start in employment with the best possible prospects, three main things are essential:

1. His aptitudes, his abilities and his limitations must be carefully explored so as to decide what kind of work he is most likely to succeed in.
2. A job of the right type must be found in a suitable place.
3. He must receive such special education as will enable him to work in that job to the best advantage.

Obviously vocational preparation is a much wider thing than vocational education or training; it is going to involve team work both inside and outside the school. Its complexity can make it at times seem impossible. It is difficult to start training a child for an employment until one knows whether work will be available in that employment after he leaves school. It is not, however, possible to find the right employment for him until one knows his abilities and so on in some detail, while detailed assessment of his abilities may be impossible until one knows what employment is planned and can test him specifically.

In most cases, however, the position is better than it may seem. A provisional assessment of the child's general powers, mental and physical, can be made during his early school years, if his disability is congenital, or within two years of the onset of an acquired disability. This need not go into great detail; it is sufficient to consider at first the approximate level of his general intelligence, the presence or absence of useful sight or hearing for speech, his prospect of being able to make a good range of skilled movement with one or both arms and his probable ability to walk about stably or to stand for substantial periods. On such lines as these it should be possible to make certain forecasts of a negative kind by the time he is ten or eleven. To say at that age that he will be unable in the long run to do certain things will at least make it possible to rule out certain types of employment as quite outside his powers.

If his limitations are likely to be substantial and severe, it is sound common sense to bring into consultation at this stage the careers adviser, who will make a reconnaissance of suitable employment possibilities. It may be that no employment within his scope is available within a reasonable distance from his home; if so there is plenty of time to plan for alternatives and to prepare both child and parent for the idea that he may have to live in a hostel after leaving school. This, however, is likely to happen only where the disability is exceptionally severe or the home is in an isolated rural area. The commonest result of this preliminary investigation is that a possible field of employment is defined in general terms.

The next step is to continue the child's general education on lines suited to the prospective type of employment and to watch for any light which his response to general education may throw on his aptitudes. Though accurate specific aptitude tests are not yet well developed, the skilled and experienced teacher can draw conclusions. Manual dexterity, memory, potential mathematical ability, a talent for drawing and other things are tested by even the ordinary school curriculum up to the age of eleven or twelve. In secondary education between the ages of eleven and fourteen the beginnings of science and language instruction will give other potentialities a chance to show themselves. This, too, is the age when woodwork and even metal work appear in the school time-table and make it possible to test more precisely the manual dexterity which has been roughly guessed at an earlier age.

Specific vocational training need not be considered until the last two years in school, beginning at about the age of fourteen. Not all authorities favour it. Some contend that since the child's handicap has already interfered with his general education to some degree the emphasis should be on bringing him up to the general educational level of a normal school leaver. It has been found occasionally that children who have received vocational training while at school have suffered on leaving because they lacked the general educational attainments to enter and succeed in higher technical training courses; they have had to settle down as competent artisans when their innate ability would have justified careers as skilled technicians. There is always the purely practical objection that the small number of pupils in the average school for the handicapped makes it economically difficult to provide an adequate range of workshops and expert instructors; there is a tendency to provide vocational training in only three or four crafts or trades and to train the children in those without full regard to what their abilities and prospects might be in other fields.

The large special school is better placed and can hope to provide a range of workshops which, while not reproducing the full range of industrial work, can teach the elementary processes which form the common basis of industrial and other skills. In such a school there is a good possibility of 'vocational exposure' and as the child tries his skill in the various workshops it is possible not only to discover his likes and dislikes but to carry out in a far more precise way the assessment of his abilities and disabilities which has hitherto been only provisional and approximate. Some schools which are unable to provide adequate vocational training are now trying the interesting experiment of allowing some of their senior children to work part-time in suitable local workshops during the last months of their school life. This may point the way to future developments in vocational assessment and training in schools which are fortunate enough to be situated in areas where there is a variety of local light industry.

It must not be forgotten that the normal technical school is a place in which a wide variety of training is given for many occupations. It is, therefore, often worth considering whether a handicapped child of suitable ability might not leave his special school for a technical school for the latter part of his school career. Much will depend on whether he has received the necessary basic education in time; if he is much below the attainment standard which the technical school requires he is likely to find it too difficult to keep up with the normal pupils. It certainly seems that some handicapped children have passed their maximum need for the special environment of a special school by the time they are twelve or thirteen years old and there is something to be said for reviewing all such children annually after the age of eleven to see whether they might be suited for a trial in the wider field of a technical or even an ordinary secondary school. It is not impossible to provide for a part-time trial in the area in which the special school is situated.

In most cases, by one or other of the means indicated a fairly good assessment of suitability for work can be made by the time the child reaches the age of fifteen. This leaves the careers adviser a year in which to carry out final negotiations with employers. At this stage it is useful to remember that the child is a person and he should be brought personally into those negotiations. He should meet the appropriate members of the employer's staff, visit the place of employment and be given a pre-view of what he has to face when he leaves school. Not only will it arouse his interest but it will make possible the discussion of various personal problems—

transport to and from the place of work, mobility at work, the carrying of loads etc.—so that solutions can be sought in advance.

Assessment must, above all, be realistic and this presents a problem to the teacher, particularly in the special school. The teaching staff have had the job of bringing out the latent abilities of youngsters who have often been reluctant to try for fear of the humiliation of failure. To do this, most teachers, very properly, have to treat their geese as if they were swans, praising and encouraging them a little beyond their just deserts. The risk is that sometimes both pupil and teacher can become convinced that the goose is indeed a swan, so that the pupil's ambitions and the teacher's ambitions for him rise beyond the level of reality. In the surroundings of a special school this is only too easy for they tend to favour swan-like performance. A youngster may be able to do admirable manual work, but if he takes four hours to produce one quality article and a factory expects its workers to turn out eight of them in a day, then he will not be an acceptable employee in that factory. If he can produce quality in quantity in a place where all the chores of daily living are made easy or even done for him, will he be able to stand the strain of that production when he has to take upon himself most of those chores? Is it realistic to educate the highly intelligent severely handicapped youngster to degree standard over a period of painful years when his 'output potential' will prevent him from making full use of his academic training? (Remember the case of Hubert in Chapter 3).

It is for such reasons as these that there is a need for special assessment provision outside the school, perhaps in special adolescent centres or in adolescent units attached to adult centres —even, if there is no alternative available, in an adult centre— and certainly in surroundings which approximate more closely to those in which the handicapped youth would finally have to live and work. However, some of the troubles in this field could be reduced if, as I have suggested, the world of work and the world of school had closer contact and if that contact were between shop foreman, pupil and class teacher rather than between managing director and headmaster.

Where it is decided that the need for general education is paramount, consideration should be given to letting the child finish his education in a special school and then take vocational training in a special training college. This is often a happy solution for the fairly severely handicapped young person whose general education has been grossly interrupted but whose general ability warrants his being trained in one of the more specialized technical subjects which may range from radio engineering to book-keeping.

Throughout his last years of education it should be remembered that the change from the sheltered conditions of school to open employment is a dramatic one which carries with it considerable risks of strain. Any practical or technical education which he receives should be considered not merely from the point of view of assessment and training but also as a preparation for independent working life. In his last years at school or college the workshops should have something of a workshop atmosphere and it may well be that the experiments in part-time release to open employment which I have already mentioned could be profitably expanded with this important point in view.

For the moderately handicapped, who have missed a substantial amount of general education, much can be done by making use of existing facilities for further education in technical colleges and similar establishments near to their own homes. Sometimes adjustments in the curriculum or other concessions may have to be made, but these should be no more difficult—and may well be easier—than in ordinary schools. (It may be mentioned that severely deaf young people, because of their need of an interpreter, may be at a special disadvantage, but this need not be insuperable.) If there is no technical college near the youngster's home it may be possible to accommodate him in a hostel or in lodgings in the nearest town where such a college exists. The advantage of attendance at an ordinary technical college instead of a special, and usually residential, college for the disabled are the wider range of subjects available and the fact that the adolescent, at a time of life when he needs to adjust to life in the world at large, is not isolated from the community.

### Education in Living with a Handicap

Those who like technical terminology might prefer to use the term 'education in (or toward) social adjustment', but the simpler phrase is more expressive and pointed. Some of the handicapped resent their disability and fight strenuously to lead a life which is even more 'normal' than that of those who are not handicapped, wearing out their bodies and spirits in desperate competition against odds. Others surrender to self-pity and luxuriate in the pity of others. Either of these courses is disastrous; the only sane and safe way of living is to face one's disability frankly, assess one's limitations and powers and shape life accordingly. Nothing in formal education, whether academic or vocational, is in the long run more important than this.

Handicap strikes its victim in a variety of ways. Some, handicapped from birth, never know normal living. They have much to learn, but nothing to unlearn. Perhaps those whose handicap strikes suddenly, out of the blue, after years of growing up normally, have the hardest task, because they become all at once strangers in a world which they know and have loved. What they have had and what they have learned is still theirs, but it may often make their new life more bitter by contrast. To a third class handicap comes slowly and almost insidiously over the years. Theirs, in theory, is the easiest task for they have time to adjust themselves progressively to the new life. Yet slow farewells are often harder to bear than swift partings and the gradual but irrevocable giving up, one after another, of the things one has enjoyed to the full, while watching one's friends and contemporaries continuing to enjoy them, makes special demands on courage and resolution.

Adjustment to handicap, however and whenever it becomes necessary, starts with a deliberate and realistic appraisal of the situation. For the young child this must first be made by those who are acting for him—the parents, doctors, teachers and others who form the team so often mentioned in this book. Even the older child cannot do it initially for himself because he can see life only in terms of what he has himself experienced before his handicap developed.

This part of his education begins in the home and the home will have a continuing responsibility for it even after he starts school life. The chapter on Parent and Child sets out some fundamental principles, not least among which is the encouragement of independence from the start.

Every child has ambitions; it is these which encourage him along the road to maturity. They may begin as insubstantial daydreams but they gradually become more concrete as time goes on, and even the most fantastic among them can act as a spur. They are valid, however, only so far as they have some possibility of fulfilment. For the normal child the world is his oyster. Anything is possible and the realization that some possibilities are outside his reach comes gradually and fairly painlessly with experience. For the handicapped child some normal ambitions are utterly impossible from the start and the knowledge that he cannot even dream the dreams of his normal playfellows is a persistent reminder that he is different. From the outset, therefore, his aims must be turned toward those things which can have a possible concrete meaning to him so that he will be striving toward that which he has some chance of reaching.

Parents, too, have ambitions and before they can rightly influence their child they must modify their own thinking. It is not easy for parents who, before the birth of their child, have had visions of him as a successful lawyer, a brilliant scientist or an outstanding athlete to reconcile themselves suddenly to his being a manual worker, a modest clerk or a mere spectator of sport, but this is the critical point from which all else begins. The child is not born with ambitions. For the first years of life it matters nothing to him whether his career will involve a white collar or no collar, dirty hands or clean. He would rather be an engine-driver than a barrister. Ambition is only part of something much bigger—sense of values—and what matters is that the handicapped child should grow up in an atmosphere in which the sense of values is consistent with his potentialities.

The home must put high earning power in a secondary place. Intellectual parents who have a dull child must let him see that high thinking and brilliant conversation are by no means the only things they value. The 'low-brow' home which has no interest in books and learning must give proper place to things of the mind to encourage its young but intelligent cripple. Even un-musical parents must be ready to acknowledge music as the gate to a new world for their blind daughter and devotees of radio or television try to foster and share interest in books with a deaf son. And here I must give an important warning. The search for different values must not be confused with a lowering of standards. Once the range of the child's possibilities has been accepted, nothing but the best within that range is good enough. It is fatally easy for parents to assume that because the child is handicapped he is basically inferior and the child himself, seeing that he is inferior in some respects to his normal fellows and knowing that success involves hard work, may tend to use his disability as an excuse for not making an effort. He must be patiently encouraged, urged and even, when necessary, pressed to put forth all his powers; however easy it may be to find excuses for slackness, it must not be tolerated.

It is not overly difficult to teach the young handicapped child this philosophy of acceptance from the start. A much greater problem will be faced when a child already established in a normal way of life, perhaps with career ambitions already beginning to crystallize, is suddenly handicapped by disease or accident. It is almost inevitable that for both child and parents there will be a period of darkness and despair. Youth, fortunately, is resilient. The child will readjust and make good unless the parents allow their own shattered hopes to infect him with hopelessness. For both parents and child the best tonic is convincing evidence that others have faced and overcome the same obstacles. They must, as soon as possible, meet such people. Those who are helping them must make a point of this and they will receive ready assistance from the many voluntary organizations which exist to aid the handicapped. Membership of an active association of parents of similarly handicapped children can provide encouragement for the parents, while personal success stories will slowly but surely give the child new goals and ambitions.

In most cases it is good for the child who acquires a severe handicap to go to a special school as soon as possible. Apart from his educational needs as such, he has a lot to gain from being in the regular company of others who have already come to terms cheerfully with his kind of disability. This may seem too obvious to mention in the case of the blind and the deaf; only by experience does one learn that a minority of parents refuse to accept the obvious and by indecision or deliberate opposition delay the child's going away, so that invaluable time is wasted.

Genuine doubts may arise in the case of acquired physical handicap, especially where the disability is not very severe. The ideal is for the child to return to a normal school, but if he goes straight back with his new disability to the place where he has previously led a perfectly normal life he may find it difficult to adjust, since every hour of every day points the contrast between what he used to be and what he now is. Particularly where the patient is a boy who has been keen and competent in sport there is much to be said for letting him have a year or two in a special school as an adjustment period, with the intention that he should go back to an ordinary school later. The boy who has been more interested in studious pursuits will probably make an easier readjustment to an ordinary school. As a rule the continuity of activity and environment in the things he *can* do helps to support him, but once or twice I have found it better to send him to a different normal school from the one he attended before. Girls, to whom sport is less fundamental, usually find their old environment less distressing, but may have difficulties at the 'dating age', a point which is considered later.

Training in living techniques is discussed in the chapters which treat specifically of the various types of handicap, but its general importance must be stressed here. The dependence or independence of the handicapped person is shown in the little things of life as well as in the big ones and because the little things are present all the time they assume special importance. It is not very hard to accept the fact that one must be pushed about in a wheel-chair or guided from place to place; what is persistently embarrassing and even infuriating is the need to have help with feeding or with using the water-closet. The use of various aids and 'gadgets' is always helpful and quite a wide variety of such things is now available. The home and, later, the school, must persevere in teaching the child to help himself by all possible means of this kind. Neatness of dress and cleanliness of person are also important in giving confidence in social contacts. The modern tendency to tolerate informality in dress is useful—it reduces the importance of shoe-laces, buttons, ties and so on. But informality must not be allowed to lead to slackness and untidiness.

I have explained in detail in Chapter 7 the importance of recreation to the handicapped. Education for recreation is no less important than education for employment. It begins with that training in a sense of values to which I have referred above. Boys in particular set much store by prowess in a limited range of physical sports, most of which are difficult or impossible for the handicapped. Every handicapped child should have a chance of 'recreational exposure' comparable with the vocational exposure considered in an earlier part of this chapter. If football, tennis, cricket, baseball and the like are out of the question, swimming, fencing, cross-country running and other 'secondary' sports may still be possible. If these fail, there are still non-physical competitive games which can be considered.

The field of non-competitive hobbies and pursuits is unlimited and there is literally no handicapped person who cannot engage in one or more of them with success. Special schools, to their great credit, are increasingly making a point of exploring children's interests and abilities in the widest fields and of giving them skilled guidance and teaching in developing them. Once the idea has been conveyed to the child that there is just as much to be proud of in competence in the less common sports or in hobbies as there is in ability in the most popular recreations confidence and morale can be steadily built up.

As I have previously pointed out, it matters much to the handicapped person is to know that in some field he is as good as or even better than the normal person. For this reason it is part of his education to let him—more, to encourage him—to join with normal people in his recreations. Probably no more important help exists than what is being done in many countries by the Boy Scout and Girl Guide movements. In the well-run Scout or Guide troop there is something for everyone with help, teaching and esteem in an enormous variety of activities. In some severe disabilities, such as blindness and paraplegia, it is probably best for the handicapped child to start in a special troop organized by the special school, but sooner or later even such gravely handicapped children should begin to share the activities of a troop for normal children.

Again, the child who acquires handicap at or after the age of ten or so will have difficulties in making a readjustment. He already has interests and standards and will find it hard to give them up and acquire new ones. Some children take the opportunity of serving in the sports or hobbies which have previously interested them. The disabled boy who was fond of cricket may become umpire or scorer to his team, the footballer may help with the secretarial work of the club, the amateur actor, boy or girl, assist in stage lighting or the making of costumes. This may well prove a useful step on the way to new interests. It is not, however, possible for all, and as in the field of work and general living, the personal help and example of someone who has already been through the experience and succeeded is invaluable.

Last but not least, something must be said about learning to get on with the opposite sex. Boys are fortunate in that it never seems impossible to find a girl who will take an interest in a handicapped boy and, ultimately, to find a wife. Whether the motives which impel a young woman to marry a handicapped youth are always those which make for successful marriage may be open to doubt; it may be dangerous for a woman to marry a man mainly because she pities him or wants to 'mother' him. But the more he mixes with girls at the appropriate age the more likely he is to find the right one and if he is early encouraged to overcome self-consciousness in girls' company and to take part in mixed recreations he has a good chance of finding someone with whom he has many interests in common.

Though the handicapped boy may arouse a girl's maternal instincts, there would seem to be no corresponding instincts in the boy which respond to handicap in a girl. Up to the early 'teens the handicapped girl may adjust to her disability better than a boy because she is not confronted with the sport-worship which is natural in most normal boys' communities. Then, quite suddenly, she finds herself at a hopeless disadvantage compared with normal girls in that particular competitive field which is most important to her sex. Even a mild disability may handicap her if, without necessarily restricting her activities or abilities, it makes her ungainly or unbeautiful. At this age the effects can be permanently damaging to her emotional development.

There is no ready answer; it is indeed doubtful whether there is ever going to be any adequate answer at all. Probably all that can be done is to start in good time to encourage career ambitions rather than marriage ambitions, though still stressing the importance of taking pains with her appearance in dress and person. If the worst comes to the worst she will join the many women who have lived successfully wedded to their careers. Experience, however, does offer one hope. More than a few handicapped girls who have concentrated on a career without apparent hope of marriage have come to emotional ripeness and fulfilment in their work and have then encountered men whose own maturity made them respond to the deeper qualities which handicap obscures in the sight of the young male. On such encounters many happy marriages have been founded.

### FURTHER READING

*The Education of the Handicapped Child*
Association for Special Education. What is Special Education? Heinemann & Spastics Society.
Devereux, H. M. Housecraft in the Education of Handicapped Children. Mills & Boon.
Miller, E. J. and Gwynne, C. V. A Life Apart. Lippincott & Tavistock, London.
Segal, S. No Child is Ineducable. Pergamon.

# CHAPTER 9

## After-School Problems

In the chapter on Assessment in Practice and also in the chapters on individual disabilities some reference is made to the long-term outlook and to difficulties which may arise in adult life, but some special comment on the years of adjustment, as they may be called, is necessary.

The middle-aged adult, looking back on himself or herself when young, is inclined to wear rosy spectacles and to think 'those were the glorious days'. In fact, for most young people, adolescence is a mixture of heaven and hell, a time when one reacts quickly and feels deeply, when a little passing pleasure may be a wonderful delight but when a trouble or disappointment which is really only trivial may look as if it is bringing with it the end of the world.

The normal young person, from the onset of puberty—which may begin as early as the age of eleven—to the end of the 'teens' is undergoing a process of continuous physical change. He may grow steadily but is more likely to do so in a series of spurts and the endocrine glands, some of which are only just beginning to come into action, are showing their influence in very uncertain ways, now over-active and now under-active. The secondary sexual characteristics—breaking of the voice, the growth of body hair, the development of the girl's breasts—and, of course, the onset of menstruation can be personally and socially embarrassing. Muscular strength may lag behind one's ambitions and desires to take part in adult activities, producing annoying and even frightening bouts of tiredness.

New personal problems arise. In the field of personal relationships, the awakening of sexual impulses at a time when society frowns on their gratification produces a whole crop of difficulties. The process of becoming a person in one's own right conflicts with the previous dependent parent-child relationship; one alternates between asserting one's independence of the family and wishing to shelter oneself inside it as one used to. It has to be accepted as one of the facts of life that most children 'grow away from' their parents for a time before they come back to a new understanding each of the other as people who are worth knowing and respecting. From the ordered life of school, with one's daily doings planned to a time-table, with responsibility carried by other people and with its simple ethical code of blacks and whites, one moves suddenly into a new world where one orders one's own affairs, carries responsibility for one's own actions and has to live by a code which has infinite shades of grey and which can twist right into wrong and wrong into right in a moment. Many observers believe that a substantial number of normal children go through a phase of 'school leaving shock' which can do marked emotional and social injury which may have lasting effects.

Some of the handicapping disabilities can actually become worse during adolescence. A stabilized diabetes or epilepsy may suddenly become unstable for a matter of months or even for a year or two. The vision of the myope may suddenly deteriorate as growth changes the optical characteristics of the eye. Asthma may become more severe, a damaged heart fail to cope with the circulatory needs of a larger body or bony deformities become more marked. The maladjusted child who seemed to be doing well may be greatly disturbed by the emotional stresses to which he is subjected, the child whose stammer was apparently cured suffer a severe relapse. Even if the disability itself does not get worse, its effects may be more serious as the child moves out of the school environment which he had learned to live in and enters a world which will not accommodate itself to his needs. This is obvious in the case of a child who has been in a special school and some steps can be taken in advance to reduce its impact. What is less often realized is that the child with a moderate or even a minor disability who has got on quite well in an ordinary school and whom one has ceased to regard as handicapped may, when he leaves school, suddenly find that he has a handicap after all, in that he cannot compete successfully with non-handicapped people in their own environment, whether at work or at play.

In brief, we subject the handicapped child to an intensification of his handicap and to a set of complicated stresses at just that time in his life when he would be specially vulnerable even if he had no handicap. What is more, our administrative systems are such that at this point of special need we cut him off from the people and the agencies which have up to now given him support

—the school and the teachers, the school health service and its doctors and nurses—and hand him over to the care of a new set of people and agencies. That these people may be highly skilled and thoroughly understanding is somewhat beside the point. What matters is that they are new to the child and the family and that the right supportive relationship needs to be developed; it cannot suddenly spring up in a moment. At a time of crisis and uncertainty it is naturally to the people whom we know and understand, and who know and understand us, that we turn.

The Working Party on the Handicapped School Leaver, to whose report I have referred in several places, gave special attention to this last point and among other things, recommended strongly that the school health service should have continuing responsibility for handicapped children after leaving school up to, at any rate, the age of eighteen. In practice more than a few school doctors, school nurses and teachers are already informally taking a constructive and continuing interest in these young people, but it would certainly strengthen and encourage them if their efforts were formally recognized and if staffs could be increased to make this work generally more practicable. Continuity of care is, however, only one part of the whole and there are quite a lot of things which can be done to make these problems of adolescent adjustment less difficult to deal with.

Can they, in the first place, be prevented from arising? Complete prevention in every case is an impossibility, but there are some lines of approach which can usefully be followed. The suddenness of the change from the school to the after-school environment is an important source of trouble; can it be made rather more gradual? The new environment is the more difficult to settle down in because it is new; can we prepare the child to face it more confidently? Each child is unique; is it possible to forecast in advance which are likely to have settling-down problems and what form those problems are going to take?

First, gradualness. I have emphasized in Chapter 8 that one of the disadvantages of special school education is that it isolates handicapped children from normal children and, in boarding schools, interferes with their relationship with the family and the neighbourhood to which they will have to return. It can be argued that boarding education may actually help a child in the process of 'growing out of the family' during adolescence and this certainly happens in a number of cases (this is an important reason for trying to meet each child's potential difficulties on a personal and individual basis). The ideal would be to give children in special schools a 'hardening-off' period of whole-time or part-time attendance in ordinary schools during their last two years of school life. In considering special handicaps I indicate those which offer the best possibilities in this direction, but the idea is worth considering in the case of every individual child, whatever his disability, provided that one makes this a counsel of perfection which cannot always be adopted and does not turn it into a dogma.

I have already stressed that the need for sound basic general education limits the extent to which vocational training can be given during the school years, but there remains the possibility of making introduction to employment progressive after leaving school. The adolescent with a handicap is already conscious that by staying whole-time at school longer than normal children he has 'lost' a year in comparison with his contemporaries but it is generally accepted that part-time further education by releasing employed young people for one or two days a week to attend technical colleges is sound policy. It might be worth while to vary this system for the handicapped and to make the year immediately following the last year of compulsory schooling one during which the adolescent might continue to attend a day special school part-time but go to work for a progressively increasing number of days each week until he is adjusted to whole-time employment.

The suddenness of change is hazardous not only because of the fact of the change but because of its nature. Part-time introduction to work means that the youngster is facing factory conditions on only two or three days out of the five in the working week, but even so the contrast between an eight-hour day under factory conditions and a five-hour day under school conditions is considerable. Up to a point a factory may be able to modify its work-schedule for the newly-engaged handicapped school leaver, but even where this is impossible there should be acceptance of the need for him to be intelligently handled by the management. His disability may not prevent him from doing certain types of job but it may easily make it hard for him to learn the job as quickly as a normal person. There is, in fact, evidence that some young people, particularly those with impaired intelligence, sight or hearing, are not infrequently rejected by industry after a trial period because they have not learned at the end of, say, six or eight weeks a job skill which the normal young person acquires in a month. Had they only been taught in the right way and had the employer persisted for a few weeks longer they might well have made good.

There is a gap here between management and practice. The official policy of an employing firm may be tolerant enough at top level but the actual business of hiring and firing is usually determined at shop floor level. Some special schools, appreciating this, have made it a practice not only to cultivate the management of local firms but to invite under-managers and foremen to visit the school both to meet in advance the prospective leavers who may be coming to their factories and to discuss with the school staff the general and individual problems of people with that particular kind of disability. This has met with most encouraging success and is well worth more general adoption.

Gradual transition and preparation cannot entirely be separated. The social and vocational experience which the child gains in this gentle introduction to the post-school world is valuable education for living. Something more, however, is needed. It is now becoming more generally realized that education in personal relationships should be part of the education of every child and this is slowly being introduced into the curriculum of ordinary schools. Many special schools have intelligently perceived the particular needs of their pupils and are giving the subject special attention. If staff resources and staff training are—which seems likely— going to be inadequate for some time to come to allow all schools to do this properly, then special schools should be given special priority. It should not, however, stop with the pupils. The handicapped child, in this field as in so many others, must not be subjected to the extra strain of having to solve his problems by a process of trial and error. He can be helped substantially by a programme of parent and family education and this must be another objective for the good school. Again many special schools have already made a start, but ordinary schools which have handicapped children among their pupils are not yet fully seized of its value. Where it is possibly most urgently needed, in the case of children at boarding schools, it is probably most difficult and least done. There is a serious responsibility on the school health staff and others in the child's home area to make sure, after consultation with the school, that parent-preparation is properly carried out.

It is, though it ought not to be, necessary to comment on certain very practical aspects of preparation for school leaving. That a child goes to a special school automatically tends to take off his shoulders certain responsibilities which normal children in ordinary schools learn imperceptibly to carry. Such items of simple daily experience as travelling alone on public transport, going shopping, alone for minor things or with parents for major ones, using the telephone and managing one's pocket money may be either ruled out altogether or, at any rate, substantially cut down. This is specially unfortunate since they are activities which may, in later life, be made more difficult by the child's disability. Some of these, especially activities like travelling and shopping, have to be taken particularly seriously. Because they may involve extra stress and exertion, it is not enough to know how they are ordinarily done; it may be necessary to work out special techniques for doing them and it is usually desirable to learn how to plan one's life so as to reduce the need for them. And, once again, it is important to remember the inter-relationship of different parts of living. It is by no means uncommon for an apparent failure in job-placement to occur not because the job is the wrong one but because getting to and from work, though possible, is worrying or because the mysteries of feeding in a works canteen or 'clocking in' have not been properly explained.

In theory it ought to be possible to detect in advance those children who may be specially vulnerable during the post-school adjustment period. This should be considered particularly at any case-conference which is held before leaving-time, but it should certainly not be left until the case-conference is due, perhaps less than a year before leaving; it should be part of the continuous assessment process which is going on all the time. Some of the questions which one must ask are obvious—is the disability likely to worsen at this time, either spontaneously or under stress, are special aids or gadgets likely to be useful and so on. Probably not enough attention is yet given to personality assessment, particularly such qualities as drive, perseverance and adaptability, all of which are liable to fluctuate during adolescence. The child's relationship with his family should also be assessed. During his school-days the school will itself have done a good deal to absorb the repercussions of school stress, but it is not to be expected that the factory will be equally understanding and elastic about work-stress. It is a commonplace that the adult who is unsettled or unhappy at work gets rid of his frustrations and aggressions on to the family at home, but if the adolescent's relationship with the family

D

is, as so often happens, a little precarious anyway, home may not be able to provide him with this safety-valve. Most of the foregoing, if detected in time, may be dealt with by a combination of preparation of child and family, special care in job-selection and arrangements for the right kind of support after leaving school.

Accepting the impossibility at present of getting continuity of all the helping and supporting services during the school-leaving and adjustment stage, what can one do to effect some bridging of the gap? The one normal continuing influence is that of the family and I have said enough to make it clear that this cannot guarantee stability, even though it may be helped to do so. I would go so far as to say that most adolescents need a friend or adviser or some equivalent outside the immediate family circle. Normal youngsters find one for themselves but if we can help the handicapped to find one it makes things easier.

It is quite common for this friend to be found in the outer circle of the family in the person of an uncle, aunt or older cousin. If such a relationship already exists, it should be encouraged. Or the friend may be found through a club, a scout troop or some other organisation. Some handicapped children may find their school relationships a source of considerable strength and they often like to lean on this support for some time after leaving. The day special school is well placed to effect a sort of weaning process and the leaver may go back for frequent visits during the first months, with the visits gradually tapering off as time goes on. Some schools run a kind of informal old pupils' club, meeting once a week or so in the evenings. It can be argued that this may tend to perpetuate dependence, but whether this actually happens depends much on the staff members who are in charge. In any case, if a boy or girl is still relying on the school and its staff for support and assurance a year after leaving, this is an important and significant fact which gives evidence that either the child is basically insecure or the other supporting services are not equal to their task. Some boarding schools, especially those for maladjusted children, have found it useful to have rooms available for their ex-pupils to come back for an occasional week-end visit, an idea which is deserving of wider adoption.

What is quite certain is that the professional workers who may have to give help and support after leaving school—the mental welfare officer, the home teacher of the blind, the missioner to the deaf and the social welfare officer to the physically handicapped—

should be brought into close association with the schools and should make their contacts with child and family long before school leaving time. This will help them to understand both the collective and the individual problems of handicapped children and to become accepted by the child and his parents before they have to take over major responsibility. It brings them into the picture not at a point when a case conference decides that they might be interested but before even the evidence which is to be placed before the case conference has been gathered. If they help in the gathering they will be better able to take part in the conference; if they share in the planning for the child's future they will be more successful in implementing the plan in practice.

The obvious importance of these changes in the child's surroundings and in the people to whom he must look for help and support must not make one overlook the equally sudden change in his activities. For the great majority of children the things which they have done in their schooldays, whether in the classroom or outside it, tend to disappear from their lives or at least to dwindle into the the background. They continue to read, it is true, but only desultorily or in those fields which directly affect their careers; they write, but only in so far as their jobs require it or in occasional letters; they do sums, but only where these are immediately necessary at work or elsewhere. History, geography, science and the other subjects outside the three Rs are virtually finished. In a period of radical change in one's life *any* continuing thread is an aid to stability and for even one thing which one has found interesting before the change to be continued and developed during the period of flux helps the process of adjustment. I have already written about the importance of recreation for the handicapped and I would add here that it is in the field of recreation that this continuing thread can very often be found.

Paul (Chapter 7) joined the local swimming club before he left school and kept up his swimming after leaving. Roddy, a severely maladjusted boy in a special boarding school, had achieved some adjustment by the time he was sixteen, but his teachers viewed with some alarm the prospect of his going back to his home town, two hundred miles away, where his contacts had dwindled and where it would be difficult because of distance for the school to keep in touch. In each of his last two years at school he was the athletics champion and he certainly had unusual athletic capability for a lad of his age. The school health department in his home area got into touch with the local athletic club and arranged in advance for Roddy to meet some of its members. The lad had been quite frankly scared of leaving school but the knowledge that when he went home he would have facilities for and coaching in his favourite recreation changed his attitude completely. He went home with confidence and has made good in his job and his social life; he is also fulfilling his athletic promise.

Whatever the recreation may be, it carries the prospect of continuity and the prospect of friends. The handicapped child at the day school should be encouraged not only to follow his hobby at school but to join the local club or society if it will accept him—and even those with no special junior section will usually make an exception—before he leaves school. For the child at a boarding school, the advance contact that was made for Roddy in athletics can just as easily be made for the youngster whose interest lies in photography, music or painting. If only Frederick (Chapter 7) had been given an interest in natural history before he left school instead of after, he would have been saved three years of stress and unhappiness. It is easy to make the excuse that bird-watching was a somewhat unlikely interest to develop in a crippled schoolboy, but there should be no need to seek excuses. To spend time and trouble in seeking and arousing leisure-time activities is an essential part of education and a worth-while investment.

FURTHER READING

*After-School Problems*
British Council for Rehabilitation.   The Handicapped School Leaver.
Herford, M. E. M. Youth at Work.   Heinemann.
Hunt, P. (Ed.)   Stigma.   Geoffrey Chapman.

## CHAPTER 10

# The Principles of Assessment

From what has been said of the problems and needs of handicapped children it is possible to infer some general principles which should be borne in mind in assessing the child and his handicap. Though the detailed application of those principles will vary with the nature and degree of the handicap, it is worth while to summarize them at this stage.

The words 'of a child and his handicap' are used deliberately, because the child and the handicap cannot be separated; they are indissolubly wedded for life and each will affect the other. The essentials of assessment are precisely those which govern an enquiry into, say, a business concern which has got into difficulties and involve the drawing up of a balance sheet. On the one side are set down the liabilities and on the other the assets; the problem is to minimize the liabilities and expand and develop the assets.

The first step to be taken is to measure, as accurately as possible, the most obvious liability, the handicap itself, as it stands at the time. This may be easy or difficult, but all possible means must be used to make sure that the estimate is as correct as it can be. The next stage is to consider what action can be taken to reduce the intrinsic disability. Is it likely to yield to medical or surgical treatment? If so, how much is it likely to be reduced? Is treatment to be undertaken at once or later? If later, at what age? Is the treatment to consist of a single short procedure, is it likely to cover a long, continuous period or will it involve a series of operations with considerable intervals between them? The need to have some estimate of this last is important right from the beginning, because nothing is more essential than to plan well ahead, especially when education is involved and the start of education may be postponed or its course interrupted by periods of treatment.

The child's immediate liability investigated, it is necessary to inquire into his personal assets. The physically handicapped child will have to make brain do for him what brawn cannot and an

91

intelligence assessment should be a sine qua non for every physically handicapped child. This need not be elaborate in the beginning, but it should at least be enough to show whether he is above average, average or below average in general intellectual ability. It is important to consider general intelligence, too, in the deaf child and the blind child, not forgetting that dullness of mind may magnify apparent hearing defect and vice versa. The very young child will not have had much chance, at the time of assessment, to show whether or not he possesses special aptitudes, but the youngster who acquires a physical disability or loses sight or hearing during his school days may already have manifested some special qualities to a discerning teacher.

A knowledge of intelligence and aptitude will give some indication of what sort of education, general and vocational, the child should receive and it will also prevent waste of time and resources in following unrewarding lines of education. It is also important to realize that the purposeful education of a child can to some extent reduce the impact of handicap. This applies not only to such things as the learning of Braille by the blind or the development of lip-reading by the deaf but to economy of movement and the acquiring of substitute movements by children with motor disabilities.

The child's personality must, of course, be taken into account, since it may make a vital difference to his prospects in the long run. Personality determines how he approaches the whole business of living with a disability, how he co-operates with those who offer treatment, education and other help and how he reacts at those critical moments of decision which are bound to occur from time to time. But, while it is easy to talk about the necessity of assessment of personality it is exceedingly difficult to make the assessment in practice.

The weakness of a muscle, the limitation of movement at a joint, the acuity of vision or hearing, are all capable of more or less precise measurement and reasonable estimates of the prospect of response to treatment can be made. Intelligence, in spite of the way in which its manifestations are sometimes disguised by various disabilities, can usually be assessed approximately and is something which is likely to stay constant, within fairly small margins, in the majority of children. By contrast, none of the tests at present available for assessing personality has the reliability of even intelligence tests, let alone of audiometry or vision testing, and this is specially true in respect of children with physical or intellectual disabilities.

The reasons for this uncertainty are obvious. One's personality is made rather than inborn and the making process goes on through the whole of the formative period of childhood and early youth. Even in adult life it can be modified by major illness or by drastic changes in environment, though the main basic personality traits generally determine themselves in childhood. To make an accurate and detailed personality assessment in the early years of childhood is rather like assessing a book by looking at its title page or guessing what will be written on a virgin blackboard during a lesson which has not yet begun. If we know the title, the author and the publisher of a book we can perhaps imagine something of its contents; if we know the qualifications of the teacher and the title of his lesson we can expect that certain things will be said and written. But in neither case can we be sure in advance of just how the subject will be treated, how much ground will be covered and where emphasis will be laid.

With a child's personality, we may guess early, from knowledge of the parents and of the nature of the disability, what degree of basic stability or instability may be produced by heredity and constitution. Moreover, knowledge of the home and family background may tell us whether the influences which will act on the child in the first years of life will tend to stabilise or unsettle. Broadly speaking, the two things which will concern us most will be the risk of emotional maladjustment and the presence or absence of that quality which is generally called 'drive'. Some hints may be obtained within the first three or four years of life by shrewd observation of the child's response to the challenges of life, but during that period the challenges are usually limited so far as a handicapped child is concerned and it may well be that our views will have to be radically revised during his school years. Moreover, the possibility of influencing personality development in the right direction is considerable—often much greater than the possibility of reducing the basic disability by treatment.

Reference has already been made to the importance of the family's economic position. In a country with comprehensive social services it may be less significant, but not all countries yet have adequate provision throughout their area and the family may have to buy some or all of the things their child needs. The size of the house can be important and so can the presence or absence of a garden. If the child's handicap is such as to make the mother's task more exacting and laborious, much may depend on whether she can afford to hire assistance in either domestic work or the care of the child himself. Toys are part of the equipment needed for the informal education of every child; the well-to-do home can provide them on a larger scale than the poor one. Though the family car is not always an unmixed blessing to the handicapped child his prospects of getting about will be better if the family own one. Educational prospects in most countries depend less than formerly on family income but it cannot be eliminated as a factor. Even if the State takes responsibility for general schooling and higher education, the family must be able to afford the loss of the child's possible earnings while he is in a University or Technical College. And if his handicap is severe it may be important that he can be more or less permanently subsidized by his family.

Parental standards of behaviour and social background may be important, especially in their effect on the parents' attitude to the child's problems. Intelligent, highly educated parents, for example, find it exceedingly difficult to accept and be realistic about a mentally subnormal child; artisan parents of modest intellect often seem to receive the news that their child is a dullard in a quite matter of fact sort of way. The educated parent has, however, a much readier grasp of the way in which trained intelligence can make up for physical disability. Any tendency in either parent to neurosis or instability has to be entered in the 'liabilities' column. The handicapped child needs stability and firmness in the home background possibly more than the normal child and certainly over a longer period. One of the things which he will need from the parents is patience with his clumsiness and slow progress; and it is important to know whether this can be relied upon. The parents' basic attitude toward the child is discussed in detail elsewhere. Whether it is satisfactory or not, and, if not, whether it is capable of modification is clearly a matter of major importance.

The other children in the family enter into the assessment. If the handicapped child is an only child he can obviously receive more of the special attention he needs, but he stands in danger of receiving too much of it. If he comes as the baby into a family whose other children have all reached school age he is likely to have the best that life offers to the only child without the worse disadvantages of the only child. If, however, the gap between him and the other children is as long as, say, ten years, he runs the risk of alternately being spoilt and being dismissed as a nuisance by his brothers and sisters. The prospect is best when the family is not too large and when the child next oldest has passed the stage of making maximum demands on the mother but is not so much older that he will never be a playmate for the handicapped one.

If the handicapped child, on the other hand, is the first-born, and if his handicap is congenital, though he can rely on a flying start, while he is the only child, problems will arise when other children are born and have to share the mother's care. This is particularly the sort of case in which the family's future conflicts of loyalty and priority must be considered in advance.

Is the home in town or in the country? This affects at once any questions of continuing hospital care and treatment as out-patient or in-patient. It will become very important as the years go on and the question of special schooling arises. The day special school is an excellent compromise between the child's special educational needs and his need for home life, but is available only if he lives in or near a town. Long-term prospects, too, may depend upon urban or rural environment. The country village can easily find work for the physically fit simpleton and will accept him into the community's life in a way which the town cannot. On the other hand, village life cannot usually provide the sedentary skilled job which offers the best prospects to the intelligent youngster with a physical handicap.

When should assessment be carried out? The obvious answer is 'as early as possible', but this is, perhaps, a little too obvious. At any particular time the evidence on which assessment is based is limited. One can usually look ahead with some certainty for a period of weeks or months, but the further into the future one peers the dimmer is the picture in the crystal ball. Of a few things one can often be certain. A mentally subnormal child will not suddenly become a genius, a child without legs will not grow new ones, a blind child whose retina or optic nerve has been destroyed will never be able to see. Even so there may be advances in the teaching of the subnormal or the blind or vast technical improvements in the design and manufacture of artificial limbs.

Where the disability is one which can be treated, a shrewd guess can be made as to the child's prospects of improvement under treatment and even as to the possibility of new treatment techniques being developed out of those at present in use; one cannot make guesses about the possible discovery of new 'wonder' drugs or machines but this kind of miracle happens only rarely and there is nothing to be gained and much to be lost by taking it into serious account. A few years ago, for example, when epilepsy was being treated by rather heavy doses of sedative drugs, it was reasonable to assume that before long there might be drugs which would damp down the fits without dulling the child's consciousness. These are now coming into use, but it is not yet reasonable to look forward to the coming of a drug which will effect a certain and complete cure in all cases. The use of transistors has made it possible to produce smaller, lighter and more effective hearing aids but it is improbable that aids will come in the near future which will give the child with severe hearing loss the equivalent of normal hearing.

In the social field the future is even less predictable. That a family may break up, that a parent may become severely ill or die, that a father may lose his job and the family fall on bad times —all these are accidents that are part of the normal course of human life and may happen to anyone. It would be quite wrong to base one's forecasts on the assumption that any or all of them might happen and yet the possibilities cannot be ignored.

Presumably the really prudent doctor would refrain from making an assessment that looked beyond the immediate future, but this kind of extreme prudence is no virtue. The parents have to come to terms with the problem of bringing up and living with the child and if they are to do this realistically they must be told, as early as possible, what the long-term outlook is, so that they know both the best and the worst. Education cannot be arranged on a hand-to-mouth basis, with a sudden change at every crisis; it is desirable to look ahead, at any rate for a period of two or three years.

The practical course is to be frank in the beginning, to say that certain things are definite and will not change or be changed but to make it clear that some of the long-term forecasts are only guesses. From then on, the child's whole life is to be considered a period of continuing assessment with the regular observations of parent, family doctor, consultant, school M. O. and teacher noted and correlated. In any case, there should be a general review of the assessment at certain points—a few months before the child reaches compulsory school age, when he is due to transfer from infant to junior school or from junior to secondary, at least a year before he is due to leave school and, of course, whenever there seems to be a worsening of the disability or a period of special treatment has to be undertaken.

Parents will press the doctor for firm forecasts and dogmatic advice, and who can blame them? In spite of what I have said in the last paragraph, there are occasions when it is the lesser evil to be definite and risk being proved wrong by events; the choice depends on one's judgement of the parents. But on the whole, parents tend to prefer the honest doubter, provided he explains clearly why he is uncertain. This course pays valuable dividends when, as not infrequently happens, the time arrives when a decision needs to be taken by the parents themselves at a critical point. If they have been accustomed to letting someone else do their thinking they may well be out of their depth.

I recall the case of a boy who was mentally handicapped and somewhere on the borderline of suitability for education. The father was faced with a crisis in his career. If he were to follow his ambitions he must accept a period of service overseas and though his family might follow him after an interval the possible educational facilities for the child in that place were not likely to meet his needs. Should we get the boy into a boarding special school and let the rest of the family follow father overseas, bearing in mind that the special school placement might turn out to be wrong and that a change might have to be made while the parents were abroad? Should we let father go abroad and leave all his family in England indefinitely, with the possible social and emotional risks for the other members of the family? Or should father sacrifice his ambitions and make his career in this country, keeping the family together?

This involved exploring the possible facilities available in England. There were two places to which he might go. Enquiry showed that one of them might be able to provide day training centre facilities but had no suitable day special school; the other had both day training centre and day special school available within fairly easy reach. This last offered the best prospects for the boy, in the sense that he could be kept with the family and that his placement in school or training centre could be genuinely regarded as a trial. The father decided to settle for this and accept the rather less attractive career prospect for himself, and a little negotiation with his employers ensured that they would be prepared to leave him in his new post for at least three years. What will happen in the end to child and family remains to be seen, but if there should be any fleeting regrets for missed opportunities they may be the less bitter because the decision was a considered one made by the family.

Much harder to counsel was the widowed mother of a handicapped child, who was considering re-marriage and wondered whether to marry this man at this time was the right thing to do in her child's interests. She was the only person who could make the decision, but nevertheless the chance of talking to someone else and having as many as possible of the pros and cons brought under review was useful to her; though in the end she would follow the counsels of her heart it was important that heart and head should, so to speak, consult each other.

The essential point which I hope to underline here is that there should be, readily accessible to the parents, some person who knows the child and his circumstances well, has a good grasp of the whole theory and practice of the care of handicapped children, and has established a relationship of confidence with father, mother or both. Precisely who this person should be is not to be dogmatically laid down, but often it may happen that the hospital consultant sees the child and parents infrequently and does not really have the close contact and intimate knowledge, while the family doctor, though knowing the family and enjoying their confidence, has limited experience with children having that type of handicap. A special responsibility, therefore, often lies with the school medical officer or a specialist medical officer of the local authority, who should be able and ready to exercise it—in collaboration, of course, with consultant and G.P.

# CHAPTER 11

# Assessment in Practice

Special considerations apply to the assessment of children with different types of handicap, and these are commented on in the appropriate chapters. In the last four or five years, however, there has been a good deal of experiment in and criticism of assessment procedures and the results are worth setting out here.

Obviously, the first question to be asked is 'What is wrong with this child and how serious is the disability?' Sometimes the answer is obvious, but as our knowledge of the subject increases it is becoming clear that some disabilities are being detected far too late. This is partly due to the fact that some disabilities are inherently hard to detect and define in young children—a very good example is high-frequency deafness. But it is also due to the fact that sometimes, where a child has more than one disability, a prominent one can 'mask' others. The case of Alice, referred to in Chapter 24 is a good example of this.

If it were possible for the physical, mental and social development of every child to be closely studied by an expert or a team of experts, the problem would be solved, but the resources for this are neither available now nor likely to be so in the near future. It is, in any case, an extravagant use of skilled man-power to think in terms of detailed study of all children over a long period when probably not more than one in a hundred is likely to have one or more of these subtle disabilities. If, however, there were some way to select for special study only those children who were likely to have disabilities the situation would be more manageable.

Three lines of approach have been tried in the past few years. The first is the 'risk register' or 'special care' register. It appears that most of the children who suffer from congenital brain damage or sensory handicaps—probably 75 or 80 per cent—have been exposed to certain risks before, during or immediately after birth. It is possible in theory that if maternity hospitals, family doctors and midwives notify the child health service of every child who has been so exposed and those children are closely observed and specially examined as may be appropriate, this special surveillance of possibly one-quarter of all children born may lead to the early detection of three-quarters of disabilities of these kinds. If the list of risk factors is kept short, the proportion of disabilities detected will be smaller; if the list is too long the number of children to be watched will become unwieldy. The right compromise has not yet been found, but there is no doubt that this approach has some value at least as a method of alerting doctors to the possibility of handicap in a worth-while number of cases.

The second method is specific screening. This is the use of tests for the detection of early signs of various disabilities. If it is possible to devise a test which takes only a short time and, which can be applied by someone who does not need a great deal of special training there is clearly going to be a considerable saving of man-power. It is essential that the test must have a 'fail-safe mechanism' built into it. By this one means that if the result is negative this must give a virtual guarantee that the child does not have the disability. It must err on the side of selecting those children who may *possibly* have the disability, so that they can be referred for more detailed investigation to make sure whether it is actually present. Tests of this kind are now available and in common use for several kinds of disability, including phenyl-ketonuria (an uncommon type of mental disability) and for congenital dislocation of the hip, both of which can be used on all new-born infants, and tests for hearing impairment can be effec-tively used on all children at the age of six to eight months.

The third method is detailed developmental examination. It is now generally agreed that a detailed examination by a specially trained and experienced doctor should be carried out in early infancy. Some people favour an examination of this kind in the first week of life but the majority opinion is that it is most reward-ing if carried out when the child is about six months old. The first examination must, of course, be supplemented by further develop-mental checks at intervals, but if the child was found to be quite normal on the first examination the subsequent ones need not be quite so detailed and annual examinations may be sufficient.

To get the best results one must use a combination of methods. From the assessment point of view it certainly makes sense to replace the old 'child welfare clinic' system of frequent superficial routine examinations by less frequent examinations by better-trained doctors who have more detailed knowledge of developmental paediatrics, but the well-baby clinic will continue to offer useful support and advice to many mothers, and the doctors and nurses who work in those clinics, whether in general practice or otherwise, will have opportunities of keeping an unobtrusive watch over the children who attend them and of acting as 'scouts' for the assessment service. Probably the service of the future will work through a new type of 'child health doctor' whose task it will be not only to undertake full developmental examinations as required but to receive, integrate and interpret information from all sources—clinics, family doctors, health visitors, the staff of nurseries and nursery schools and social agencies—and to carry out a running assessment of the physical, mental and social development of all children who are at risk, vulnerable, or suspected of being or known to be handicapped.

This doctor will be more than an assessor; he or she will be the supervisor and advisor with a continuing responsibility for the handicapped child throughout his childhood in an integrated child and youth health service which watches over him through his school years and into the adolescent years of adjustment to life in the community.

The words 'unobtrusive watch' must be stressed, especially during the early years before disability has been finally diagnosed. The parents in this period must never be allowed to get the impression that their child is probably handicapped; they must understand that the special watchfulness is, in many cases, to make sure that an improbable disability is not in fact present. When a disability has, in fact, been diagnosed, the continued watchfulness is being maintained less because the disability is grave than because the observation offers the best hope of its effects being minimized.

The 'risk register' idea has come under criticism in practice, partly because some workers have made their list of risk factors too long, partly because liaison between the people concerned in its operation has often not been good enough but probably even more because too much has been expected of it. It is not in itself a system of detecting disabilities but rather a means of enabling screening tests, systematic observation and specialized investigations to be carried out more purposefully and more economically. Unless it is thus seen in perspective it can actually waste effort and be misleading in its results.

When the defect is discovered and the necessary specialist help has been brought in to define its severity and consider the possibilities of treatment, true assessment begins. How and where should the first assessment be made, and by whom? In discussing the principles of assessment I have stressed that a great many things have to be taken into account and that a number of people are involved. At one end of the chain we have the child welfare doctor, the family doctor and the health visitor, who have a good knowledge of and good contact with the home, but who may not have the specialised knowledge and resources to investigate all the possibilities in detail. At the other end we have the knowledge, experience and facilities of the staff of a specialised children's hospital who, unfortunately, have no direct contact with the home and may be many miles away from it.

Not every child is so difficult to assess that the full range of specialized facilities is essential; indeed the majority can be dealt with quite satisfactorily in their home locality by the health department staff, the family doctor and the consultants at the local hospital working together as necessary. A small minority will need such comprehensive and elaborate investigations that they must be referred to the kind of specialized centre which is at present to be found only in London and the largest provincial teaching hospitals, even at the risk of losing the value of close team contact. Quite a substantial number, however, fall somewhere in between and attempts are being made to provide for these.

It is important to remember that assessment may require that some of those concerned should see the child not once but several times over a period. The greater the distance between the child's home and the place of assessment, the more difficult it becomes to arrange for a series of visits. Again, it is sometimes desirable that he should have a spell of continuous observation by skilled people, and admission to hospital is not always the ideal way of providing this.

At the moment, attempts are being made to work out a compromise solution and some people are already experimenting with assessment centres situated in well-chosen places within easy reach of most parts of the district served. In one sense, these centres may be 'satellites' of the regional specialized hospitals which I have mentioned above, with the members of the hospital staff visiting them regularly. They are also convenient bases for all the local staff who may be involved and the local authorities concerned are arranging for doctors on their own staff to have special training and experience so that they may be able to co-ordinate the work. Such a centre can have a day nursery unit to which handicapped children may be admitted for observation periods of varying lengths and, indeed, the nursery unit may provide special care and therapy for a number of the children.

## Assessment for Education

The inital assessment will probably have included a rough forecast of the child's educability and of the probable type of education he will need. Particularly in the case of blindness or hearing impairment, a first decision may well have been taken, for some blind children and many who are deaf or have only partial hearing can profit by and need a start of special education of some kind at the age of two—or, in some cases, even earlier. (This is discussed in the appropriate chapters.) Most handicapped children, however, will not be likely to start school much before they are five.

These children need a detailed re-assessment at some time during their fifth year. The questions to be asked are: 'What kind of special education is he likely to need for a start?'; 'Will he be ready to start when he is five or should he be given a little longer to become mature enough for school life in the educational, social and physical sense?' and 'Is the programme of treatment which is planned for him likely to affect his educational programme?'

The first question demands a choice between the facilities available—ordinary school, day special school, boarding special school and home tuition—and it cannot be answered without taking into account the answers to the other two questions. For example, if we know that a child who is nearly five years old is likely to have to go into hospital for an operation when he is five and a half or six, we might think it undesirable for him to start going to a special school and then have three months off school just as he is beginning to settle down, and it could be a good idea for him to start attending an ordinary school until the operation takes place and transfer to a special school when he has finished treatment and convalescence.

At the time of this assessment it is important to have recent reports from all the specialists who may have been involved and a special visit to a hospital department may be justified if the child is not due for an ordinary 'follow-up' visit. The parents and the family doctor must be brought fully into the picture and, if the possibility of the child's going to a day school, whether ordinary or special, is under consideration, the head teacher of the school should also be consulted. It is always better to have too much information rather than too little and negative information can often be as valuable as positive. While the child's first school placement should always be regarded as provisional and his response to the school environment is in itself an important part of the assessment process, it is desirable to avoid frequent changes, which can be very unsettling. Accordingly, the assessment should try to look at any rate two or three years ahead in the hope that the child will stay at the school which he first enters for at least that length of time. In case of serious doubt it may be wiser to defer a decision for six months or a year, rather than risk a wrong placement and the disturbance which could ensue.

### Intermediate Assessment

When this will be necessary must depend on circumstances. Most special schools are flexible in their organisation. Their 'infant' and 'junior' sections overlap and some are 'all-age', so that a suitably placed child will rarely have to change school until he is eleven and may be able to stay in the same school till he is sixteen. Even where transfer to a different school for secondary education is necessary, the junior special school can usually contrive to keep a slow-maturing child for an extra term or two and the secondary special school will be ready to accept him after the age of eleven.

All parties—school, school medical officer and specialists—must keep in touch and report to each other any significant happenings or developments  This is usually easy when the child is at a day school but even so failures of communication can happen, possibly because some member of the team does not realise that something which to him is not very important might be significant to someone else or because he thinks that what he has noticed is important only in his part of the field  It is the putting together of two or three apparently isolated happenings which can give the early clue to some development of potentially serious consequence. A slight falling off in a child's educational progress may be just one of those temporary phases which every teacher is accustomed to in normal children but it might be an indication that there is some worsening of his disability or that something is going wrong with his home care or his emotional well-being

When the child is at a boarding school contact is less easy to maintain and communication between the school and the 'sending authority' often leaves a lot to be desired. School reports may be scanty and infrequent and sometimes they reach the office of the authority and stay there without being passed on to the school medical officer who was responsible for the child's original assessment and still is the person who ought to be keeping an eye on his welfare. The medical officer should make a point of seeing the child at least once a year when he is home on holiday and having a chat with the parents. It is also important for the M.O. to listen to the parents' complaints, if any. True, most complaints about Mary's being unhappy at school or Tommy's not wanting to go back after the holidays may be just manifestations of parental fussiness or anxiety, but even if this is the case it is necessary for the parents to be encouraged and reassured. And there is always the possibility that something may be genuinely wrong. Placing a child in a special school is not just a matter of sending him to a place which takes children with that particular disability; even the best of schools may fail to establish the right rapport with an individual child.

However well things may seem to be going, there should be a complete reassessment when the child is ten or eleven years old. This is most important when a change of school at secondary age will be needed. A child who has been getting on well at an ordinary school in the junior stage may not be able to stand up to the special stresses of an ordinary secondary school and might need to change to a special school. Senior special schools vary somewhat in the character and bias of their curricula and it is as well to make sure that the handicapped youngster is going to get, in his last five years, the education which will best fit him for the sort of career which will best suit him. But even if the child is at an all-age school and can, if necessary, stay on there till he is sixteen, though a full assessment may be deferred until a little later a careful check should still be carried out somewhere about this age. Puberty is an unstable time for any youngster, handicapped or not, and to take stock of the child and his needs before the pubertal stresses begin can be a sound investment.

## Assessment for Leaving School

The problems facing the child on leaving school have been discussed in Chapter 9. A mistake at this point in life can easily cancel out much of the good which has been done by skilled care and education in earlier years. At no stage is there more need to look ahead and, as always, this is far from easy. We have the advantage of knowing more about the child than at the earlier assessments. On the other hand, at each previous assessment we have known more than a little about the possible environment which the child was going to enter—nursery, ordinary school or day or boarding special school—and we have always had the prospect that if we made a mistake in our choice of school or recommendations for care there was a chance of making a change before it was too late. Moreover, the people who were going to be in charge of him were knowledgeable and experienced and would be likely to notice early signs that things were not going well.

When he leaves school he is going into an environment which is much less predictable. The works foreman is not, however kindly and understanding he may be, as expert a judge of handicapped young people as the special school teacher. And if we make a mistake we have far less opportunity of putting it right. This assessment is, in fact, often the most critical of all and it must be approached in that spirit.

At this stage the questions one has to ask are: 'Is he going to need any medical or surgical treatment in the near future?'; 'What sort of job can he undertake with the prospect of success?'; 'Are there any special problems which he will have to face in matters of daily living?' and 'What sort of social support and after-care is he likely to need?'

All these need to be asked in good time, at least a year before he is due to leave. Like the questions one asks before school entry, they may be interdependent. Suppose that a period of hospital investigation or an operation is necessary. Should this take place while he is still at school so as to avoid the risk of interrupting his first job? On the other hand, can he afford to miss two or three months' schooling in this last year? If the investigation or treatment is done before he leaves school will it improve his chances of making good in suitable employment, or will it make ordinary daily living less of a strain or a burden?

The forecasting, in general terms, of a programme of medical or surgical treatment at this stage of a young person's life is not very difficult. There are only two aspects of the forecast which are conditional on other things. The first of these is the timing of the programme. What we particularly want to avoid is dislocating our youngster's social progress by requiring him to spend three months in hospital just as he is beginning to settle down to a suitable job. This usually gives us a choice between postponing the treatment until he is well settled or postponing the start of work until he has had the treatment. In many ways the second is to be preferred, but it must be remembered that there are some kinds of treatment, notably certain orthopaedic operations, which give the best results if they are carried out at particular ages or stages of growth and that to have them too soon or too late may mean that we risk a second-rate result.

The second special aspect of the problem is that sometimes there is a choice of methods of treatment of disability during adolescence and that one of those methods might have a direct bearing upon suitability or unsuitability for certain employments. Assume, for example, that an orthopaedic surgeon may have in mind two alternative operations on a patient's arm, one of which would leave the limb with greater strength but limited movement, while the other would allow a wide range of movement but limit muscle power. If we have good reason to believe that a particular job is available which would suit the patient admirably and that, for that job, range of movement is much more necessary than muscle power, this might determine the surgeon's choice of operation.

Assessment for employment is specially important for reasons which can be inferred from what I have written in Chapter 6. Unfortunately it is by no means as easy as we could wish. Some aspects are simple enough, of course. A large number of lightly handicapped people have the capacity to adjust themselves to almost any type of job. Certain disabilities, by their very nature, rule out work of certain kinds. Blind people cannot drive motor vehicles, deaf people cannot become piano-tuners; such specific major barriers are dealt with in chapters covering particular disabilities. But one of the important trends in this field in recent years has been the realisation that given the right selection and the right opportunities many people—and this applies particularly to the young—can be trained for and fitted into jobs which used to be regarded as the preserve of the able-bodied.

In the sort of ideal world which some people have in mind it would be possible to specify in detail the exact requirements for adequate performance in any individual job—vision, hearing, mental capacity, range of movement at particular joints, muscle power, fatigueability and every other factor which might be relevant. One would thus chart for each handicapped school leaver all aspects of his abilities and disabilities. It would then be a simple matter to feed all the data into a computer and, within minutes, to get an answer which said that John Jones was ideally suited to be the third man in a working team which made left-handed thermal combobulators for hydro-electric parcel-loaders as used in certain aircraft. So John Jones would be given such a job (assuming it was available at the time) and at the end of a month would be sacked because he and the foreman were temperamentally incompatible!

The assessment of individuals' physical powers is not very difficult and elaborate systems of analysis, awarding points for this, that and the other have already been worked out. The assessment of personality and temperament is quite another story, expecially when we bear in mind that the practical expression of A's personality depends not only on A himself but on the personalities of B and C, with whom he may have to work or live. Moreover, what one does on the job is only part of the story; getting to and from work, having meals inside or outside the workplace and, of course, home life, can make the critical difference between success and failure. In the last resort, therefore, job placement is going to depend on skilled assessment, detailed knowledge of the labour market and diplomatic negotiation by a professional placement officer, usually the Careers Adviser, who must be given all the information he may need for the purpose and must be in close touch with everyone who might have some contribution to make.

The Report of the Working Party on Handicapped School Leavers studies this subject in detail and ought to be read by all who are interested in this work, but some of the points which it makes are worth mention here.

The child's teachers should know him well so far as education and personality go, but are not doctors or industrial experts. The School M.O., helped by the doctors who have been looking after the child, by his colleagues in the School Health Service and by the teachers, should have a good all-round picture of the child but may well know less about local industry than does the teacher. The Careers Adviser has had experience of placing normal as well as handicapped school leavers in employment and can have an almost encyclopaedic knowledge of work-opportunities over a wide radius, with the understanding needed to make use of what he knows; his medical knowledge, however, will be strictly limited to what he has picked up in the course of his job and he will be not better than any other lay person at translating medical technical terms into the idiom of his own profession.

That these three—and others who may be involved—should meet to talk over their problems is obviously desirable. Sometimes all that is needed is that each of the officers should be ready and willing to telephone to or call and chat with a colleague on some specific point. When a child presents a difficult or complicated problem, a case conference among the people who know him and can offer help and information is an excellent way of trying to find an answer. These conferences may be called together *ad hoc* but there is much to be said for using, in the right circumstances, the method adopted by certain special schools which hold a case conference every term on the children who are due to leave when the term ends. Some of the children present no serious problem and their cases may be dealt with in a minute or two; others may need a substantial period of detailed discussion.

The obvious advantage of this scheme is that it ensures the holding of an adequate discussion about every child who may need it, an important point because it can sometimes happen that only when the members of the group get together in discussion does it emerge that a case conference is needed. The procedure is, however, one which will be easiest in a day special school which serves a not-too-large area, so that the number of people involved will not be very great and all of them will live near enough to be present. The isolated boarding special school, which is the one where communications tend to be least effective, draws its pupils from such a wide area that it is virtually impossible to bring together all those who ought to attend a case conference. The procedure also carries the risk that discussion of problems may be deferred till the child's last term when it should have begun a year or two earlier. This can be avoided if the people concerned look on the routine case conference as primarily a final check over what has already been done.

In any event, a case conference must be preceded by study and the exchange of information. At present the weakest link in communication is probably that between the School M.O. and the C.A. Too often all that happens is that the S.M.O. sends the C.A. a simple form which contains very little information. In part this is due to the lack of a common technical working language to which I have referred above, but it is also partly due to a medical conservatism which makes doctors reluctant to tell their lay co-workers all they might. The Working Party suggested that a functional assessment scheme might be devised which would overcome the language barrier and made some concrete suggestions. The Department of Education and Science and the Ministry of Labour took up the idea and a functional assessment schedule is now in general use. A copy of the current schedule is included as an appendix to this book.

For the traditional conservatism which withholds information there is no excuse. Information which is not necessary and might be embarrassing to child or family should properly remain strictly confidential, and the disclosure of medical information to a prospective employer without the consent of the child's parents is to be strongly discouraged. But the C.A. is working as a colleague of the doctor in the child's interests and is a professional person who is accustomed to be trusted with confidences. If parents give their consent to the passing of information well and good, but they not infrequently refuse such consent. In those circumstances it is grossly unfair to the C.A. that he might be asked to find a job for a child when he is ignorant of something which might be of cardinal importance. Not only may it embarrass him but it may end in the child being placed in unsuitable employment from which he may have to be discharged or withdrawn, with traumatic results.

Sometimes the C.A. might find himself in possession of information which it is desirable the child's employer should know. That such information should go to the employer without the parents' consent remains wrong, but the C.A. should at least have the opportunity to talk to the parents about the matter and try to persuade them to agree; in the last resort he may deal with the matter by refusing to handle the case.

No form which can be devised will ever be adequate for all cases. In the more difficult or complex ones it is no substitute for a person to person discussion of all the issues involved and the M.O. should always consider whether a letter should be added to amplify some of the points or whether he should ask for a talk with the C.A. or even call a special case conference. The holding of a routine case conference is, as I have said, a useful procedure but it must be remembered that such conferences only suggest answers to problems and do not guarantee that they will succeed; all those involved must remain in touch until the young person concerned is not only placed in employment but is showing evidence of having adjusted to both work and living in general.

## FURTHER READING

*Assessment*
The Early Detection and Treatment of Handicapping Defects in Young Children. World Health Organization, Regional Office for Europe, Copenhagen.

# CHAPTER 12

# Blindness

Of the total population of Great Britain nearly one-quarter are children under the age of fourteen. Of the 100,000 or so blind people in Great Britain only about 3,000 are children under fourteen, while 50,000 are more than 70 years old. There are two reasons for this disproportion. One is that the commonest causes of blindness are the accidents, diseases and degenerations of middle and later life. The other is that some of the conditions which at the turn of the century were causes of blindness in childhood are now far less common. It is possible that medicine and surgery may still further reduce the risks of blindness in childhood, but the next steps in such reduction will not be spectacular. Even so, three thousand is not a great number, and from the point of view of size—and, therefore, cost—the provision of adequate care for blind children presents a manageable problem. Present provision is, in fact, good. It could and should be improved and extended, but such failures as occur are due less to lack of provision than to failure to make the best use in a particular case of the resources which are there to be used.

But, parallel with this slow decrease in numbers there is an increase in the complexity of our problem. This is one of the many parts of the field in which improved medical and surgical techniques are allowing children to survive hazards occurring before, during and after birth but not preventing the occurrence of disability and several of the conditions which produce congenital blindness are liable to cause other damage to the child. The result is that the number of blind children who are also deaf, mentally handicapped or physically handicapped—sometimes suffering from all these disabilities simultaneously—is growing. The number of these children is not great but their total disability is very serious and, particularly so far as the deaf-blind are concerned, requires the development of new techniques in education.

Broadly speaking, the position in Britain is typical of that in all the highly-developed countries. It is not unreasonable to say that in countries in an intermediate stage of social development the problem of blindness is coming under control. The diseases which are the most prolific causes of blindness are, happily, diseases which disappear at an early stage in the development of organized public health services. In the public mind, too, blindness is something which excites ready sympathy and this leads to public readiness to provide social services for the blind while corresponding services for other groups of the handicapped remain in abeyance.

There are, however, many regions in which some of the old major causes remain rife and in which prevention still has enormous scope, while in these very countries limited resources for the care of the blind are overwhelmed by the number of people requiring care. This is a field in which the fortunate countries have great opportunities to help the less fortunate ones and it is encouraging to see this moral obligation being increasingly accepted.

## Definition

Superficially it would seem easy to define blindness; a blind person is, obviously, one who cannot see. In actual fact, however, the working out of an adequate definition sorely puzzles the experts. Absolute blindness could be defined as an inability to distinguish between light and darkness, but it is obvious that many people who can tell light from darkness do not possess vision which is of any practical use in daily life. For the adult blind, Britain has long used the practical definition of 'inability to perform work for which sight is essential' but in recent years it has been shown that many jobs which were formerly regarded as essentially for sighted people can be performed by blind people suitably trained and provided with suitable apparatus. Often whether such a job can be done by a particular person depends not only on his sight but on his intelligence, his temperament and the acuteness of his other senses. An arbitrary definition of blindness in terms of sight-testing type is unpractical, as vision of 6/60 or less may be adequate for certain purposes. One definition expressing the outstanding practical disability of the blind—'inability to find one's way about in unfamiliar surroundings'—has found some favour but is, again, valid only for certain purposes. In practice it is necessary to compromise and use different definitions for different purposes. Educationally a child must be considered blind if his vision is so defective that he cannot be taught by visual methods, but even this is not a complete definition. It does not cover the case of the child who has useful vision but whose sight is likely to deteriorate to a point at which he cannot be taught by visual methods. It also leaves out the child who has a little sight but who, in later life, will have to rely to a considerable extent on techniques which are taught only in schools for the blind.

In childhood, therefore, it is best to regard as blind the child who can be best helped, in consideration of all the circumstances, by the services which are provided for the help of blind children, though as much use as possible must be made of such sight as he possesses.

## Causation

The classical causes of blindness over the world and through the centuries have been smallpox, trachoma, ophthalmia of the new-born and vitamin A deficiency (Keratomalacia). In the highly developed countries all these have been virtually eliminated; they persist in parts of Africa, Asia and Latin America, though in the last few years there has been a substantial decrease in the prevalence of smallpox and there is a possibility that it may soon become a rare disease in all the continents. In the developed countries at the present time some 80 per cent of cases of blindness in children under the age of four are due to congenital and developmental causes. Some of these are hereditary and it is likely to be a long time before the laws which govern the inheritance of blindness are well enough understood to make prevention a universal practicability. Virus infections during pregnancy can cause blindness but there is a good prospect that the development of vaccines will soon make this type of blindness a thing of the past. Birth injury and injury after birth—whether injury to the eyes themselves or injury to the brain—should become a less common cause as techniques of obstetrics and of treatment improve. Some blindness is caused by certain forms of cancer and, in spite of the antibiotics, it sometimes still happens that blindness results from infection.

In the nineteen-forties there appeared in some Western countries an alarming new condition—retrolental fibroplasia—appeared, blinding hundreds of new infants every year. It was discovered that this was due to a new life-saving technique in the care of premature infants, the giving of intensive oxygen therapy. Once this was realized, the risk was guarded against and the condition disappeared but there are signs that it is beginning to occur again. There must be occasions where the virtual certainty of death has to be weighed against a possible risk of the loss of sight. But the tragedy of retrolental fibroplasia has its value as a warning against complacency and over-enthusiasm; this is not the only part of the field of medicine where the introduction of a new technique or a new treatment has brought new risks of disability and it is by no means impossible that there may be similar episodes in the future.

## Treatment

It is obvious that if early and effective treatment is given in the infections which cause blindness the sight may be saved. The same applies to the treatment of certain injuries to the eye. But once an eye has actually become blind treatment has little to offer. Corneal grafting can sometimes be brilliantly effective in cases oi gross corneal damage, and operation on an eye with congenital or acquired cataract can restore useful, though much impaired, vision. The majority of blind children must, however, face irrevocable blindness and planning for their future need take no account of provision for treatment or its consequences.

## General Management and Care

The completeness and irrevocability of blindness has at least this compensation, that the worst is known quickly and that a good deal of the doubt and speculation which surrounds many of the other handicaps is absent. It is clear from the start that the blind person will be unable to do certain things and that he will have to have certain kinds of help at various stages of his life. The basic task of preparing him for the fullest possible life within an inevitably restricted field can, therefore, be started at once. His basic needs are for confidence, competence and independence—precisely as with any child with any handicap—and these must be borne in mind from the beginning.

The first question to be asked is 'where should the young blind child be brought up?' and to that question there are various answers. It is important to remember that for the blind child in particular the home is faced with many problems.

The normal child starts to learn everyday things by watching what others do and imitating them; he cannot learn by listening to what he is told or by asking questions until he acquires a vocabulary. The blind child is, therefore, at a considerable disadvantage in the first three or four years of life. Most of the activities of the brothers and sisters and others with whom the blind child would normally play depend largely on sight, so that he will tend to be isolated from other children.

Possibly the most important disadvantage is that every home is full of physical hazards for young children—the chair in the middle of the room, the curled-up carpet, the unstable occasional table, the edge of the half-open door, the edged and pointed kitchen tools and the dangling corner of the table-cloth are all notoriously things which bring bruises, cuts and burns to the sighted child. But the sighted child can see these causes of risk and soon learns to avoid them; to the blind child they are hidden and unavoidable menaces which punish him for every little excursion into which normal curiosity tempts him, with the result that he decides that ventures are dangerous and, in the extreme case, may sit all day apathetically on the floor, his confidence desperately injured.

The unremitting care and watchfulness which can guard against this are difficult to practice in any home and well-nigh impossible in a home containing some lusty sighted children. The highly intelligent mother with ample time can, given skilled assistance, start her young child's informal education through the senses of touch and hearing, but only a minority of mothers are in a position to do this well. It is by no means unknown for other children to rally to the aid of a blind child and give him comradeship, but this cannot fairly be expected of the average four- or five-year-old. Unless, therefore, he is very lucky, the blind child in his own home runs a very serious risk of being retarded, timid, isolated and withdrawn by the time he is five. It is for this reason that great stress has in the past been laid on the desirability of letting the blind child start life in a special nursery school—the so-called 'Sunshine Homes' are typical—at the age of two or as soon after as practicable.

Opinions are changing. It is accepted now that too-early separation of the child from the mother carries emotional hazards which are not to be ignored. Ideally, the child's social and emotional development in the early years should be a gradual process of widening relationships—first with the mother exclusively, then with the other members of the family and later with other children and adults in the extended family and the neighbourhood. The blind child who has no other serious disability has a unique combination of a special dependence with a general physical competence that offers a high potential degree of independence; the disability which makes him specially dependent operates from the first months and there is always the risk that it may hamper him very severely in realizing his potential for widening his circle of relationships during the vital first five years of life.

Given the right circumstances there is no doubt that the young blind child can develop satisfactorily in his home. Those right circumstances depend on the parents' intelligence, understanding and attitude to the child, perhaps especially on their ability to find the right middle course between doing too many things for him and encouraging him prematurely to do things for himself, remembering that it may well be necessary to press him toward self-reliance in a way which may seem to them almost brutal. They depend also on whether the number and ages of their other children allow them the time and the energy to give him the help he needs, on their economic situation and on their physical surroundings—the character, the size and the situation of their house in particular.

Not even the best of parents in the best of homes can do this difficult job without specialist help and support and probably the most important factor which must be taken into consideration in deciding whether the child should stay at home is whether this help is available in the necessary quantity—and of the right quality. What is needed for young blind children is a type of social worker who is specially suited by temperament and is specially trained for the task, and without in the least decrying the admirable work done by home teachers for the blind one must say that their training has hitherto been mainly centred on work for the adult blind, who are, of course, more numerous and no less in need of help to meet their special difficulties. So few, comparatively, are the numbers of the young blind, that it is doubtful whether there is any real possibility in the near future of providing special home teachers for them except in the larger urban areas where one such teacher can give adequate time to several of them. It seems probable, therefore, that only the fortunately-circumstanced few can hope for really adequate specialist help and that the residential nursery unit will continue to offer the best prospect for a considerable number of blind children. This will be specially true for the blind children who have a second substantial disability.

Before the blind child leaves the home and in the home during holiday periods there is still much that can be done to help. Nothing trains the sense of touch so well as toys and even in the earliest years some of the standard nursery toys—the posting-box, the nesting beakers, hammer-pegs and so on—can be invaluable. He must learn to recognize common domestic objects by touch and be taught to feed himself with simple table utensils. To free the whole of the house from risks of accident is well-nigh impossible, but it is often practicable for him to have, even as a toddler, a room of his own where everything has its regular place so that he can move freely and find and put away his own toys and other articles. Such simple aids as a loudly-ticking clock or a ball with a bell inside it help him to find his way about by sound. Concentration can be developed by the telling and reading of stories and this also can begin very early. The reading and reciting of simple nursery rhymes, even before he is of an age to understand them, will give him the idea that speech is something worth listening to.

I have mentioned that it is always bad to anticipate all the needs of any handicapped child and that doing too much for him delays development. This is specially bad for the blind child; certain things which he obviously cannot do and can never learn to do must be done for him, but he should start early learning to do anything which in the long run he is likely to be able to do, even imperfectly. In particular it must be remembered that one of the chief things that makes a child learn to speak is the need to ask for things! Blind children are more liable than sighted children to develop habit-movements—head-scratching, nose-picking, eye-rubbing and the like—and these need to be tactfully checked. The best way of discouraging them is undoubtedly to provide the child with plenty to do and to keep his fingers and senses occupied.

The fact that the blind child tends to be timid in moving about leads not only to his becoming emotionally 'shut-in' but to his becoming generally physically lazy. Simple indoor physical exercises are a 'must' and regular outdoor walks holding father's or mother's hand are no less important. For mother to take him when she goes shopping combines physical exercise with experience of new sounds and smells and new things to touch. A fairly large, smooth lawn to play on is invaluable, but something which a flat or a working-class house cannot often provide.

A few words might be useful about the so-called 'sixth sense' of the blind. It is believed by many people that the blind can develop an extra sense by which they perceive persons or objects in their neighbourhood and some suggest that this is a 'normal' human sense which lies dormant in sighted people because they have no need for it. It is, however, much more likely that this faculty is due to the skilled development of the ordinary senses. I have met one blind man who, on entering a strange room, could guess its size as accurately as most sighted people, but he would not venture an estimate until he or someone else had spoken; he considered that his guess was almost certainly based on sound reflections. One brilliant young blind woman, who is a remarkably successful ice skater, makes deliberate use of a small 'clicker', which she carries in her hand and clicks from time to time, listening to the reflection of the sound. Some blind people sense nearness to large objects such as buildings by either the warmth of the object of the reflection of the sun's heat from it on a warm day. Others are helped by noticing air currents and eddies. Probably most of the practised blind use several of these techniques more or less consciously. Nothing could more strongly stress the need for opportunities of sense training and for letting the blind child and young person have as much and as wide experience as possible.

Intensive research is going on into the development of new aids for the blind. From time to time rather extravagant claims appear in the popular press because they obviously make good news stories but they usually tend to be grossly exaggerated. In theory it ought to be possible to make use of some kind of 'radar' by developing an instrument which sends out radiations which can be reflected from objects and received by a mechanism which turns them into sounds. The techniques of micro-electronics certainly ought to allow of instruments of this kind being produced which are not too bulky or heavy and it is fair to say that current experiments in this direction are promising. Some workers suggest that a few blind people are able to 'see with their finger-tips' and that this faculty might be helped to develop by the use of some electronic device. It is hard to say what process is involved, but the suggestion cannot be summarily dismissed out of hand. It would, however, be over-optimistic to imagine that any new aids are likely to come on to the market and revolutionize work for and with the blind in the next decade or so.

This consideration of care and management has concentrated mainly on the child who is born blind or has become blind in very early childhood. Many of the general principles hold good for children who lose their sight later in childhood, but some special points have to be borne in mind.

E

The child who has had sight before he became blind has both advantages and disadvantages. Nothing can take from him his wider experience of life and the consequent knowledge of things. He has already learned certain skills which will stand him in good stead. What he has been taught in school will stay with him, though he may not be able to continue his education seriously until he has learned Braille.

On the other hand, some of the skills he has learned will be quite useless in his new life and he will have to start, at his comparatively advanced age, learning from the beginning things which the congenitally blind child has more or less mastered at that age— feeding himself is only one example. Almost certainly he will have neglected his senses of hearing and touch in favour of sight; he will now have to start cultivating them. He will have learned the sighted way of life and must not only learn a new one but unlearn much of the old. He will have lost many of his old pleasures and even if he does not lose his friends and associates he must learn a new relationship with them. The older he is, the more difficult some of the changes will be and if he is past, say, the age of ten or eleven he will have to give up the future of which he was already dreaming and build himself a new one.

In general—there may be rare exceptions—the sooner he goes to a special school the better. Not only is it important for him to start learning the new techniques quickly, since he has less time in which to learn them, but he is likely to find it easier to get used to the world of darkness if his immediate surroundings are not those which he has learned to associate with the old world of sight.

It is amazing to see how quickly a child can make this great adjustment and, incidentally, how much longer his parents may take to accept the new state of affairs. It might be expected that in the case where blindness comes on slowly, over a matter of a year or two, readjustment for both child and parent would be easier than in the cases where it comes quickly; there is, in theory, time to prepare and plan. Experience, however, suggests that the opposite often happens and that it is the quick shock which is best borne by all parties. Skilled help and counselling can help a great deal in the cases of slow onset and it is essential that doctors, teachers and all concerned should be realistic from the beginning and not postpone breaking the bad news in the hope of letting child and parents down lightly. So long as there is a probability that useful sight will be saved, optimism is justified, but the moment the probabilities swing in the opposite direction it is dangerously misleading kindness to conceal the facts.

## Education

The blind child cannot be taught by the visual methods on which ordinary schools rely so heavily. Not only will he have to be taught substantially by other methods but he will have to learn to read and write in Braille. Apart from acquiring knowledge of school subjects he must also be trained to make skilled use of his other senses to compensate for the absence of sight. He must, even more than in the pre-school years, be able to acquire confidence and freedom of movement. He must be able to join in the games and social activities of his fellows as an equal partner. This combination of specialized education by skilled teachers in an environment where hazards are minimized and convenience of activity is facilitated and where all the pupils can work and play as equals can be provided only in a school designed, equipped, staffed and organized for the blind. In essence, for the blind child for most of his years of schooling, a special school undoubtedly provides the best opportunities for learning not only school subjects but the special way of living which he must acquire.

Experiments are being made in trying to provide for blind children in ordinary schools and there is evidence that in some cases this can be reasonably successful. Where special school provision is not available or where, in an individual case, there are strong reasons against letting a child go away from home to a special school, this may be an acceptable second-best, but the policy of special school provision as a general rule for blind children is undoubtedly the right one at the present time.

In this country all special schools for the blind are boarding schools. There are good reasons for this. Since the total number of blind children is comparatively small it is manifestly impossible to provide day special schools within a reasonable distance of all such children's homes and daily travel to and from school has its obvious difficulties. In any case, the blind person, more than any other victim of handicap, needs education not only in academic and technical subjects but in a special technique of living and he will get this best if his out-of-lessons time is spent in a place where everything contributes to this end. There is, however, no absolute reason why the whole of his school life should be spent exclusively in a boarding special school and, indeed, there is a case for relaxing the regime in the later school years. The sudden change from a completely sheltered life to life in the community when he leaves school can be overwhelming and anything which makes it gradual is worth considering. If his home is good and if the problem of transport can be solved, it should not be impossible for him to live at home and attend the special school daily for, at any rate, the last year or two of school life, though this will be practicable only for the minority whose homes are within a few miles of a special school.

The success of 'integrated' units for the partially hearing—special units attached to ordinary schools, which are referred to on page 145—arouses speculation as to whether similar units might be developed for the blind. The idea that blind children should go to a special class in an ordinary school and, while staying in that class for the 'visual' subjects, should join the rest of the school for the mainly oral subjects is theoretically attractive but has its practical difficulties. Because of the comparatively small numbers of blind children, such a unit would have to have a wide age-range and it would not be easy to give the members of an all-age group the education at different levels of attainment which they needed. Again, even the mainly oral subjects of an ordinary school are taught on the assumption that the children have had basic education in fundamentals, which is generally partly visual. Only the older blind children would have reached the necessary level to be able to join in profitably. The answer may lie in arranging for special schools for the blind to be affiliated to neighbouring ordinary schools and for the children to go to those schools for selected lessons. Some experiments on these lines have been made and their results are sufficiently promising to justify their extension.

### The Prospect for the Blind

In the last twenty years there has been a radical change in the position regarding employment for the blind. In the nineteen-thirties the majority of blind people would have to be content with simple crafts, such as basket-work and brush-making, in sheltered workshops. A few of the more intelligent might be trained for and settle down in physiotherapy, piano-tuning and switch-board operating while a mere handful of near-geniuses might find a career in the law or some other profession. During the 1939-45 war the acute labour shortage led employers to experiment with blind workers in jobs previously done by sighted people. There were doubts and misgivings, particularly with regard to accident risks, but the event proved that blind workers in suitably chosen jobs had an output rate higher than sighted workers and that their accident rate tended to be lower.

There was no miracle about this; it was simply the operation of the principle of 'compensations' which was mentioned in Chapter 1. On the question of output it is worth quoting the comment of a blind worker in a Lancashire engineering factory: 'When you're blind you can't see whether t' foreman's watchin' you or not, so you've got to keep at it!' Accidents are as often as not due to failure of concentration because of some momentary distraction; let the blonde with the tea-trolley come into the workshop and all the sighted workers look up, while the blind ones go on with their work. There are indeed some jobs where touch or sound is a more accurate guide than sight and the use of the eyes may mislead the worker. For these and other reasons the experiment succeeded and much though by no means all of the reluctance of employers to take blind workers disappeared.

Once blind workers began to succeed in open industry, efforts were made to bring more and more jobs within their reach. There was a deliberate search for work which might be within their powers and it was discovered that a considerable number of processes, or parts of processes, which had been carried out by sighted people were within the scope of the blind. The redesigning or modification of gauges and instruments so that they could be 'read' by touch extended the field considerably and it became worth while to provide skilled blind workers with transport or guides between their homes and their workplaces. But perhaps the moral victory was the most important thing; the public's belief that blind people were suitable only for brush- and basket-making was shaken and there was a willingness to give them a chance in many other types of work.

By no means all the public or all employers are yet converted and the story is not one of unrelieved success. Some blind workers have failed because of faults of temperament and personality, often due to mistakes in their early education and management. In any case, by the law of averages some blind people are bound to be limited in intelligence and to make other senses do the work of sight in skilled employment demands not only general intelligence but courage and perseverance beyond the average.

Persons who, if sighted, would be capable of only unskilled or semi-skilled work, cannot overcome blindness sufficiently to enter open industry with success, because the jobs within their powers of intelligence demand sight; fetching and carrying, loading and unloading vehicles and trucks and kindred tasks are out of the question. For this quite substantial number of blind people the old types of craft work in sheltered workshops will still be necessary.

The essential practical disabilities of the intelligent blind person are few, and some can be by-passed or overcome. They cannot undertake work which requires them to find their way about alone in unfamiliar places; they can, however, be guided or transported to regular places of work and for occasional tasks in new places it may be practicable to provide them with guides. They cannot communicate in writing with sighted people who do not read and write Braille and they cannot, of course, read books unless they have been translated into Braille, which cuts them off from new books and periodicals in their professional work; the blind professional worker needs at least a part-time secretary. Anything involving the making or use of engineering or architectural drawings is beyond them, quite irrevocably, as are tasks requiring colour- or pattern-discrimination.

This, however, still leaves plenty of scope and it is interesting to see experiments being made in giving blind children part-time industrial work during their latter school years and in providing industrial training workshops to prepare blind adolescents for 'open' employment.

Employment apart, the long-term outlook for the blind is encouraging. As I have mentioned, the blind traditionally attract special sympathy and over the years the notable achievements of blind people have accumulated to encourage not only the blind themselves but those who live with them, work with them and encounter them in any place. Most countries give them direct or indirect economic help in the way of pensions and tax reliefs to offset the extra expenses in which they are inevitably involved, and substantial voluntary funds are available to provide aid in cash or kind or to subsidize skilled welfare workers. Such apparatus as Braille books and 'talking books' are at their service. Guide dogs are becoming increasingly available.

Perhaps the most critical need for their fulfilment is marriage to an understanding partner but this seems often to come of itself, more easily than to the deaf, with their difficulty in communication, or to some of the severely physically handicapped. They can be adequate—indeed, model, parents.

True, there are unhappy, querulous, neurotic and even malicious blind people, but these defects are encountered among physically normal sighted people, and where they afflict the blind it is usually those who have become blind in middle life. Those who are born blind or who become blind in childhood usually grow up competent, confident and serene. It is no accident that among those who have done the finest work for the welfare of blind people all over the world there are many who have known sight only for a few years of childhood or who have always lived in physical darkness and who have, with the right help, found their own inner illumination.

## FURTHER READING

*Blindness and Partial Sight*
Gibbs, N.   The Care of Young Blind Children.   Royal National Institute for the Blind.
Lightfoot, W.   The Partially Sighted School.   Chatto and Windus.
Monk, P.   Though Land be Out of Sight. (The early years of Chorleywood College). R.N.I.B.
   The R.N.I.B. has also published a number of pamphlets and handbooks for the guidance of parents and teachers of the blind.
   The College of Teachers of the Blind (Bristol) publishes handbooks for home teachers and school teachers of the blind.

## CHAPTER 13

# Partial Sight

Once again, the definition of a handicapping condition has to be expressed in terms of practical expediency. From the educational point of view, the partially sighted child is one who can be taught by visual methods but needs special aids or special techniques which are not available in ordinary schools. From the social point of view, the partially sighted child is one who, while not blind, is restricted in doing things for which sight is essential, and much the same applies in respect of employment

Translating this into terms of ordinary, everyday abilities we can say that the partially sighted child can find his way about and will have no great difficulty in coping with most of the general activities of daily living, such as feeding himself and dressing himself. His distant vision is likely to be poor and he is likely while young to have trouble in tasks which demand acute 'fine' sight, like reading ordinary print. The consequence of this is that his education will be impeded and, in fact, his most serious problems will be educational. In the long run, it will be easier for him to find employment than for the blind person to do so and the only activities which will be completely barred will be those which demand good sight at long and middle distances.

## Causation

The commonest single cause of this type of visual defect is high myopia. Knowledge and opinions on this subject have changed considerably in recent years. Not very long ago it was believed that 'eyestrain' played a very large part in the development of myopia and myopic children were subjected to very drastic restrictions of activities of all kinds. They were placed in special 'sight-saving' classes in schools, reading and 'close work' out of school were virtually forbidden and even moderately strenuous physical exercise was frowned upon. Years of careful study of the subject, however, have shown that many of these restrictions were of little value and that they did not prevent the myopia from increasing.

The modern view is that most myopia is, so to speak, inevitable. The tendency is often inherited and as the child grows, the myopia automatically becomes more severe. Since myopia is an optical fault in the eye and essentially due to the eyeball being longer than average, so that the lens is further from the retina than in the normal eye, this is to be expected. Whatever one may try to do to prevent it, the eye, like the child's bones, will grow steadily to whatever length is natural for the particular child and then stop growing. There is no evidence that over-use of the eye muscles causes the size and shape of the eye to become 'worse' or that 'eye exercises' can preserve normal size and shape. During the years in which the child's general growth is most rapid the eye grows more rapidly and the myopia progresses more quickly; in the middle and later 'teens' the progress of the myopia is slower and in the end it becomes almost stable.

It must still be regarded as possible that the very myopic eye is more prone to accidental physical damage than the normal eye and that strenuous physical activity might cause such disasters as detachment of the retina, but on the whole there is little or nothing to justify the very severe restrictions of activity which used to be considered necessary for moderately myopic children.

Other conditions which leave the child with only partial sight include injury, infection, congenital deformities or defects of the iris and congenital or juvenile cataract which has been treated by removal of the lens. The albino, though his eye is complete and he may have no error of refraction, lacks natural pigment in the eye and may be dazzled by ordinary light to a degree which seriously impairs his vision. All these conditions are non-progressive.

Some of the diseases and disorders which cause total blindness may be very slow in their progress, so that the child passes through a longer or shorter period during which he is partially sighted before he becomes blind. Such a child may present special problems, because direct treatment of the condition which is causing the deterioration will sometimes be necessary and this, by involving substantial periods in hospital, may disorganize both his general life and his education.

## Treatment
Medical and surgical treatment as such have a very limited place

in the care of the partially sighted. They are virtually confined to operations for the removal of the lens in cataract, corneal grafting and operations to minimize the after-effects of injury.

The vast majority of partially sighted children will, however, be much helped by the wearing of suitable spectacles, the lenses of which need to be changed at intervals. The myopic child in particular needs very close supervision from this point of view; during the periods of rapid progress re-examination may be needed as frequently as every six months. It ought not to be necessary to stress that for this purpose the care of a good ophthalmologist is necessary, but some members of the public do not seem to understand the difference between a sight-testing optician and a doctor-specialist and, unfortunately, there are some opticians who will not recognize their own limitations.

No less important is the proper care of the spectacles which have been provided. Young children are often rather feckless creatures and neglect to clean their lenses, so that they may be trying to look through glasses which are semi-opaque. Spectacles are prescribed so that they give the best results when the child is looking through the centre of the lens, with the lens parallel to the eye and with the lens at the right distance in front of the eye. No-one has yet invented a completely child-proof spectacle frame and metal frames, which are desirable because they are less liable to accidental breakage, have a tendency to bend rather than to break. A random check on a group of young children wearing spectacles is likely to show lenses tilted, frames slipping down the child's nose, one lens well away from the eye while the other is touching the eyelashes and lenses facing inwards or outwards instead of to the front. Even if the spectacle frame is straight, as the child grows his eyes become a little further apart so that instead of looking through the lens centres he is looking through the outer halves of the lenses. These faults must be constantly watched for and corrected.

The child with a minor visual defect often neglects to wear his spectacles regularly. The partially sighted child usually wears them constantly for the very good reason that he knows he is helpless without them. But because they may get broken and have to be sent away for repair and adjustment it is essential that he should have a spare pair *in good condition*. The last three words are emphasized because it is not unknown for a child to put on his 'stand-by' pair when his regular ones are damaged and for the repair of the regular ones to be forgotten or postponed.

In recent years much progress has been made in the manufacture and fitting of contact lenses and some partially sighted children can obtain considerable benefit from them. More experiment will be needed before their scope and limitations can be fully defined, and not all children can tolerate them or use them intelligently. The decision as to whether they should be tried in any particular case is, of course, a matter for the ophthalmologist.

## General Care and Management

The partially sighted child has useful sight and the important thing is to prepare and train him for life as a sighted person, even though his sight may be limited. In most cases his difficulties will not begin during the early years of life. There are two reasons for this. The first is that most children are born long-sighted and progress to normality during the first ten years or so. The child who is going to be myopic is, therefore, likely to have normal sight or even long sight in the beginning and his myopia will not show itself till he is four or five years old. The second reason is that very few indeed of the normal activities of a child under the age of four or five require fine vision; they are 'coarse' tasks which can be accomplished with only moderately acute sight. Only the albino and the child with a lens defect which has not yet been operated on will have serious difficulty in this early period.

As time goes on the important thing is to follow the general principle which applies to so many handicaps—the child must be encouraged to practice and develop the things which he can do and must be taught to find in them the satisfactions which he cannot expect to get from the things which he cannot do. A substantial number of myopes end by being quite capable of doing close work competently, especially if provided with suitable spectacles and special aids for fine work. Naturally, except for the albino, good lighting is important.

There has been some controversy over the care of the child whose partial sight is known to be a stage on the way to total blindness. Some people have suggested that preparation for sightless life should begin early in these cases, but the majority view now inclines in the opposite direction. So long as a person has useful sight he finds it comparatively difficult to learn Braille. More important, however, is the desirability that so long as he has sight he should have every opportunity of making use of it to acquire a store of knowledge and experience, which can be done so much more easily with sight than without. He should, of course, be encouraged to use touch and hearing as much as possible, but as supplements to rather than substitutes for sight. In particular, he should be encouraged to develop independence and habits of free movement, so long as he has the sight with which to avoid dangers and obstacles.

## Education

First steps in the school education of the partially sighted child are comparatively simple. Up to the age of seven schools in general follow a policy of introducing the child to and preparing him for formal education. Much of the activity in school has a quality of 'play'. The development of number sense is encouraged by the use of toys and such objects as counters and when figures appear they are written or printed so large that a child who is quite severely visually handicapped can distinguish them. The beginnings of reading similarly come through letters printed or written large and even the books which the child begins to use in the infant department have large, clear print. The great majority of partially sighted children, therefore, can make a start in an ordinary school and more or less keep up with the average until the age of seven.

The next phase of normal education is a very different thing. Writing cannot continue to sprawl in large printed characters but must be disciplined to standard size and form. Arithmetic is no longer done by moving counters or match-sticks on a table but must be brought to tidy normality in the exercise book. Books contain longer words and therefore smaller print and are no longer used merely for reading exercise but have become sources of information. Blackboard work and the use of other visual aids in class have to be based on the seeing capacity of the normal child. And, not least important, the leisureliness of the infant school has gone and an element of urgency comes in, for in three or four years' time decisions regarding the child's future education and career will have to be made and his academic attainments must have reached a certain standard or else he will be permanently educationally retarded.

The intelligent partially sighted child can, in the four years between seven and eleven, cover the same educational ground as the fully sighted child, but not under standard school conditions because the educational methods which have to be used for full-sized classes of normal children do not meet his needs. During this period he should have education in small classes, where individual attention is possible. Reading aids such as direct or projection magnifiers make it possible for him to read ordinary print but he will have to have a good deal of large-scale blackboard work and more use must be made of oral methods of teaching than is customary in an ordinary school. A typewriter may be of some value at this stage. It is, therefore, easiest for him to spend these days in a special school or class.

Whether he remains for the rest of his school career in a special school or class will depend upon special considerations in each case. A substantial number of these children, having acquired the basic skills in a special school by the age of eleven or twelve, can then return to an ordinary school, using their reading aids and receiving such special consideration as a seat near the blackboard, a little individual help with some of the more complicated parts of the curriculum and some indulgence for their still large and untidy writing and figuring. Some, because of the severity of their disability or minor intellectual shortcomings, may take five or even six years to cover the normal four-year programme but can then transfer to an ordinary school. Permanent special schooling is, however, inevitable for the remainder. Probably the best principle that can be followed is that the special school should have as its ideal aim the preparation of as many children as possible for normal secondary education standard.

## The Prospect for the Partially Sighted

The ultimate outlook for many partially sighted children is very fair. Some of the conditions which produce this disability leave the eye permanently susceptible to grave injury, and in such cases strenuous exercise or heavy work will have to be permanently forbidden. In most cases, however, by the middle or late 'teens the condition is finite and stable and the child can go on to do anything which is within his powers. Many types of employment are quite within his scope and he has vision enough to succeed in the majority of the activities of daily living.

# CHAPTER 14

# Deafness

Though it is difficult to define 'blindness' in strict terms and to distinguish it from 'partial sightedness' it is both possible and convenient to make at least a working distinction. Deafness presents a more difficult problem. Some enthusiasts have claimed that there is no such thing as a totally deaf child and that every child has some hearing if only one looks for it sufficiently thoroughly; this is undoubtedly going too far. The distinction which has been made in the educational classification of children with hearing defects between the 'deaf' and the 'partially hearing' is based on educational provision and distinguishes less between children than between the types of school which is best likely to meet their needs. It is best for practical purposes to think of deafness as something which has a wide range of gradation from the moderate through the profound to the total. And even this is not the whole story. In some children it is possible for the degree of their deafness to vary. In some one has to consider the quality as well as the quantity of the deafness. So for the purposes of this book there is no virtue in having separate chapters to consider the deaf and the partially hearing.

As I have indicated elsewhere, in considering any kind of disability one has to be aware of what it does to its victim and in many ways deafness can be regarded as the cruellest of all. Human contacts and human relationships depend most of all upon communication by means of speech. Whatever their limitations, sufferers from other disabilities can communicate with their fellows. Even the brain-damaged child with a severe speech disability can hear what others say and make some kind of answer by other means. The profoundly deaf cannot converse, in the ordinary sense of the term, with other people unless those others have learned to use sign language, and it is obviously impossible to expect everyone to do this. The moderately deaf can converse and communicate only imperfectly and with difficulty and in doing so they make demands on the tolerance of their friends and work-mates which are certainly not conducive to easy relationships.

The deaf person soon realizes that to many of those he meets he is a joke or an embarrassment and the embarrassment soon becomes mutual. He is understandably reluctant to exhibit his disability and this commonly leads to disastrous human conse-quences—aggressiveness, petulance, even withdrawal from con-tacts with others unless these are absolutely necessary for basic practical purposes. He may even reject the very help which could make life easier; it is all too common for the deaf to refuse to wear hearing aids, since to do so is to advertise their deafness and induce embarrassment from the start in those whom they meet.

What we can do for the deaf in the way of training, education and practical help can, in fact, be nullified unless from the start they are taught to live with their disability among hearing people and unless hearing people are also taught how to live with the deaf.

## Causation

Though our knowledge of the causation of deafness is widening, much remains to be discovered and understood. Twenty years ago the commonest single cause was undoubtedly neglected chronic infections of the middle ear. These followed acute infections in the first five or six years of early childhood which continued to smoulder, were fuelled from time to time by colds and catarrh, and ultimately produced severe destruction of the ear mechanism. The introduction of antibiotics made it possible to treat the first causes of the trouble—usually throat infections—and either to prevent the infection from reaching the middle ear or to cure it before any appreciable damage had been done.

Ten years ago the experts were claiming with some confidence that deafness due to infection was no longer a problem. Only within that period has it been realized that the problem has not been eliminated but merely changed. Many mysterious cases of deafness in young children—in the pre-school or early school years—are now known to be due to a condition which has come to be known as 'glue ear'. Ironically, the increase in its prevalence is due to the very means of treatment which have 'saved' children from chronic middle ear infections. Antibiotics are used to clear up a first attack of earache, produce rapid improvement and are discontinued. There is another attack of earache and the same happens again. There is no continuing discharge from the ear to remind parents and doctor that something is wrong and so the inflammation is never really fully controlled. And so, in time, though there is not necessarily the destruction of the middle ear mechanism which followed the old and more obvious infections, there is an interference with the working of that mechanism which is equally damaging to the sense of hearing. Much work is now going on in the treatment of glue ear and there are surgical techniques which offer considerable improvement. But whether and how it can be prevented or totally and permanently cured remains to be seen. What matters is that the possibility of its occurrence must always be borne in mind and that for this purpose it is important that attacks of slight, transient deafness, or insidiously developing hearing impairment in the pre-school child must be watched for and carefully investigated.

This apart, acquired deafness after the first days of life is becoming quite uncommon. Meningitis can now be regarded as only a rare cause. Profound deafness is most likely to be due to inherited factors or to virus infections—usually rubella (german measles)—in the mother during the first two months or so of pregnancy, to brain damage during labour or to the jaundice caused immediately after birth by rhesus incompatibility. These last are specially important because the factors which produce the deafness may also produce other disabilities so that the child is multiply handicapped.

The outlook is certainly improving. It is now possible for those women who have never had rubella to be vaccinated against it before they reach child-bearing age, so that this infection in the unborn child should soon be eliminated. Techniques in dealing with rhesus incompatibility are steadily improving. We can hope that advances in obstetrics will further reduce the occurrence of brain damage during birth, though it is also to be expected that these advances will continue to favour the survival of some brain-damaged children who would otherwise have died.

### The Nature of Deafness

In considering deafness we are dealing with a disability of unique complexity. It is always tempting to think in terms of handicap as a matter of damage to a particular organ; nowhere in the whole field of handicap can this error be so damaging or even disastrous, whether we are considering the help we give to an individual or the nature of the provision we make for all those who suffer from that particular disability. Deafness is important in itself but even more important in its consequences. In all but the mildest defects of hearing, substantial or severe secondary handicaps are the rule rather than the exception. These secondary handicaps are in some degree inevitable and if they are to be minimized action must be taken early in the child's life.

True, the immediate consequences of a hearing defect are by no means unimportant. Inability to hear a motor car horn, a bicycle bell and certain other noises may be a cause of serious physical danger. Inability to hear music or bird-song deprives one of pleasures which mean much to many people. These, however, are modest in their effect compared with impairment of hearing for speech.

Deafness must, in fact, be considered as essentially a part of the total business of communication, which is fundamental to the business of daily life. Communication is always to be regarded as a two-way activity. It is not enough to receive; there must be response as well as reception. For proper communication, sounds must reach the ear and their essence must be clearly conveyed to the brain. Their significance must be interpreted in the brain. At that stage, if the message received calls for immediate action that action must be taken. If the message conveys information for storage the information must be stored. If, as commonly happens, the message requires that there should be a reply, that reply has to be given in a form which the original communicator can understand. For practical purposes, therefore, hearing, understanding and speech cannot be considered separately. And even this somewhat over-simplifies the situation. 'Understanding' involves two processes, first the analysis of the sounds received— 'discrimination' is the term commonly applied to this—and then the more intellectual business of conceptualizing what they convey. 'Speech' requires not only the physical use of the organs of speech but the employment of them to produce language, the basic medium of communication.

Intellectual deficit and speech disabilities can exist without any hearing disability; these handicaps are considered separately in other chapters. What we have to bear in mind here is that defective hearing can of itself be a cause of delayed intellectual development, of impairment or absence of speech and of poor acquisition of language.

With these considerations in mind we can now begin to analyse, admittedly in simple terms, what deafness is and what it does to its victim.

Sound waves enter the ear passage and strike the ear drum. The middle ear contains a chain of little bones which pick up the vibrations of the drum and pass them on to the inner ear. This is a kind of 'coding' device, which turns the vibrations into nerve impulses and passes them on to the brain via the auditory nerve.

Blocking of the ear passage, usually due to the accumulation of wax or the presence of foreign bodies, prevents the waves from reaching the drum. This produces overall difficulty in hearing; it can be relieved without great trouble by removing the obstruction.

Damage to the drum itself or anything which interferes with the normal movement of the bone-chain in the middle ear, prevents the transmission of the vibrations to the middle ear and also produces a degree of overall deafness. This kind of trouble usually follows infection; if taken in hand early it may be quite successfully treated but if neglected it may produce incurable damage. It is possible, even if the middle ear is irretrievably damaged, for sound vibrations to be conducted through the surrounding bone to the inner ear but they reach it in a very much weaker form than if they go through the normal mechanism.

Conductive deafness—the term usually applied to deafness from these causes—usually interferes with the hearing of sounds of all kinds to a similar extent. When we come to consider perceptive deafness, which is due to faults in the inner ear and the auditory nerve, we meet a more complex problem. People are now familiar with the idea that sound waves come to the ear in a range of frequencies. In music the bass notes have a frequency as low as about 20 cycles per second, a point at which they can almost be felt as vibrations as well as heard as notes. The treble notes have frequencies which go as high as 20,000 cycles. From the point of view of musical appreciation, the extremes of the frequency range are not very important. All except 'Hi-Fi' fanatics are usually happy if their record reproducers function adequately from 50 cycles up to about 16,000 cycles.

Most of the sounds of daily life, which contain a mixture of frequencies, fall below the 10,000 cycle level. Essential speech sounds have an even smaller range; good hearing from about 250 to 8,000 cycles is adequate for speech reception. Unfortunately, however, while vowel sounds have frequencies mainly below 1,000 cycles consonant sounds involve frequencies which may be as high as 6,000 or 8,000 cycles. Quite often, hearing loss in moderate or even fairly severe deafness is not even over the whole range of useful frequencies and is commonly much greater in the higher frequencies. The effect of this high frequency deafness is obvious; the victim will hear vowel sounds well but will have difficulty in hearing consonants or in distinguishing between them.

The implications of this are important. He will hear the ordinary noises in his surroundings and he will also make some response when he is spoken to. It is obvious that he is not 'deaf' in the ordinary colloquial sense of the term. But virtually all words contain consonants as well as vowels and, in fact, it is the consonants which mainly distinguish one word from another. So, while the child may, for example, be able to detect a difference between 'cat', and 'bee' and 'bow' he will be unable to go much further. He will not distinguish between 'cat' 'hat' and 'mat', between 'bee', 'see' and 'flea' or between 'bow', 'low' and 'go'.

Most cases of deafness in childhood fall into these two main groups—conductive and perceptive. There are, however, a few in whom the fault is in the brain. We know that in most of these children the 'reception', 'coding' and nerve transmission mechanism is functioning normally and that sounds of all frequencies can be heard. They are, however, incapable of appreciating speech sounds as speech. This condition has been called 'word-deafness', but nowadays it is more often spoke of as 'congenital auditory imperception'. What the actual fault is and where it lies nobody yet knows.

This description, as I have said, over-simplifies, especially in that the types of deafness are not always 'pure'. It is by no means rare to find both conductive and perceptive deafness present together and a child with congenital auditory imperception may also have either conductive or perceptive difficulties. However, it does give the basis for a working understanding of what their deafness does to its victims and how they may be helped.

Children learn through using all the five senses. Any barrier or obstacle in any of these gateways will slow down intellectual, emotional and social development. Hearing has a special importance. We are not born with speech; we acquire it by listening to and imitating others. It follows that any child with any hearing defect will be slow in learning to speak and that if the defect is severe enough he will not spontaneously learn to speak at all. For the young child, the understanding of speech and the use of speech are closely interwoven and in the early years communication by speech is the most important way in which anyone learns anything, especially about the fundamentals of 'how' and 'why'.

It is obviously important that any degree of any type of deafness should be recognized as early as possible, so that anything that can be done to help the child will be done. There is a special urgency in the case of deafness in that evidence is accumulating to suggest strongly that there is a critical period in the child's life during which he learns to hear and speak and that if the deaf child does not receive help before he is about five years old it will never be possible to get optimal results, whatever one may try to do.

There is always a risk that any child who is developing slowly may be suspected of being intellectually subnormal, and it is by no means unknown for deaf children to be wrongly classified in this way, so that suitable care and help is delayed or not provided at all. The child with conductive deafness is not greatly at risk; if his deafness is substantial someone is almost certain to realize that he has difficulty in hearing any type of sound. The mistake is easiest to make when the child has high-frequency deafness. He has been seen to respond to sound from quite an early age, so it is obvious that he can hear. He tries to imitate speech sounds but produces only unintelligible monosyllables. He listens but understands little of what he hears. These are characteristics of the mentally handicapped, notoriously late in developing speech and generally slow in the uptake. But they can result just as easily from the fact that the child with high-frequency deafness hears speech distorted and mutilated and imitates the mutilations he has heard and from the fact that the speech he hears is to him largely incomprehensible and so largely not understood.

### Diagnosis and Assessment

If there is one thing that stands out above all others in efforts to help deaf children it is that the sooner those efforts are started the better the results. We want to prevent them from falling behind in general development or developing wrong behaviour patterns which will have to be laboriously unlearned. In particular we want them to develop speech, so far as they can, and to make the fullest use of whatever hearing they may have and we must make a beginning on this during the critical period of the first years of life. And our assessment must be as accurate as possible; the great majority—even many of the profoundly deaf—have some remnants of hearing and we must try to define who much they can hear at various parts of the frequency range.

The accurate map of a person's hearing, the audiogram, defines his hearing loss in terms of units of loudness (decibels) of the quietest sound he can hear at six or eight selected frequencies between 250 cycles and 800 cycles, the range of frequencies covered by speech sounds. To prepare an accurate audiogram requires from the patient a degree of patient and understanding cooperation which cannot be expected of young children. An expert, using special techniques, may be able to prepare one for an intelligent child of perhaps four years old; more often it is not possible to do this until a child is five or six years old. Even four is late to offer the best prospects for care, training and treatment. Efforts have therefore been made to find ways of getting a provisional assessment of hearing in very much younger children.

The parents' suspicions that a child may be deaf may not be aroused, even if the deafness is severe, until the latter part of the first year, and in moderate and mild deafness nothing may be suspected until very much later. The ideal to be aimed at, therefore, is some kind of test which can be applied fairly quickly to *all* children in early life. This kind of screening test must be so designed that it will miss no child who has any substantial hearing loss. It is better to have a test that will arouse some suspicion of deafness, which can later be eliminated by more accurate testing, in some normal children than to have one which will fail to pick up substantial deafness in any child.

Experiments are now going on with audiometry in new-born children. If a fairly loud noise is made close to a new-born child he is likely to blink or show some other reaction if he hears it. This is a crude technique but it may offer promise of detecting some cases of substantial hearing defect and even suggesting whether that defect is mainly on high or on low frequencies.

The most practical method of early childhood screening in young children in this country, however, is that of arranging for health visitors to test children of between six and eight months old by making some simple and familiar noises (e.g. rattling a spoon in a cup and crumpling a piece of paper) near to the child but out of his sight and noting whether he tries to look in the direction of the sound or shows any other reaction to it. Children who fail to react are referred for more detailed investigation and some simple tests of hearing are now usually included in the routine developmental screening tests mentioned in Chapter 11. These tests are proving on the whole very effective, so much so that many areas claim that virtually all children with substantial hearing defects are found well before they reach school age.

Some localities make a habit of carrying out group hearing tests, using simple audiometers operating on four or five selected frequencies, on all children during their first year at school. This system has proved of value at times. Recent studies suggest that it detects very few cases of deafness which are not already known to the child health services, an excellent testimony to the potential effectiveness of young child screening. It is not yet possible to make a final judgement on the value of this 'sweep testing', as it is commonly called. Some children who have been found to have normal hearing in the first year or two of life may develop deafness for various reasons (e.g. 'glue ear') during the later pre-school years and may not have attended child health clinics and received screening examinations during that period; sweep testing on school entry certainly offers a fair chance of detecting these. I would certainly be reluctant to advise abandoning sweep testing in places where it is done as a routine at the present time, and there may be a case for starting it in places where it is not yet done.

Probably the most rewarding procedure is to select children for more detailed and comprehensive individual tests on a basis of history and observation. Factors which produce other disabilities may also damage hearing and any child with any type of substantial congenital disability should be regarded as having some possible hearing handicap. Such children must be watched for any signs suggestive of deafness and specially tested if these signs appear. Desirably they should be specially referred for audiometry at the age of 3 or 4 and be tested annually thereafter until it is certain that they have no hearing disability.

The teacher, who is giving her class some oral teaching every day, is ideally situated as an observer to detect signs of hearing impairment and to refer children for detailed testing. Sometimes, however, through no fault of her own, she may fail in this. The intensity of sound varies inversely with the square of the distance from the source of that sound. This means that the teacher's voice can sound four times as loud to a child in the front row of the class as it does to one in the back row. Also, a child with a slight hearing disability or one which is developing slowly may spontaneously develop considerable facility in lip-reading. I have known such children who were lucky enough to be allocated front seats pass as having quite normal hearing until a move to a new class and the allocation of a back seat revealed their disability. This is rather less likely to happen with the new techniques of infant teaching, where the children move about in group activities and the teacher moves among them, but it is still a possibility.

The teacher, therefore, must be on the alert not only for direct evidence of deafness but for signs of its possible consequences or of things which might cause deafness. Slowness in speech development or in progress in learning, especially in oral subjects, may of course be due to intellectual defect but may, as already indicated, be due to hearing impairment. Wandering of attention, in class or at play, especially in a child who has seemed earlier to be normally attentive, a falling off in attainments in a child who has previously done well, a reluctance to concentrate in a child who has previously seemed attentive—all these may have several causes but they may well be early signs of developing hearing defect.

Just as the presence of another disability may suggest the possibility of deafness, so the presence of deafness may suggest the presence of other undetected disabilities. The principle that all apparently dull children should have a hearing test holds good in converse; all deaf children should have intelligence tests and careful general checks. If the deafness is at all substantial, then the help of the expert staff of an audiology unit should be invoked, for even in the interpretation of non-verbal intelligence tests experience in working with deaf children counts for a great deal.

Finally, no less than with other handicapped children—in many cases even more—assessment involves the assessment not only of the child's assets and liabilities as an individual but of his family and home assets and liabilities. The parents can do invaluable work with the child in the first years of life. Their role is critical in the first two years or so and even when the child is getting expert help the success of that help depends very much on whether the parents are positive and understanding collaborators. Most people with experience in helping deaf children have found to their disappointment that parents can remain neutral or even be actively hostile.

## Care and Education

Medical and surgical treatment have little to offer to the majority of deaf children, especially those whose deafness is congenital. Their principal role is to curb or cure chronic infections which are causing deafness and to prevent infections, whether acute or chronic, from making worse deafness which is due to other causes.

The positive approach to the deaf child is to make use of whatever remnants of hearing the child possesses—and most of them do have useful remnants—and by building on what remains and using a variety of techniques to develop the child's hearing skills, his speech and his employment of language whether in speech or otherwise. In achieving this, care, management and hearing are so closely interlinked that they must be considered as part of the same total process.

The power to hear is the first thing to be considered. If it can be increased, so much the better, and hearing aids can be invaluable. However, they have their limitations. They are at present least effective in children whose deafness is uneven over the frequency range. If an aid magnifies sounds of all frequencies, then by the time its volume control is turned up to the point at which a child with high-frequency deafness might hear the high-frequency sounds it is likely that the volume of the low-frequency sounds may be intolerable. Tone-control mechanisms cannot yet be applied to hearing aids as effectively as they can to record-reproducing amplifiers. It is probable that new micro-miniature circuit techniques may make it possible in the fairly near future to tailor a child's hearing aid to the precise frequency-loss from which he suffers, but this stage has certainly not yet been reached. Otherwise, recent developments have greatly improved the effectiveness of aids. The old types which had a large box for battery and microphone were inconvenient, to say the least, for very young children as well as being unacceptable to many children of all ages. The new, small aids which fit close to the ear and do not require any long connecting flex between amplifier and ear-piece are usually better in every way and have the further advantage that since the child can have one complete aid to each ear he will have a chance of developing 'stereophonic' hearing and sound localization in a way impossible with the old-type aids with a single cumbersome receiver connected to either one or two ear-pieces. Their disadvantages that they are still relatively expensive and may be less robust than the older types, but it is being increasingly recognized that their virtues may outweigh the cost of supply and maintenance.

Next comes the use of the power to hear. We know that a muscle which is not used becomes weak and may need prolonged special rehabilitation care to bring it back into function and that an eye which is not being used loses its visual acuity to a degree which may cause very serious impairment of its usefulness and which may make it impossible to restore it to anything approaching normal. We do not know that the same kind of thing happens with an ear which is not used. The probability is that so long as there is any hearing at all in an ear sound waves get to it and are dealt with by the transmitting and coding mechanisms, so that in the strict mechanical sense the ear is being used. However, the impulses which are getting through to the brain from an impaired hearing mechanism may be too weak to make any impression on the consciousness and though in the strict mechanical sense they may be 'heard' they are certainly not listened to. There is no doubt that if a child with remnants of hearing does not receive help early in life the likelihood of his making use of those remnants later is considerably lessened and whether this is due to his having failed to acquire the habit of listening or to his having suppressed the auditory stimuli as an unwanted—because meaningless distraction is of little practical importance.

What does matter is that any child with a hearing disability must from the moment at which that disability is recognized receive deliberate auditory training. This demands that he must start, preferably during the first year of life, to listen to sounds and to associate sounds with meaning. The fact that he may not be able to hear all sounds, to distinguish between the between the finer details of different sounds or to appreciate at first exactly what they mean is not basically important. If he realizes that they *do* differ and that they *can* have meaning it is enough at this stage. If, through lack of training, he fails to realize this and forms the habit of relying on sight and paying no attention to sound it will be exceedingly difficult to develop what hearing he has at a later age. Speech and language training as such come at a rather later stage, but even from the start he must learn that speech does have some meaning and that people communicate through speech.

In the first eighteen months or two years the mother has an important part to play. She must accept the fact of her child's deafness and must see to it that he has constant listening practice. An individual hearing aid must be provided as soon as practicable—this has been done with success for children as young as eight or ten months. It must be constantly worn—some children are a little restive at first but at this age they quickly learn to like their aids and will not be parted from them. By contrast, children who do not receive their aids until they are four or five years old start by disliking them and finding every possible excuse for not wearing them; they have already begun to set a pattern of life in a world without sound and the sounds which the aid brings to them mean nothing at all.

The last paragraph must not be taken to mean that either mother or child has an easy task. Skilled professional help and advice are absolutely essential and regular visits to an audiology centre are probably the best way of providing this. In the beginning the centre may be able to give mother and child frequent auditory training sessions until the mother has grasped the principles and practice of what she is to try to do, but as she becomes more adept the visits will be less frequent and will be in the nature of progress checks.

Experts are not yet agreed on the relative value of the home and the special nursery unit for giving auditory training after, say, the age of two or three years. This is the age at which the normal child learns to talk freely and the only environment in which it is possible to learn speech is one in which speech is constantly used. There are plenty of reasons why even a capable and well-intentioned mother may not be able to continue to surround her child with speech after he has come to this age. She has responsibilities to her other children and he is ripe to widen his circle and play outside the home, in surroundings in which auditory training will be less deliberate. His very mobility will take him out of the range at which his hearing aid is fully effective. If any substantial difficulties arise at this stage a period in a special nursery unit should be considered. A day unit is to be preferred but if there is none within reasonable distance it may be possible to send the child to a boarding unit as a weekly boarder, going home at week-ends so that the link with home is not broken. The unit provides three important things. It has equipment beyond the range of the home; to mention only one item out of many, the 'loop amplifier' provides constantly amplified speech and other sounds to the child while he is moving freely about a large room and eliminates the need for whoever is training him to keep him constantly by her side. It has skilled and experienced staff, who can watch the child's progress closely, detect difficulties as they arise and give specific and positive help to him in those difficulties. And it gives him variety of company. The voices he hears vary, but since they are presented to him carefully and deliberately they register with him —the voices of casually-met strangers who do not appreciate his disability are less valuable in auditory training at this stage. It is socially important, too, that he mixes with other children who are his equals; the deaf child who is mixing only with hearing children may be cruelly isolated because he is not quick enough in hearing to grasp what they say and is therefore unable to join fully in their games.

If he does go to such a unit, however, the mother must not surrender her responsibility. She must visit regularly and be brought into full partnership with the staff so that when the child is at home she can continue what they have been doing.

As the deaf child comes to school age the question of more formal education has to be considered. Some children with only minor defect of hearing may already be so adept at the use of their hearing aids and so well grounded in auditory training that they can enter an ordinary school at five and, with a little understanding help, keep pace with normal children. The small minority of the totally deaf, who must rely permanently on lip-reading, 'artificial' speech and education by mainly visual methods can get what they need only in a special school, day or residential.

The majority need a progressive compromise. Since the deaf must ultimately live in the world, the ideal is that they should at some time move into an ordinary school, but it is difficult in the child's early years to forecast how soon his hearing, his speech and his educational progress will make this possible. A start in a special school is essential; a day school is preferable but if there is none within easy reach then a boarding school must be chosen. For many children a school for the partially deaf will be needed throughout school life, with their training and education built on the hearing they possess and oriented to make them as fit as possible to mix with hearing people.

Much hope, however, is encouraged by recent experiments in grafting units for the partially deaf on to ordinary schools. Many ordinary school subjects are taught largely or entirely by visual methods. It is, therefore, possible for a child to spend part of his time with normal children in ordinary classes for these subjects and to mix with normal children in play and organized games, but to go back to the special unit, with its special techniques and equipment, for the rest of the curriculum. Some children in such units gradually 'grow out of' the unit into the school and even those who need the unit permanently for part of their education become much more comfortable in the company of the normal—and much more readily accepted by the normal.

The 'home teacher' of the blind is now coming to have a counterpart in work for the deaf. A combined teacher, adviser and social worker, she can be exceedingly useful to deaf children of all ages and their families. For the pre-school child, she can aid, advise and support the parents in giving auditory and general training and for the school child she can help to see that the home understands what the school is doing and co-operates fully. She can be useful as a counsellor during the years of adjustment after leaving school. Provided that she is not used as a substitute for school, so that the child is robbed of contacts outside the home, she is likely to become invaluable in work for the deaf and the training and employment of such home teachers needs to be considerably expanded.

This section has so far had a deliberately optimistic tone, for the education of the deaf must be embarked on with confidence. I must, however, end it with a realistic comment on the end-results of education and the value of some special techniques. I have referred to 'artificial speech.' It is possible, by using special methods, to teach a totally deaf child to talk. The sounds are clipped and the voice lacks modulation, but the child can make himself understood at any rate on simple everyday matters. Even a little hearing allows him to introduce modulation and the value of 'natural' speech is such that concentration on the use of hearing remnants is justified. It must not, however, be expected that the child with a severe hearing defect will ever acquire normal speech. (A survey in 1968 in schools for the deaf suggested that less than one-half of the children had 'fairly intelligible' speech.).

Lip-reading is an essential for the totally deaf, but must be used with discrimination for the partially deaf. Since the aim of training is to make the child use to the full what hearing he has, lip-reading, which enables him to comprehend speech without listening, may divert him from the immediate task in hand. The child who has acquired deafness slowly and has involuntarily learned some lip-reading can often present great difficulties in auditory training. It is undoubtedly a useful aid in cases of severe sub-total deafness, but it is probably best not to introduce it until everything possible has been done in the way of training hearing.

Sign language, formerly the standby of the deaf, went out of fashion some years ago in the education of deaf children. Obviously, to rely on it completely restricts one's conversational intercourse to those who have acquired it, and this in itself is undesirable if it can be avoided. The philosophy of purely aural training seems at first glance rational. If the child who has some hearing is allowed to acquire lip-reading and sign language there is a possibility that he will prefer to use these skills for communication rather than to develop the much more laborious skill of learning to rely on his hearing and develop his speech. With this in mind, the trend has been to forbid or strongly to discourage either signing or lip-reading and to insist on hearing and speech as the only acceptable mode of communication.

But even the most convinced of oralists ruefully admit that as soon as their pupils get out of the class-room they do in fact use signing and lip-reading and the newer school of thought is beginning to make constructive use of these. This is not merely an acceptance of the undesirable inevitable. Speech is the use of language. Reading, also, depends on the acquisition of language. Language postulates a vocabulary. Moreover, if a child is to make effective use of what speech he has, the incentive to do this is likely to increase if he finds that he has a wide range of communication possibilities—if, in fact, he has a reasonably wide vocabulary. Britain has been for some time mainly committed to oralism but other countries have been experimenting more liberally for some years and there seems to be little doubt that the deaf child who is taught by methods which include signing and lip-reading in the early years will, by the age of six or so, have a far greater vocabulary than the child taught by purely oral means. Not only does this appear to help his facility with speech but it makes matters much easier for him when he starts to learn reading and writing and to go on to learn subjects which are taught through those skills. It seems likely that 'combined' teaching will soon become a great deal more general in schools for the deaf and special units for the partially hearing, though the ideal way of achieving the best combination still needs to be worked out.

## The Prospect for the Deaf

Eric was the severely deaf son of parents who were both intelligent and educated. Until he was 11 years old he attended an ordinary school and had special home coaching from his teacher mother. He had spontaneously begun to lip-read and had also received a little lip-reading training from a special instructor. When I first met him, at that age, he was more than two years below average in school attainment and his speech was very poor indeed, but he was certainly well above average in intelligence. The parents wanted him to be educated for one of the professions.

Obviously there was little hope of his going on to higher education unless, for what school years remained, he could have the advantages of a grammar school for severely deaf children—and have them soon. I was able to interest the headmaster of such a school in his case and to secure special and expert coaching to bring him nearer to the attainment standard which the school required of new entrants. Yet for more than two years the parents placed one obstacle after another in the way of his going to that school and only after several long and painful interviews did they finally give reluctant consent. They never fully acquiesced and though he made quite good progress the constant tug-of-war between home and school hampered him both educationally and emotionally. By the time he was sixteen it was clear that his attainments would not reach University entrance standard in time for him to embark on an academic career and he himself had developed a strong inclination to go into farming.

The thought that he should go into farming rather than enter a profession was anathema to the parents and I suspect that it was precisely because of this that he stuck to his guns and eventually wore them down. In the end, he found reasonable happiness and success in the work of his choice and ultimately the breach between himself and them was healed, I quote his case as one of too many I have met in which the parents have long and actively opposed their deaf child's best interests. Indeed, over many years I have formed the opinion that of all handicaps deafness is the one in which there is the greater likelihood of parents failing to collaborate with those who are trying to help them and their child, a specially tragic matter, since, as I have already mentioned, it is in this field that the understanding parent can play an absolutely vital role in helping the child along.

The reasons for this kind of failure are not easy to analyse. Probably one of them is that from the start there is difficulty in parent-child communication. Sometimes the parents feel that the child may be mentally sub-standard and dare not face the possibility of being told so. Sometimes they are influenced by the fact that deafness is one of the less socially acceptable disabilities. But whatever the reason, though increasing knowledge of the subject is slowly improving the situation, one continues to meet parents who find excuses to delay investigation of suspected deafness, who refuse to let their child wear a hearing aid or who stubbornly resist the offer of special education.

The risks to the child's development of speech and language and of his coming to make use of what hearing he has are obvious. No less grave is the risk of failure to develop that good parent-child relationship which is the foundation of all good human relationships throughout life, and 'inability to relate' is a potential source of failure.

Much remains to be done in exploring the field of possible employment for the deaf. There is a certain amount of prejudice and resistance to be overcome and it is hard to say whether some apparent objections to the employment of deaf people in certain occupations are truly valid. Deaf students, for example, are not accepted for training in physiotherapy. Some types of physiotherapy carry a risk of injury to the patient and it is essential that whoever is using them should hear if the patient complains of pain or discomfort, but it would be interesting to see whether a deaf person could successfully engage in certain branches of physiotherapy. There has been considerable argument as to whether the deaf should be allowed to drive motor vehicles. On the one hand it is argued that failure to hear another vehicle's horn signals might cause an accident but on the other it is contended that the deaf driver concentrates his attention on his driving all the better for not being distracted by irrelevant sounds—including the chatter of his passengers.

In practice there are probably few employments in which the fine discrimination of sound is essential; just as in the employment of the blind sound signals can be substituted for light signals, so for the deaf light signals can replace sound. The principal limiting factor is difficulty of communication with other people. The deaf person will be quite effective in a type of work in which, after initial instruction, he can go on steadily working without the need to consult or discuss with colleagues. This applies not only to manual tasks but to clerical and office work, some of it very highly skilled, in which, as in book-keeping, both the input to him and the output from him are mainly on paper. It is tempting to assign all deaf people at once to work of this type and many of them tend to accept it readily because it will obviously save them trouble and embarrassment. The temptation should be resisted. Up to school leaving age, the deaf youngster, however much he may have been encouraged to mix with normal people, has always been able, in case of need, to fall back on someone who would help him—someone who spoke slowly and clearly for his benefit, who talked in a way easily lip-read or who understood without much difficulty his imperfect or downright poor speech. Once he starts work he is dependent on himself during working hours and must learn to understand and be understood, while those who are to work with him must learn to accept him and communicate with him. If he is assigned to isolated work, this will not happen and he will sink and shrink into the solitariness which is the bane of the deaf.

It is true that a job which makes little demands on his speech and hearing may come more easily to him and help him to gain confidence in his ability, but if he is started in such work for that reason care must be taken that some of his fellow-workers talk with him during work-time in connection with his work and that he is encouraged and actively drawn into work which requires some communication with others.

A disturbing number of apparent failures in employment on the part of deaf people turn out on investigation to be due not to incapacity in work but to difficulty in relations with other people. 'A steady worker, but surly or quick-tempered' is the type of comment one receives. Part of this is due to sheer misunderstanding on the part of others; to the unthinking majority of normal people, anyone who does not talk readily is surly or sulky and they do not distinguish between those who refuse to talk and those who are simply shy of talking because they cannot converse easily. They are irritated when they have to repeat conversation, comment or instruction and their irritability communicates itself to the over-anxious and embarrassed deaf person. Better understanding and greater tolerance are the only things which will overcome this difficulty and they will come only as more deaf people enter and succeed in open employment.

The fault is not all on one side. Some deaf people are grossly and many are slightly maladjusted. They have not fully learned how to accept their handicap and their lack of free communication with normal people has prevented them from going through the normal process of adjustment through experience. This is a problem which education has yet to solve and may never solve completely. Probably the deaf adolescent needs, during the years after leaving school, the help of an experienced counsellor or adviser who is accustomed to helping the deaf and understands their emotional difficulties. I have no doubt that recreational mixing with others outside work can play a vital part in helping the deaf to adjust and it is something which should receive special attention both before and after leaving school.

Some experienced observers claim that deaf adolescents are specially prone to sex delinquency. There is no physical reason why they should be 'oversexed', but this might be consistent with their emotional problems. Any type of maladjustment in adolescence is liable to show itself in a sexual context just because sex problems are urgent at that age. Any handicapped person may seek compensations in sex to make up for the other satisfactions of which he is deprived. Difficulty in ordinary communication with the opposite sex will produce frustrations and, in consequence, the desire to express physically what cannot be expressed on a higher plane. The timid teacher or administrator, to avoid the risk of scandal, will seek to keep deaf boys and girls apart, but this is essentially illogical. The more the sexes mix in the controlled conditions of school and organized recreation the more likely they will be to establish good relations on levels other than the physical.

I have been impressed by the frequency with which emotional difficulties and outright maladjustment occur among the normal children of deaf parents. This is quite understandable. Any barrier between either parent and the child impedes the development of a normal parent-child relationship and it is obvious that a speech-barrier will be exceptionally important. It is true that the care and education of the deaf has made rapid strides recently and that few present deaf parents have had the benefit of those advances. The new generation of deaf children will probably be better parents just as they can hope to be better workers and better citizens. None the less, any child with a deaf parent should be regarded as emotionally vulnerable and the parents should be guided in his upbringing. If any signs of behaviour disorder develop, early child guidance is strongly indicated.

FURTHER READING

*Deafness*
Davis, H.   Hearing and Deafness, a Guide to the Layman.   Staples Press.
F

Ewing, A. W. G. and I. R.   New Opportunities for Deaf Children.   University of London Press.

Ewing, A. W. G.   Speech and the Deaf Child.   University of Manchester Press.

Ewing, A. W. G. (Ed.).   The Modern Educational Treatment of Deafness. University of Manchester Press.

Hodgson, K. W.   The Deaf and Their Problems.   Watts.

Ministry of Health.   Services for Young Children Handicapped by Impaired Hearing.   H.M. Stationery Office.

Sheridan, M.   The Child's Hearing for Speech.   Methuen.

Sifton, M.   Triumph over Deafness.   University of London Press.

Whetnall, E. and Fry, D. B.   The Deaf Child.   Heinemann.

CHAPTER 15

# Epilepsy

Epilepsy has been known for several thousand years and its old, colloquial name, 'the falling sickness', literally describes it as the ordinary person thinks of it. In recent years, however, it has become clear that the classical epileptic fit is only one of many manifestations of the condition, any or all of which can be present in the same person at the same time or successively. The common varieties are the so-called grand mal, with the fall, convulsions and unconsciousness which most lay people regard as typical, faints without convulsions, attacks of slight and sometimes quite sharply localized twitching, and petit mal which may range from a momentary sharp faintness to a simple moment of 'absence' or dreaminess.

## Causation

The condition is not a disease in the ordinary sense of the term. It has no specific cause and no specific cure and it may take a variable course. It is best considered as consisting of an irritability or special sensitiveness in some part of the brain which causes the brain, the nervous system and the muscular system to react abnormally or excessively to influences and stimuli of various kinds. This conception of its mechanism has been in a large degree confirmed by the recent use of electro-encephalography in the study of the electrical reactions of the brain and the electrical currents which pass through the brain tissues. The tracings obtained by the machine show that the waves of electrical activity tend to fall into certain patterns in epileptic patients. Not every epileptic shows the specific wave-pattern and wave-patterns of the specific type are sometimes found in persons who have shown no signs or symptoms of epilepsy. These special patterns do, however, occur far more often in the electro-encephalograms of epileptics than in those of other people, so that there is no doubt of their relation to epilepsy.

The investigation of case histories has suggested that epilepsy undoubtedly can 'run in families' and electro-encephalography has added the new information that the apparently non-epileptic relatives of epileptics tend to have the same abnormal pattern of brain activity. It is, therefore, very probable that there is often some inherited factor in the causation of the condition and that this factor is an unusual excitability of the brain; whether someone who inherits the factor will actually become an epileptic and which sort of epileptic he will become depends upon the degree of the excitability and on the strength of the stimuli to which he is exposed.

This excitability may be increased or, it would seem, may be caused in the first place, by injury at birth or later, by damage to the brain by the toxins of disease or even by chemical poisons circulating in the blood. How these work is uncertain, but there is some evidence that in cases of injury, at least, there is some interference with the blood supply of the brain. The stimuli which precipitate the attacks are many and varied and it is often difficult to determine what they are and precisely what part they play in the total picture. Among them are worry, fear, fatigue, physical or emotional shock, illness and dietary factors; it is quite possible that some of these act rather by increasing the excitability of the brain than by actually stimulating it into activity.

### The Clinical Picture

More than three-quarters of all cases of epilepsy start in childhood or adolescence and about half of them show the first fits before the age of ten. A good many children have 'convulsions' of some sort in the first two years of life. The parent is the chief source of information and this kind of history may be very unreliable. 'Teething convulsions' are a commonplace of the mythology of child care and precisely what the term means is anyone's guess. Temper tantrums, respiratory obstruction in laryngitis and so forth may be interpreted as convulsions and, of course, a young child suffering from any of the acute infectious diseases may have a spell of 'twitching' during the feverish stage. It is, therefore, difficult to fix the age of onset definitely. Some investigators believe that a far higher proportion of cases than suggested above begin in early childhood and that perhaps half of all cases start in the first three years of life. But where the history is doubtful the only possible way of getting a definite answer must be by electro-encephalography and unfortunately the immature brain may 'normally' show the sort of wave-pattern which is associated with some degree of epilepsy in older persons. There are, of course, cases in which the E.E.G. of a young child may show unequivocal epileptic patterns but these are usually the cases in which there is virtually no clinical doubt. Until a good deal more is known about the electrical reactions of the brain, therefore, the number of children whose genuine epilepsy starts in early childhood will remain in doubt and doctors will not have the diagnostic help they would like in the doubtful cases.

The typical grand mal fit may begin suddenly, without any warning at all, or may be preceded by an 'aura'. The aura can take many forms—a general feeling of illness or faintness, pain in some part of the body, the hearing of strange noises, flashing lights before the eyes or curious smells. It is however, usually constant in character in the same person. The presence of an aura before fits strongly supports a diagnosis of epilepsy, but its absence does not necessarily reduce the probability.

The aura lasts for a matter of seconds only, after which the patient falls unconscious and the muscles go into spasm. In this period of spasm the patient may bite his tongue, cry out and empty the bladder or the rectum. Then come the convulsions, which may last from a minute or two up to as long as half an hour. When they cease, the patient may recover consciousness in a matter of seconds or may pass into a deep sleep for an hour or more. When he recovers consciousness he may feel quite normal except for a headache and will have no recollection of what has happened to him. Sometimes he may act strangely for a time after the attack, although to all appearances quite wide awake. The frequency of the fits varies considerably from person to person, but grand mal attacks, in contrast with those of petit mal, are usually separated by normal intervals of days, weeks or even months.

Petit mal is a much more variable thing. There is usually no fall and the attacks of unconsciousness last only for seconds, being sometimes so brief that they are not noticed. The aura is usually absent. Sometimes the child may be seen to stiffen for a moment or he may drop something which he is holding. In school his attention may wander from what he is doing; some cases are first brought to notice by the fact that the teacher discovers that a pupil is inattentive. In contrast to grand mal, the attacks may be very frequent, occurring as often as thirty or more times in a day. Some children with petit mal may later go on to develop grand mal, but in many the petit mal picture remains.

The natural progress of epilepsy is very variable. In some cases, particularly those of grand mal, the repeated fits may eventually cause major brain damage with paralysis. In others there is a strong tendency to spontaneous recovery, with a progressive lessening of the frequency of the attacks.

An important feature of many cases of epilepsy is so-called personality deterioration, which may consist of a steady deterioration in intelligence or of alterations, invariably for the worse, in the victim's character. In many cases this is undoubtedly due to repeated damage to the brain during attacks, but other possible explanations have to be considered. A child undergoing the usual form of treatment by sedative drugs may have his perceptions blunted by the drugs. Or—and this undoubtedly happens in a number of cases—the bewildering nature of the attacks and the chronic state of anxiety which comes from never knowing when the next fit will occur may combine to produce quite serious emotional disturbance.

These possibilities apart, there is wide variation in intelligence and emotional stability between one epileptic and another. Epilepsy is not incompatible with high intelligence or even with genius; in fact such eminent personages as Julius Caesar and Napoleon Bonaparte are believed to have been epileptics. It has been suggested that the inherent excitability of the epileptic may be associated with the special sensibility which is so often a part of genius; certainly it is reasonable to imagine that heightened perception and instability are perhaps only two aspects of the same thing.

### Diagnosis and Assessment

The diagnosis of epilepsy can, as will be seen from the foregoing, be a matter of some difficulty. It is obviously unnecessary and undesirable to take an alarmist view of convulsions occurring in a young child, and single, widely spaced fits in a child under the age of two, especially if they occur during illness or teething, need not cause any particular anxiety. If, however, there is a tendency for convulsions to occur when the child is apparently quite well, if they occur more than three or four times a year or if their frequency is increasing there is ground for suspicion.

If a child who has rarely or never had convulsions in the first two or three years of life develops them after that age, the presumption of epilepsy becomes considerably stronger. The possibility of single isolated convulsions from non-epileptic causes diminishes with age and after the age of five such single episodes rarely occur except in the course of some acute illness of the nervous system—encephalitis or the encephalitic form of one of the acute infectious diseases.

The value of electro-encephalography in diagnosis is very considerable; it is necessary to reiterate that it is not infallible but taken in conjunction with the typical symptoms of a major fit it provides very useful confirmation. It is most useful, however, in the uncertain field of minor attacks and petit mal.

The mild, major fit without convulsions is indistinguishable to the inexpert eye from an ordinary faint. Children of all ages faint from a considerable variety of causes and it would be quite wrong to begin to suspect epilepsy in every fainting child. It is even possible for a child to faint repeatedly from non-epileptic causes, but it is fair to assume that any child who suffers from 'fainting attacks' on more than the rarest occasions will be placed under medical care; repeated fainting from whatever cause is worth investigation. The exclusion of non-epileptic causes is, naturally, the first thing to be done, but if no such causes can be found the electro-encephalogram is the next resort.

Petit mal may go on for years without being detected or even suspected. It is important to remember that the child himself has no recollection of what has happened to him in an attack and that he cannot be a reliable witness. As he grows older he begins to realize that something strange is happening to him but it is difficult for him to understand and even more difficult for him to describe. Unless the attacks are very frequent indeed they may pass unnoticed until adolescence or even early adult life. Most children have moments of absent-mindedness and inattention and one would not expect even a teacher to draw special attention to them unless they were occurring very often indeed. Sometimes the presence of instability of personality in addition to fits of 'absence' may attract the attention of a shrewd and experienced teacher, but it has to be remembered that the bright, imaginative child is precisely the one who becomes bored by having to go through lessons at the slow pace of his duller fellows and gazes out of the classroom window and daydreams until the voice of the teacher suddenly recalls him to reality.

Some experienced workers in the field have questioned how far one should go in pursuing the diagnosis of the very mild case. They point out that in borderline cases, which are precisely those in which the greatest diagnostic difficulties occur, the electro-encephalogram may be inconclusive and that it may give a result suggestive of epilepsy in a person who is normal. Against this it is argued that 'normal' in this context is extremely hard to define and that a normal person whose encephalogram shows an epileptic pattern is, strictly speaking, an epileptic who does not suffer from overt fits. In so far as there is an answer to these questions at the present time, it is given by considerations of humanity and expediency. If the child's disability in consequence of the suspected attacks is so slight that he suffers no particular inconvenience and is exposed to no risk, there is nothing to be gained by having the label 'epileptic' attached to him. It is a label which, once attached, can never be finally removed and the mention in his medical record of a tentative diagnosis of epilepsy may have serious consequences later when he is starting out on a career. The lay mind cannot readily separate the idea of epilepsy from that of major fits and both teachers and employers will think twice before accepting anyone who has been found to be epileptic.

Assessment, as distinct from diagnosis, presents special difficulties in the case of any epileptic, whether the attacks be major or minor, frequent or infrequent. It is the only one of the common handicapping conditions in which an exception can be made to the rule that an early attempt should be made at long-term assessment. The probable spontaneous course of the condition cannot be forecast with any sort of confidence except to say roughly that the more frequent the attacks in a case of grand mal the less likely they are to disappear spontaneously. What is certain is that with proper treatment and management the effect of the disability can in the majority of cases be considerably minimised; with modern methods it is becoming the rule rather than the exception for the epileptic to be able to lead a virtually normal life. There should not, therefore, be any attempt at a long-term assessment until the child's response to treatment has been watched over a period of years. A couple of years of observation will often make it possible to prophesy with some degree of confidence. It must, however, be borne in mind that the physical and emotional stresses and strains of puberty may change the picture for the worse, temporarily or permanently, while, on the other hand, the years of adolescence are not infrequently those in which the mild case progresses to spontaneous recovery.

## Treatment and Management

In a few cases, where the condition is due to certain forms of localised brain injury, surgery can effect a dramatic and complete cure. These apart, treatment and management are closely interwoven. Sedatives of various kinds have been used to control fits. They can be very effective but have the tendency, mentioned above, to dull the child's general consciousness. Research has been going on for a number of years to find drugs which would act more strongly on the fits than on the consciousness and a considerable number of such preparations, the anti-convulsants, are now available. They are not simple to use. To produce the desired effects in any particular child may require a substantial period of hospital or special school care while the right combination of drugs in the right dosage is being worked out and re-stabilisation on a different combination may be needed from time to time as the child grows older. Experience so far suggests that while the anticonvulsants are very effective in many cases they sometimes have undesirable side-effects or otherwise fail to come up to expectations; the old drugs still have their place and the new ones are not the final answer to the problem of controlling fits while maintaining alertness.

Diet has a place in treatment, but the typical regime is strict and requires medical supervision. It is not easy for the child and the home to observe it as scrupulously as is necessary and one must not forget that a rigid system of dieting can cause a good deal of dislocation of daily living and make it hard for the epileptic to lead the normal life which is so desirable. It may still be worth a trial in some cases, but progress with the anti-convulsant drugs has so changed the general picture that dietary treatment has now moved somewhat into the background.

In the sphere of general management the accent must, in fact, be on normality, regularity and the avoidance of anxiety, fear and apprehension. This is easily said but less easily practiced. The child himself is the victim of something which he cannot understand. All he knows is that suddenly he feels a strange sensation—the aura—and that the next thing he knows is that he wakes up on the floor, possibly bruised or cut by his fall, wet or soiled, and surrounded by a group of anxious adults or children. He never knows when it will happen again and it is only too natural that he should be the victim of anxiety and insecurity. He knows that he is not as other children and he is quite likely to become shy of their company, the more so if, as sometimes happens, his playmates are shy of him or ridicule him.

The anxiety of his parents is quite a normal phenomenon. It takes quite a long time to persuade the parents of an epileptic that even a major fit, calmly and intelligently handled, carries very slight risk indeed of injury. The usual tendency is for them to be exceedingly apprehensive and to be chary of trusting the child out of their sight in case he has a fit in the middle of crossing the busy High Street or climbing a tree. The atmosphere of the home quickly becomes tense with the constant expectation of a fit and this is an effective way of making sure that fits occur, as well as of intensifying the child's psychological tangles. In point of fact, there is no doubt that in petit mal, and even in many cases of grand mal, attacks are much less likely to occur while the child's attention is absorbed by some steady, purposeful activity; it is just while the attention is focussed on crossing the street that the probability of a fit is at its least.

## Education

The best place for the epileptic child to spend his day is in an ordinary school doing normal work with ordinary children and the aim of treatment and management should be by drugs or by diet to reduce the frequency of fits to a reasonable rate and to send him to an ordinary school. Schools are sometimes reluctant to accept epileptic children, giving the almost invariable reason that the fits frighten the other children. I have vivid recollections from my own schooldays of an epileptic boy whose fits occurred, in school at least, about once in two weeks. Conceivably, the first one or two might have frightened some of the class of eight-year-olds, but before long they were regarded as welcome interludes in the course of the less interesting lessons. When arithmetic became too tedious, many were the glances thrown at young Harold in the hope that he would oblige and, in retrospect, one cannot help fearing that sometimes he anticipated the course of nature! What is quite certain is that neither in the classroom nor out of it was he feared or unpopular. The teacher, in fact, who rejects an epileptic child lest he should frighten others is probably cloaking her own fear of an unpredictable responsibility.

She is, of course, in a special position in relation to the epileptic pupil. She may, and probably does, exaggerate the risks in her own mind. In twenty-five years of experience in school health work I have met only one case of serious damage to a child in the course of an epileptic fit in school, but in that one case the child had her fit in the middle of drinking milk during morning break, inhaled some of the milk and had a fatal laryngeal spasm. It was an accident of the 'one in a million' type and could as easily have happened at home as in school, but it was none the less a distressing experience for the teachers, admirably though they managed the affair.

It is proper and justifiable for the school medical officer and the family doctor to use their persuasive powers to the uttermost in order to get a hesitant teacher to accept an epileptic child into an ordinary school. It is not justifiable, if persuasion fails, to bring administrative pressure to bear in order to enforce acceptance. This has its ethical reasons; though the risks of injury may be very slight indeed it is possible that the teacher might be faced with a responsibility greater than she could honestly bear, for not all people are equally able to bear certain responsibilities. But it has an at least equally important practical reason. To place a child in a school against the firm wishes of a teacher is to produce a situation of uncertainty and tension between teacher and child which is likely to prove the worst possible atmosphere for an epileptic youngster. In urban areas at least, it is usually possible, if the school nearest the child's home will not accept him, to find some other school within reasonable distance which will and, if necessary, transport to that school can be provided. In the country, the village school is usually a tolerant place in which all the children and teachers already know and accept the village epileptic, so that there is not likely to be much hesitation in admitting him. If he is not acceptable after attempted persuasion, then a boarding special school is the answer.

The boarding special school, however, is principally useful for the child who suffers from major fits which have not been brought under control by drugs or diet or whose disturbance of personality is such that he is unacceptable in an ordinary school. Unfortunately there are a few epileptic children in whom the character changes referred to above are marked even though the fits are infrequent; they can prove virtually unmanageable in an ordinary school. A similar group are those whose automatic behaviour after a fit is grossly abnormal, taking the form of wandering, destructiveness or assaults on other children. It may be that some of the children in the preceding group really fall into this one and that their association of unmanageability with infrequent fits is due to their having unnoticed minor fits followed by automatic behaviour. The last category of child commonly sent to a special school is the child who in addition to being epileptic is mentally retarded.

Two questions will suggest themselves at this stage. The first is whether the mentally retarded epileptic child who has his fits fairly well under control would not be better placed in a day special school for educationally subnormal children rather than in a residential special school for epileptics. The answer to this is, with reservations, in the affirmative; one reason why that course is not more often adopted is merely that the habit of categorisation is too strong among administrators and that if a child falls into the epileptic category he cannot be sent to a special school for children in a different category. The teachers in a special school for E.S.N. children, however, have already a considerable special responsibility to bear and they above all others should not be pressed against their inclinations to accept an epileptic child.

The other question is whether the epileptic child who is emotionally maladjusted and shows behaviour disorders should be given a trial in a special school for maladjusted children. Much depends on the cause and nature of the problems. There are three possible factors, genuine emotional disturbance due to the stress and anxiety resulting from the fits, actual brain damage caused by the fits and a general over-activity and restlessness—hyperkinesis— which makes the child difficult to manage and impedes his fitting in to a school regime and forming good relations with other children. These problems can be present even in a child whose fits are well controlled by anti-convulsant drugs. The permissive regime and the tolerant atmosphere of the special school for the maladjusted can, in fact, provide the right environment for such a child. Such a school will not be able to do much about brain damage or hyperkinesis, of course, but provided that the fits are well controlled it will offer the child a place where he can have a chance of settling down and receiving education and the possibility of having some of his emotional problems smoothed out.

Finally it must be said that, with epileptics as with other handicapped children, special school placement should not be regarded as always final and irrevocable. On the contrary, a substantial number of epileptic children achieve, after a period of two or three years' treatment and management in a special school, a degree of stability which makes it possible for them to go out and finish their education in an ordinary school. It is difficult to say in advance just which children are likely to be those who will need only short term special care; there are too many unpredictable factors involved. The school, however, should never lose sight of the possibility, even though it would be imprudent to raise parental hopes too high too soon.

What out-of-school and recreational activities should be permitted to the epileptic child? Obviously, the longer the permitted list the better, for restriction of recreation separates the child from his fellows both physically and emotionally. Much depends upon the presence or absence of an aura; if the child has a consistent aura which gives him three or four seconds of warning and is taught to keep cool and not to panic, those seconds give him time to remove himself from a place of danger into one of safety. (One of the best ways of preventing the child from panicking when the aura appears is actually to teach him that it is a beneficent warning which serves precisely this useful purpose.) Cycling is probably best forbidden entirely; the aura might not allow time to dismount safely, especially if riding on a busy road. Swimming is permissible provided there is an adequate aura and provided the child swims only within his depth and in the presence of a responsible older person. Climbing comes as naturally to children as to monkeys and no-one has ever yet discovered a way of preventing children from scaling walls, trees and anything else climbable. The epileptic who climbs takes a risk, though concentration on what he is doing may quite easily inhibit an impending fit. Practical counsel can probably go no further than to warn the child whose fits are major and at all frequent of the risk involved in climbing and leave it at that.

Games and sports on ground level are to be encouraged; no-one is likely to come to any harm if a fit occurs on the cricket pitch or football ground. Gymnastic work on apparatus is to be regarded in the same light as climbing, except that since it is usually done under supervision the control of such things as rope-climbing can be managed effectively. Workshop practice in school involves the child in the use of potentially dangerous tools and increases the risk of injury during a fit. The determining factor here will again be the aura; the child will be allowed to use only those things which he can be assured of being able to put safely down before a fit begins. The same applies to domestic science work in the case of girls.

The fact remains that some risk is present and that a heavy responsibility will rest on all those who are in charge of the child when he is undertaking any of these activities. There should be frank talking between school M.O., family doctor, teacher and parent and unless all four are agreed in permitting a particular activity it is probably best to forbid it. The heaviest anxiety will lie with whoever is actually supervising the child at the time and it should be remembered than an anxious watcher is often, for that very reason, not a fully effective watcher whose anxiety may also be communicated to the child. Particularly where swimming is concerned, the supervisor should be a mature and experienced person who knows the child well. And, since fatigue and illness— even minor illness—may affect the child's stability, the risky activities are better omitted altogether when he is feeling, or appears below par in general condition.

### The Prospect for the Epileptic

Some experts hope that the development of the anti-convulsant drugs may improve the prospect for many epileptics. Certainly, under the old methods of treatment, the delicate problems of whether what one gained by dosage of sedatives sufficient to control the fits was lost by the side-effect of 'doping' often tempted the doctor to keep the dosage down to a point at which the fit control was somewhat precarious. It is still too early to say whether the new drugs can, in the long term, control the fits to a point at which the patient is really safe, to himself and to others, in doing many of the things mentioned, but optimism seems justified.

The epileptic whose fits are under reasonable control is as employable as he is educable, but the considerations which govern his activities at play and in the workshop in childhood will operate in selecting his job with the addition that the safety of others is of increasing importance.

No known epileptic, for instance, can be really safe as a car driver. Even if he is alone in his own vehicle, a failure of control might cause a collision which would endanger others and in very few cases indeed is the aura sufficiently long to ensure that the patient could bring the car safely to a standstill in heavy traffic.

The same consideration would apply to such occupations as the driving of self-propelled trucks in a factory but possibly an exception might be made for the farm tractor driver within the confines of the farm provided the fits were rare and the aura adequate.

In the past, restrictions have forbidden the issue of licences to persons suffering from fits, even if those fits are fully controlled by medication and many licensing authorities have taken the further step of requiring that, in a patient whose fits have ceased under treatment should have a further period of two or three years complete freedom from fits without treatment before a licence can be granted. Such requirements offer a strong temptation to the epileptic to conceal his disability when applying for a licence and thus defeat their own intention. It is now proposed that every case should be treated on its merits and that certainly the "fit-free period without medication" should no longer be demanded as a routine. It can be argued that the driver under treatment may be irresponsible and forgetful and may fail to take his drugs, or that the drugs themselves may impair his alertness while driving. The argument has some validity, but is such a driver less of a road risk than an epileptic who has not disclosed his disability? A more flexible system which takes all the circumstances of each case into account will be more sensible and probably safer.

In many occupations the fit-inhibiting effect of absorption in the job in hand seems to operate. Some industrial medical officers assert that they have never seen an epileptic employee have a fit while at work. But important questions of employers' liability and insurance arise and third party risks are also important. If an epileptic is lifting a heavy load jointly with another worker, he may have time to drop his end of the object but not time to warn his partner, and comparable risks exist in many shared jobs. Unless, indeed, fits are very infrequent, the epileptic is best employed in single-handed work either away from machinery or with machinery which is adequately guarded.

A special hazard occurs in the case of those epileptics who have a phase of automatism after a fit. If the fit is a major one, the patient's workmates are warned and he can be watched during the minutes of risk. If, however, the automatism occurs after a minor fit, the patient may, without any warning to his fellows, either do something which involves him or them in danger or, no less dangerously, omit to carry out some safety precaution for which he is responsible. The known victim of automatism should not be

placed in any employment where a sudden lapse from responsibility might be dangerous.

Important though these warnings and prohibitions may be, they
still leave a considerable range of employment open to the epileptic
whose fits are neither major nor frequent. Initial placement in work,
however, should not be regarded as final. At the age of sixteen the
patient is still at an age when his condition may either improve even
to spontaneous cure or may deteriorate. It is likely that the years
between twelve and sixteen will have given some clue as to what
the prospect may be, but though deterioration, if it is going to be
serious, is very likely to show itself by then, a failure to show improvement at that age does not rule out the possibility of later
improvement or even cure. Improvement can be followed by
transfer to more appropriate employment, with the proviso that
the epileptic should not be set to any of the contra-indicated types
of work until he has had at least a year without a fit and that those
which involve the greatest risk to third parties should not be considered until he been fit-free for three years.

Should epileptic girls go out to work? For the girl or young
woman who has major fits there is no more dangerous employment
than domestic work alone in her home. The cooker, the electric
iron, the coal or gas fire are all dangerous instruments if mis-
handled. The risk of falling against a cooker or a fire obtains not
only in the moment of the fall but during the period of unconsciousness afterwards, when curtains or clothing might catch
alight. The isolation of the home may, by encouraging intro-
spection and worry, have a disturbing effect on the emotionally
unstable epileptic. Work outside the home not only keeps the
girl where there are others to watch over her but 'takes her out of
herself' to her considerable benefit.

There are two aspects to the question of whether epileptics
should marry. To the question 'can an epileptic make a good
husband and father?' the answer depends on simple considerations.
If he is well enough to be able to earn a good wage in normal
employment he is well enough to be a good provider and to play
his part in the general life of the family. If he is one of the minority
who are not, the question of marriage is not likely to arise. For an
epileptic woman to make a successful wife and mother is less easy.
The risks of a housewife's daily round have been mentioned.
Contrary to what was believed some years ago, pregnancy and
labour will not in themselves be likely to do any harm, but a

mother of young children has responsibilities which she cannot completely evade or delegate to others. None the less, women with petit mal and well controlled grand mal marry, make a success of marriage and can find support and stability in a happy marriage.

The eugenic aspect is a different matter. The part played by heredity in the causation of epilepsy is still not precisely determined and there is no certainty that an epileptic parent will produce epileptic children, nor is there any constant relationship between the severity of the condition in a parent and its probable appearance in the children. An epileptic married to someone with either overt epilepsy or a family history of epilepsy has a higher than average chance of producing epileptic children; marriage between an epileptic and a member of a 'clear' family may produce one or more epileptic children but is quite likely to result in normal children. Certainly for an epileptic to marry without disclosing the fact is a risky and highly unsocial proceeding. It is true that the person with severe grand mal is unlikely to find a marriage partner and to be faced with this problem, but the person with mild petit mal and even the grand mal patient who is being successfully treated with modern drugs may proceed normally into courtship and may have certain positively appealing qualities which make him or her an attractive partner. Frank and realistic discussion before marriage, preferably with medical advice, is essential and the outlook for the children as well as the alternative of a deliberately childless union must be carefully considered. A frankness which may break an engagement does not come easily to a young person in love, but a broken engagement is better than a disastrous marriage.

## FURTHER READING

*Epilepsy*
Almost all the books dealing with epilepsy are specifically medical textbooks. The best book for general reading is the following:
Fairfield, L. Epilepsy. Duckworth.
The British Epilepsy association publishes a journal and booklets on the employment and general care and welfare of the epileptic.

# CHAPTER 16

# Physical Disability

The field of physical handicap is a wide one, including conditions as different as congenital defects of the heart, progressive muscular atrophy, accidental injury and the after-effects of poliomyelitis. The fundamental principles set out in the first chapters of this book apply just as much as they do in other fields, but some new considerations have to be taken into account and these, incidentally, make it desirable to divide the subject for detailed discussion.

In the first place, defects of bones, joints and muscles and, nowadays, of the heart, are much more amenable to medical and surgical treatment than are defects of the brain and the sense organs. It is, therefore, possible in many cases of severe disability to look forward to a time when the degree of disability will be substantially reduced and in a few cases to a time when there will be no appreciable disability at all. On the debit side, the general care and education of the child is complicated by the need to make provision for treatment, either continuously or at intervals over a long period.

In the second place, much depends upon the age at which the handicapping defect arises. When it is congenital or appears shortly after birth, education and management can be directed from the start toward training the child to live within the limitations which the handicap imposes. When, however, it arises later in childhood we have to face the problem, which may be vastly more difficult, of taking a child whose life has already been shaped to one pattern and adjusting him to an entirely different pattern.

Thirdly, some physical handicaps have an effect outside their immediate field on the general physical condition and the general life of the child. Thus, the child with a heart damaged by disease or congenitally deformed will have all his physical activities circumscribed and will in addition be 'delicate' in the sense that he is more susceptible to severe damage by various illnesses which he may contract in the course of his life. He will thus need special care and will be liable to periodical interruption of his education or dislocation of his life by spells of invalidism.

Fourthly, many physical handicaps are obvious to the eye in a way and to a degree not paralleled in children handicapped in the mind or the senses. This raises important problems in relationships with other people, whether through the handicapped child's own sensitivity or through the tendency of other people to recoil from the sight of deformity and disfigurement.

Finally, though many physical disabilities may lessen with time, either naturally or under treatment, a few are inevitably progressive, leading in the end to complete invalidism and death. In these cases the constructive outlook of preparation for a reasonably full and independent life is, of course, not to be sustained.

These considerations apply to purely physical defects. Different problems arise when physical defect is combined with mental or sensory handicap. For this reason the 'spastic' child, who commonly has physical defect combined with intellectual defect, is separately considered and the general subject of dual or multiple handicaps is also the subject of a special chapter.

## 1. Crippling Disabilities

There is no wholly satisfactory term to cover the whole of the largest single class of physical handicaps. 'Orthopaedic defects' is often used, because the physical repair of the defects is within the province of the orthopaedic surgeon, though not necessarily within his province alone. 'Musculo-skeletal defects' covers many of them, for the muscles and bones are commonly involved, but would not strictly apply to defects of joints or to nerve injuries. 'Crippling defects' is loose, colloquial and, again, not precise in its limits, but it has the merit of conveying to the reader the right kind of mental picture, that of a defect or deformity which, in some way or other, impedes the body or limbs in action. It may, therefore, be the most satisfactory term for the present purpose.

## Causation

In the most highly-developed countries the majority of these defects as they occur in children at the present time are the results of paralytic poliomyelitis. Bone and joint tuberculosis, which twenty-five years ago held first place as a cause in this country, has receded into the background, though it is still important—more important than poliomyelitis—in many less advanced countries.

Rickets, a common producer of bone deformities fifty years ago, is a vanishing disease in the highly-developed countries and is beginning to respond to preventive measures wherever in the world organized child health services are beginning to do something about infant nutrition. Crippling from all these causes, as well as from certain tropical diseases, is preventible in theory and in practice, but experience shows that practice tends to lag behind theory. For reasons not yet fully understood, poliomyelitis is more prevalent in countries in an advanced stage of social progress. It is probable that vaccination against this disease will, within the next decade, make it a rarity in the advanced countries, but it is also possible that in less advanced countries the disease may, for a time, increase with social progress more rapidly than vaccination can control it.

A substantial amount of crippling is congenital. Some of this is the result of 'developmental failure' and some the result of damage to the child in the uterus or during birth. Developmental failure is essentially the failure of a bone, a joint or a muscle to grow and mature as it should do. It may account for a limited deformity such as the absence of one of the bones of the forearm or the lack of an adequate joint socket in some cases of congenital dislocation of the hip, or it may be responsible for the complete absence of a finger, a whole limb or even more than one limb. Little is known of its causes, but in view of the way in which some virus diseases which affect the mother during pregnancy have been shown to produce defects of the eye and ear it is now being suggested that these diseases may also affect other parts of the body of the developing child. Damage to the child in the uterus may occur for such reasons as the umbilical cord becoming twisted round a limb or the child being cramped in a distorted posture. Damage during birth is becoming much less common with the advance of obstetrics, but is still responsible for some cases of paralysis following pressure or tearing injuries of the brain or nerves.

Accident is another fruitful producer of crippling defects and has become more important in recent years. This is partly due to certain other causes having become less important, but though surgery is becoming more and more effective in minimizing the damage which remains after accidents, the progress of cililization is providing more and more opportunities for accidents to occur.

Infantile hemiplegia, a paralysis, more or less severe, of one side of the body, caused by brain haemorrhage and analogous to some kinds of 'stroke' in adults, can occur quite early in life. The fact that a child has had one of these haemorrhages does not seem to indicate that he will have others and the intelligence is commonly not impaired. So-called 'transverse myelitis', in reality usually an abscess adjoining and compressing the spinal cord, can produce paraplegia (paralysis of both legs and other muscles from about the level of the waist). The muscular dystrophies are particularly distressing, though fortunately uncommon, conditions in which there is progressive degeneration of the muscles which tends to spread until virtually all the muscles of the body are involved and death in late adolescence or early adult life is to be expected.

## The Clinical Picture

The clinical picture is considerably more definite in crippling diseases than in many other handicaps. To begin with, the disability is commonly more obvious. It is usually visible even to the untrained eye and the risk of its being overlooked and opportunities for treatment being missed is correspondingly smaller, though the risk does exist and, for instance, it is by no means unknown for a congenital dislocation of the hip to remain undetected until the best opportunity for early treatment has been lost. In the majority of cases, with the obvious exception of the progressive diseases, the defect itself will not get worse, though there is a chance of secondary deformities developing, as, for instance, when deformity of the spine follows faulty posture consequent on a defect in the leg. Most important of all, except in cases where a part of the body is completely absent there is a probability that surgery will produce substantial improvement, if not complete cure, while plastic or transplantation operations and the provision of modern artificial appliances can mitigate the effects of the absence of a digit, part of a limb or even a whole limb.

Except in cerebral palsy, handicaps of this type are almost always essentially physical and restricted to the affected part. The child is a normal child with one part functioning badly or not at all and there is no automatic secondary handicap like, for example, the speech disability which invariably threatens the deaf child. But secondary problems can arise and they are the more likely to do so because the primary disability is so manifestly physical and limited. There is no real paradox here. What happens is that because the disability is obvious, is physical and is likely to yield in some degree to treatment, the physician, the surgeon and the parent may concentrate their attention on the disability and forget the child, only to discover later that social, educational or emotional damage has already been done.

The clinical picture must, therefore, be amplified to include certain common secondary effects. The crippled child is likely to be educationally retarded because the crippling defect and its treatment have substantially interfered with his education. He will probably be self-conscious and may express this in either abnormal timidity and shyness or abnormal aggressiveness. He may also be socially immature in a general sense because his disabliity has restricted his experience and his human contacts. The treatment of these complications is important, but it is even more important to know that they are important dangers and to take steps to prevent them arising or at least to minimize their extent.

### Assessment

We have seen that in all types of handicap assessment must be dynamic rather than static and that it must include an element of long-term planning. This last is specially important in considering crippling defects because the new element of long-term treatment to reduce the amount of essential disability is characteristic of this class of handicap.

The orthopaedic surgeon's contribution to the assessment is considerable and complicated. He must indicate what he regards as the most favourable long-term prospect if treatment is as successful as possible and also what he regards as the least favourable long-term prospect. There should be no attempt to spare the parents; candour is essential. In fact, if a range of possibilities is sketched out in this way and it is made clear to the parents that what they do and how they do it will have a profound effect on the point within the range which the child ultimately reaches, the effect on them will be highly beneficial. This forecast should, of course, be made in functional rather than anatomical terms. Will there be disability in moving from place to place? Will the patient ultimately need a wheel-chair, crutches, calipers, braces or merely a walking-stick? Is he likely to be able to stand for long periods? Will he be able to lift weights? If an arm is damaged will it be useless, will it be adequate for coarse movements (e.g. steadying an object on which the patient is working), will it be capable of fine movements or will its overall strength be impaired? These are only examples of the practical questions which must be answered.

Next must come a plan for treatment. The essential points here are what type of treatment is needed and an indication of its stages and their timing. If a series of operations is going to be necessary, how many will there be, at what ages will they be carried out and how long will each of them compel the child to stay in hospital? Is the child going to need a long period of continuing physiotherapy? If so, what will be the period? Will periods of intensive physiotherapy be needed after each of the series of operations?

This casting of an orthopaedic horoscope is made more complicated by the fact that the improvement of the child's physical condition is likely to be progressive—he may have two years in a wheel chair and several with crutches or calipers before finally reaching the 'walking-stick stage'. Needless to say, the making of a detailed forecast runs contrary to the ingrained habit which most doctors have of talking in detail only of the immediate future and leaving the distant future very indefinite and one has the utmost sympathy with the surgeon who is asked to outline a twelve-year plan for a four-year-old patient. It is, however, so important that something of the sort should be done that the surgeon must take the risk of doing it. Often he will prefer to wait until the first of the series of operations has been carried out or until the child has had a substantial period of treatment before he dares to be prophetic in detail, but this does not entirely preclude an early rough forecast.

He cannot, of course, make it alone and it is important to stress at this point that as soon as it becomes clear that the child will have a substantial and lasting disability there should be frank and direct consultation between the orthopaedic surgeon and the school medical officer. Correspondence via a hospital almoner is not enough. At the present time even this last is too often lacking; it is not unknown for a hospital to treat a child for years before it finally communicates with the school health service saying, in effect, 'We have now finished with this child, having done all we can. Will you please take over?' The words 'substantial and lasting' also need generous interpretation. If there is a probability that the child will be virtually normal by the age of sixteen but may have difficulty before that age in attending an ordinary school, assessment and planning are just as important as if there is a prospect of permanent disability.

The planning must be joint because the programme of treatment has a degree of elasticity and can and should be adapted to the social and educational programme. In particular, there are certain critical points in a child's educational progress at which a prolonged interruption might be disastrous; either the surgeon's programme must be adjusted so that interruptions come at times when they can be fitted into 'quiet' periods of education or the educational programme must be adjusted to fit around the surgeon's fixed points.

It ought not to be necessary to emphasize that the child's intelligence and educability should be taken into account at the initial assessment, but this point can easily be overlooked. A complete investigation, using the full battery of intelligence tests, is not always necessary, but it is essential to know from the start whether the child is going to be able to make a career for himself by using his head rather than his body. In the case of the child crippled by disease or by accident after the age of six his school career up to then will give a fair general indication of his potentialities. If his initial treatment is given in an orthopaedic hospital school, the teachers there will be making their own estimate of him. The experienced school medical officer, however, will be able to form some opinion even if neither of these sources of information is available and should lose no time in doing so. The good orthopaedic hospital should welcome the S.M.O. concerned as a visiting colleague and the Education Authority should encourage him to visit. If the first approximate assessment of intelligence and educability leaves an element of doubt, a complete intelligence test should not be long delayed.

The child's home also enters into the assessment. Is it a 'good' home in the material sense? Are the parents going to be intelligently co-operative over the necessary long period? Is the child-parent relationship good? If it is, how can it be maintained during the child's periods in hospital? If it is not, how can it be developed?

If there is going to be substantial permanent disability it is necessary, at quite an early age, to consider the home and surroundings in relation to employment. He will need physical care and protection well into early adult life and this, ideally, is best given in a good home. Will it be possible for him to find near his home the sort of work which he is going to be able to do? What sort of work is actually available there? Can he be trained and educated with that sort of work in view? Might it be best for the family to consider moving to a place where his prospects would be better?

These are questions which need answer years before he is ready to leave school.

In this field perhaps more than any other, the initial assessment, though it should be as detailed and accurate as possible, must be subject to regular review as the work of the orthopaedic surgeons succeeds or fails. If the first requisite, the defining of the best and the worst prognoses, has been properly provided, the plans of the surgeon, the S.M.O., the education authority and the youth employment service will have been made flexible enough to cover the whole zone of possibilities. As time goes on and the zone of possibilities narrows, the plans will become progressively more definite until they reach their final form.

## Care and Management

The point has been made and emphasized that each individual handicapped person has to find his own way of life, with a maximum of activity and achievement within the limitations imposed by the handicap. This is no less true of the child with a crippling defect than it is for the blind, the deaf and the epileptic, but the cripple has often a special problem to solve. In the western countries at the present time the majority of crippled children are the victims of accident or poliomyelitis. They are, therefore, children who after a longer or shorter period of normal life find themselves facing a restricted future. It is true that in other fields of handicap disabilities may arise in later childhood but where that is so—as, for example, in epilepsy—the disability is not constant and it may very well begin in a mild form and become severe only with the passage of time. Accident or poliomyelitis strikes quickly, out of a clear sky. There is no period of warning during which the victim can prepare himself for the changes to come and reconcile himself to the probability that some of his dearest ambitions will never be realized. He is suddenly and irrevocably cut away from his friends and from his own self of yesterday. Not only has he to learn to live a special life but he has to unlearn the life to which he has grown accustomed and must day by day compare what is with what might have been.

Obviously, the task will be easier for the young child and harder for the child whose disability arises in his later schooldays. There is no hard and fast critical age above which readjustment becomes specially difficult, but there would appear to be something of a dividing line at the age of starting group life in school. Before then the child is an individual who has not learned the importance of being able to do the same things as his contemporaries and if he can start his new life as a cripple while he is still in the individualistic stage he may be able to consolidate his position before he joins a group. A second critical phase, particularly important for boys, is that at which the youngster has acquired certain physical skills, especially in the sphere of sport. If he is disabled before that stage is reached, while he may envy the normal boys their agility and prowess he will not find it too difficult to make his own world alongside theirs; if he is disabled after that stage is reached he is subjectively and acutely aware of what he is missing. To envy others is the normal human lot; what really hurts is not the knowledge that someone else has something which we never really hoped for but the knowledge that we have been robbed of that which we had and treasured.

For the child who is crippled congenitally or from an early age, the general principles of care and management hold good. They may in fact be easier to apply than in the case of certain other handicaps, for to the crippled child his disability is real, obvious and finite. The blind child, as we have noted, lives in a world full of hidden and unpredictable hazards, while the deaf child is mystified by the lack of a means of communication  normal to other children. The crippled child, without these bewilderments, sees as clearly as a normal child what he wants to do and goes ahead and does it to the best of his ability. If he cannot do it the orthodox way he will do it the unorthodox way and the skill which he can develop has to be seen to be believed.

This very fact is not infrequently a source of trouble. A child who could walk with difficulty and should, indeed, be trained to walk may become so adept and agile in crawling or 'crabbing about on his keel' that he will resist any attempts to teach him to walk. His logic is quite simple and unshakeable. Within his little world he can move from A to B quickly and safely by the technique he already knows; why should he waste time and trouble learning a new technique which will merely enable him to do the same thing more slowly? He does not yet realize that there is a wider world in which even a halting or impeded walk is far better than no walk at all. Again, in convalescence from poliomyelitis or recovery after an operation on a limb there is a stage at which the use of the affected muscles or the treated limb in the normal movements of everyday life is better treatment than even the physiotherapy department can offer. During the acute stage of the poliomyelitis, however, or during the period when the limb was encased in plaster after the operation, the child learned to manage without it or with minimum use of it and he has no obvious incentive to start training himself to use it again.

There is a conflict here between two principles. Most certainly the child needs to be trained for independence and to this end it is better that he should be able to do things for himself moderately well than that he should have them done for him exceedingly well. If, instead of letting him do something the wrong way, we are going to train him by degrees to do it the right way, he is inevitably going to be somewhat dependent on others while he is learning. It is vitally important to decide at this stage what are the essentials and what long-term results can be expected and to act accordingly.

Take one simple example. For many reasons it is better to be right-handed than left-handed. The old prejudice against the left-hander is dying out, but a great deal of the physical apparatus of living and much industrial machinery is designed so that it will be most effectively used by a right-handed person. Should a child who has a damaged or defective right arm or hand be encouraged to use the left—which he will naturally have started to do—or should he be trained to use the right? Most adults have one skilled arm and hand, usually the right, which they employ for precise, delicate or detailed work and use their other arm and hand for supporting, carrying etc. The left hand is the semi-skilled mate or labourer for the right. The essential question to be asked about our hypothetical child's right hand is 'can it, with training and practice, become as adept as the right hand of a normal person?' If it can, then everything possible should be done to encourage or even compel the child to develop it. If it cannot, then the correct policy is to train the normal left hand for skilled work and let the right serve as the assisting limb.

How does one encourage a very young child to use a damaged limb? The really hard work is done in the home and it is on the parents rather than on the staff of the hospital that the responsibility will lie. The fundamental need is to convince him that there is profit to himself in using it and this is to be done by observation rather than by argument. Again, a few examples will show how this can be done. Suppose the problem is to make him use a weak or damaged arm and hand. The answer is to set him tasks which attract him and which cannot be carried out with one hand only. What the tasks are will depend on his age and capacity. One may serve his favourite food in a manner which requires him to use both spoon and pusher to eat it or offer him sweets in a box which must be steadied with one hand while the other opens it. He should be given toys which need both hands for their successful manipulation, or he may be placed so that he has to use one hand to steady or support himself while he uses a toy with the other. Rarely it may be necessary to take the extreme step of splinting or restraining the better arm so as to compel him to use the other, but to do this is to confess failure to find a more positive solution.

The same principle applies in getting the child who is an adept at crawling to stand or walk. Toys and other things which he wants should be placed just out of reach, so that to get them he must stand, his play-pen, a sound chair or some other support being handy for him to steady himself. Even for a small child, a tricycle can be invaluable in making him use a weak or damaged leg; he may be able to do the hard work of pedalling with his good leg, but unless he keeps the weak one on the pedal and makes some use of it, it will get in the way and prevent him from making any progress.

The more such a child mixes with other children the better, for he will be encouraged to imitate their two-handed techniques, their standing and their walking. Nothing convinces a child that walking is better than crawling, or that two hands are better than one, more quickly and effectively than seeing that other children do things that way. But here one enters the caveat which appears in so many parts of the field; if the child is among others whose skill and ability is beyond anything which he can hope to attain he will be discouraged rather than stimulated. A challenge brings out the best in us only if it is a challenge which is within our capacity to meet.

Behind all the training of the young crippled child should be the concept of the life which he is ultimately going to lead. The emphasis should constantly be on the things which he *can* do and will eventually be able to do well. Of the total range of their abilities and their aptitudes most people develop only a fraction, the others remaining latent. The small child has no set standards. His life is almost all future and he has no reason to consider drawing, painting and music less satisfying than cricket and football. If his aptitudes can be explored and those within his prospective powers encouraged and developed he will at quite an early age learn to be satisfied with what he has. True, no crippled boy will ever grow up without at least a passing phase of envy for those who are good at games, but if he has already the support of the knowledge that he is good at other things he will come to no harm.

The parents can and must school themselves to keep sympathy within bounds, seeing the child not as an abnormal person nor yet as a fully normal one, but as a normal person within a restricted range. Within that range he should be encouraged, disciplined and even, when necessary, punished as a normal child would be. The making of allowances for him should be confined to occasions when he might be necessarily required to do something beyond his powers and care should be taken that such occasions do not often occur. His biggest danger may come from people outside the immediate family circle who cannot resist gushing well-meaning sympathy over him, and this danger is, perhaps, greater for girls than for boys.

The risk may often be best avoided by giving the child contacts with others in a place where the problem is understood—for example in a good nursery or nursery school—but such places are not always available and even if they are they cannot accept a very seriously disabled child. Its possibility is something which must be borne in mind when considering whether a child should or should not go to a special school.

Most of the children who have a serious handicap early in life spend a substantial part of their early years in hospital. The orthopaedic hospital which has a considerable number of such children can and usually does start their early social training on the right lines, but it is not unknown for a physically handicapped child in a general hospital or an orthopaedic unit catering principally for older children and adults to have the spoiling process initiated by the hospital staff and the other patients. Even in the good orthopaedic hospital it is possible for the wrong child-parent relationship to be developed.

The key to the situation lies in frequent visits by the parents to the child and in the hospital's enlisting the parents from the start as important members of the team. The parents who see their child in a hospital bed naturally think of him as sick and suffering and the less frequent their visits the less likely are they to develop a constructive attitude. If, instead, they see him in the physiotherapy department or the hospital school and are taken into the confidence of the people who are dealing with him daily the positive side rather than the negative will be stressed, and they will have some idea of what they themselves should be ready to do to help when he returns home.

## Education

The maxim that a child should be sent to a special school only if he has some essential need which cannot be otherwise provided for holds good with the crippled child but can present some very difficult problems of decision and interpretation. In theory a child can be educated in an ordinary school if his sight, his hearing and his intelligence are within normal limits and if one of his hands is capable of the movements involved in writing and drawing, but it is essential not to lose sight of the fundamental need for considering the whole child in relation to all the circumstances.

Impaired mobility is not in itself a valid reason for sending a child to a special school. Much depends on the nature and degree of the impairment. A severely crippled child who is unable to walk more than a few steps may be able to move about quite well in a wheel-chair. If he cannot get to the nearest school by wheel-chair, special transport can be provided by the education authority and his chair can travel with him or a special chair be kept for him in the school, and in a single-storey school he will be able to move about sufficiently for purposes of basic education. Such a child will not, however, be able to join in physical education, free play and organized games. In the case of a girl this may be only moderately important, but a boy is every day forcibly reminded that he is not as others and that he is inferior to his fellows in something which is important to him and to them. He may, therefore, make a better social and emotional adjustment if he is placed among his equals in a special school.

So far as it is possible to generalize, then, one might say that while a boy with this degree of handicap would be best placed in a special school from the start, it would be justifiable to give a girl a trial in an ordinary school with single-storey premises and a constructively interested staff, moving her to a special school if the trial did not seem to be successful. An important exception occurs in the child of 'grammar school' calibre. It is not easy for grammar school education to be provided in a special school and a clever youngster of either sex whose prospects of a sedentary career on this level were good would probably be better off attending an ordinary grammar school, in spite of the social difficulties, than receiving an education below his or her capacity in a special school.

A difficult problem may also arise when a child already well established in a normal school is suddenly crippled to this sort of degree. He is faced with the need to adjust himself quickly to an entirely new life with new prospects. Can he do this in surroundings which constantly remind him of what he used to be and what he has lost? On the other hand, will the change to another school add to his difficulties and perplexities? Experience suggests that, as a rule, a change to the environment of a special school may make the re-adjustment easier, but it is worth adding that if he is already nearing the end of his school life it may be better to leave him where he is; if he goes to a special school it will be some months, at any rate, before he is sufficiently settled to start reaping the full benefit.

Where the impairment of mobility is only moderate and the child can move about tolerably well with the aid of a stick or a caliper, there is a strong case for a trial in an ordinary school before special schooling is considered. It is not uncommon to find teachers reluctant to accept such a child. The teacher has, of course, some responsibility, legal as well as moral, for the physical safety of children in his care and is afraid that the rough and tumble of the playground may bring injury to the cripple. In practice this fear seems to have little foundation. There are some 'tough' schools where the weakling cannot survive but as a rule children—even the roughest and rowdiest—are exceptionally tolerant to the cripple and will go out of their way to be helpful and protective; sometimes they are, indeed, over-helpful and over-protective. What some children with calipers can achieve in the way of physical activity has to be seen to be believed and though they rarely hurt themselves the damage they do to their appliances is phenomenal! The case of James (Chapter 1) is evidence that the moderately mobile boy may sometimes run into serious difficulties because of his inability to join fully in games and sports, so that all youngsters in this class should be carefully but unobtrusively watched. The chance of their making good without special schooling is sufficient to justify a trial in an ordinary school and the risks of failure are probably greatest when, as in James's case, the disability starts during early school life with a prolonged illness causing absence from school and consequent educational retardation.

The child with mobility unimpaired or only slightly reduced—usually a child with deformity of the spine or trunk or with one arm crippled—has little to gain from a special school. If he is educationally retarded because of prolonged absence from school it is theoretically possible that the smaller classes in a special school might enable him to get more individual tuition, but this does not always work out in practice. In the case of a boy the problem of impaired participation in sport may still arise and placement among his equals become socially necessary, but with a little skill and ingenuity some acceptable social outlets may be found for him. A boy with a disabled arm may find scope in football, athletics or cycling and if his disability is more serious it is likely that membership of a local Scout troop will provide him with plenty to do in good company.

It is not possible to consider schooling without taking into account the informal education which the good home gives. The aim of all education for handicapped children is to make them as far as possible independent among normal people while, as we have mentioned elsewhere, there is a natural tendency in parents to protect their handicapped offspring. The handicapped child attending a normal school may, therefore, find himself in a situation in which the school and home are at cross purposes, the school encouraging him to venture and be independent and the home pressing in the opposite direction. Such a conflict is exceedingly bad for the child and can sometimes only be resolved by sending him to a boarding special school where both inside and outside school hours he has the right sort of management. This step, however, should not be lightly taken.

William, at the age of ten, had an attack of poliomyelitis but after a period in a good hospital school was discharged home physically fit except for a partly disabled left arm. He started in a normal secondary modern school, a grade appropriate to his average intelligence. Unusually, the parents strongly pressed for his admission to a special school. They had satisfied themselves that he was not as other children and imagined that a special school could provide him with more than a normal school. He was happy at school, his educational retardation was no more than could be counteracted by a little special coaching and the teachers, the youth employment officer and the educational psychologist were satisfied that the school could give him all the special training that was needed to fit him for employment in which he could make a satisfactory career. In sport he took well to cross-country running, though he was naturally somewhat out of training. The parents forbade him this exercise and rarely allowed him to go out of the house alone. He had been a keen cyclist before his illness but the parents would not allow him to cycle on the grounds that his weak left arm would prevent him from braking in emergency. Prolonged argument between the school medical officer and the parents produced some softening in their attitude, but eventually the provision of a cycle with a back-pedal brake released him from his captivity and enabled him to get out with his normal friends in his spare time and paved the way for adjustment; his own achievements were the best refutation of the parents' arguments!

Hetty had poliomyelitis at the age of two, when she was living in London. The paralyses were severe and widespread and she went into a long-stay orthopaedic hospital, remaining there even after the parents had moved out into the country. Liaison with the hospital was good and when she was six it was decided that since she now needed more education than the hospital could give her and since it was high time she got back to her family she could return home and start attendance at an ordinary school. The village school was prepared to take her and door-to-door transport was arranged when at the last minute we discovered that liaison with the hospital had not been good enough; in the surgeon's opinion she still needed daily intensive physiotherapy. This was not available within fifteen miles of her home and after consulting the physiotherapy department we found that if she were to have the treatment she would at best have to miss afternoon school each day. At this stage the educational sacrifice was not worth while and instead we arranged for her to go to a boarding special school which had its own physiotherapy unit. After two years of steady progress, physical and educational, she came to a point at which physiotherapy twice a week would suffice; it was now reasonable for her to go home and attend the village school, since missing two afternoons a week was a moderate price to pay for the advantages she would now gain.

This kind of case is not very uncommon. Where the child lives in a town it may be possible to arrange for the necessary therapy at the end of the afternoon and thus not to lose more than half an hour a day of schooling. Some of the larger day schools may have physical education staff who are able to give, if not physiotherapy as such, remedial exercises which can be adequate for the later stages of physical treatment. Occasionally the need for continuing expert therapy may be so great and prolonged that for the sake of this alone it may be necessary to choose permanent boarding

G

school education. On the whole, however, it is more likely that, as with Hetty, the need will be for a moderate period of intensive care and treament and the prospect of bringing the child back to an ordinary school should always be borne in mind.

The crippled child, unlike the blind or deaf child, needs no special educational techniques which cannot be provided in an ordinary school. In many cases the tendency is for his disability to become less with the passage of time and even if it remains stationary he will be learning tricks and techniques which reduce its handicapping effect. Thus the need for the facilities of a special school may well diminish and the practicability of a return to an ordinary school increase. This possibility should always be borne in mind, and the school medical officer should keep in close touch with the special school. If, as often happens with boarding schools, the school is too far away for him to visit regularly, he should receive copies of all school reports and should see the child at least once a year during the holidays. It is no reflection on special schools to say that their small size, which is so valuable in giving the child a chance of individual attention during his early years, limits the range of vocational and technical education which they can provide and that particularly where boys are concerned career prospects can be much improved if the last two or three years of education can be spent in a technical or a progressive secondary modern school. If a boy has learned to adjust his way of life to his handicap during his special school years, a final spell in an ordinary school may be a gentler introduction to the normal world than transition straight from a special school to employment. Furthermore, since his ultimate need is for suitable employment near his home, the youth employment officer may find it easier to place him if he is on the spot for a year or two before he starts work.

It is fair to warn that sometimes a child who has made admirable progress in the sheltered environment of a special school has difficulty in re-entering life in an ordinary school and that the difficulty may be greater if he has never been to an ordinary school but has spent his whole school life in a special school. For this reason care should be used in selecting the ordinary school to which he is to be transferred and some special consideration should be given to him in the settling-down period. In large towns it may be possible to attach a special 'transitional unit' to a secondary modern school, to introduce such children gradually to normal school life.

Home tuition has been briefly mentioned in an earlier chapter as a possible alternative to special school education. Its dangers cannot be too strongly emphasized. The need of the crippled child is to get out of his home, which is likely to be over-protective, and to mix with other children; home tuition tends to confirm his status as a prisoner in the home and to make him less social and more dependent. The more protective and possessive parents will try to press for it as an alternative to a special school but this pressure should be resisted.

There are, however, four main types of case in which it is legitimate. Sometimes a young child or one newly disabled may not be able to enter a special school at once, either because the appropriate school has a long waiting list or because he is receiving regular treatment in a local out-patient department. In such a case it is all to the good that his education should be begun or continued at home during the waiting period so that he will not have too much leeway to make up when he finally starts school. Again, a child recently discharged from hospital may have a good prospect of entering an ordinary school after six months or a year of convalescence, possibly with treatment; it may be better for him to have home teaching in the interim rather than be sent to a special school for a comparatively short period. It sometimes happens that the surgeon's programme for a crippled child involves a series of operations with intervals of a few months between them; home tuition during the intervals may be better than repeated short spells in a special school. Finally, there are the rare but distressing cases of children with such diseases as the progressive muscular atrophies. In these a stage inevitably comes when even education in a special school is impracticable. When this occurs the child will be happier in his own home and though education for a career is out of the question an hour or two a day with a home teacher will give him an interest in life and make living a little more tolerable.

## 2. Congenital Cardiac Deformities

The outlook for the child with a congenital heart defect has been radically changed for the better since technical advances made cardiac surgery safe and practical. It is not yet possible to say that all, or even nearly all, deformities of the heart can be remedied by operation, but the prospect for many children with such defects is now good in the sense that their hearts can be so successfully repaired that they will ultimately be able to lead virtually normal lives. It is, therefore, essential that their condition should be diagnosed as soon as possible—not very difficult when the deformity is substantial—and that a specialist cardiac surgeon should be consulted early.

Where the prospect for surgery is good, the problem of care and education can be simply stated. It is simply that the child must be guarded from undue stress and strain and exposure to infection until operation is carried out. Nature herself may well take care of the former, for the infant's physical activity will automatically limit itself to what the heart will comfortably stand, but the common illnesses of childhood which the normal child takes in his stride will all present special hazards to life, so that any disease—measles, whooping-cough, influenza and even german measles and chicken-pox—is potentially dangerous. In many of these cases surgery can be carried out before the child is of school age, so that questions of special education will not arise.

One interesting incidental feature of congenital cardiac handicap is that the child is slow in reaching the physical milestones of life. Because his heart will not accept the strain he will be slow in sitting up and slow in beginning to stand and walk and he may even be incapable of 'pot-training' because he is unable to sit on the pot for long enough. It is not unknown for mental subnormality to be suspected in consequence, but after the heart has been repaired at operation he will quickly make up for lost time. (See Chapter 24).

Where the surgeon decides to defer operation to a later age, the effect of the cardiac handicap on education has to be considered. The child will at best be unable to share the ordinary physical activities of a normal school and may, at worst, be unable to make even a short journey to and from school. In this connection it is worth remembering that travel to and from school in bad weather and travel by public transport among people with colds and other infections may carry risk. If the child has not long to wait before operation, the start of school life may be postponed, but to delay this for two years or more is to expose the child to educational retardation and strain or difficulty in later years in making up for lost time. Home teaching, for reasons discussed elsewhere, is to be considered only as a short-term expedient. The choice will generally lie between the provision of special transport to an ordinary school, special transport to a suitable day school for 'delicate' children and admission to a boarding special school and the general principles outlined in Chapter 8 will be applicable in making the choice.

There remain some children whose congenital heart defects will not be amenable to surgical treatment. The point is already almost reached when the surgeon can say what the prospects for any particular child will be with present surgical resources, so that it is not common for these operations, when carried out, to be grossly disappointing. It follows, therefore, that in cases where operation is not considered advisable or where operation fails to give appreciable improvement it has been known from the start that the child would remain seriously handicapped. A prospect of this kind is to be faced in the same way as any permanent disability, with a forecasting of the child's prospects as he grows up and a general preparation for the life he is likely to be able to lead.

The essential practical effect of congenital heart defect is that it limits the amount of physical activity in which the victim can engage. Certain types of activity may be quite impossible and there is a limit to the length of time for which the patient can engage continuously in those which are possible. It has been found over the years that where the defect is not very serious the heart can be trained to stand up to quite considerable activity, but in some cases of this kind the prospects for surgery are so good that operation is virtually certain to be undertaken. Education offers the triple choice mentioned above in the consideration of operable cases, but the question of long-term planning must influence the choice.

Unless the disability is very slight indeed, the child has to face a future in which all physical activities must be carried out on a reduced scale. This makes life in an ordinary school difficult, especially for a boy. The child with a damaged leg or arm can find some activities to provide physical outlets, but the child with a severely deformed heart cannot, either at work or at play. There is, therefore, a strong case for putting him among his equals in a special school, allowing him to find out by a process of trial and error what he can do and what he cannot do and educating him toward the full use of the resources he has while reconciling him to the limitations he must accept.

## 3. Acquired Cardiac Defects

The amount of heart invalidism resulting from disease is steadily decreasing as improvements in general health, the control of infectious disease and the use of the antibiotics in the treatment of disease reduce the commonness and the severity of the conditions which cause heart damage. It can, indeed, be said with a good deal of truth that the biggest risk run by the child with acquired heart damage is that he will be given more protection than is necessary.

The education of the public proceeds only slowly and it is still popularly believed that any person with 'heart disease' is likely to fall down dead at any moment on the slightest or no provocation. The mere mention to a parent that a child has even some suspicion of heart disability is likely to make the parent immediately set about turning the child into a permanent invalid, and though successful cardiac surgery is modifying this where congenital defects are concerned it is still little changed in respect of acquired defects. Two dicta of the late Sir Thomas Lewis have proved their truth with time. They are that a scar in the heart is not necessarily more damaging than a scar anywhere else in the body and that a young person with a heart injury will sit down and rest long before he is ready to fall down and die.

The disease-damaged heart possesses great powers of recovery and unless the damage is very serious this compensation may bring the child virtually back to normality. If it is manifestly serious and permanent, then the treatment of the child will be much as outlined above for serious congenital heart disability—education and management on a much reduced scale of physical activity and preparation for a life with some permanent restrictions. With slight or moderate damage, however, the aim should be to train the injured heart to accept activity on a scale as near to normal as possible. It is, therefore, desirable that a child in this category should attend an ordinary school and participate as fully as he can in its physical activities. There are three main grades of regime—restriction of activity to normal walking and standing in ordinary class activities, participation in play and normal physical education but abstention from competitive physical activities and games, and the full regime of the school. In the early weeks or months after the initial illness the first of these may be required, but it should be possible to progress to the second stage before very long.

In the second stage the child is not too rudely reminded of the difference between himself and the others and the emotional effects of isolation and physical inferiority will not be very marked. Much, however, depends on whether this stage is approached in a negative or a positive way. The positive approach is to regard it as a quite deliberate and progressive training of the injured heart to compensate for the injury and a great deal of good can be done if the people responsible for physical education in the school handle the child intelligently in this way. Unfortunately, there is still a shortage of teachers fully trained in physical education and many schools, especially of the primary and secondary modern types, are not yet able to give individual attention in physical education. Where this is the case, it is probably worth while for the child with this kind of cardiac disability to have a period in a day or boarding school for delicate children, with the understanding that he will progress from there to an ordinary school as soon as his condition improves.

## 4. Asthma

Much more still needs to be known about the subject of asthma in children. Some authorities have long held that it is mainly an allergic condition, while others are equally insistent that the principal factors in producing it are emotional. However good progress is being made toward a more eclectic concept. There is no doubt asthma tends to run in families and the view which is now being generally accepted is that in most cases the asthmatic child has a constitutional instability of the air passages of the 'bronchial tree' and that a number of factors may trigger off a construction of those passages. Undoubtedly allergy, emotional stress and infection are among those factors, but their relative importance varies both from case to case and from time to time in the same individual. Exercise can also provoke attacks, though the amount and even the nature of that exercise seems to differ from case to case.

The evidence is complex and conflicting. One investigation showed, for example, that asthmatic children tend to have severe attacks causing absence from school during the first week or two of each new term, a period when children coming fresh from home to school are suddenly exposed to nose and throat infections. This is, however, most marked at the beginning of the autumn term when, after the summer holidays, resistance to infection ought to be fairly high. But the autumn term is the first term of the school year, when most children are promoted and therefore have to face a change from the class teacher to whom they are accustomed and meet a new teacher about whom rumour, school being what it is, has circulated alarming stories. An insecure child, facing this new and possibly alarming prospect, may well have some emotional disturbance.

Of the three components the allergic one is in theory the most susceptible to investigation and specific treatment and it is commonly good policy to investigate it first, so that either by desensitization or by avoidance of the substances to which he is sensitive the child may be freed from this part of his trouble. Since the constant threat of distressing attacks of breathlessness is in itself enough to cause emotional upset, asthma has within itself the potentialities of a vicious circle and it sometimes happens that when the allergic component has been dealt with the emotional component is for that reason much more amenable to treatment.

Edward, aged ten, was the son of a farm foreman. He appeared to be an insecure and emotionally unstable child but when his asthma was investigated from the allergic point of view it was shown that he was sensitive to various substances associated with cattle, notably cattle-hairs. The prospect of successful desensitization was considered poor and it was found insufficient to keep Edward away from the farm and its buildings—undoubtedly his father was carrying home on his person and his clothing a sufficient amount of the allergens to precipitate the boy's attacks. The choice lay between sending Edward away from home and pressing the father to change his work. The latter was socially and economically impracticable; a man with a wife and children who is well established in a skilled job simply cannot leave it and make a fresh start as a learner in a new field. In spite, therefore, of the risks involved to Edward's emotional stability in separating him from his family he was given a trial in a boarding school for delicate children. His first term was somewhat stormy, but the attacks of asthma were less frequent than they had been while he was at home. A few weeks after the start of his second term he began to improve rapidly and he soon became asthma-free at school, though remaining liable to minor attacks when he went home for the holidays.

The emotional component presents problems as diverse and complicated as any other type of emotional disturbance in childhood. It may be quite a minor part of the whole, possibly resolving itself as the child grows older and more confident or being dealt with simply by minor changes in the environment or in the parents' handling of the child. At the other extreme, asthma may be one of the manifestations of deep and severe maladjustment, so that the child must be considered first and foremost as maladjusted.

Tony, a 'chesty' child, suffered a good deal from coughs and colds with occasional frank attacks of asthma. Not every cough had asthmatic complications, but observation over a period showed a definite pattern in the attacks. His mother—he was an only child—was a good mother who was compelled to work as well as look after him and her work from time to time took her on trips of several days' duration. If he was well when one of her trips was due, nothing went wrong, but if he had a cold or a cough at the time a severe attack of asthma invariably occurred. So far as was compatible with her career the mother modified her arrangements, though it was clearly impossible for her to cancel her business trips at a day's notice. In the end the problem solved itself as Tony grew stronger and older and his resistance to infection built itself up.

Martin, by contrast, was the son of a neurotic and unstable father who complicated matters still further by moving his family about and having seven homes during the boy's first twelve years of life. His asthma was severe and continuous. The father was reluctant to accept the idea that his child needed psychiatric treatment and even when he did accept it the changes of residence interrupted treatment. The boy was admitted to an ordinary boarding preparatory school, where the stability of his environment produced some improvement in the symptoms. Eventually, however, for general reasons it became necessary for him to be transferred to a special school for maladjusted children.

The long-term outlook in juvenile asthma is undoubtedly good. There is no foundation for the popular superstition that children who are asthmatic in the early years 'grow out of it' at the age of seven, but improvement usually starts in later childhood and in most children the attacks cease, or become very infrequent and less severe, by late adolescence. This is to be expected. Emotional and physical instability and susceptibility to infection are all natural features of childhood and as the child matures his body and mind learn to cope with the incidents and accidents of life and he acquires greater stability all round.

Desensitization often eliminates and generally reduces the allergic element. Drug treatment, change of environment and enlightened emotional and social management are, perhaps, less 'cures' than things which keep the asthma under control until the child's process of maturing is complete and the condition disappears because the provoking factors are no longer operative. Very often the modern methods of treatment are so effective that the child can live at home and attend an ordinary school. In these cases there is a risk that the asthma may be regarded as cured, when in fact what has happened is that it is not manifest in the child's present environment. When he leaves the ordered atmosphere of school, with its secure routine and limited responsibilities, for the new and somewhat frightening experience of life in the workshop, factory or office, possibly in an atmosphere which may be physically conducive to 'chestiness', there may be a recrudescence of the asthma, possibly in a quite severe form. The asthmatic youngster, therefore, should be watched carefully during the first year or two after leaving school, so that he may have whatever treatment, advice or support may be needed to help him through his readjustment period.

## 5. Diabetes

The original British Handicapped Pupils Regulations named the diabetic child as a special category but after some years of experience the revised regulations made no special provision. This was quite in accordance with modern knowledge and practice, for a child who suffers from diabetes but whose insulin balance is controlled by diet, the administration of insulin or both is, in fact, a normal child for all practical purposes. His only disability is that from time to time because of the progress of the disease, because of the endocrine disturbances which accompany the process of growing up or because of changes in his activities the balance will be upset and it will be necessary to re-stabilize him. This can usually be done at the cost of a short period in hospital at not very frequent intervals, and the disturbances of schooling or general life are not serious.

Occasional difficulties arise, however. Some homes are quite incapable of giving the child a satisfactory and suitable diet. They should not be unduly criticized for this. Skill and labour are involved in dieting the diabetic and not every overworked housewife with a large family can be expected to cope with the problem. In such a case, where the choice lies between keeping the diabetes under control by careful dieting with a small dosage of insulin and controlling it by larger doses of insulin with a more normal diet, the latter, especially with modern long-acting insulin, may be the better expedient. Diet, however, cannot be neglected and the regularity of meals may be as important as the amount of the ingredients. The child with a long journey to school is at a disadvantage, because the intervals between his main meals are thus considerably increased. If he takes school dinners it may be possible to adjust his helpings to his needs but difficult to provide him with alternatives to certain forbidden dishes. Sometimes a home is so completely disorganized or incompetent that it cannot or will not co-operate at all in dieting a diabetic child. In such cases an alternative to the home must be provided. There have been experiments with hostels for diabetic children, the children living in the hostel but attending ordinary schools in the neighbourhood and these are probably a better proposition than sending the child to a special school as such. The number of diabetics in need is not great enough to justify special schools for diabetic children and such children do not usually need the full range of special facilities provided by special schools.

Though the difficulties mentioned in the earlier part of the last paragraph are not often insuperable in themselves, they may sometimes complicate the problem of re-stabilizing a child whose balance has been disturbed by one of the factors mentioned above. If that happens, the short hospital period of restabilization may become a series of short spells in hospital alternating with trial spells at home and at school. A useful alternative is to send the child to a diabetic hostel and place his stabilization in the charge of a hospital near the hostel; six months or so of this regime may do what is necessary without too great dislocation of schooling. Again, if the home is unable to do its share or the difficulties arising out of a long journey to and from school are serious, the answer may be provided by a 'normal' boarding school which can give special attention to general regime and diet. This particular problem is, perhaps, likeliest to arise in the case of the country child who needs a grammar school education but may have to spend an hour or two every morning and evening travelling back and forth to the nearest grammar school. It is better for him to go to a boarding grammar school than to sacrifice his education and be content with a secondary modern school nearer home.

Insulin balance is, of course, complicated by questions of exercise. A spell of hard physical activity may have as much effect as a quite substantial dose of insulin and the normal school regime of a child consists of alternations of long periods of rest with bursts of vigorous exercise. What is to be done in a particular case depends on the child, the home and the school. The exercise of a child with a cardiac disability will restrict itself automatically, but the diabetic child feels quite normal and will, like all children, play 'all out' so long as he feels well; by the time he has exercised himself until he feels faint or ill it is too late. It is never good to tell a child that he must not do the things his schoolmates and friends do and it is often futile to expect him to obey such instructions. The older and more intelligent child may co-operate at least to the extent of adjusting his diet or taking extra carbohydrate before or during exercise and it is, of course, the older child who is more likely to go in for vigorous sport. If it becomes necessary, particularly during one of his un-stable periods, to restrict his exercise and confine him to a more regular life a spell in the more organized and regulated atmosphere of an open-air school may be worth trying, for there, at least, he will be doing as the others do and will not feel that he is being singled out as an invalid.

Formerly it was true to say that diabetes in children was more severe and more dangerous than diabetes in adults. Modern knowledge, modern techniques and the new varieties of insulin have materially reduced the danger and the diabetic child has every prospect of surviving into adult life. Once the instabilities of adolescence have been overcome, the prospect for the diabetic child are precisely those for a diabetic adult with the same degree of insulin deficiency, and no special hazards have to be faced. It is sufficient to say that a steady, regular life, intelligently managed, will meet his needs and the only point which needs to be emphasized is that care should be taken to prepare him for and direct him into a career which will provide him with a regular job within his physical powers.

### The Prospect for the Physically Handicapped Child

The person with a cardiac defect can perform every action of which a normal person is capable. His trouble is that the more vigorous of such activities tire and strain him to such a degree that he may not be able to complete them and certainly will not be able to perform them rapidly and repeatedly. The 'chesty' person—like some people with cardiac defects—is capable of substantial periods of normal activity but will from time to time have periods of days, weeks or months during which he is a complete or partial invalid. Both these types of handicapped person are perfect examples of the axiom that circumstances determine handicap. If the person with a cardiac defect can contrive to live under conditions in which he is relieved of strenuous activities, everything which he does do will be done as successfully as any normal person could do it. He leads, as it were, a normal life in miniature. Proper choice of employment, suitable housing (not too far from the place of work or the shopping centre and preferably in a bungalow or a ground floor flat), help with the heavier household duties and a little planning to make his head save his legs will solve most of his problems.

The chesty person can be considerably helped in the same sort of way, but requires an environment which will also reduce the emotional strains which play a part in asthma and which will limit the risks of infection and allergy. Thus he will be barred from all-weather outdoor work and may benefit by changing his place of residence. He will need an employer who is tolerant of his periodical breakdowns and an employing organization with a generous sick-pay scheme. (Registration as a disabled person will often make him more acceptable to such an organization.) Help in the home during his or her 'off' spells will also be needed.

In both these types of case the final success or failure of the person in making good depends on the accuracy with which the long-term difficulties have been forecast and anticipated and on the effective-ness with which the home and school have combined to teach the person to accept the prospect of life in miniature. There is no reason why a high degree of success should not be achieved in the great majority of cases.

The cripple has a different prospect to face. There will be some normal activities which he can undertake as skilfully, as vigorously and over as long periods as any non-handicapped person. There will be other activities which he can perform with less than average skill and vigour over short periods and there will be still others which he cannot attempt at all. He will lead not a normal life in miniature but a life which is maimed, incomplete and, above all, unbalanced. Physical, emotional and social stability ideally require a balanced life with all the faculties of body and mind receiving exercise. If some are over-exercised and others not exercised at all, stability may be in danger.

Not all the body's resources are fully used in normal life. Most manual activities in practice demand one skilled arm and hand and one less skilled one as a steadying and supporting apparatus. Thus, one strong arm and one weak one are as good for most purposes as two normal ones and practice and ingenuity in sharing tasks between the arms and hands can reduce the partial crippling of both or the severe crippling of one to a comparatively modest practical handicap. The legs are used for two purposes, moving the body from place to place and supporting it while it is stationary, so that legs which are of little value for walking may be quite adequate for standing, at least for limited periods.

Physical appliances to aid weak or deformed limbs or backs can be valuable and may make a substantial or even critical difference. Braces and calipers can enable a person with a leg disability to stand, walk and even take some part in sport and the possibility of their use, either constantly and permanently or for specific purposes, should always be explored. Not all cripples take kindly to aids. They may be uncomfortable in use; this can be due to bad initial fitting, to failure on the patient's part to take the time and trouble to get accustomed to his appliance or to failure to carry out the necessary periodical checks for fit, possible damage and so on. They may be useful for one purpose but a hindrance in other ways—a caliper may be admirable for walking in but an uncomfortable nuisance when one is sitting down at school or at the office and the wearer may fail to make full use of it or to wear it regularly for just this reason. Sometimes aids may be spurned because they advertise one's disability or represent to the patient a surrender of the spirit. A person who could move about tolerably well with two sticks or a crutch may prefer to hobble about in pain or even to give up all but the most essential movements rather than feel that he is publicly owning that he is a cripple; he fails to see that his acceptance of unnecessary restrictions is an equally public announcement of disability.

On the other hand, appliances and aids, while admirable servants, are tyrannous masters. If walking is painful, troublesome or tiring, a wheel-chair is a great practical boon, but it is easy to become so addicted to the wheel-chair that one does not even try to do the little walking of which one is capable and with lack of practice and exercise the remnants of mobility shrink still further. It is often worth while for a handicapped person to accept a little strain and effort for the sake of physical and spiritual exercise. It is better to depend on aids and appliances than to depend on other people, but better than either is to depend on one's own skill and ingenuity. The essential purpose of an aid is to enable the cripple to do something which otherwise he could not do at all or could not do without the help of other people, a principle which applies to the whole range of aids from the motor-car with special controls to the long-handled shoe-horn or the knife or fork with a special grip. Otherwise aids must be used with discrimination. One which cuts down the time involved in some regular daily chore from fifteen minutes to five minutes is usually legitimate but one which does something which the patient could learn to do for himself with only slight effort and loss of time is of doubtful value.

This question of aids and appliances is stressed in some detail because it is an important part of the business of adjusting circumstances to abilities. It must not be forgotten that both abilities and needs change with the passage of time and that the nature and amount of help which the cripple needs must be kept constantly under review if he is to make the most of life. This applies both in his private life and in his working life. While the blind and the deaf may start in their late 'teens on the job which they are going to keep throughout their lives, the physically handicapped person may need modification or change of work at intervals.

Most of the crippling disabilities are, fortunately, non-progressive. For the unlucky few with the muscular dystrophies the prospect is bleak. There still seem to be a few people who think that because these youngsters have no career prospects investment in their education is not worth while. I prefer the contrary view that because their lives are going to be short in any case it is our duty to give them the change of getting as much as possible out of the years that are left to them. If we can find even one interest and aptitude which they can develop and continue we are doing something worth while. Maude, for instance had an aptitude for languages and we arranged for her to go to a grammar school for two half-days a week, in her wheel-chair, to take French until she was eighteen. By then she was, in any case, becoming home-bound but we were able to provide a home teacher who gave her a little continued help with the language. She died at twenty-two but I like to feel that even in her last year of life, when all she could do was a little reading while someone else turned her pages for her, life still had some interest for her and even had some challenge for her undoubted talents.

A final word is indicated on the subject of marriage and parenthood. As I suggested on the chapter on Education, the crippled girl is less likely than the normal girl to get married at all. It may be that as public opinion becomes more enlightened her prospects will improve, but it is hard to be sanguine. If she does get married the chances of her becoming a good mother and wife are very fair if she is given the help, whether through personal assistance or the provision of equipment, to bring her domestic work to a point within her powers. (It is possible, by thoughtful attention to such things as the lay-out of the kitchen, the height of the cooker, the working-table and the cupboards and the use of ramps for steps to enable quite a severely crippled woman to do a most efficient job around the house, especially if she has the help of a fit husband.)

The woman with a cardiac or respiratory disability has, unless it is very severe, a fair prospect of finding a husband, but may have a poorer prospect as wife and mother than the crippled woman. Pregnancy and childbirth carry some risks for her; it may, indeed, be necessary to forbid them. Housework is notoriously an employment which allows little rest and the woman with a cardiac defect or asthma is not always free to sit down and rest when the sudden need arises. The 'chesty' woman's probable periods of substantial illness will interrupt the smooth running of her home. But if the home is organized on the basis of first things first and if help is available when special difficulties arise, she will probably manage fairly well.

Unless their disability has brought them considerable personality disturbance, most physically handicapped men find wives, however severe the disability. From what I have said elsewhere it will be plain that the motives for which women marry disabled men are not always those on which the happiest and enduring marriages are founded, but there is no need for general pessimism.

Some obvious problems do arise. The physically handicapped husband may feel acutely the fact that he cannot do those things about the home that normal men do—saving his wife some of the heavy work, doing 'handyman' jobs about the house and looking after the garden—and hiring outside help is not the complete answer. It is a particular joy for a father to share his sons' sports and games; if this is impossible both father and sons miss something. The father's employment must have first claim on his physical abilities and energies and home must be the place in which he gets the rest he needs, even if the activities of the rest of the household have to be restrained or curtailed so that he can have it.

These considerations are not all peculiar to the physically handicapped. They underline the fact that the handicap of one person may affect intimately the lives of several others. Though perhaps fewer than three per cent of the population of a country may be actually handicapped, ten or fifteen per cent may have their lives complicated by their own disability or that of others. Whether the problems I have just outlined are great or small, soluble or insoluble, depends very largely on how the handicapped person has been taught to live with his handicap but they should also remind us of the need for the handicapped to learn to live with others— and for others to learn to live with the handicapped.

## FURTHER READING

*Physical Disability*
Various Authors.   The 'Chesty' Child.   Chest and Heart Assn.
Clarke, J. S.   Disabled Citizens.   Allen and Unwin.
Le Comte, E.   The Long Road Back.   Gollancz.
Mallinson, V.   None Can be Called Deformed.   Heinemann.
Franklin, A. W. (Ed.).   The Care of Invalid and Crippled Children.   Oxford University Press.
Goldsmith, S.   Designing for the Disabled.   R.I.B.A., London.
   The Central Council for the Care of Cripples publishes a guide to services for the physically handicapped and a summary of legislation on the subject.

# CHAPTER 17

# The Delicate Child

The British Handicapped Pupils Regulations divide children into categories on a primarily administrative rather than a clinical basis, each category comprising children who, if they need special education, will go to the same sort of special school. For convenience this book has followed the divisions generally, but has telescoped into one the two classes of 'Deaf' and 'Partially Deaf' and has included the asthmatic or 'chesty' child with the physically handicapped though such children are often administratively classed as 'Delicate' since it is delicate children who are accepted in open-air special schools.

The majority of children who are formally ascertained as delicate are not handicapped in the sense in which that term is generally used. They are not necessarily suffering from a disability of mind or body which is going to be permanent or even from one which is certain to persist throughout their schooldays. They are, in fact, children who for some reason or other—not always a major reason—are likely to profit by a period of education in a slightly modified school environment and who cannot be conveniently brought into one of the other categories. The expedient is typically British and provides a most valuable piece of elasticity in what might in other circumstances have been a somewhat rigid legal framework.

There do actually exist children who are permanently sub-standard constitutionally for reasons which are impossible to define. They may have a low resistance to infection, coupled with poor recuperative powers so that for them life under ordinary conditions is a continuous process of illness, slow convalescence and further illness. Such a child, exposed to the many miscellaneous infections which are always present in an ordinary school will be absent from school more often than he is present but in the closed community of a small school, with a generally favourable environment, he will get through his education with a minimum of interruption. Furthermore, there is always a possibility that as he grows older he will tend to become stronger and more resistant. To what extent the 'open-air' aspect of the special open-air school is of direct value to him is a moot point.

Most delicate children, however, are in a temporary phase of debility. They may be convalescing after a long illness or a series of illnesses. They may be malnourished. They may be passing through that stage of puberty which is colloquially known as 'overgrowing one's strength', a term which is not without literal meaning in some cases. Growth is a notoriously uneven process and a period during which the child is rapidly growing in length but developing adequate muscles only slowly is quite likely to produce strain, tiredness and debility. What such children need is a combination of good food, general care and a regime which will allow them adequate rest. A convalescent home can take them for only a short period and will have difficulty in providing education; an open-air special school is a sound compromise.

A substantial number of children in open-air schools are not, however, delicate in any genuine sense of the word but are sent there deliberately because there is something lacking in their home environment. They may have slum homes or homes on the poverty line. Not uncommonly they are children neglected in their own homes by feckless, inefficient parents. Occasionally a child who is, strictly speaking, maladjusted is sent to an open-air school; this will happen where the child is not sufficiently maladjusted to require the full resources of a special school for maladjusted children but where the home environment is likely to produce emotional instability if the child remains at home.

The choice between a day school and a boarding school for children in this group will depend on circumstances. For the genuinely delicate child with a good home and understanding parents the day open-air school, if one is conveniently available, will often prove quite adequate. Where the fault, for whatever reason, lies in the home it is obviously futile for the child to go home each night so that whatever good has been done by day may be undone. In such cases the boarding school is the answer. Again, one of the child's needs may be for a spell in a more gentle climate than his home town provides, whether in the way of warmth, dryness or sunshine; if so, a boarding school in the appropriate place is obviously the answer. But perhaps more than in any other group of handicapped children the 'delicate' child's case must be kept under review and his special school placement regarded as essentially temporary.

The long-term prospect for these children is usually good and presents few special difficulties. Most of them are restored to normal health before they leave school and can face normal life without qualms. The fact does remain, however, that, as was specifically mentioned in the case of the 'chesty' child, an occasional youngster who has been in stable physical and mental equilibrium in the sheltered environment of school finds the sudden transition to employment, coming, as it does, with the other strains of adolescence, too much for him. The art here lies in watching the child closely and continuously during his schooldays and noting anything which might suggest that he may be vulnerable to such strain. If vulnerability is suspected not only will he need observation after leaving school but the type of work which he enters should be carefully chosen and, no less important, he should, if possible, be placed with an employing firm which studies and provides for the welfare of its workers.

# CHAPTER 18

# Mental Handicap

## Causation

Mental handicap, like any other type of handicap, may be inborn or acquired. In by far the greatest number of cases it is inborn, arising either from hereditary defect or from damage to the child before birth.

Very little is known about the inheritance of intelligence or lack of intelligence, largely because the nature of intelligence is ill understood. It can, however, be said with some certainty that a pair of mentally subnormal parents will not have children of normal or higher-than-normal intelligence. It is by no means equally certain that a pair of highly intelligent parents will have children who are all of their own level. In a community in which persons of all grades of intelligence are free to mate and have children it is, therefore, natural that a proportion of children should inevitably be mentally handicapped. Apart from this, which is a matter of natural variation among human beings, truly inherited mental subnormality is confined to certain rare degenerative diseases of the nervous system.

'Mongolism', now coming to be known as 'Down's Syndrome', is a type of subnormality in which the child has a slant-eyed appearance (hence the original name) and certain other physical peculiarities including short fingers and a large, creased tongue. It is comparatively common, occurring in about one child out of every six hundred born. The cause is uncertain. Such a child is as likely to be born to mentally normal parents as to subnormal ones and usually the other children in the family are normal. There is an abnormality of the chromosomes, quite possibly associated with parental age—most mothers of mongols are rather older than the average—but it is suggested that pre-natal infection may also be a factor.

Damage to the child before or during birth, arising from many possible causes, may affect the brain just as easily as any other organ. Virus, bacterial or other diseases of the mother at certain stages of pregnancy may produce mental defect. So may physical brain injury during birth, interference with the oxygen supply to the child during birth, or the administration to or taking by the mother of various drugs during pregnancy or labour.

Haemolytic jaundice of the newborn, referred to in the chapter on brain damage, can produce severe brain injury but can be anticipated by Rhesus-testing of the mother during pregnancy and the carrying out of an exchange-transfusion on the child at birth (though not all such children are born alive). Cretinism, formerly a fairly common cause of mental defect, is due to a failure of metabolism associated with the thyroid gland and the newly-discovered condition of phenylketonuria is a rare phenomenon also associated with metabolic faults; both these can be cured or much alleviated if diagnosed and treated really early.

'The commonest cause of mental handicap occurring after the new-born period is virus encephalitis. This may be due to viruses which specifically affect the brain or to the encephalitis which sometimes occurs as a complication of the infectious diseases which are common in childhood, especially measles. Bacterial meningitis, thanks to modern methods of treatment, has virtually disappeared as a cause of severe brain damage in the highly-developed countries, but it is by no means rare in countries which have as yet only scanty medical services.'

In a book such as this, only two other causes need be specifically mentioned. Epilepsy is quite often associated with mental deterioration; some epileptics are mentally subnormal from the start and others become so by steady progress. The reason for this is uncertain, but is believed to be recurrent damage to the brain during fits. Precisely how the fits damage the brain has still to be discovered.

The last cause is physical injury to the brain caused by a blow or a fall. It is possible for this kind of physical injury to produce haemorrhage into or around the brain, with consequent damage to the brain cells or to produce fracture of the skull with irritation of or pressure on the brain. In actual fact, proved mental subnormality from this cause is rare. Most parents who find that their child is mentally handicapped seek to discover some reason for the disability which will not reflect on their own intelligence and which will be intelligible to other people with a minimum of embarrassment to all parties. They have little difficulty in recollecting some fall during the child's early years, for the good and sufficient reason that every child, normal or handicapped, has falls as part of the ordinary process of learning how to move about, climb stairs and sit on chairs. The mentally handicapped child may have fallen because he was mentally handicapped and therefore clumsy in relation to his size or he may have fallen merely because he is a child. Though it is possible that he is handicapped because he fell, it is highly improbable.

### Definitions

So far we have been dealing principally with conditions in which a sharp line separates the normal from the abnormal. The blind child, the deaf child, the child with a paralyzed limb and the child with a damaged heart all have some obvious and definable difference from the normal child. 'Normal' intelligence, however, is not an obvious physical thing. Intelligence cannot be measured as accurately as hearing and sight and its importance is directly related to its use. We must, therefore, work out a compromise between arbitrary standards and convenient social approximations. This has been done and it works reasonably well in practice. It is, however, subject to occasional errors, some of which may be quite serious.

The average height of Englishmen is five feet, seven and one-quarter inches. But if we take a thousand men at random and measure them we are not likely to find that more than a handful of them measure exactly 5 ft. $7\frac{1}{4}$ in. About half of them will be shorter than the average and about half of them taller. If we take the shorter ones and group them into those who are between 5 ft. $7\frac{1}{4}$ in. and 5 ft. $6\frac{1}{4}$ in., those between 5 ft. $6\frac{1}{4}$ in. and 5 ft. $5\frac{1}{4}$ in. and so on, we shall find that the first of these groups is the largest, the second contains fewer men, the third fewer still and by the time we get to the fourteenth group, the men of about 4 ft. 6 in., we shall have very few indeed. The same applies to the men of above average height; the taller the fewer. The great majority are within three or four inches of the average in either direction, while giants and dwarfs are rare enough to be curiosities.

Much the same is true of intelligence which is, in a sense, mental stature. The great majority are quite close to the average and the further one departs from the average the smaller is the number in the group, the genius and the grossly mental defective being both uncommon. For reasons already mentioned there are many more defectives than geniuses but the principle of their distribution in the population still holds good. Even if there were some exact and infallible means of measuring intelligence, the standard which we used for deciding who was mentally handicapped would be difficult to set. We should have to think not just in terms of those who were below the average but rather of those who were so far below the average that they were notably worse than the majority of the population.

Naturally one sooner or later asks the question 'What is intelligence?' It cannot be seen, touched, smelt, weighed, put under the microscope or analysed in the chemical laboratory. Looking at its functions, we see that it includes many faculties such as memory, reasoning power and the ability to see and understand relationships between similar or different things, between similar or different ideas and between things and ideas and it is easy to split hairs in the argument as to where one part stops and another begins. Colloquially, we speak of 'the intelligent use of' a physical tool, a personal skill, a concept or a facility but we are making a purely practical judgement; what we mean is that whatever it may be is being used to the advantage of the user or other people, with economy of effort and a minimum of waste or undesirable side-effects.

Many angels have wisely—or, should one say, intelligently?— refrained from treading in the field of definition of intelligence and I have no intention of attempting it myself. It is, however, still worth while to take a look at intelligence in action in the hope of seeing how it works and even how it develops.

Let us begin with something so simple and commonplace as a baby's first encounter with chocolate. If he meets it in very early infancy it is just a pleasant taste. A little later, however, when sight and touch are being brought into play, it becomes a brown substance of moderate hardness which tastes delicious and which 'melts' when one sucks it. Later still comes the feel of it between the newly acquired teeth. There are plenty of other things which are chocolate coloured and if they are left within baby's reach or if he can crawl to where they are accessible he will most certainly seize upon them in hope. Fortunately, though many common chocolate-coloured things have either an unpleasant taste or none at all the average house is not likely to contain any which are highly poisonous. Our infant, therefore, will probably survive his experiments and add to his knowledge of chocolate and non-chocolate. He now comes, in effect, to a point at which, when he encounters a brown object, he asks himself whether it is the same colour, size and shape as the things which he has come to know as pieces of chocolate, or whether there is something about it which more resembles the pieces of linoleum, formica or painted wood which he has found in the past to be so unprofitable. Before long he is able to make an unerring snatch, without conscious thought, at certain chocolate objects which are thoroughly familiar to him, but he may still have to think when he meets wrapped chocolate, chocolate in unfamiliar shapes or chocolate disguised in a non-chocolate though edible covering.

Putting this into general terms, the child's encounter with a piece of potential chocolate is the encountering of a situation. He analyses the situation and looks back into his own experience to see what there is in the situation which he knows and what there is that he does not know. If he then comes to the conclusion that the situation is a familiar one he remembers what he did last time and what happened. If what happened last time was pleasant, satisfying and successful he does it again; if not, he either takes no action or does something different. This is the pattern of living. Virtually every voluntary action we take involves this process of analysis and comparison with experience until we come to the stage at which some of the actions are so familiar that they are to all intents and purposes automatic.

This is the first and most elementary use of intelligence—dealing with the immediate situation as it presents itself. The second degree takes us further into looking ahead at the more distant consequences of the action. Our baby can now recognise chocolate and eat it, which he does with avidity. If mummy is not present and the whole box or packet is accessible he goes on eating it until some very unpleasant feelings arise and he is sick. The idea that too much chocolate makes one sick develops more slowly than the original idea that chocolate tastes good. It is bound up with some rather complex matters—a certain amount of chocolate is harmless, but more than that amount makes one sick—the 'safe' amount varies with the type of chocolate and also varies according to the quantity and nature of what one has eaten recently and how long ago one ate it. This demands a much higher degree of judgement than merely deciding whether a particular object is pleasant to eat. Whether with chocolate or with other things in life, this consideration of consequences and whether they are or are not acceptable always requires conscious thought and considered action.

Whether one should eat the isolated object or not and whether one should eat more chocolates or stop eating them are both matters of dealing with a present and concrete situation. The third degree of intelligence takes us to the realm of situations in the rather more distant future, which may be real or hypothetical. Still in the simple world of chocolate and knowing one's capacity when faced with a boxful, does one eat to one's capacity now or does one eat only three now with the idea that there will be three more tomorrow and three more on other future days? Or, bringing in the subject of money, with its complications of choice, does one buy a small quantity of cheap sweets now or save up for a week or two and buy either more or better things? And, as the child grows older, there come even more difficult forward-looking problems such as whether one should economise on chocolates or go without them altogether in order to be able to buy, next month or even in six months' time, the attractive toy one has seen in a shop window.

These three degrees of intelligent activity were recognized in the old Mental Deficiency Acts. 'Feeble-minded' persons were those who required care, supervision or control for their own protection and the protection of others; in other words, they were so lacking in judgement and foresight that they were liable to make serious mistakes if they were not properly guided by others. 'Imbeciles' were 'incapable of managing themselves or their affairs'; broadly speaking, they were unable to look beyond the moment. 'Idiots', the lowest grade, were those 'unable to guard themselves against common physical dangers'; they could make gross errors even in dealing with some of the simplest problems of life even at the moment of occurrence. These definitions have now ceased to have legal standing but they remain useful yard-sticks to bear in mind in making preactical assessments.

## Intelligence in Action.

The foregoing neither defines nor explains the nature of basic intelligence, but it does suggest that intelligent behaviour depends to a considerable extent on the systematized and purposeful use of stored experience. This requires essentially:—

1. The capacity to store experience.
2. The acquisition of experience to be stored.

3. The storing of that experience in an ordered and connected manner.

4. The ability to draw on that store quickly and effectively.

All four of these elements are interdependent and if any one of them is impaired the value of the others is reduced. We still know so little about basic intelligence that we cannot say to what extent any of them is inborn or acquired but undoubtedly several of them may be in a considerable degree determined by circumstances.

1. *The capacity to store experience.* Memory mechanisms are as yet imperfectly understood. We do not know, for example, whether defective memory is due to an insufficiency of the right type of brain cells to hold an adequate amount of experience or whether it is due to an inability to retain experience in storage. However, since the intellectually handicapped child common needs to have learning experience more often repeated, it certainly seems possible that there is an element of inability to retain experience in storage or an organic defect which impairs the ability to receive memory imprints. The defects of memory which develop after brain injury or the deterioration of memory which comes with ageing certainly suggest that storage capacity does play an important part in determining memory effectiveness.

2. *The acquisition of experience to be stored.* By contrast, this is substantially determined by environment. If the child does not have access to experience he cannot store it. The over-protected child and the isolated child—the child, in fact, who is in any way deprived of normal contacts—is obviously at risk. 'Experience' is by no means confined to things which one personally sees, hears and does. It includes second-hand experience, the advice of parents and teachers, what one reads in books and newspapers, what one hears on the radio and sees on television. So interrupted formal education or cultural deprivation in the home can also be involved.

It is important to note that the acquisition of experience can also be impeded by non-intellectual disabilities. Physical handicap can delay the start of schooling and, no less important, can prevent the child from learning by play and routine activities during the early years. A defect of vision or hearing can obstruct one of the gateways through which experience is gathered.

3. *The storing of experience.* The storing of experience must be systematized, and connected in an orderly and useful fashion. To take a simple instance, a child may very early learn that flame

burns. He will also learn that glowing coal burns, and, as he becomes more adventurous, discover also that things which neither flame nor glow can burn. He will come to learn that things which are hot enough to burn are to be found in certain places. A dull object which is likely to burn is usually to be found in a fireplace—a piece of coal in the coal-scuttle or a poker which is hanging on a stand can probably be handled with impunity. Until, therefore, he has acquired the primitive experiences and learned to connect them in his memory he is not ready to go on to the more advanced and sophisticated experiences. Either the child with poor storage or the child who is deprived of experience will consequently be a slow learner; the poor storer will remain slow in learning while the child who has been essentially deprived has a fair prospect of becoming a quicker learner as essential experience becomes more available to him.

4. *The ability to draw on that store quickly and effectively.* Only practice makes perfect. Imagine a child who has adequate reading skills being given the run of a library. Here is a store of information indeed, but he will initially be quite bewildered; he will at best pick at random and at worst may be too daunted to pick at all. But he will, if he is helped, come to know which books are in particular sections and eventually be able to go almost automatically to the correct shelf or even directly to the desired book; even indeed to related books which are needed for supplementary reference.

The child who has the opportunity, the incentive and the stimulus, the child, especially, who is offered challenges beyond—though not too far beyond—his past experience will tend to be considerably quicker in his intellectual development than the child who is not getting enough practice.

The picture of intelligent behaviour which emerges is certainly complex. There is no doubt that there are constitutional limiting factors. Each child has a certain potential beyond which he cannot develop but whether he does in fact attain that potential is determined by things which have nothing to do with 'intelligence'.

There is no agreement upon which are the basic constitutional limiting factors, though probably they include memory capacity, memory retention, comprehension and the power to appreciate certain relationships. Sensory handicaps, perceptual difficulties and a wide range of social and environmental factors impede intellectual development; these may be cured, alleviated or their effects moderated. Illness, both physical and emotional, may lower one's level of intellectual function and slow down one's mental processes, thus temporarily retarding development; if the illness is substantially cured it will not take long for the child to reach his potential level of performance.

It must also be remembered that there is an expressive side to intelligent behaviour. Intelligence can be manifested only in speech and in the movement of the limbs. Certainly lack of speech and movement will restrict social intercourse and in some degree limit experience, but it is quite possible for a person with these disabilities to realize the greater part of inherent high intellectual potential and yet to be too easily classed as severely mentally handicapped because only a small part of what is in the intellect can find expression.

Our essential purpose is to help the child to make the best of what he has. To fulfil that purpose it is certainly desirable to explore his basic potential, inexact though our means may be and however we may lack precise definitions. If he has a mental handicap then it is important that the most appropriate means shall be used to encourage and foster his development. We are on surer ground in seeking to identify the many adventitious factors which may be hampering him. It is true that we may find it difficult to discover exactly how much each factor may contribute to the total picture but to find and remove, cure or alleviate such factors must inevitably do some good. This is the essential aim of assessment, something very much more comprehensive than 'measurement of intelligence'.

## Assessment

The first part of assessment consists of the taking of a careful and comprehensive history. The child's physical developmental progress is important. The child of below-average intelligence usually shows delay in reaching the 'developmental milestones'—he is later than the average child in sitting up, standing, walking, feeding himself, acquiring bladder control and bowel control and learning to speak. If a child is up to average in reaching all the milestones, then it is improbable that he is mentally handicapped. Conversely, if he is later than average in reaching all of them there is good reason to suspect mental handicap. If he is only slightly late in reaching some of them but grossly late in reaching others there is a distinct probability that some factors other than lack of intelligence have been at work. Indeed, such cases as that of Alice (Chapter 24) confirm that physical factors may account for substantially delayed all-round physical development in a quite intelligent child.

Social development is more difficult to assess. Again, the child who is well up to average in social development is probably not appreciably mentally handicapped, but it is quite common for delay in social development to be due entirely to causes independent of mental handicap. Though the social history may give useful indirect evidence about intellectual development, its principal importance is in indicating the presence or absence of the many social factors which may, as discussed in the last section, interfere with the manifestations and progress of the development of intelligent behaviour.

It is becoming usual to record developmental history, physical and social, on child health clinic record cards and to pass on a summary of the salient points to the school health service. However, one cannot rely on this; though most children attend child health clinics in the first year of life the frequency of attendance falls off rapidly as the child gets older and it is not uncommon for the record to be discouragingly blank during the third, fourth and fifth years of life. Even if there is a fairly full record it is important to discuss the child's medical history with the parent and also to supplement the record with information from the family doctor— with, of course, the parents' consent to approaching him. Incidentally, the prudent doctor, when assessing a child who has been suspected of mental handicap for the first time after he has started school life, will not rely too much on the summary record of pre-school health which has been passed to the school health service but will have a look at the complete pre-school record if it is available. It is always possible that it contains relevant information the significance of which may not have been appreciated at the time when the record was summarized.

There should be little need to refer in detail to the next step in assessment, the carrying out of a physical examination. If the child has had a complete medical examination in the child health clinic or on school entry within, say, a year of his being assessed, the findings of that may be used as a basis, always provided that the child was found to be free from defects at that examination and that he has had no illnesses in between. The operative words are 'as a basis'. A physical check should never be omitted completely and there are two elements to which special attention should be paid.

One is a test of vision. Apart from the fact that it is not easy to test vision accurately in young children, it is possible for vision to deteriorate in various ways between the ages of, say, three and seven, and a child who appeared to have normal vision on the last test may have developed a substantial defect since that test was carried out. The other is even more important. Hearing impairment, temporary or permanent, may undoubtedly impede intellectual or social development and, incidentally, affect response to intelligence tests. A special source of trouble is high frequency deafness—discussed in Chapter 14—which, in a normally or even highly intelligent child, can produce delayed speech development and failure of comprehension, two of the cardinal signs of intellectual deficit. It should be an absolute rule to insist on referring a child suspected of mental handicap for audiometric assessment before investigation of his mental handicap begins. Failure to do this can involve the doctor in difficulty and embarrassment; more important, it may result in a disastrous mis-assessment for the child.

The second part of assessment is the intelligence test. Early in the present century Binet and Simon worked out a series of tests to measure not intelligence itself but the way in which intelligence is manifested. The tests covered manual dexterity, discrimination of shapes, memory, recognition of common objects and pictures of objects, understanding of the spoken and the written word, comprehension of ideas and the forming of judgements. These tests have been extended and elaborated by other workers until they form a very complete battery. They have been standardized on the basis of what the average child can be expected to achieve at a particular age. If a child under examination succeeds in the tests which are average for a child of a given age, then he is said to have the corresponding 'mental age'. His mental age, expressed as a percentage of his chronological age, is his intelligence quotient, familiarly known as 'I.Q.' If a child of ten years passes tests only at the five-year level his mental age is five and his I.Q. is 50. If he reaches the ten-year level his I.Q. is 100 and if he reaches the fourteen-year level his I.Q. is 140.

The idea of being able to measure inherent intelligence and express it in figures is certainly an attractive one. Those who pioneered testing were probably too optimistic in their hopes and in recent years there has been a good deal of criticism of tests in general. The criticism has been worth while in that it has led to a reappraisal of tests and their use. It is fair to say that, properly used, they will give an accurate measure of intelligence in the majority of cases and a good approximate measure in most of the remainder. In a few cases they are sadly inaccurate or even useless from the measurement point of view, though even there they may give valuable information about the child. The vital thing is their proper use; they must be used with a full understanding of their limitations and the user must remember all the time that he is assessing the whole child and not just a disembodied intellect.

The most obvious of the limitations is that the tests have been standardized on normal children, who have had normal upbringing at home and at school. They do not take into account the environmental factors which have been discussed in the earlier part of this chapter, so that whoever is responsible for assessment has to bear these and their possible effects in mind. Nor do they make allowance for defects of vision, hearing, co-ordination and so on; these again must be watched for and their effects considered. A further flaw is that the most comprehensive and effective of the standard test systems depend to some extent, especially in the case of older children, on vocabulary and ability to read and do simple arithmetic. This places the normally intelligent child whose education has been interrupted for any reason at some disadvantage and for this reason it is always desirable to use some non-verbal tests in the assessment.

Since intelligence testing must be a time-consuming process, there have been attempts to simplify it, especially through the devising of group tests which enable a number of children to be tested simulataneously by a kind of examination paper which they complete under supervision. A test of this kind cannot make allowance for individual differences and does not provide any real contact between the tester and the child, so that at best its results can be only approximate and at worst they may be quite badly wrong. It is, however, a useful 'screening' procedure provided that one does not expect too much of it. On the whole it is fair to say that a child who passes a group test at or above the level of his chronological age is most probably of average or higher intelligence. On the other hand, a child whose score in a group test is below his chronological age is not necessarily below the average in intelligence; his 'failure' should be taken as an indication that he ought to have an individual test.

The individual intelligence test, properly carried out by a skilled and experienced tester, is an effective and reliable means of diagnosis; much more reliable, in fact, than many of the tests on which physicians and surgeons base quite drastic and far-reaching decisions about physically ill people. It is true that the results may be influenced by the many things which have been discussed in the last few pages as liable to affect the child's manifestation of intelligence and, in consequence, his test performance but because the tester meets the child in person and can see him in action and because, also, information about the child's physical and social disabilities will be available to him, it will be possible to take these into consideration. Of course, experience counts for a great deal, but with it the tester can be sure in the majority of cases of making a sound and accurate estimate of the child's intelligence—accurate, that is, to within ten per cent—while in the small remaining minority of cases he will not only know that his estimate is incorrect but will also have a shrewd idea of what incidental factors are interfering with the child's response.

It is not the function of this book to deal in detail with the technique of testing, but a few comments may usefully be made. It is important, for instance, that testing should be done in favourable surroundings in which both child and examiner can be at ease and secure from both interruption and distraction. The examiner must have the child's confidence, which is not always easily gained on a first meeting in circumstances which can be a little strained. Without this confidence it is best to stop the tests and adjourn the examination to another day. It may, indeed, be a good thing for the examiner to arrange to meet the child quite informally on one or more occasions before the test is actually carried out. Where there is reason to expect temperamental or emotional difficulties he should make a point of trying to establish this informal contact and if he feels that he and the child cannot reach emotional *rapport* he may do wisely to ask someone else to carry out the tests.

In Britain the formal assessment examination of a school child with a view to special education must be carried out by a doctor, a reasonable provision, since the child's physical health has to be taken into account. If he wishes, the doctor may arrange for a psychologist to carry out the intelligence tests, but without in the least wishing to disparage psychologists it is necessary to point out

H

that there is an important risk in doing this. The tests, in addition to their primary value in measuring intelligence, have an important secondary value; the child's behaviour under test, his response to the test situation, his approach to the tests and his reaction to success or failure can, to the skilled examiner, be little less illuminating than the tests themselves and may give the clue to various anomalies which appear in the test results. It is, therefore, important that the person who is to make the summing up of the assessment as a whole should have himself observed the child under test and should not rely on second-hand information. Having said this, however, I would add that in cases of doubt and difficulty the examining doctor should never be afraid of asking a psychologist to carry out an *additional* examination. This is particularly desirable when the history and the initial examination suggest that there may be some specific educational disability or when it seems that some physical, motor or sensory handicap may be complicating the picture.

When test results have been obtained they have to be interpreted. The actual form of the result has significance. It is not usual for a child to pass all the tests up to one particular year-level and to fail at all those above that level. A child with a mental age of ten, for example, is likely to pass all tests up to the nine-year level but may fail in one or two of the ten-year tests and pass one or two of the eleven-year ones, failing completely at the twelve-year level. If this zone of partial failure spreads over more than three years it is probable that there is either some specific educational difficulty or some emotional block. The probability of this being so is even greater if the child is consistently successful in tests of one particular kind and consistently unsuccessful in those of another kind.

The present age is one of reverence for figures and the idea of being able to express intelligence in terms of a precise figure and to classify the child and plan his future on that basis is certainly attractive. But practice, as usual, betrays theory. The most one can say is that a child with an I.Q. between 100 and 80 will almost certainly be capable of being educated in an ordinary school, that if his I.Q. is between 70 and 55 he will probably be educable in a special school and that if it is below 45 he is not likely to be educable at all in any academic sense, though he may profit by some practical craft training and social guidance. We are left with two borderline groups of children, those with I.Q's. between 80 and 70 and those with I.Q's. between 55 and 45.

There are two principal reasons for this. One is the accepted fact that the tests have at best a five per cent margin of error. The other is that educability does not depend solely on whatever it may be that intelligence tests measure. A child may have some defect of perception, may be emotionally unable to adjust to school and receive education or may have been brought up in a home in which education is ignored or despised. In deciding on his assessment of a borderline case the examiner needs additional evidence. Part of this may be provided by a school report; if the child has already had a trial in school and has shown that he can accept education this is proof indeed. If his previous school life has shown that he does not respond to education this has some evidential value but is not conclusive; while his failure may be his own fault it may be partly or wholly the fault of the school or the teacher or the consequence of an incompatibility of temperament between teacher and child.

There is seldom any great urgency about the assessment of the borderline child or the child over whom the examiner has serious doubts and a little time can profitably be spent in investigation and observation. The first need is to eliminate or confirm any suspicions of physical disability which may be affecting the way in which the child uses or manifests his intelligence. This can sometimes be done quickly but in certain cases in which partial deafness is suspected in addition to definite subnormality of intelligence it may take a considerable time to clarify matters. If emotional blocking is suspected, the advice of a child guidance clinic must be sought.

The golden rule of assessment, however, is 'if in doubt, watch.' It may be sufficient to leave the child in his home or in his present school during this observation period. A reasonable principle is that if one is in doubt about which of two grades a child should be placed in it is better to give him a trial in the higher of the two, but this should not be slavishly followed. A child who is having difficulty in keeping pace with his fellows in an ordinary school may make notable advances if he is given a period of work at a slower pace in a good special school. In the lower of the borderline groups a child whose test scores and general response appear low because of social factors may improve in the social environment of a good training centre. In some special categories—the spastic child, the subnormal child with a hearing defect and the subnormal child with a visual defect—a period in a special assessment centre may be necessary.

These comments on assessment can appropriately include a note on the so-called 'late developer'. It is the firm belief of many lay people that some children may have markedly subnormal intelligence in their early years but at a later age improve rapidly and end with average or higher-than average intelligence. This belief has no real foundation in fact. Classical instances are quoted of men and women who have achieved success and fame but who were backward in their schooldays. The evidence of backwardness rests only on their academic records; no intelligence tests were available when they were children. Closer study reveals that the intelligence was there all the time, though it was manifest outside rather than inside the school walls. It is true that where illness, dual handicap or environmental factors are impeding the manifestation of intelligence, special attention to those factors may improve the I.Q. by ten or even, occasionally, fifteen points, but the improvement is rarely more than that. What is important is that skilled assessment, including, where necessary, observation and investigation, will indicate what is wrong and point the way to its remedy.

## Care and Management

Good care for the mentally handicapped child, as for any other child with a handicap, must be founded on the parents' courageous and realistic acceptance of the situation and their intelligent co-operation. The factors which can impede this have been generally considered in Chapter 3 but certain special aspects of the matter need somewhat more detailed mention here.

The great majority of mentally subnormal children look perfectly normal at birth. Some of the more seriously handicapped ones will show early signs of their defect in the first weeks of life—reluctance to suck at the breast or bottle is one—but there are plenty of other explanations for such shortcomings. In most cases of moderate mental handicap the first real signs, such as slowness to reach the milestones of development, will not be recognizable before the middle of the first year. Normal variations among normal children make it necessary to allow a certain amount of margin and unless the defect is gross not even the expert will diagnose it with certainty until the end of the first year or the early part of the second. From the parents' point of view, they have started with what they considered to be a perfectly normal child. Other people may have suspected that something was wrong and may have told them of those suspicions, but there has been little evidence to convince *them*. They have known children who were late in sitting up, late in standing and late in walking and slow in beginning to talk but those children turned out all right in the end. Their own child is only a little slower and he is certainly making *some* progress.

The parent who wants to defer acknowledgement of his child's mental handicap has plenty of reasons for doing so and desire can fight a rearguard action against reason for years. Most parents do in fact want to defer that acknowledgement, and it is hard to blame them. It is bad enough to have to surrender one's ambitions and hopes for an eagerly-awaited child, but in the case of mental handicap the feelings of guilt which I have mentioned earlier seem to have exceptional significance. The widespread belief that mental subnormality is inherited has something to do with this; husband and wife each wonder whether it is their family which has produced the 'taint' and are not quite able to smother the suspicion that it is the other side of the family which is responsible. Venereal disease is associated in the popular mind with mental disability in the children, so that remorse for possible past sexual irregularities or fear that one's partner may have been unfaithful cannot be entirely suppressed. Feelings like these coupled with guilt over the use of contraceptives or vague attempts to terminate pregnancy or even over sex relations in general, combined with fears that later children may also be mentally handicapped, can build up to a formidable total.

The child has been accepted as a child before suspicions were aroused; it is the acceptance of the situation which is delayed. Some parents who are themselves notably dull can reconcile themselves to it quickly, but they are, of course, less likely to bring intelligence to their task. A minority of highly intelligent parents also accept quickly and do excellent work. But on the whole the parents of the mentally handicapped child are especially likely to go from one adviser to another seeking for crumbs of reassurance and clinging to the most tenuous hope that some mistake has been made.

It is a mistaken kindness to be otherwise than frank with them. There is no need for that frankness to be unnecessarily brutal, but to encourage the belief that the child will grow out of his disability is merely to make the inevitable realization harder when the time comes for it to be faced. No doctor likes to be the one to break the news and it is probably best for the family doctor to leave the task to a specialist, whether consultant paediatrician, psychiatrist or school medical officer. Certainly the parents will be more ready to believe someone with special knowledge and experience.

So long as there is reasonable doubt whether the child is normal it is probably best to keep silence, neither alarming the parents by voicing suspicions nor lulling them into optimism by insisting that he is normal. As soon, however, as the doubt is resolved the doctor should break the news gently but firmly, telling the parents that the child is going to be permanently backward. If he can broadly categorize the child, so much the better; he may indicate that the child will probably be educable to some extent, that though ineducable he may be capable of some training or that he is never likely to rise above infantile level. With the young child, however, up to the age of five or so, the error in estimating may be appreciable and it is best to be judiciously general in forecasting unless it is obvious that the child will be of very low mental grade indeed.

For all practical purposes of care in childhood the mentally subnormal fall into three groups, those who are so severely handicapped that they are certain to need institutional care for most of their lives, the idiots and imbeciles of the traditional classification, those who while ineducable are capable of training to a point at which they can lead happy and moderately useful lives if they are shielded from the crises and complications of existence and those who will be capable of being educated in special schools and becoming largely self-supporting.

For the first group in general the earlier the child can be taken into institutional care the better. Parents with feelings of guilt may compensate to themselves by lavishing extra affection on the child and becoming inordinately attached to him, so that the break, when it has to come, is considerably more painful. But, a point of more practical importance, the severely subnormal child demands so much care and attention for so much longer than the normal child that the other children of the family may be neglected and the strain on the mother lead to her breakdown. Where a grossly defective child is the first-born of normal, intelligent parents they may become so absorbed in his care that they do not dare to have the normal children whom they could have and whom they desperately want and need.

Both the other groups will normally spend their early years in their homes and, indeed, they should do so unless the parents are under stress from some other cause or are ill or disabled. The parents must appreciate that the children will grow and progress in the same way as normal children but at a much slower tempo, taking eighteen months, two years or even longer to do what a normal child does in one year. They will learn the simple skills of living slowly, needing longer and more patient teaching, but it is important that they should be given the chance to do so. The mother must resist the natural temptation to do things for the child rather than wait and teach him to do them himself; this will consume more time, but the time is invested and not just wasted. It is equally natural to keep the child at home rather than to take him out shopping and thus parade him before the neighbours, but going out with mother is part of every child's education.

Important difficulties, however, may arise in the home and in certain circumstances are almost inevitable. The mentally subnormal child with normal brothers and sisters may get on well with them up to a point and profit by their company. But there comes a point at which they begin to grow past him intellectually and from then on true companionship in the things which matter to children is no longer present. In other ways, family relationships may suffer. Edgar was the mentally handicapped child of normal parents. They were not educated beyond ordinary working-class standards but with a little help they faced their problems realistically and obtained a good deal of insight into them. The usual guilt reactions and fear to have other children were courageously overcome and when Edgar was three another son was born to them. For a time all promised well. Since Edgar's I.Q. was in the region of 50, his mental age was three when the new baby was chronologically three and in fact during the second and third years of the younger brother's life the two were more or less equals. Then Edgar saw his little brother growing beyond him into activities and relationships, including the fellowship of other children in the neighbourhood, for which he could not hope. He became moody, resentful and demanding. To some of his demands at least the mother had to yield, whereupon the younger brother began to show *his* resentment at being deprived of his proper share of mothering. The temporary admission of Edgar to a junior training centre by day made things a little easier, but the final improvement for both children did not come until he went on to a residential nursery school, by a generous dispensation which allowed him to go there after the normal age, and, later, to a boarding special school.

In some way or other, the home is always likely to need help after the mentally handicapped child reaches the chronological age of five and it may need such help even earlier. Understanding advice may meet the need for a considerable time but has its obvious limitations. The child must have the companionship of his equals and it is important to find a way in which this can be given. In some places small groups of parents of mentally retarded children find means of bringing their children together frequently. Training centres can make provision for 'infant' groups. A 'normal' nursery school or nursery class or a day nursery can often accept one or two children who are moderately mentally retarded, if the administration responsible is prepared to interpret its rules and regulations with a little elasticity.

To counteract some seeming pessimism in the foregoing, it is necessary to mention that in the majority of cases the difficulties which I have just mentioned are not very serious. As we saw at the start of the chapter, the number of children who are severely mentally handicapped is smaller than those who are slightly handicapped and many children with I.Q's. between 65 and 75, especially if born to parents who are not too intelligent and ambitious, may follow a pattern of development not too far removed from the average. Not until they start school at the age of five is their lack of intelligence disclosed by their inability to keep pace with the others in their class. As I have already suggested, there is much to be gained by allowing these children to go along the normal road with a minimum of interference, though they must be closely and unobtrusively watched. As their disability becomes manifest their educational future must be considered and planned for, with each case considered on its merits.

### Education and Training

The child of normal intelligence becomes ripe for the beginnings of education somewhere between the ages of four and six. It seems, in fact, that even simple systematic schooling requires a mental age of approximately four-and-a-half or five. The mentally handicapped child with an I.Q. between 60 and 75 will therefore be ready to start special education at about the age of seven. His response to it will initially depend very much upon what has been done to prepare him socially, in the home and outside it, in earlier years and if that preparation has been imperfect he will not merely get little profit from the special school in the early months but may be a disturbing influence in the school and thus impede the education of others.

The first year or so of ordinary education in most countries is not academically strenuous and for the substantial number of mentally handicapped children who make a start in an ordinary infant school there is no great urgency about transfer to a special school. Unless a child is grossly retarded or is showing serious behaviour disorders the first years of infant school life can be used as an assessment period, especially if he is in the hands of sympathetic teachers with not too large classes. At the age of seven-plus, when his contemporaries move on to the more academic 'junior' stage of education, he can transfer smoothly and without any disturbing break to the special school and a good deal of useful, practical knowledge about him can be passed on from the infant school to the special school.

It has been a considerable weakness in the British system that the provision of services for the mentally handicapped has been divided between the health departments and the education departments of the Local Authorities. It has been necessary administratively to classify children, as soon as their mental handicap was recognized, into those who were 'educable' and could therefore be admitted to appropriate special schools and those who were 'unsuitable for education' and would be admitted to training centres or institutions for the 'severely subnormal'. Broadly speaking, children with an I.Q. of 55 or over were classed as educable and those with an I.Q. below 45 as unsuitable for education.

This classification, intelligently applied, is not unreasonable as a provisional guide; the fault in the old system was that because of the administrative structure it was difficult to use it provisionally. Training centres, conceived as appropriate places for children who had little academic potential, provided very little education. As more became known about the effects of environmental and social factors on manifest intelligence it was realized that an appreciable number of children whose I.Q. was apparently in the region of 40 or lower had learning capacity equivalent to children with a substantially higher I.Q. It was also becoming recognized that there were children with an I.Q. which undoubtedly placed them in the 'educable' range but whose social development and behaviour would have made it difficult for them to fit into the regime of a special school.

It was obviously desirable for more education to be provided in training centres. It was also important to make arrangements for the less mentally handicapped who were socially immature to have the opportunity of a period of 'socialization' in the environment of a training centre before they were admitted to a special school; the administrative structure made it necessary for them to be formally classified as unsuitable for education before this could be done and formally re-classified as educable before they could be transferred to a special school. Not only could this cause delays, but it was understandable that parents would often resist this classification and refuse to accept a placement in a training centre. Some enlightened authorities introduced a policy of informal admission to a training centre, which made transfer easier when the time arrived for it to take place. Many authorities set up 'assessment units' which were linked to special schools but provided a regime half way between school and training centre and would admit children for six months or a year to see how they responded to that regime and defer final classification until the assessment period was over.

However, the logical solution was eventually adopted and training centres for children up to school leaving age are now under the management of the education authorities. 'Trial placements' and transfer between schools and training centres are now possible without administrative and legislative impediments and it has become the duty of the education authorities not only to expand the educational element in the training centre regime but to provide appropriate education in 'special care centres' and in hospitals for the mentally subnormal which provide for the more severely mentally handicapped and for those whose severe mental handicap is complicated by physical disability.

The principles of special education for mentally handicapped children may be inferred from what has already been said in this chapter. Learning in school is like learning to live; it consists of instruction and practice in dealing with situations, some of which can be more complicated than they might seem at first sight. A child may, for instance, have dealt successfully with some such arithmetical problem as 'George has three apples, Billy has two and Edward has four; how many apples are there altogether?' He now meets the question 'Mary has five oranges, Alice has one and Betty has three; how many oranges are there altogether?' Not only are the numbers different, but there has been a change of sex and a change of fruit; he has to decide which of the changes is relevant and which is not. The dull child will sit slowly worrying this out long after the brighter ones have grasped the idea that all that matters is the number. Or, the child has learned that 'rough' spells 'ruff' and 'tough' spells 'tuff'; meeting the word 'plough' he renders it as 'pluff'. If he is bright he will fairly soon grasp the idea that 'ough' can be pronounced in quite a variety of ways and will be prepared for almost anything. If he is dull he is more likely to be discouraged and feel that the English language is so full of pitfalls that it is not worth trying to learn it.

The more concrete instruction can be and the less it has to do with abstract ideas the better will be its results with the young retarded child. While boys and girls or apples and oranges may make arithmetic more appetising for brighter children, the duller ones will make a better start if they learn by manipulating blocks, rods of differing lengths and other objects. And in the reading field, it is not surprising that some teachers of backward children are finding that the Initial Teaching Alphabet, which takes some of the worst inconsistencies out of English spelling, is enabling them to make better progress. The school must in general take the child along the road of learning in shorter steps than the average and must be prepared to repeat steps time and again as may be needed. The pace which is set must not be so slow that he does not feel the satisfaction of making progress nor yet so fast that he feels that he is failing to keep up; either of these may well bring him to a halt. One must reach the compromise which is right not only for the individual child but for the child at the particular age and stage of development. Small classes, flexible organization and infinite patience in all the staff are important.

The ultimate target should be based on the child's capacity, remembering that even if his I.Q. is as low as 60 he will come in the end to a mental age of nine or thereabouts and that the simple skills of the 'three R's' should be within his reach. But he will also need to be educated in those basic practical aspects of daily living which most children pick up in their stride and, since he must rely on body rather than brain for earning a living, there should be stress on the crafts and manual work.

Should the educable mentally handicapped child go to a day school or to a boarding school? Because mental handicap is common, day school provision is made on a large scale in most countries which have seriously attacked the problem and the difficulty of finding a day special school within a reasonable distance of the child's home is less than in many other kinds of handicap. In the majority of cases the decision will depend upon the nature and quality of the home. If the home is sound and stable and the parents have a matter-of-fact approach to the child, then the day school is undoubtedly the answer. Unfortunately, the parents of some subnormal children are themselves notably unintelligent and are feckless and incompetent in the home; where this is so, boarding education is often to be preferred. The intelligent parent who is not reconciled to the child's disability may not be able to provide what is needed at home, and the same may be true of the intelligent parent whose feelings of guilt or whose rejection of the child are producing stress and strain in the home. In the case of the retarded child who has very clever brothers and sisters, the return each evening from the place where he is among his equals to the place where his inferiority is only too manifest may be a cause of emotional disturbance. In such families, boarding education may be the answer.

Special problems may arise in the case of the child living in the village or very small town. If the nearest day special school is ten or fifteen miles away, transport problems are serious. A child with a mental age of six and with limited social experience cannot be expected to travel alone by public transport and the provision of special transport may be impracticably costly. The arguments advanced against private tuition in the home for children with various other handicaps are valid for the mentally handicapped child; it should be used only as a last resort and then preferably as a temporary measure. Even in these days of increasingly mechanized farming, the rural community can still provide suitable work for the occasional simpleton and can and does still take the simpleton to its heart and regard him as a village responsibility. To break the link with a good home and a community by sending him to a boarding school is something not to be lightly undertaken. The good village school is often ready to accept him and is able to give him something educationally up to the age of eleven or twelve and it is often wise policy to leave him there until that age when, if his handicap is not too severe, he may be able to use public transport to a day special school. If he does not reach this stage of independence, it is still worth while to see if an ordinary school near his home can tolerate him, though boarding education must be used in the end, as the lesser evil, if nothing else can be found.

Whatever terminology we use—and however kindly we may intend it to spare the feelings of the handicapped—there is no getting away from some basic truths. In the sophisticated and industrialized society of the western world a certain degree of literacy, of technical skill and of social understanding is needed if one is to be economically self-supporting and able to 'manage oneself and one's affairs', a phrase which must include being able to cope with the machinations of the social predators who live by taking advantage of their neighbours. For these practical purposes there will always be some people who are not only academically but socially ineducable. The training centre, originally known as the 'occupation centre' and intended to keep the mentally handicapped out of mischief and relieve the parents of part of the burden of their care, has made its task much more one of training in basic social skills and in comparatively simple and semi-skilled crafts. This is realistic. If a handicapped person cannot be economically self-supporting it is nevertheless worth while to make him less dependent on others for support and protection, partly to take some of the load off the others but, no less important, to give him some sense of usefulness and also to make him more socially acceptable. It is a sense of uselessness and a feeling that one is not socially tolerated that so commonly lead the mentally handicapped into unsocial or downright anti-social behaviour.

The day training centre has been standard practice. It is open to the same objections as day special schools. It may be too far away from the child's home for him to travel daily, an important point since the training centre child has a lower mental age than the special school child. If the home is unsatisfactory, then lack of home co-operation with the training centre reduces the effectiveness of what is being done. The child's low intelligence level may make it difficult for him to establish any social contacts with his contemporaries near his home and he will, of course, be a more serious problem for his parents than the educable mentally handicapped youngster. Residential training centres and hostels associated with training centres are so far only in the experimental stage, but their potentialities are considerable and are well worth exploring.

Institutional care has been provided on a large scale for the severely mentally handicapped and has, indeed, been suc- more severely mentally handicapped and has, indeed, been successful in a way and up to a point. For the child who is obviously going to be permanently dependent upon others, especially if his natural home is not going to be able to give him adequate support, it makes adequate provision. The difficulty is that for many mentally handicapped children it is impossible to make an accurate forecast on these points. Certainly for the most severely handicapped it is as good a type of provision as has so far been found, but for the more numerous children and young people who lie within the I.Q. range of 40 to 55 it is always possible that something else might be found which would be more suitable to their needs. Institutional care is, however, so much a long-term matter that it is perhaps better considered in the next section of this chapter.

### The Prospect for the Mentally Handicapped

The outlook for the subnormal person is by no means as bleak as it sometimes appears, but great care and hard work are required from those responsible for helping him.

Employment ought to present no very great problem, if the person is physically fit. It is true that machines are increasingly taking over the function of the unskilled worker, but some unskilled labour will always remain to be done. Mechanization itself is now reaching a point at which the machine often does the really skilled part of the work and the man or woman is a semi-skilled machine-minder or a performer of simple repetitive work. More than a few industrial jobs are so dully repetitive, in fact, that they would be intolerable to a person of intelligence and imagination. Domestic service in hospitals, hostels and other large establishments can be organized so that one skilled person supervises and organizes the work of a number of unskilled ones who may quite happily and quite effectively carry out the routine chores.

Careers advisers, however, report substantial difficulty in placing mentally handicapped boys in industrial work and girls in other than domestic work. The reasons which employers give for reluctance to accept the mentally handicapped are probably not always the true ones, and alleged incompetence may cover a multitude of things. The prejudices and fears of fellow-workers are certainly of some significance. These, and the employer's preconceived idea that a mentally subnormal person cannot be an efficient worker probably prevent many of these youngsters from getting a fair trial. The important thing is that any type of work, however unskilled it may appear, has to be learned. The adolescent of average intelligence learns it so quickly that those who teach him do not realize that they are teaching. The mentally subnormal boy or girl will learn it more slowly and will have to be taught deliberately. When the employer, the foreman and charge-hand in the workshop and the housekeeper in the hostel or hospital appreciate this, things seem to work out quite well. The point certainly emphasizes the desirability of the child being given an introduction to simple manual or domestic work in the school or training centre.

Such an introduction has other functions besides training; it allows for some exploration of special disabilities or aptitudes. While serious mental subnormality is usually associated with a depression of all the various faculties which go to make up 'intelligence', that depression may not be uniform over the whole range. Thus of a group of mentally handicapped people of similar overall intelligence some will be better than others in rote memory or in spatial discrimination and some more capable than others of reading or doing simple arithmetic. There is also considerable temperamental variation—some are more patient, more biddable and more amenable to teaching than are others.

The range of work which the mentally handicapped can do and the quality of that work is somewhat surprising to the uninitiated and can lead to false hopes and errors of assessment. What I said at the beginning of this chapter about the nature of intelligence will explain this. Much work of even a fairly skilled character is largely repetitive; even those who practice the learned professions spend a great deal of their time applying routine techniques to familiar problems and thus solve those problems without needing to take much special thought. For success, however, it is necessary to be able to distinguish the familiar situation from the unfamiliar one and it is precisely this that the mentally subnormal person finds it hard or impossible to do. Where the work involves planning ahead and dealing with possible or hypothetical situations he is at an even greater disadvantage. Thus, a man may be able to earn a living wage by unskilled labour—he may even, because he is lacking in imagination and ambition, do that work more thoroughly or uncomplainingly than a highly intelligent person— but he may still be incapable of laying out his earnings to his own best advantage, the victim of his own caprice or the cunning of others.

A woman may be a competent houseworker yet quite unable to deal with the recurrent major and even minor crises which are an inevitable part of the bringing up of children. The brightness of the prospect depends not upon earning capacity but upon social capacity, which determines social competence.

The mentally handicapped person will be able to lead a successful life only if he is placed in surroundings which will materially reduce the chance of his finding himself in an unfamiliar and difficult situation or if there is some person or organization always at hand to provide, when necessary, the judgement which he lacks. The good home can provide those surroundings and help, but it may not unaided be able to give the specially skilled help which is sometimes needed and as the child grows through adolescence and becomes adult the burden on the other members of the family may become very heavy. In the past, many markedly mentally handicapped children did not survive childhood but recent advances in medicine and surgery have made it probable that most of the mentally handicapped will outlive their parents and thus reach a point at which the support and protection of the family is no longer available.

The mental deficiency institution, for these and for other obvious reasons which need not be laboured, has hitherto been a ready solution to the problem. It provides a simple routine life with no anxieties, it allows the patient to do some sort of more or less useful work and it prevents him from straying into the community to the risk of himself and others. It is there permanently and there need be no anxieties about what might befall the inmate if his relatives die. For many of the severely subnormal it may very well be the best thing, but of late there has been much discussion as to whether institutional care is the most effective, the most economical or the most humane provision for those only moderately handicapped. Experiments in release on licence, over a considerable number of years, have proved that suitable patients, while nominally under the care of an institution, can be boarded out in families or in such places as general and special hospitals where they do domestic work, gardening and the like. Because of the shortage of institutional accommodation, attempts have been made to employ social workers—mental health officers—to help families to care for their mentally handicapped adolescent or adult son or daughter whose case was not sufficiently urgent to secure quick admission to an institution.

Out of this experience, as well as out of rarer trials of such things as hostels for the mentally subnormal, village communities where they mix with normal people and 'fostering out' in families, there is growing a new concept of community care. Expert opinion in Britain is that perhaps one-third of the patients in mental deficiency hospitals need something less than the complete care those hospitals provide and that given competent guardianship outside the hospital they may be able to become self-supporting in employment and lead reasonably normal private lives. Such radical advances toward community care will be successful only when hostels have been built and staffed, when expert social workers are available in large numbers, when the people who will care for the mentally handicapped, whether hostel staffs, foster parents or their own natural parents have had some training and when the prejudices of the public at large have been broken down, but the development of community care certainly offers exciting possibilities. Perhaps those countries which are only now developing their services and are not yet committed to an institutional policy may have an opportunity to take the lead.

For those severely mentally handicapped people who are still going to need hospital care, the question of marriage does not arise. For those living in the community—including many who are only moderately handicapped—marriage, however, is an important question. Some are so obviously handicapped and so unattractive in appearance that they are unlikely to find a partner, but it is possible for a mentally handicapped person to be quite good-looking and to have a shallow vivacity which is quite attractive to someone without critical tastes. Again, as I comment in another place, the mentally subnormal girl stands a higher-than-average chance of becoming illegitimately pregnant and being faced with the prospect of a 'shotgun marriage'.

The risk of producing mentally handicapped offspring is not a valid reason for generally prohibiting the marriage of those affected. We know that much severe subnormality is not inherited. There is also, according to geneticists, a tendency to 'regress toward the mean' by which it seems that parents who depart from the average in either direction are quite likely to have children somewhat nearer to the average. In simple language, this means that if two moderately mentally handicapped people mate, their children are likely to be no more severely handicapped than either parent and may be slightly less so. The sterilization of mentally handicapped persons, often advocated by ill-informed enthusiasts, would not greatly reduce the number of mentally subnormal members of the community.

The strongest argument against their marriage is just that question of social competence which has been considered above. Study of 'problem families' has shown that in a majority of the families which fail to fulfil their function of bringing up the child satisfactorily and become largely dependent on public support, even to the extent of the children being taken from the home into the care of public authorities, the mother is significantly mentally handicapped. It is the mother's handicap which seems critical. A man of modest intelligence who is fortunate enough to marry a normally intelligent and capable woman may have little serious difficulty in life; he will earn enough to provide for most of the family's material needs and his wife will manage the household affairs and look after the children. But a husband, however intelligent, who has to work at a whole-time job cannot also run the home and look after the children if his wife is mentally handicapped and unable to do more than simple cleaning, cooking and so on. The conclusion is inescapable that marriage for the mentally handicapped girl is fraught with risk for her children and for the community if not for herself.

## Delinquency and Subnormality

The association between delinquency and subnormality cannot be dismissed with cursory consideration. It is a matter of observed fact that the proportion of mentally subnormal men and women among the population of our gaols is higher than in the general population. Studies of juvenile delinquency also show a high correspondence between anti-social conduct and backwardness. The statutory classification of mental defectives until recently included a group of 'moral defectives', those who combine mental defect with 'strong criminal or vicious propensities.'

It was formerly believed that criminal tendencies as such were inheritable, and nineteenth century observers, notably Lombroso in Italy, but including also Galton in this country, thought in terms of hereditary 'criminal types', even going so far as to indicate that certain minor physical peculiarities were indicative of the types. Parallel with these theories went a belief in an inborn 'moral sense' which enabled the normal person to distinguish right from wrong, the original moral defective being a person in whom that sense was inherently defective or absent. Neither of these beliefs is now tenable in its original form and few would dare to advocate them, but there is still enough of the old superstitions remaining for persons who hold otherwise balanced views to believe that moral defect, in terms of its present definition, is sufficiently constantly inherited to justify sterilization of the moral defective.

There is little, if any, foundation in fact for such a belief. Certain well-known nineteenth-century studies of families certainly showed that moral defect appeared in successive generations of the same family, but the data on which the studies were based were incomplete and open to serious criticism. In no instance has it been possible to show undisputably that apparent inheritance of moral defect could not have been equally due to the effects of environment upon a person who had inherited nothing more sinister than simple mental subnormality.

How, then, does the association between delinquency and subnormality arise? Part of it may well be apparent rather than real. Statistics show only those crimes which are recognized as such and only those offenders who are found guilty of offending. There is no doubt that many intelligent people are able to break the law without detection and with impunity over long periods in ways which are outside the compass of the subnormal; these latter are capable only of the simpler and thus more easily detected offences. Again, in any group of persons committing the same offences, those of lower mentality are likely to be the ones who are caught. These considerations apart, however, there are certain definite and well-known processes which are likely to bring the person of low intelligence into delinquency.

The first of these is purely social in its mechanism. Every human being must earn a living somehow, but to earn an honest living in twentieth century urban England demands some measure of strength, intelligence and skill. If it is difficult for an individual to earn an honest living—to find and keep a good job—he will drift into the ranks of the wasters, whose chief concern is to live without working, and will come to imitate their practices. In short, the defective, being unacceptable to the respectable sections of society, is forced into bad company, with the natural consequences.

The second factor is one to which reference has already been made, the readiness with which the defective follows the lead of others. He can be the ideal catspaw for the gang of children, adolescents or adults, doing what he is told to do without understanding its full significance and implications.

This latter consideration is an important factor in its own right. Every child learns the laws of cause and effect by bitter experience—fire burns, glass breaks and knives cut. At every age he—or she—is liable to make errors of judgement because of failure to foresee the more remote causes of an action or mission. Playing around a parked car may precipitate a serious road accident; the leaving open of a gate may lead to the ruin of a farmer's crop. In many ways, what is regarded as delinquency in an adult may be childish thoughtlessness or experiment in a child of nine or ten. But the defective is, as he grows up, a child of ten faced with the responsibilities of an adult and because he cannot bear those responsibilities he will act in ways which, for one of his chrono-logical age, are unsocial or anti-social, or, in the more formal language of the law 'show criminal or vicious propensities'.

This is notably the case where sex delinquency is involved. It is natural and normal for a child to have sexual curiosity and to experiment in order to gratify that curiosity. Fortunately, by the time a boy or girl reaches puberty the normal intelligence is sufficiently developed to permit some understanding of the social implications of sex and the development of acceptable standards of behaviour. When, however, puberty bursts upon the subnormal adolescent, all its bewildering urges have nothing to control and direct them but the mentality and understanding of a much younger child.

Again, the mentally subnormal youngster is a misfit in what ought to be his normal social setting. Neither in lessons nor in play can he compete on equal terms with his contemporaries, while he is too big physically to mix acceptably with children of his mental age. Robbed, therefore, of the normal outlets for his energies he seeks substitutes. Again, since it is in the nature of a child to vie with his fellows, he may try to outdo them and justify himself to himself in some activity in which he can be successful.

An appropriate and typical illustrative case was that of Sammy, aged twelve, who was brought to my notice by a clergyman to whom his mother had taken her troubles. For some years after the death of the father Sammy, his older brother and the mother had lived in tranquillity but Sammy had suddenly taken to stealing and had become quite an accomplished bicycle thief. It seemed, at first sight, that his motive was simple cash gain, since he also stole small sums of money and invariably sold the bicycles he stole. Further enquiry showed that most of the money was spent on cigarettes, of which he gave most away to his schoolfellows, keeping only a few for himself. His school career had appeared normal and his teachers were as shocked and surprised as anyone else when they discovered his offences.

On examination he was a bright, cheerful, co-operative lad with an I.Q. of 75. His brother, whose I.Q. was 105, was two years older and had just left school. Sammy had followed his brother through successive classes while teachers could still remember him, and Sammy's comparative failure in class was ascribed to laziness, so that he was constantly being exhorted to follow his brother's example and do better. He could not do better at school, but he found an out-of-school activity in which he was undoubtedly successful. Furthermore, by becoming a generous provider of forbidden cigarettes to his schoolfellows he obtained a substantial position in the boys' hierarchy. Moved to another school, where his brother's shadow did not fall on him and where his history was unknown except to the head master, he finished his schooling in a 'C' class with modest effectiveness and after leaving school he was successfully placed, with some appropriateness, in the shop of a local cycle dealer, where he turned out to be a steady assistant and mechanic.

Last among the major factors, but by no means the least of them, is the influence of the home. It is a truism—but a profound truth—that it is in the home that standards of conduct are determined. Most mentally subnormal children come from homes in which one or both of the parents is also subnormal, homes, therefore, in which care and management of the children are likely to fall substantially below what is desirable. A normally intelligent child in such a home would be unlikely to receive the informal education in good social conduct which he needs and would be in danger of becoming un-social or anti-social; a subnormal child never has a chance. He inherits the parents' low intelligence, but he follows the pattern of their life by unconscious imitation.

Probably the best way of summing up the whole of this question of delinquency among the mentally subnormal is along these lines. Society is a complex and highly artificial thing, whose rules are far removed from the simple logic which a child's mind can under-stand. There are times and places and degrees in which certain actions are good, neutral or, at worst, venial, but there are other times, places and degrees in which those actions are anti-social or criminal. The good citizen is the one who has learnt when and where to do certain things and where to draw the line; the delin-quent is the one who has not learnt that lesson. The moral defective is not lacking in inborn moral sense. He is simply defective in social understanding.

## FURTHER READING

*Mental Subnormality*

Adams, M.   The Mentally Subnormal.   Heinemann Medical Books Ltd.

Buck, P. S.   The Child Who Never Grew.   Methuen.

Cheshire Education Committee.   The Education of Dull Children.   University of London Press.

Clarke, A. M. and A. D. B.   Mental Deficiency, the Changing Outlook.   Methuen.

Gulliford, R.   Backwardness and Educational Failure.   National Foundation for Educational Research, London.

Gunzburg, H. C.   Social Rehabilitation of the Subnormal.   Bailliere, Tindall & Cox.

Levinson, A.   The Mentally Retarded Child.   Allen and Unwin.

Loewy, H.   Training the Backward Child.   Staples Press.

Loewy, H.   The Retarded Child.   Staples.

Minski, L.   Deafness, Mutism and Mental Deficiency.   Heinemann Medical Books Ltd.

O'Connor, N. and Tizard, J.   Social Problems of Mental Deficiency.   Pergamon Press.

Schonell, F. J., Richardson, J. A. & McConnel, T. S.   The Subnormal Child at Home.   Macmillan.

Tansley, A. E. and Gulliford, R.   The Education of Slow Learning Children.   Routledge & Kegan Paul, London.

The National Association for Mental Health has published numerous advisory leaflets and booklets on this subject.

# CHAPTER 19

# Maladjustment

The terms used by doctors in describing mental illness are as yet very imprecise. They all relate to degrees and types of emotional disturbance and though there are certain types of severe disturbance which can be given specific labels, it is still difficult, even in dealing with these, to be sure whether the severity of the condition justifies the use of the term concerned. The most severe degrees and types are the psychoses. Some of these are due to toxic or infective conditions but they may also be due to disorder of function. The neuroses are less severe in degree and are probably due to failure in function rather than to organic damage. Because all kinds of mental illness involve failure to fit into the community and develop satisfactory relationships with other people, they can be regarded as evidence of 'maladjustment'.

A few children are sufficiently mentally ill to be truly called psychotic; reference is made to these in Chapter 22. Most emotional trouble in childhood is, however, much less severe than this. It is possible—indeed probable—that many disturbed children are in the early stages of a process which, if nothing is done about it, may lead on to the development of neurosis and even psychosis. It is equally possible that many of them may be going through a temporary phase of trouble which could resolve itself without specific help. Because, however, it is difficult to be sure in the early stages what the outcome is likely to be, maladjustment in childhood is something which must be taken seriously.

It is easy enough to indicate a general definition of maladjustment but well-nigh impossible to find a precise one. The word itself, with its suggestion of failing to 'fit in', is apt enough; human life is not a matter of mere physical existence but involves the delicate art of living with other people. We are all born individuals, conscious of nothing outside our immediate personal needs, yet we must learn to give as well as to take and to balance our personal desires against the desires and the necessities of others. We are all born utterly dependent on others, yet we must learn to achieve a good deal of independence and to be stable enough for others to depend upon us. Inevitably some people fail in one or both of these and the failures—the misfits and the immature—are those who have been 'unable to adjust'.

In every other field of handicap there is some recognizable standard of normality or at least of average powers or attainments. In the emotional field there are no such standards. Very little of the irregular behaviour of a maladjusted child is absolutely wrong. Aggressiveness, for example, is a natural human characteristic which is often of positive value and the aggressive maladjusted child is merely showing a normal quality at the wrong time or in the wrong circumstances. Bedwetting is often a symptom of maladjustment, but all children wet their beds in their early years and achieve control over their bladders only as they grow older. It is perfectly normal for that control to be lost occasionally by a perfectly normal older child or adolescent. Every parent knows what an irregular process is the growing up of a child and how at any time the baby may bewilderingly appear in the would-be adult teen-ager.

Some people have tried to define adjustment in terms of conformity, but such a definition, though attractive, has its dangers. The person who does not conform can be a nuisance to himself and to others but in a society in which all conform there is no progress; cranks and eccentrics are as important in the working of the social machine as they are in the working of the motor-car. In any case, who in a diverse community shall say what is the standard to which the individual should conform? Some eccentricity or irregularity is often the safety-valve which makes it possible for the individual to conform in the remainder of his life.

Perhaps we may think of the mentally healthy person as one who is leading a reasonably happy personal life, who is fulfilling his social duties to his family and the community without undue strain and whose behaviour does not interfere with the happiness and well-being of others. If we accept this, then we may define the maladjusted child in practical terms as one who is having so much difficulty in progressing toward this end that he needs the help of someone with special skill and experience.

## Causation
It is no less difficult to set out in precise and logical form the causes

of maladjustment. To begin with, there is no clear understanding of the parts played by heredity and environment. In the nineteenth century much stress was laid on hereditary factors and some classical family studies seemed to give support to the idea that they were paramount, but reconsideration of these studies suggests that the importance of environment was underrated.

Some eminent authorities believe that certain qualities of temperament can be inherited but it can be argued that these traits may also be infectious in the sense that a child is very likely to imitate the characteristics of the parents with whom he lives. Probably the most that can be said with certainty is that some people are inherently more emotionally stable than others and that some quality of stability can be passed from parent to child. Stability, however, is always relative and in the end depends not only on what is inborn but on the kind and degree of the forces which play upon it. It is also worth remembering that unstable parents will have difficulty in providing their child with a stable home environment in his formative years.

It is in the home and in the early years of life that maladjustment begins. Emotional development is essentially a matter of learning to live with other people. The child learns by experience, which is a process of trial and error. He begins in the limited circle of parents and brothers and sisters. Then he grows into the 'outer circle' of the family—the uncles and aunts, cousins and grandparents—and graduates into the wider world of the neighbours' children and, in due course, school. During the process he has experience of both his contemporaries and his elders and he is able to make his first mistakes in an atmosphere of love, tolerance and understanding rather than under the strictly critical eye of strangers. This growing out process applies not only to matters of personal relationships but to questions of social conduct; it is, indeed, often hard to say where one ends and the other begins. The family must, therefore, provide not only love and understanding but standards of truthfulness, standards of respect for persons and property and standards of ethics and morals. It is not enough for the family to provide a miniature world for the child to grow in. It must also interpret the outside world to the child in terms which he can comprehend.

In the beginning the child has a close and exclusive relationship with the mother. If he is to develop satisfactorily, this must become less close and exclusive as relationships with other people begin and extend. Much the same applies to the home as a whole. It is his entire world for a start but it must progressively turn into a secure base from which he can venture out into the world at large and to which he can come back for rest, refreshment and the tending of his emotional wounds. The term 'emotional wounds' is used deliberately. As the physical body learns to protect itself against infections by repeatedly taking in doses of infection small enough to do no lasting harm and as the individual learns to guard himself against accidents by discovering that hot things burn and sharp things cut, so the mind learns to deal with the shocks and stresses of living by suffering and overcoming minor emotional injuries.

The incomplete family will obviously have difficulty in giving the child what he needs. It is incomplete if either parent is missing, or if the child has no brothers and sisters. If one parent is absent from home for long periods, as when the father is a sailor, or if the intervals between the birth of the children are too long, the problem of incompleteness can arise in quite a serious degree. Even the absence of an outer circle in the family may cause difficulties.

The emotionally insecure family is a potent producer of maladjustment. It is unnatural for parents to be unwaveringly patient and long-suffering day in and day out—it is, indeed, salutary for a child to discover that even father and mother can sometimes be pushed to exasperation—but it is important that they can be fundamentally reliable in crises. If the child 'never knows where he is' with his parents then he has no secure base for his ventures.

The importance of the mother-child relationship has been greatly stressed in recent years, probably to a point at which the dangers of separating mother from child have been over-rated. Sooner or later he must become independent; what matters is that the process must be a gradual one. There is no doubt that sudden separation at too early an age may do serious damage, but to preserve the exclusiveness of the mother-child relationship for too long is to pave the way for equally serious damage when separation inevitably comes. Essentially, emotional upset in itself is not dangerous. What really matters is that the child shall not suffer emotional shocks for which he has not been prepared and to meet which he is not sufficiently mature.

It is often possible to associate the onset of maladjustment with some single outstanding emotional shock such as removal to hospital, loss of or long separation from the mother, or the birth of another child into the family, but it may be that in such cases the spectacular event merely brings to a head the effect of lesser shocks long continued or of the wear and tear of chronic insecurity. There is good reason to believe that children who are already well adjusted can survive without lasting emotional damage experiences which would in theory be likely to be very damaging indeed.

Most maladjustment shows itself after the child is of school age. It is probable that this is partly due to the fact that when he starts school the child comes under skilled observation and that had such observation been exercised beforehand the diagnosis would have been made sooner. But this is only part of the story. Going to school is one of the major events in a child's life and involves a radical change in his way of living. Quite suddenly he has to spend a large part of his waking life on his own among strangers who are likely to be less indulgent than his family. He has to fit into a system which is necessarily less elastic than his home. If he is unable to cope with this situation he becomes unpopular with his schoolmates and his teachers. The more unpopular he is the less happy he becomes and the harder he finds it to adjust, whereupon his acceptability to children and teachers is lessened and a vicious spiral begins, sooner or later producing gross emotional disturbance.

The whole of this outline has necessarily over-simplified the picture. It is possible, if not common, for an ill-adjusted child to find in the system and discipline of school a security which he has sought in vain in his early years at home, and to go on spontaneously to fairly good adjustment. Or, some special adverse factor in a particular school may initiate maladjustment in a child who has hitherto been quite well adjusted. In general, however, one finds some evidence of pre-school failure to adjust and as that failure becomes worse during school life the blame for it lies partly on the home and partly on the school.

## Assessment

The assessment of maladjustment is a highly delicate and specialized business and the psychiatrist plays a greater part in it than do the physicians and surgeons in other types of handicap. This is because the handicap and the illness which produces it are quite inseparable. The care of the maladjusted child, social and educational, is a great part of the treatment of his emotional ill-health. Though the school medical officer, the family doctor, the school nurse and the teacher can contribute, the child guidance team of psychiatrist, psychologist and psychiatric social worker will do the bulk of the work and will be mainly responsible for advising on care, treatment and management.

Diagnosis is easier as the trouble becomes more marked; for reasons already mentioned it is often almost impossible to say whether slight or occasional departures from the normal are really evidence of true maladjustment. One is, indeed, continuously adjusting throughout life and the only way of discovering whether a phase of emotional disturbance is going to persist or is a natural phenomenon which is about to resolve itself may be to wait and see. If there are obvious factors in the child's background which would predispose to instability, the chance of the trouble resolving itself is less and action of some kind is indicated.

When maladjustment is established, the identification of its causes is important. In no part of medicine can treatment be started with optimism and confidence if the causes of the illness continue to operate and this is probably truest in psychiatry. Psychiatric treatment can never cure mental illness in the sense in which, say, an antibiotic can cure an infectious illness. It can, in many cases, help considerably but it must fail or its effects will not last unless the child's emotional surroundings can be modified. Even where an emotional shock has been the principal cause it is impossible to let the child start life anew as a baby and re-live it without the shock. The contribution of home and school to the maladjustment must be carefully assessed and their susceptibility to advice and their ability to change in the child's interests have to be minutely considered.

## Management and Education

Most maladjusted children improve considerably with treatment in a child guidance clinic combined with more understanding care at home and in an ordinary school. It is not possible to give any general rules for such care because what each individual child needs must be worked out in detail for his particular case. The important thing is that home, school and clinic must co-operate and collaborate and that neither parents nor teachers must expect quick results nor be disappointed by slow ones. In a substantial minority of cases, however, either it is obvious from the start that something else is needed or it quickly becomes clear that the clinic, the home and the school are failing to produce results. At the present time in Britain this can occur in as many as thirty per cent of children referred to a clinic. No doubt it often happens that a child comes to the clinic too late and that had he been referred earlier it would have been much easier to help him; the moral is plain. At present, however, it is necessary to face facts and to make special provision.

A very few maladjusted children have reached a point at which they need urgent admission to a hospital unit, for they have passed beyond simple maladjustment into the early stages of frank mental illness. But as a rule, special provision is made by boarding the child with foster-parents, by sending him to a special hostel, by sending him to a special school or by combinations of these means. The principles behind their discerning use follow from what has already been said about the causation of maladjustment.

If a child is emotionally disturbed because of something in his home background and if that flaw is ineradicable or the parents are unable or unwilling to co-operate in treating him, then it is most unlikely that he will make any progress so long as he stays at home and he must obviously leave home and live somewhere else. Where he goes to will depend on whether difficulties at school are also contributing to his troubles. It is, rarely, a good idea for him to leave home but to continue to live in the same district and attend the same school. Sometimes this works well but more often it is likely to set up conflicts and confusions since he is living partly his old life and partly a new one.

He may live with foster-parents and attend an ordinary school. With the right foster-parents, who may, in fact, be relatives, this sometimes works excellently. There are, however, dangers. It is far from easy to find parents who are willing to take a disturbed child into their home from another family and willing parents may not be suited to a given child's needs. Even if the parents are suitable there may be incompatibilities between their own child or children and the newcomer. For the child himself there is the possibility that contrasts and comparisons between the new home and the old will be confusing and disturbing.

Philip, aged ten, had been brought up in a home where his artist father was absorbed in his work and his mother was more than slightly neurotic. His upbringing in his home was partly under the tutelage of two aunts, neither notably stable, who regarded him as dull and stupid and had produced a chronic feeling of inferiority. Various war-time upheavals had helped to make things worse so that he was neurotic, withdrawn yet aggressive, a complete failure both at home and in school. Arrangements were made for him to stay indefinitely with distant relations—distant in both kinship and location. He reacted favourably to the novelty of new home and new school and with special tuition made good progress. Though he remained a little 'odd' he acquired friends and seemed to be progressing toward normality. As puberty developed, troubles began. His education continued satisfactorily but his behaviour at home was unpredictable and serious food neuroses appeared. It was plain that he was benefiting in many ways but that the new home, good as it was, had not replaced in his mind his own natural home, which he had idealized as time went on. His doctor foster-father and the psychiatrist decided that in spite of this he should stay away from his natural home until he was a little older and their decision proved right in the event. When in the end he returned home at fifteen, though it was a return to the unstable environment he had left he was better able to deal with it. In particular, the five-year break from the aunts, who now found him a young man and not the child whom they had treated as a baby, was salutary. He was able to form a new relationship and had gathered confidence enough to stand up for himself. Fifteen years later, though not without stormy periods, he has passed with flying colours the examinations for a profession in which he already shows promise of a distinguished career. (The foster-family, incidentally, suffered no lasting harm from an experience which had some exceedingly trying phases!)

For most severely maladjusted children, however, the educational side of the problem is so serious that the boarding special school is considered the best place in which to seek help. Such schools vary considerably in character. The pioneer schools were small establishments of the 'free discipline' or 'no discipline' type but experience over the past twenty years or so has brought about interesting modifications. The conspicuous success of some early workers who used 'free' methods was followed by the equally conspicuous failure of some of their imitators, suggesting that the personality of the worker was at least as important as the technique which he used. It would also seem that for some maladjusted children a certain amount of discipline and regulation is necessary, perhaps to help them to a feeling of security.

None the less, the schools have something in common. They are all small, because the pupils need individual care and help and it is important to avoid an institutional and impersonal atmosphere. Their curricula are elastic. Some have no fixed time-table whatever, while others have a set time-table for certain basic subjects but allow a great deal of elasticity in the remaining subjects. The intention in either case is that the child's interest may be captured by the subjects he likes or the teacher he likes and that he may be led from that point toward more orthodox education. In all the schools class gradations are indefinite, so that a child who is notably backward in certain subjects can be taught those subjects at his own level instead of having to compete with contemporaries who are more advanced.

It is usual to allow the pupils some measure of self-government, since a constant feature of maladjustment is a tendency to rebel against authority. A common finding is that a child who resents and resists the rule of adults will acquiesce without much difficulty in a no less strict rule imposed by his equals. Most of these schools, by a process of trial and error, have decided which are the points that can fairly and safely be left to a committee of the children and which must still be under the absolute jurisdiction of the staff, though the details of the division vary from school to school and depend much on staff personalities. Art, crafts and creative and constructional activities are usually prominent. Not only do they attract the youngster who is allergic to academic activities but they provide an emotional satisfaction which means much to him. The range is wide—one school, for instance, had remarkable success with boat-building under the direction of an enthusiastic master. Which leads to the final and, perhaps, critical, common point; all these schools are staffed by understanding enthusiasts and on the maintenance of staff quality much, if not all, depends.

The case of Barry is a pretty example of how special schools work at their best. Considerably disturbed, educationally backward, hard to control and already venturing into delinquency he was taken from his unstable home and placed with foster-parents. He remained a failure at school and twice ran away from his new home. Introduced to a special school he showed no interest whatever in school subjects but gradually developed a liking for woodwork. The need for accuracy of measurement made him reluctantly embark on simple arithmetic, while he began to see reading also as a means to the end of pursuing his hobby. Slowly he began to fit into the elastic school curriculum, which adjusted itself to his waxing interests, but he remained unruly and a law unto himself. His exasperated schoolfellows ingeniously elected him to the children's committee and almost overnight he started to respect the rules which he was now expected to help to make and enforce. He ended his school career with only average academic performance but had risen to the chairmanship of the committee and was conspicuous as a steadying influence.

It would seem that one of the most important factors in the success of a special school for maladjusted children is the presence of a nucleus of children who have found their way to adjustment. Their influence slowly convinces newcomers that it is not merely proper but is actively pleasant to fit in. The new school takes time to develop such a nucleus and it sometimes happens that the simultaneous leaving of a number of stable older pupils adversely affects the school for a time.

In no type of handicap is it so important that the individual child shall be suited to the school and the school to the child. The school medical officer and psychiatrist who send the child must know the school and the school must have the fullest particulars about the child before it can accept him. A school which might in theory be right for a given child may, at a particular time, have other children with whom he would, so to speak, combine to form an explosive mixture.

Because, sooner or later, the child must come home, close and continuing contact between the school and the home is important and the sending clinic and its helpers may well be able to do something to improve the home while the child is away. Whether he should return home for holidays has to be decided in the light of circumstances; occasionally it may be unwise for him to do so and alternative provision has to be made. Much the same applies to visits by the parents to the school. If possible, visits by the parents and their willing co-operation with the school are helpful but cases occur in which parental visits may be disastrously unsettling. Moreover, the child is changing and developing so that what meets his emotional needs at one time may not do so later.

The day special school for maladjusted children is still something of a novelty. In theory it should admirably meet the needs of children whose emotional problems are mainly associated with education or the school environment but whose homes are basically sound and whose parents will co-operate with the child guidance clinic and the school. With carefully selected children it succeeds, but the number of suitable children is limited and except in large cities it is doubtful whether it will ever be possible to find enough children living within an easy distance of the school to provide the thirty to forty pupils necessary to justify the provision. Educationally, there is little difference between the day and boarding special schools, but naturally the day school does not provide the same range of out-of-school activities.

Some experts consider that the integration of school life with life outside school is fundamental in helping the maladjusted and have doubts as to whether the day school can ever be fully successful. The idea is too recent for any definite assessment to be made, and it should not be either wholly accepted or wholly rejected on theoretical grounds. The need for careful assessment of the child's suitability and, even more, of the potentialities of the family for improvement and stabilization, is exceptionally important.

Many maladjusted children are of higher than average intelligence. It is a weakness of the small special school that it cannot provide advanced education in a wide enough range of subjects to bring all the highly intelligent pupils up to University entrance standard. Some of them, it must be conceded, are so disturbed and so educationally retarded that even with specialist teachers they could not hope to reach that standard. It is now becoming the accepted practice with some clever maladjusted children whose problems are not primarily in the educational field to send them to 'ordinary' boarding schools. The word 'ordinary' is used with reserve, for life in many of the traditional British boarding schools would probably make maladjustment worse. There are, however, a few of the smaller boarding schools which are able to provide special attention, care and sympathy for a boy who is not too grossly disturbed and it is worth while to give the very intelligent youngster a trial period in such a school.

Hostels, from which the children attend ordinary schools, are often useful. Well run and staffed they are not inferior to good foster homes and if they establish a good relationship with the neighbouring schools they do excellent work. But ordinary day schools have large classes and overworked staff and cannot do all that is necessary for any child with substantial educational problems and, as already mentioned, most seriously disturbed children do have educational difficulties. Hostels, therefore, have only limited value.

## The Prospect for the Maladjusted

The long-term prospect for the maladjusted child is difficult to assess. In the special school he has lived in a sheltered environment

I

and when he leaves it he has to make good in a world which can be quite harsh and intolerant. When he leaves school he may have to go back to the very home where his problems originated. A recent survey by one well-established school showed that rather more than seventy per cent of the children who had left were, three years later, settled in suitable and permanent employment and were in general as 'normal' as one could have wished. This figure compares quite well with the way in which the average child from the secondary modern school settles down to after-school life. The case of Philip which I have quoted shows how a disturbed child can re-settle in a virtually unchanged home.

Unobtrusive after-care is, however, essential. In the experience of the school just mentioned, continuing contact with the school after leaving seems very useful indeed and it is common for former scholars to go back there for a few days' stay; the idea that their friends the staff are still 'with them' is a valuable aid to confidence. The selection of the right job in the right place is vital, for happiness and security in work can enable one to survive crises of unhappiness and insecurity outside work. A few, ripe for work, are not yet ready to go back to their insecure home and must go to hostels or be settled in lodgings with understanding families. The child who has once been seriously maladjusted may be liable to break down under strain at any time within five or ten years after leaving school so that just as in earlier childhood he should not be exposed to strains which may overtax his powers and he must always have someone to turn to for advice and help if strain arises.

Education for leisure, so often stressed in this book, is important here. To be accepted as an equal and respected for his competence by his friends outside the place of work is an essential steadying factor. The school should have regard to this and the pains taken to see that the maladjusted school leaver has some continuity of leisure interests should be little if any less than those taken to find him suitable employment. Almost invariably maladjustment carries with it serious inferiority feelings and self-confidence and self-esteem are rooted in self-fulfilment.

Relations with the opposite sex naturally present difficulties, because maladjustment, if not arising from sex problems, often produces and precipitates them. Every adolescent is perturbed and puzzled over sex matters and there is good reason to believe that 'sex delinquency' is common among normal teen-agers. (Whether it is true delinquency or merely natural experimentation with newly-acquired powers depends on the point of view of the observer!) The general instability of the maladjusted youngster may produce an excessive interest in both the theory and practice of sex and there has been a consequent tendency to avoid co-education in secondary schools for the maladjusted. The prudence of this is plain, but it robs the boy or girl of the chance of getting to know the opposite sex in the general context of school life—a pity, because this could be a vital part of that learning of the art of human relationships which is fundamental to mental health.

Whether maladjustment leads to preoccupation with sex, to sexual guilt, lack of interest in sex matters or open or concealed homosexuality it can produce strains and tensions in the sexual field during the very vulnerable years of social adjustment outside the protected environment of school. Normally adjusted people do not always pick the right spouse for their particular needs, but their emotional stability enables them to make their marriage work tolerably well. It is vital that the maladjusted should find suitable partners, since their comparative instability limits their chance of making the best of a bad job, but because of their emotional uncertainties they have a higher-than-average prospect of making the wrong choice. The continuing wise guidance after school which I have already mentioned may avert some of the risk; much depends on the closeness of the rapport between the counsellor and the counselled, because readiness to discuss one's work with another person does not necessarily betoken readiness to discuss one's relationships with one's fiancée.

Anything which brings the adolescent of doubtful stability into contact with the opposite sex in the company of others is useful. The value of mixed clubs and mixed groups for the pursuit of hobbies is particularly great. They not only put the other sex in perspective but help to make sure that permanent pairing, when it comes, is based on some community of outlook and interest. None the less, it is probably unwise to leave everything to nature unaided and the engaged adolescent who has been maladjusted will gain much from the help of the 'marriage preparation groups' which are being organized by Marriage Guidance Councils and similar bodies.

Because maladjustment may be partly due to inherent in-stability there remains, even after adolescence, the possibility that someone who seems to have become well adjusted may find trouble if he or she happens to be subjected to undue stress in any aspect of life. If so, the cycle is complete and the emotional tensions and neuroses in the home which prevented him from adjusting in his childhood emerge again in his own household to place his own children in jeopardy. But the outlook need not be too pessimistic. Experience suggests that maladjusted people who have acquired insight into their troubles and have co-operated with those who were ready to help them are better prepared than the average to detect emotional disturbances early and are less reluctant to seek help for themselves or their children. This is by no means the only part of work for and with the handicapped in which the best understanding comes through personal, subjective experience.

### FURTHER READING

*Maladjustment*
Bowlby, J. Maternal Care and Mental Health. H.M. Stationery Office.
Burbury, W. M., Balint, M. and Yapp, B. J. An Introduction to Child Guidance. Macmillan.
Burns, M. Mr. Lyward's Answer. Hamish Hamilton.
Gets, S. B. & Rees, E. L. The Mentally Ill Child. Thomas, Springfield, Illinois.
Jones, H. Reluctant Rebels. Tavistock Publications.
Lenhoff, F. G. Exceptional Children. Allen and Unwin.
   The National Association for Mental Health has published various reports, booklets etc. on the subject.

# CHAPTER 20

# Brain Damage

Medical understanding of the nature, the causes and the effects of brain damage in children has increased greatly in the past twenty years, though there is still much more to be discovered and explained. The term 'spastic' has been in common use for quite a long time to refer to children suffering from two particular types of such damage. One was the child suffering from 'Little's disease'. His most obvious disability was spastic rigidity of the limbs and especially the legs whose tight muscles pulled them together or, quite commonly, across each other in the so-called 'scissor-leg' deformity. When Little first described the condition he mentioned slight or no impairment of intelligence, but as it became more widely diagnosed it was obvious that many of the children affected were below average in intelligence, some of them severely so. The other classical type was the child with athetosis or 'mobile spasm', a condition in which the limbs are incoordinated and have frequent bouts of writhing involuntary movement, also accompanied by impairment of intelligence. Both types of children improved little as they grew older, were usually unable to develop co-ordinated and purposeful movement and had some degree of speech defect which might be very severe. Treatment in general was limited to surgery aimed at reducing spasm, correcting gross deformities and giving the patient some modest amount of mobility. It was widely held that no further treatment was justified for the severe cases, since they were too mentally defective to receive worth-while education or to become useful citizens.

A new outlook began to develop in the middle nineteen-forties. Phelps of Baltimore started to work out a combination of education and corrective training which showed results and there were some spectacular successes in individual cases by doctors and even by unaided patients in many parts of the world. These indicated that many spastics who had been considered grossly mentally defective might have average or even superior intelligence and that special techniques of curative training could so far alleviate the disability in a substantial number of cases as to enable the patients to grow up to lead virtually normal lives.

The natural result was that a wave of enthusiasm and optimism swept the Western countries and spread even into lands where little had been attempted for any handicapped children. Parents of spastic children leaped from despair to wild hope that their children, too, were geniuses in disguise. There was a rush to elaborate new theories, methods and techniques both inside and outside the fields of orthodox medicine and education. Considerable voluntary funds were raised to 'help spastic children' and pressure groups began to urge the appropriate and even the inappropriate authorities to provide more facilities for spastics. A good deal of effort was wasted, but experience began to accumulate and brought a considerable amount of realistic knowledge. Some of the funds raised were, wisely, devoted to research, and information from a wide variety of scientific and medical fields was painstakingly brought together to throw new light not only on spastics but on the whole subject of child development, normal and abnormal.

Criticism is now tempering enthusiasm and work for spastics in general is becoming more realistic. There is still some confusion and uncertainty and unequivocally clear guides to further progress are not yet available. It is certain that much more can be done for many of these children than was ever dreamed of twenty years ago, but various schools of treatment still differ widely from each other and are not yet prepared to substitute synthesis for rivalry. Such synthesis must be achieved and there may have to be radical changes of thought and practice as knowledge grows.

It is, however, possible to give a general outline of the present situation, though this is made difficult by some uncertainty of terminology. Brain damage can be of many kinds and degrees and can have many causes. Indeed, the term 'damage' itself is open to criticism, because it conveys the impression of something which has at one time been normal but has been injured by some agency, whereas part or the whole of the trouble may have been due to imperfect development, but it is convenient to keep the word as an omnibus term.

Anything which damages or affects the development of the brain may affect any part of the brain, not only those which control the movement of muscles but those associated with co-ordination of movement, of position sense, and of the interpretation of what one sees, hears and feels, as well as the parts which deal with what is generally known as intelligence. In addition, some of the things which interfere with the normal development of the brain may also affect the development of other organs, so that a child with developmental 'damage' to the brain may have some eye, ear, heart or limb disability.

In spite of this, it does not inevitably follow that a child with brain damage will have multiple disabilities. Many types of mental subnormality may occur without any physical handicap whatever. Brain haemorrhages in infancy, which though uncommon are by no means rare, may paralyse one side of the body in a greater or less degree or, perhaps, affect the speech centre in the brain, without in the least impairing intelligence. Nor, when there are multiple disabilities, are they all equally serious. It is, indeed, a matter for sober thought that in some cases of brain damage some of the resulting defects are so minor in comparison with others that they may be overlooked and not receive attention at the time when most could be done about them. The moral to be drawn from this is that when any child shows evidence of any form of brain damage there should be the most careful general investigation to detect or exclude other damage or disability whether in the brain or elsewhere.

Because the term 'brain damage' connotes so much it is desirable to try to divide it into various parts whether for purposes of clinical or educational classification or for purposes of teaching.

Since 'spastic' means literally 'undergoing contraction' and should be used only of a muscle or muscles which are in contraction, it is obviously a vague and sloppy term to apply to a person who is the victim of brain damage. However, it is now well entrenched in the language and will have to be forgiven as a convenient colloquialism, provided that its limitations are remembered.

A better term now being used for some kinds of disability in this field is 'Cerebral Palsy'. It is far from ideal, because it literally means only 'paralysis due to brain damage', but it has become necessary to follow the example of Humpty Dumpty and say that a word must mean what we intend it to mean provided that there is some general agreement on the meaning and that the accepted meaning does not distort the original meaning too violently. In this particular case, Cerebral Palsy is now regarded as covering substantial defect of muscle use caused by some defect in the brain, whether the muscle disability is the original type of severe spasm found in Little's disease, the writhing uncontrollable muscle activity of athetosis, or the failure of muscles to do their job not because they are in spasm or involuntarily over-active but because something is wrong with the parts of the brain which deal with the co-ordination of muscular activity.

There is a tendency to use separate terms for the effects of the more sharply localized kinds of brain damage. Paralysis or weakness of one or more limbs due to brain haemorrhage, if it is not accompanied by any other evidence of damage, though literally 'paralysis due to brain damage' will usually be spoken of as Monoplegia (one limb paralyzed), Hemiplegia (arm and leg on the same side affected) or Paraplegia (both legs affected). Muscular incoordination due to damage to the cerebellum is 'Ataxia' and speech failure due to damage to the speech centre 'Aphasia'. If, however, any of these occurs as part of a wider panorama of disability, the term Cerebral Palsy will be used for the whole and the specific term for the particular part of the disability which it connotes.

A new term, '*Minimal Brain Damage*', has been coming into use in the past four or five years. It has been found that a substantial number of children who have no appreciable muscle weakness or spasm and who, indeed, appear at first to be quite normal, turn out, as they grow, to have a combination of slight disabilities of a kind which might be due to brain damage. Separately the disabilities may be trivial but together they can add up to something which can be a major problem both educationally and socially.

**Causation**

Much still remains to be discovered and defined in the causation of brain damage. It can happen before birth, during birth, in the period immediately following birth or, less commonly, during the early years of life.

Damage before birth may be due to failure of development from genetic causes. There is good reason to believe that it can be caused by virus infections of the mother during pregnancy, rubella (German measles) being a particular offender, by the taking of certain drugs during pregnancy or by excessive exposure of the unborn child to X-rays. So far as the two latter are concerned, women vary widely in the sensitivity of themselves and their children to these things and only a very tiny minority are likely to suffer from drugs or radiation in the amounts normally used.

Damage during birth is probably the most important single cause. It can happen if labour is unduly prolonged or unduly rapid, it may be caused by the use of instruments or it may happen if anything interferes with the child's oxygen supply during labour. Blood abnormalities arising out of Rhesus incompatibility may damage the brain. Modern techniques of dealing with this danger-ous condition are usually successful in saving the child's life, but the poisonous substances circulating in the blood, though they have not been there long enough to cause death, may have been present for a sufficient time to injure the brain tissues.

Premature babies are also exposed to risk. No incubator seems to be able to give a child, during the eighth and ninth months of development, an environment as satisfactory as that which nature provides in the womb, so that the mere fact of being out would seem to produce some risk. The recent use of high-concentration oxygen in the care of premature babies, especially if it was sud-denly discontinued when the child seemed to be ready for life in ordinary air, caused retro-lental fibroplasia and it might be that brain damage also could follow the injudicious use of this method of care. But an important riddle remains to be solved—is it possible that some of the things which cause a baby to be born prematurely, whatever those things may be, are themselves capable of producing injury to the developing brain and thus ensuring that even if the care of premature babies were ideal some of them would have this kind of disability?

Most of the common infectious diseases of early childhood have been known to be followed by cerebral palsy, though the relation of cause and effect is not always certainly known. Gastro-enteritis, middle ear infection, the encephalitis sometimes complicating measles and mumps and even whooping-cough and scarlet fever have at times been reported to produce the condition during the first two or three years of life.

But though the specific causes may not be exactly known there is no doubt that the majority of causes are, in theory at any rate, preventable and that better ante-natal care and obstetrics and better control of the spread of infections are likely to bring about a material drop in the incidence of brain damage.

In view of the emphasis laid in recent years on the importance of spastic children, it is easy to wonder whether children with brain damage are in any way 'special' or 'different from' other handicapped children. The answer is that it is dangerous to generalize and that, according to the circumstances such a child may or may not be special. The following points should be considered whenever the question is raised.

1. If a child's brain damage mainly affects the intellect and the physical disability is very slight, then the care which he needs will not be appreciably different from that which other mentally subnormal children need. Much the same applies to his general education.

2. In some types of physical disability produced by brain damage, and particularly some forms of monoplegia and hemiplegia, if the intellect and senses are normal the care, education and even treatment of the child will be much the same as if he had been crippled by, say, poliomyelitis. In other cases, while care and educational needs are like those of physically handicapped children, special kinds of treatment and educational therapy may be needed.

3. Where, as is often the case, the brain damaged child has several substantial disabilities, intellectual, motor or sensory, the combination of handicaps will necessitate providing some special care and the education provided in a school for the 'pure' mentally or physically handicapped will probably not meet his needs.

4. The most important consideration is that special attention must be given to diagnosis and assessment. If a child shows any one disability which might be due to brain damage, then it is possible that he may have other disabilities which are less obvious and the most assiduous search must be made for these before it is decided that he has only a single substantial disability. Moreover, since some of these less obvious disabilities may show themselves only after a few years have passed, the first assessment must be only provisional and he must be kept under constant surveillance.

After these general observations on the whole question of brain damage, we can now go on to consider the subject in more detail, dividing it, for convenience, into 'Cerebral Palsy' and 'Minimal Brain Damage'.

## Diagnosis and Assessment

If the damage caused by cerebral palsy is sufficient for the sufferer to need special care and treatment, the diagnosis will become obvious in due course. But the spastic child has two things in common with the deaf child—early neglect can lead to the missing of vital opportunities and the first signs of his disability may pass unnoticed or may be misinterpreted as evidence of something else. The problem is less diagnosis as such than diagnosis at the earliest possible stage, and diagnosis in itself is not enough; one must know as soon as possible the relative extent of the damage to intellect, the damage to the motor nervous system and the extent to which the powers of sight, hearing, muscular co-ordination and spatial perception may also be affected.

It is, therefore, sound policy to suspect the possibility of cerebral palsy in any child who has been exposed to any of the things which I have mentioned above as possible causes and to arrange for such children to be seen as a routine, quite early in life, by someone with special experience in dealing with the condition. In many if not most cases where the damage is substantial some suggestive signs will be apparent to the watchful in the first few months of life. Where none of the probable causes is known to have existed the possibility that a child will be a spastic is, naturally, less and it would be superfluous—as well as a cause for unnecessary anxiety in the parents—to expect and look for cerebral palsy in all children! It is, however, sensible to bear the possibility in mind in investigating *any* apparent slowness in physical or mental development in infancy.

At whatever age the child is brought to the notice of the doctor or the nurse one important question has to be answered—how much of the total disability is motor and how much intellectual or sensory. In so far as the child may be permanently physically handicapped it will be necessary for him to earn his living by the use of his brain; in so far as his disability may be curable by special training, the success of that training will depend upon the extent to which he can understand what has to be done and co-operate in doing it. The outlook, in fact, depends very largely upon the child's intelligence, though it is, of course, considerably worse if a sensory defect such as deafness is also present.

Intelligence, as I have pointed out in other chapters, cannot be measured as an entity but only by its manifestations. If a child is able to do certain things which normal children of his age can do it is fair to assume that his intelligence is normal. The spastic child, who will have been lying on his back inert while other children have been sitting up playing, who will have been kept at home while other children have accompanied their parents on shopping expeditions and so on, will lack experience of life, so that some of the standard intelligence tests will be meaningless to him. His speech is almost certainly affected, so that he will be unable to answer questions or show how big is his vocabulary. He will be unable to control his hands and make them obey his wishes, so that his response to non-verbal performance tests will be poor. Social isolation and physical disability may, in fact, so mask innate intelligence that a spastic child with an I.Q. of 125 may respond to formal testing at feeble-minded or imbecile level.

One case will serve as a useful illustration. Timmy was first brought to my notice at the age of three, when an experienced paediatrician pronounced him ineducably mentally defective. Examination by a doctor skilled in the use of intelligence tests confirmed this; his I.Q. was about 45. The only practical course seemed to be to ask the orthopaedic surgeons to do what they could to reduce his deformity and then, at some later date, to get him admitted to an institution for mental defectives. He entered an orthopaedic hospital and surgical treatment began, but after a few months he contracted scarlet fever and was removed from the hospital to an infectious diseases unit under my care. First impressions confirmed the original findings of my colleagues, but as he became convalescent and began to try to play with the lively normal children in the ward I began to suspect that his intelligence had been rated too low.

Two months later I visited him at the orthopaedic hospital and tried to test his intelligence; tested in familiar surroundings by someone whom he knew he responded better. His I.Q. on test was 60 and I was sure that this was an under-estimate, especially since he was responding to training and making attempts to walk with support. Treatment finished, the hospital discharged him to his home and a few months later he was reviewed by the selection panel of a school for spastics. By this time, lack of expert care in his isolated rural home had produced physical deterioration and though the special school psychologist estimated his I.Q. as 70 he was considered unsuitable for admission to that school. A further spell of hospital care produced more progress, to a point at which he could walk with sticks, but after his inevitable discharge home he regressed once more. By now, however, he was old enough for admission to an ordinary school for physically handicapped children and in spite of the physical deterioration I was convinced, on re-testing him, that his I.Q. was probably over 80.

A place was found for him in a boarding school for the physically handicapped, he settled down quickly and well, and his progress was most gratifying. His response to special education suggested that even my estimate of 80 for his I.Q. might be too low and that he was probably of virtually normal intelligence. Unfortunately the story ends rather less happily than one would have wished. After a couple of years of promise his performance began to deteriorate and he lagged behind his contemporaries, with an apparent fall in his I.Q. Detailed investigation showed that he had some marked difficulties in perception; these had been unimportant and had not shown themselves in his 'infant school' stage but they impeded him when he had to make a serious start on the three Rs. Moreover, as he found school work more difficult he became unsettled and slightly emotionally disturbed, which made his work even less satisfactory.

Timmy's case shows up several of the pitfalls of assessment in cerebral palsy. The first is the masking of intelligence by physical disability and lack of social experience, to which I have already referred. The second is that intelligence tests for older children are often partly dependent on education and that educational retardation may lower the test response. The third is that some of the disabilities which occur in cerebral palsy become obvious only when the child's activities have advanced to a point at which he has to do things or show skills with which those disabilities interfere. His degree of perception difficulty might or might not have been detected by special tests when he was younger, but I certainly have an uncomfortable feeling that if he had gone to a school specializing in cerebral palsy someone would have found it within a year or so. This kind of problem must be borne in mind when one is considering whether brain-damaged children with disabilities which are mainly physical should go to 'ordinary' schools for the physically handicapped. Timmy, in fact, was transferred to a special school for spastics, where he did fairly well though without justifying my initial optimism.

A single examination in unfamiliar surroundings, however skilful and experienced the examiner may be, may give a misleading impression. A child who shows up well in such surroundings is undoubtedly intelligent, but a child who fails must not be rejected out of hand. It is probable that assessment of spastics should ideally be made in a residential centre over a period of from one to three months.

Naturally, preliminary assessments by some shorter procedure will have to be made. The worst way to make them is by applying intelligence tests in a clinic and my own personal preference is to see the child in his own home, with the mother present. The examination should take the form of a 'play session', preferably on the floor, with his familiar toys scattered around; what the examiner loses in dignity by crawling about on all fours he will make up by opportunities for assessment under ideal conditions. In the course of play it is usually possible to introduce the equivalent of some standard performance tests—simple block building and form boards, for example—or even tests of object and picture recognition or ability to count, but the child's failures in the tests cannot be taken at their face value. In the chapter on mental handicap I have stressed the importance of following the prescribed procedure in applying intelligence tests, but in testing the spastic child some relaxation may be allowed. The time allowed for a particular test may, for example, be increased to allow for sheer physical difficulty in performing it or the child may be allowed several attempts. It is reasonable to allow the mother to 'interpret' the child's speech, even if her interpretations sometimes err on the optimistic side.

The fact that the child fails in a particular test is interesting but not conclusive; what matters is to watch him closely and try to see *why* he fails. His use of toys can be most illuminating from this point of view. If, for example, he pushes his toy motor-car across the floor instead of making use of its built-in drive, is it because he does not understand the idea of such a drive, because he cannot learn how to operate the drive or because his hands cannot manipulate the drive mechanism? The examiner will play *with* the child, working the toys and using them himself and noting whether the child appreciates what he is doing and tries to imitate him. And what applies to tests and toys applies equally to simple games as well as to ordinary activities of daily living. It is obviously impossible for anyone to draw valid conclusions from this sort of a session with a spastic child unless he or she has had considerable experience with normal children and their play, but I have dealt with it in a little detail because the school doctor, the school nurse or health visitor and other people can, over a period, make an appreciable contribution to the assessment of a particular child. The 'screening panel' of a special school, when they see a child for the first time, can be much helped by crumbs of information from those who have been looking after him previously and even an assessment centre can be assisted in its initial approach to a child taken in for assessment.

Most of the really doubtful cases and particularly those on the borderline between educability and ineducability will need assessment in a centre. Tentative estimates of intelligence may have to allow wide margins; whereas in the borderline case of a simply mentally handicapped child one may say with some assurance that his I.Q. is between 45 and 55, in the case of a spastic child one may have to suggest a possible range of from 40 to 70. In such a case, to follow the principle of letting him have a trial period in a special school is probably to take too great a risk of failure. There has been some argument on the relative merits of day and residential assessment centres, and the balance would seem to come down on the side of residence. It is true that there is a risk that the child's going away from home may produce emotional disturbance which will prevent him from showing his true self in the early weeks at the centre, but continuous observation by experienced people through his whole waking day is much better than observation for a mere four or five hours daily. It can also sometimes happen that under observation in a day centre the child has difficulties in adjusting himself to two different environments at the same time and that the daily alternation between home and centre may confuse or disturb him.

The assessment of social background is also of special importance. Because the spastic child is handicapped physically as well as mentally he will present his parents with complex problems of care and management and their ability to handle these problems has to be carefully judged. Their attitude to the child, their intelligence and education, the time they can devote to him in the home and outside it, and their financial resources may all be important. Among other questions to be answered are whether physiotherapy and other special treatment are readily available in the neighbourhood of the home and whether the family doctor, the paediatrician, the school or child welfare medical officer and the school nurse or health visitor have the right understanding and appreciation of what is involved in the child's special and general care.

Though all initial assessment of all handicapped children is provisional, this is most important in the case of cerebral palsy. Even if the assessment centre suggests a particular school, the suggestion must have a provisional element and his first years in that school are as much years of observation as of education. It is always difficult, if not impossible, to guess in advance what prolonged physiotherapy, speech therapy and neuro-muscular education may achieve in the way of removing the physical barriers to the manifestation of the child's intelligence or what mechanical aids, such as the electric typewriter, may do to allow him to express what he has within him. As in Timmy's case, there is the possibility that disabilities which were at first latent may become obvious, and even when defects of coordination and perception are found early their practical significance may not be assessable for some years. And because the social background and the need for skilled parental care are so important, changes and developments in the home may also profoundly affect current care and training and the long-term outlook.

## Treatment

As I indicated in the introduction in this chapter, ideas on the treatment of cerebral palsy have changed radically during recent years and are still in a state of flux. Surgery still has some place, in the correction of severe established deformities, in tendon transplants and in the cutting of motor nerves to relieve gross spasm, for example, though anticipatory therapy and management may reduce both the likelihood and the severity of such conditions. Physiotherapy is much more in vogue, although much remains to be done both in devising and in evaluating techniques. Some experienced physiotherapy experts doubt its value while others are enthusiastic. Enthusiasm has done much to stimulate ingenuity and to make people persevere with the most unpromising cases; it has also led to some unfortunate discord between advocates of special techniques. It is certainly fair to say that physiotherapy has in many cases produced substantial benefit and unfair to argue at length whether the effort involved has been jusitfied by the results which have been achieved, since it is impossible to say in the event just what would have been the condition of the child had the treatment not been given. It may be, as some have said, that the success of physiotherapy depends largely on the personality of the therapist, for not all techniques are equally successful in different people's hands. Sadly, extravagant claims have been made for some techniques which have not been at all borne out in practice, so that parents and children have paid a heavy price in both money and disappointment; this, fortunately, cannot be said of any techniques which are in wide use in this country.

Of course, any treatment which can be given to alleviate other disabilities which are present simultaneously with cerebral palsy must be given and speech therapy is often both necessary and effective. But much treatment in cerbral palsy consists of physical education and re-education, which must begin in the early years of life and must be an integral part of the whole of the child's education.

## Care and Management

The general principles of care of the mentally handicapped child and the crippled child apply also to the care of the spastic child, but special attention must be given to seeing that he is not deprived of the normal stimuli of his environment. His physical disability, as already mentioned, will tend to rob him of some of these; even such an apparently simple thing as helping him to sit up in a good position at the right age may play a critical part in the development of his intelligence.

Simple special equipment in the home is immensely useful. A special chair, made to his individual requirements by a specialist manufacturer with the guidance of the orthopaedic surgeon and the specialist in physical medicine, can be invaluable. A walking aid is often equally important. Some pieces of apparatus of this kind are rather expensive, but in Britain the local health services can help in their provision and elsewhere there are various private and public funds which can be tapped. Simple and quite inexpensive minor 'gadgets' play a part in helping him with general needs. Among these are such things as built-up handles for spoons and other table utensils, table drinking mugs with wide bases and suction discs to hold plates in position at mealtimes, and racks or frames to hold toys and other things on the table. An ingenious parent or local handyman can devise and make some of these with little trouble or expense.

Physiotherapy and speech therapy are likely to be important in his life from quite an early age, and here the parent can do much to help. The work of the physiotherapy and speech clinics can often be continued and supplemented in the home by simple exercises and the mother must co-operate with the therapists by learning these exercises and seeing to it that they are carried out.

Much of what I have said in detail about the care and management of the crippled child may be applied directly to the care of the spastic child in respect of his physical disability and need not be repeated here, but certain special aspects of the subject need emphasis. When the crippled child is learning by experience to do simple every-day things he is working toward a limited objective. If he is teaching his left hand to do what his crippled right hand ought to do, he will within a reasonable time have a competent left hand which will do its work admirably. If he is learning various shifts and 'trick movements' to make a limb which is weak or has a limited range of movement do certain specific things, once each thing has been learned all is well.

The disability of the spastic child is not as a rule confined to a single limb. Moreover, while the cripple's damaged limb is, so to speak, a passive passenger the spastic's damaged limb is often more in the nature of an active opponent. Even after he has learned to make use of it for a particular task there is always a possibility that it may betray him, especially in moments of stress and strain. In brief, he will learn more slowly than the cripple and in many things he will never acquire a finally reliable skill. It follows that he needs special patience from those who are teaching him, in the home as elsewhere, and that there must in the end be many activities in which he will always need help.

Take as an example such a commonplace matter as feeding himself. His first efforts with a spoon will be hopelessly inadequate. The spoon will be loaded only after much trouble if at all. Some of its contents will be lost as he raises it and he cannot even be sure of conveying what remains to his mouth. The prospect of his taking in, by his own efforts, enough food to meet his physical needs is small and it may well be years before he can feed himself effectively without help. Yet he must try to learn. He is not merely developing a technique of using a spoon—he is training brain, nerves and muscles toward a co-ordination which will be of value in using all the various implements and tools which may serve him in later life. Even if the mealtime ends in his being fed with what remains on his plate, it must include a patient period of encouragement of his own efforts.

Though I have taken feeding as an example of all activities, it has a special importance in that eating is a social activity and to the adult the inability to share a meal with other people is a very substantial social handicap. The lightly handicapped spastic may ultimately learn to eat with no great difficulty but the heavily handicapped spastic may always be a 'messy eater'. The more this can be taken as a matter of fact in the home the better for all concerned; the fight for supremacy between self-consciousness and confidence in this, as in other things, is first fought in childhood at home.

Dressing and undressing probably ranks next after eating. One must consider not only the putting on of clothes in the morning and their removal at night but the need to adjust clothing before and after attending to bodily needs. Anything which can be done to simplify the manipulation of clothing is all to the good. Slip-on shoes, elastic and zipp-fasteners in substitution for buttons, and open-neck shirts are now socially acceptable wear on all but the most formal occasions, and the moderately handicapped can learn to manipulate them.

For the more severely handicapped spastic, however, some form of help from others will always be a necessity and one of the social responsibilities of the home is to teach the child how to accept help gracefully. It is possible as time goes on to find out which things he will never be able to do for himself and to assess the amount of help he will need. The help of friends and relations outside the immediate family circle must be enlisted, so that he will learn to take as a commonplace simple assistance when he is among strangers.

### Education

Cerebral palsy, as already mentioned, has received a good deal of special attention in recent years. One disadvantage of this is that stress has been laid on its uniqueness to such an extent that many people assume that all children handicapped in this way need a peculiar type of treatment, education and care which has magical results with all spastics but is of little value for non-spastics, and, in particular, that all children with any kind of cerebral palsy should go to special schools for spastics. This is by no means a true picture. The facts can be roughly summarized as follows:

1. In many cases the disability of movement has a special character, which may require special techniques of treatment. In other cases—some hemiplegias, for example—the nature of the trouble and the appropriate treatment are no

different from those which might be needed by a child crippled by poliomyelitis.

2. Where the disability is in a considerable degree due to defects of perception or co-ordination it is probable that some special techniques of education or training will be needed.

3. If there are defects of vision or hearing, these are not in themselves different from such defects in non-spastic children.

4. Any defect of intelligence is also, in itself, no different from defect of intelligence in other mentally handicapped children, but its effects may be exaggerated by the presence of other effects of brain damage.

The special problems created by cerebral palsy arise from the fact that these various disabilities may be present in combination —one has, as it were, a cocktail of disabilities with the ingredients in widely varying proportions. Some of these children may have virtually normal or higher intelligence and only slight physical disability; if so, the fact that they are technically 'spastics' need not prevent them from being educated in ordinary schools and some of them get on admirably in such schools. Others may have substantial mental handicap but only moderate physical disability; they may do quite well in special schools for E.S.N. children, provided that the nature of their physical disability does not call for special treatment techniques.

At this point we might consider some of the special aspects of intelligence in children with cerebral palsy. There is no getting away from the fact that they are likely to have some defect of intelligence. Among normal children some 25 per cent have I.Q.s of 110 or over. In children with cerebral palsy the percentage is probably less than 5. At the other end of the scale, among normal children only about 3 per cent have an I.Q. below 70; with cerebral palsy this figure increases to something in the region of 50 per cent. It is generally assumed that children with a mental handicap only may benefit by education in E.S.N. special schools even if their I.Q.s are as low as 55, but it must not be assumed that because of this a large proportion of the under-70s with cerebral palsy are similarly educable.

The tests on which these percentage figures are based have been used in surroundings and have included techniques which reduce to a minimum the other effects of brain damage, physical and sensory, which would impair the children's performances, so that, as far as possible, they measure 'pure' intelligence. In practice, we are concerned with intelligence as it works in the surroundings at the time, and it has not been possible as yet to produce school surroundings and teaching methods which eliminate the reaction of other disabilities on mental handicap, so that educationally speaking the school potentialities of the child with cerebral palsy may easily be anywhere from five to twenty points below the I.Q. he shows on special test. This means that at present somewhere about half of all spastics fall below the point at which they would be considered educable by even ordinary special school standards. It is quite probable that within the next few years educational techniques will advance and that the number of spastics 'unsuit-able for education' will fall to 40 per cent or even less, but one cannot forecast with certainty.

This aspect of intelligence has further importance in respect of the long-term outlook for the spastic. However far test techniques and educational methods may improve, in the long run the spastic will have to live and work in circumstances which can be modified in his interests only to a limited degree, so that his practical intellectual ability will be likely to remain below his theoretical capacity. His capacity to benefit by education will not truly reflect his capacity to use his intelligence and education after school, and both the design of his education and the forecasts of his potential which are made during his schooldays must take this into account and not be unduly optimistic.

What applies at the lower end of the intelligence scale applies also at the higher. The 4 or 5 per cent of spastics with over-average intelligence may well have physical disabilities which bring their learning potential and their long-term living and work-ing potential down to or below the average. Nevertheless, in spite of the obvious difficulties the attempt to make maximum use of this high intelligence is justified. Such a child will need facilities available in very few schools. Apart from his requirements in the physical field—physiotherapy, speech therapy, physical aids and appliances and so on—he will need intensive education by methods adjusted to his physical disabilities, which may virtually amount to individual coaching and will certainly demand teaching in very small groups. Emotionally he is probably at greater risk than his less intelligent fellows because of the conflict between his aware-ness of what is within him and his limited capacity to express it;

from his higher intelligence may come either complete failure to reconcile himself to what he sees as the cruel injustice of his fate or —often by painfully slow degrees—realistic acceptance of such fulfilment as is possible for him. To explore, develop and exploit his potentialities is a task demanding the highest skill and much human understanding.

We are left with two substantial groups whose needs have to be specially considered and for whom much can be done. The first consists of children of average intelligence but suffering from marked physical handicap. These have much in common with ordinary crippled children and only two major issues arise. Does the child need a type of physiotherapy combined with physical re-education which cannot be provided in a school for the physically handicapped? Has he some perceptual disability which will require educational technique outside the repertoire of the ordinary P.H. school?

If either or both of these obtains, then a special school for spastics is the place for him. But many schools for the physically handicapped provide intensive physiotherapy of various kinds within the school and if one of these can give the spastic child what he needs there should be no qualms about sending him there. As a 'normal cripple' he will gain something from the school's accent on normality and will not be unnecessarily taking up one of the as yet limited number of places in special schools for spastics. One warning, however—that implicit in the case of Timmy. Because some perceptual disabilities may declare themselves rather late, the school must be on the watch for the possible presence of this kind of thing.

The second group, that of children whose handicap is severe in both the intellectual and the physical fields, is large and presents a considerable problem. More than in the case of purely physical crippling defects, the relief of physical disability in the spastic makes severe demands on the subject's understanding, patience and perseverance, and until quite recently it was considered that the markedly physically handicapped spastic child with an I.Q. of less than 100 had very little prospect of making good educationally. His moderate or low intelligence, impeded in operation by his physical defect, made him unacceptable to a school for the physically handicapped, while his physical disability made him no less unacceptable to the special school for the mentally handicapped.

There are now a number of special schools which cater specially for the spastic child with marked disability of both mind and body and their experience over the few years for which they have been operating is modestly encouraging. It is not fair to judge them as yet for their work is still in the experimental stage and opportunities are only just being perceived and techniques devised and tried. One can, however, say without hesitation that their combination of effort in general education, social education, physical education and appropriate therapy is able to give a substantial number of children something worth having and though it may not offer many pupils the prospect of being independent and self-supporting in the future it helps them toward some degree of happiness, usefulness and self-fulfilment.

Home tuition for the spastic child has no larger place than home tuition for any other handicapped child. I have found it useful in ensuring that time spent waiting for a vacancy in a special school was not entirely wasted, and, occasionally, in making a running assessment of a child while at the same time providing some preparation for formal schooling. Susan, for example, was the child of a father whose employment compelled him to move from one place to another and in her young days she never came, for any worthwhile length of time, under the continuous care of any hospital or school health department which was ready and able to give her what she needed. One attempt at special school education had been a disastrous failure, largely because the school concerned, though admirable in dealing with ordinary physically handicapped pupils, could not meet her requirements. At the age of twelve she was severely crippled, though able to get about in calipers, virtually illiterate and grossly maladjusted. I estimated her I.Q. as in the neighbourhood of 100 and possibly slightly higher, but it was improbable that any school would accept a girl of that age who had not reached even infant school standards of attainment. Had a school been prepared to take her Susan would have been a disruptive influence and her academic inferiority to her contemporaries would have intensified her maladjustment.

A home teacher—a retired infant school headmistress with infinite patience and perseverance and a fine sense of humour—agreed to make an attempt to give her the rudiments of education to prepare her for entrance to a suitable special school. It took a long time to conquer her distrust of teachers and dislike of schooling but patience won and it became clear that her intelligence was at least of average level. In two years she had reached a standard which, though well below the attainment level of the normal fourteen-year-old, gave her a chance of finding her feet in a special school. At this stage, unfortunately, various family problems intervened and though a suitable vacancy was found it was not taken up. Still, Susan could at least read and write and had begun to enjoy books, while her emotional disturbance was less and she was considerably more at ease with strangers. Though the experiment failed of its avowed purpose, it was not entirely without results, and Susan will undoubtedly have a happier life because of her teacher's efforts. I do not, however, mention her case just to indicate what home teaching can do. It is more apposite as a warning that even in Britain the handicapped child of intelligent and fairly well-to-do parents can escape the meshes of the net which the various services spread to protect and help such children. Susan was a spastic child; a similar story, with an even less happy ending, could be told of deaf, partially sighted and physically and mentally handicapped children. The legal duty of the parent to provide education suited to a child's age, ability and aptitude must be supported by the legal and moral duty of the school medical officer, the child welfare medical officer and all their colleagues to seek the handicapped child and his parents and to guide and advise them appropriately.

## The Prospect in Cerebral Palsy

Twenty years ago the child with severe cerebral palsy was virtually a 'write-off'; the child with less severe disability might hope for some surgical help and for a few years of more or less perfunctory education in a school which was neither staffed nor equipped to meet his particular needs. Fifteen years ago the first special schools for spastics were coming into being, but the accommodation was far from meeting the potential demand and the only thing that prevented them from being overwhelmed was the fact that still too few spastics were being detected and assessed really early. Not until the middle nineteen-fifties was the spastic child with marked disability in both the physical and the intellectual fields assured of a reasonable probability of the right sort of education starting at an early age.

The present situation is, therefore, that no spastic child born before 1945 is likely to have had treatment and education suited to his potentialities which has started early enough and gone on long enough for him to have made the best of his physical and mental assets, such as they are. A minority of those born between 1945 and 1950 will have been more fortunate, but it is fair to say that most spastics over the age of twenty have had a good deal less help than they needed at that stage in their lives when help, whether in treatment, education or general management, could have done most for them. It follows that the prospects for the spastic child of today must not be judged on the basis of what the average adult spastic of today is and does.

The public image of the adult spastic is still a distressing one. He is someone unbeautiful to look at, uncouth and unkempt, prevented by speech disability from free communication with others, painfully clumsy and slow in every movement of which he is capable, virtually confined to a wheel-chair, doing at best a little work of poor quality and needing help with most of the activities of daily living. Of course, the public image depicts the worst cases, simply because they are the ones who impress themselves most forcibly on the situation. Equally of course, some of these unfortunates are so severely disabled that no special treatment or education could have helped them and it would be foolish to assume that the number of such severe cases will decline greatly in a short time.

But the development of adult centres in the last few years has shown encouraging results. People who fitted this description, with no education to speak of and with their personalities and capacities further diminished by years of being home-bound or, worse, years of incarceration in hospitals for the chronic sick or the mentally subnormal, have been rescued from their vegetable life. For more than a few of them physiotherapy has improved mobility and the use of their hands, speech therapy has brought rudiments of speech to some who were completely unintelligible and occupational therapy and training have given an interest in life. Some have gone out into open industrial work and more have achieved something in sheltered workshops. No less important, living with other people who are facing similar problems has made them more social in behaviour and outlook.

Apart from the benefit to the individuals, this is producing a slow improvement in the public image and as more spastics show themselves to be employable and socially acceptable so employer-resistance diminishes and social tolerance increases. It would seem obvious to ask whether if centres for adults are getting results with human material which had been 'spoiled' before admission, the newer generation of spastic children who have had the right care in infancy and the right education later may not be expected to have very much better prospects when they grow up. In the long run, the answer must be 'yes', but a great deal will depend on progress in educational methods. Without in the least minimizing the admirable work that special schools have been doing, it must be said that hopes have not yet been fulfilled of making the most of children in the 60–75 I.Q. group with fairly severe physical disability or difficulties of perception.

## MINIMAL BRAIN DAMAGE

This is certainly a bad title. It suggests that the child's brain has been normal or, at any rate, was developing normally up to a certain point, and that some factor has interfered to cause injury or to prevent normal development from continuing. In fact, children in this class suffer from various disorders which *can* be caused by brain abnormality but it is not always possible to prove that such abnormality exists. In some of these children there is evidence that something has happened which could have produced brain injury, even though the existence of injury cannot be proved, but in others there is no such evidence. In 1962 an expert study group, after considering the subject, came to the conclusion that it would be a good idea to drop the term 'minimal brain damage' and to substitute 'minimal cerebral dysfunction' which means, in effect 'something seems to be slightly wrong with the functioning of this child's brain, but we do not quite know what it is.' Since that date the only new information which has come to hand is that slight attacks of encephalitis which follow some of the common minor infectious diseases of childhood, such as mumps and German measles, and apparently clear up completely, are associated with electrical disturbances of the brain at the time of the acute illness. It may be possible to infer from this that every child who has suffered from one of these diseases (which means most children!) has been exposed to the risk of brain damage, but it would still be going too far to assume that actual damage does occur in all these cases.

Broadly speaking, the symptoms of the condition can be divided into three groups.

Group 1 consists essentially of children who have minor degrees of cerebral palsy of either the spastic or athetoid type and some authorities also include 'hyperkinetic' children who show constant and marked over-active behaviour.

Group 2 includes, among others, children with retarded speech development, children with specific difficulties in reading and writing and the so-called 'clumsy' children. Group 3 includes children showing distractability, variability of behaviour, impulsiveness, irritability, anxiety and emotional immaturity.

It will be seen that this classification depends to some extent on the degree of disturbance. In group 3 in particular, any of the symptoms mentioned may occur for a time in a child who is in general normal, and even when they are marked and continuous it would not need a great deal of ingenuity on the part of a psychiatrist to explain them in emotional rather than organic terms. Even in Group 1, moderately hyperkinetic behaviour could be partly or even wholly accounted for in terms of emotional disturbance and, of course, whether this kind of behaviour tends to get worse or to improve may well depend on the reaction of parents and teachers to the child—and the child's consequent response to that reaction.

If it is possible to detect actual evidence of brain damage, or if there is something in the child's history which strongly suggests exposure to damage, then the term may be literally used. But there is no doubt that in all these children, whatever the cause of of the trouble may be, we are dealing with a situation in which the wrong environment can make things worse and the right environment might well make them better.

## Diagnosis and Assessment

It follows automatically that early diagnosis and assessment are vitally important for these children. Unfortunately, of all groups of the handicapped they probably present the most difficult diagnostic problems. Unless there is some obvious physical disability or some special feature which is inevitably likely to cause concern —repeated mild epileptic fits for example—the symptoms are such as not to arouse special anxiety in the family doctor or the parents because, as I have mentioned, any of them may occur as a passing phase in a perfectly normal child. It is by no means uncommon for the trouble to be ignored or passed over lightly until the extra stresses and strains produced by entry to school make it obvious that something is really wrong.

Kevin was a fairly typical case. His father was a solicitor whose office was in his own house and his mother, too, was a well-educated person. His brother, two years older, was well above average intelligence and physically normal. Kevin was big for his age—nearly as tall and strong as the brother—but he was unlucky enough not to have a prepossessing appearance. At the age of five he started to attend the same private school as his brother, with whom he was naturally compared to his own disadvantage. He failed to make progress and caused a certain amount of trouble among the other children, so that after a couple of terms the school asked the parents to remove him. He was clumsy, but could the clumsiness be due to the fact that his physical size made him physically awkward? He was slow to learn, but could that be due to shortcomings in the teaching? He was an annoyance to other children, but when he barged into them and knocked them down it might well have been due to an affectionate nature combined with clumsiness. He was over-active and had difficulty in concentrating, but how far did this reflect his anxiety in the school situation and could it indeed have reflected the parents' anxiety over his failure to come up to his brother's standards?

The local state infants school admitted him but the reception class was large and it was impossible to give him individual attention, so that things went from bad to worse. He obviously enjoyed the company of other children so that when kept at home he resented the isolation and it became increasingly difficult to prevent him from interfering with his father's professional work and his mother's domestic routines.

Intelligence tests were inconclusive because of poor cooperation, but it seemed as if he might be in the low normal or high E.S.N. range. The child guidance clinic confirmed this but was sure that there was some emotional disturbance into the bargain. He was not unduly clumsy in ball games or the other general activities usual to children, but he seemed to have some problems of co-ordination and space perception. At this point he had two or three epileptiform fits, but the electro-encephalograph showed no very marked disturbance and the fits had occurred at times of special stress in the home. The parents appreciated that something was wrong, but it was difficult to discuss the problem with them, precisely because one could not point to anything clear-cut and definite. This illustrates a not uncommon problem, which deserves a little comment. The uneducated parent is usually likely to accept the doctor's authority uncritically. The intelligent and educated parent, by contrast, wants to have things explained in detail and it is important that this should be done if one is to get the fullest possible understanding co-operation. The doctor, by virtue of his professional training and experience, is able to see the significance of a number of signs and symptoms, none of which is conclusive in itself but which when taken together build up at any rate a strong presumptive case. Non-medical people, like Kevin's parents, are conscious of the fact that when the evidence is broken down into its separate parts none of those parts can stand alone. Perhaps in this case the father's legal training made him specially critical of what seemed to him the 'flaws' in the medical reasoning, but in this particular field of work with the handicapped the evidence inevitably contains a lot of 'ifs' and 'buts'. Eventually the parents consented to Kevin's going away to a residential assessment unit. The detailed study which was made there did not add much to the picture which had been built up previously; its chief value—and this was quite considerable—was that it confirmed that nothing serious had been overlooked and it produced that little extra expert authority which was needed to make the parents realize that the boy's troubles would have to be taken seriously.

The end of Kevin's story is not a very happy one. He was admitted to a special school which had had considerable success in dealing with children of his type and for a while he made appreciable progress. His schooling was, however, interrupted by episodes of illness and he became difficult to manage. It is impossible to say whether there may have been some intellectual deterioration or whether his troubles were largely emotional—I suspect the latter—but eventually the school asked for his withdrawal. He came home and attended a junior training centre but the behaviour problems continued and he is now in a residential unit for disturbed and mentally handicapped children.

Note that there was no single aspect of Kevin's disability, until the fits occurred, which could not have been consistent with his being generally 'normal'. Only an over-anxious parent would have been likely to seek medical advice sooner and in all probability the family doctor would have noted the parent's over-anxiety and have made light of the matter. Even the fits, had they occurred earlier, might have been discounted and it would have been hard to blame a doctor who preferred to wait a little while and see if they recurred. Not till the combination of stresses produced by school—change of environment, the need to mix with other children, unfamiliar and somewhat demanding tasks, the call for special skills—made all the parts of the disability combine simultaneously to produce manifest trouble which could not be ignored, was the need for action imperative.

Some children in this class have in their history one or more of the things which are taken into account in 'special care registers'. If so, then the regular developmental examinations and checks which are carried out are likely to arouse suspicions by the time the child is three years old or, possibly, earlier. The majority, however, will have no such history and until our knowledge of the subject is greatly increased it will be unrealistic to hope for really early diagnosis. At the present time, there is a feeling in certain quarters that the first school medical inspection, now carried out between three and six months after the child starts school, should be replaced by a detailed examination six months before he is due to enter school. If this became standard practice it would probably lead to the earlier detection of this kind of disability and make it possible to avoid the school entry stresses which can so easily make things worse. In the meantime, however, probably all that can be done is to alert all those who might be concerned to the possibilites and to seek advice on all children who have difficulty in settling down in school. It must be borne in mind that such things as specific reading and writing difficulties and trouble in learning the finer skills are not likely to be observed until a child has been at school for some time and that children with these problems may well be found normal at the first school medical inspection. The consequent risk of their being left without a medical check until their next routine inspection is due emphasizes the need for close and understanding contact between the school health service and the teacher.

## Care, Management and Education

Medical or surgical treatment as such has not a great deal to offer to these children, though the use of the anti-convulsants and similar drugs may be of some help in reducing the excessive activity. General management and education are the things which can help most. Note that the different parts of the total problem react on each other. Failure to learn will produce frustrations in the child and make him even more distractable and irritable and, in consequence, reduce his ability to learn. Failure at school will produce tensions and anxieties in the home and the child from a tense and anxious home will have even more trouble in settling down at school. Anything which reduces stress will be beneficial and probably the most important ingredient in care is infinite patience and tolerance, something which is far easier to prescribe than to provide.

Where, as in Kevin's case, the family expects more of the child than he can perform, the realistic acceptance of the facts by the parents will be a considerable step in the right direction, but even so the actual problems created by his behaviour disorders in the home will make it hard to produce the needed calmness. If there are specific learning difficulties, then it may be that special attention to those difficulties will break the chain reaction on the educational side and allow of gradual settling down. If the learning difficulties are more general and associated with limited intellect, then admission to an E.S.N. special school may be the answer. The less demanding atmosphere of the school and the slower pace which it sets will be likely to diminish the tensions arising out of education; a difficulty here is that because the child may not be notably and obviously below average in intelligence the parents may not easily reconcile themselves to his going to such a school and may not co-operate with the staff. If so, the tug of war between home and school can be disastrous.

In a considerable number of cases the stresses in the home seem to be the most important single factor, which raises the question of whether the child can be expected to make good at all while he is still at home. With the right guidance many parents can adjust themselves to the child's needs, but this is a tough job, not to be taken lightly and may be made impossible by home circumstances. In Kevin's case, for example, the domestic set up made it impossible to adjust the running of the house—and the father's professional work—to his needs and a boarding special school had to be the answer. While he was waiting for a vacancy we achieved the rather uneasy compromise of letting him attend a small village school half-time and arranging for a half-time home teacher, but this was made tolerable for all parties only by the knowledge that it was a temporary arrangement.

There is certainly no standard answer to the problem and it is likely that a process of trial and error will have to take place in most cases. So far as it is possible to generalize, one may say that it is unlikely that the ordinary state primary school will meet these children's requirements in the beginning, because the present size of classes make some standardization of educational methods inevitable, while most ordinary private schools though their classes may be smaller, still do not have the teachers whose special knowledge and experience can give the child specific help. Remedial teaching in the home by a suitable specialist teacher if one is available and if the home circumstances permit may often be the best practicable measure. Early diagnosis, however, offers the best hope, for the more one sees of these children the more one feels that the year or two of consistent and unexplained school failure which so often precedes diagnosis has done damage which makes the whole situation substantially worse and which is extremely hard to repair.

## FURTHER READING

*Cerebral Palsy*
Carlson, E.   Born That Way.   Evesham, James.
Dunsdon, M. I.   The Educability of Cerebral Palsied Children.   Newnes.
Illingworth, R. S. (Ed.).   Recent Advances in Cerebral Palsy.   Churchill.
Morgenstern, M., Low-Beer, H. & Morgenstern, F.   Practical Training for the Severely Handicapped Child.   Spastics Soc. & Heinemann.
Neal, E.   One of Those Children.   Allen and Unwin.
Saunders, J. and Napier, M.   Spastics in Cheyne Walk.   Pitman.
Schonell, F. E.   Educating Spastic Children.   Oliver & Boyd.
Spastics Society (Loring, J. A., Ed.)   Teaching the Cerebral Palsied Child. Heinemann.
Woods, G.   Cerebral Palsy in Childhood.   Wright.

The Spastics Society, formed by the amalgamation of the British Council for the Welfare of Spastics and the National Spastics Society, has published a variety of booklets and pamphlets on the subject. It also publishes, in association with the Association for Special Education, a journal, Special Education, intended primarily for teachers and other workers in the educational field and a journal intended for medical readers, Developmental Medicine.

# CHAPTER 21

# Speech Defects

A few—a very few—children have an organic defect of the speech mechanism. Sometimes this is a defect of the palate or mouth—cleft palate or hare lip or both combined. Very rarely there is a defect of the larynx or the nerves which activate it. Rather more often the disability is due to some kind of damage to the brain. But the overwhelming majority of children with speech defects have a disability which is more correctly described as a disorder of the use of the speech mechanism.

Speech is not inborn. As already mentioned in Chapter 12, a child learns to speak by listening to the sounds which other people make and by imitating those sounds. Anything which interferes with the speech learning process will delay the acquisition of speech and may result in failure to speak properly. The failure may range from complete inability to speak (a consequence of the most severe forms of deafness) through varying degrees of intelligibility to persistent 'baby-talk', inability to produce certain speech sounds or a slight persistent lisp. The sounds, of course, must not only be produced but must be produced to order in the right place and at the right time, and even in the normal child there may be a considerable time-lag between learning how to make a particular sound and using it correctly in spontaneous speech. Furthermore, it is normal for a child to be able to recognize and understand words for quite a long period before he is able to speak them recognizably.

Stammering, the commonest of the seriously handicapping speech disabilities, seems to occur in about one child in a hundred. It is not to be confused with 'cluttering' in which the words pour out so rapidly that they, so to speak, fall over themselves and become a tangle of indistinctness. Some occasional hesitations in speech are normal. They often occur in young children who have not yet become fluent and it is perfectly natural for older children and adults to be slightly at a loss for the right word in circumstances of stress or excitement. The stammerer knows what he wants to say and has the right word ready to his tongue but something out-side his will makes him repeat the initial sound or even prevents him from uttering the word at all.

### Developmental Failure

So many factors influence the development of speech that it is impossible to be precise in defining 'milestones'. During the latter part of the first year of life the child is experimenting with the making of sounds and may jabber away quite eloquently. His jabbering inevitably contains some monosyllabic words, but it is usually the beginning of the second year when he shows, by look-ing at or pointing to a person or an object, that the words are being used deliberately. By fifteen months he will probably speak any-thing up to six recognizable words and will understand many more. Toward the end of the second year he will begin to put words together in groups of two or three. By $2\frac{1}{2}$ years he has acquired a much wider vocabulary including some of the pro-nouns (I, me and you) and some prepositions. At three years his vocabulary may be 250 words or more, he uses plurals and pro-nouns and though he still misuses some sounds, substituting easier ones for difficult ones, most of what he says is intelligible to strang-ers. By the age of four his pronunciation is fairly mature, with only a few substituted sounds, and he is accustomed to putting words together in sentences which, though short and simple, have the elements of proper construction.

It is not difficult to understand the causes and the consequences of failure in speech development. Sounds cannot be imitated unless they are heard. The totally or severely deaf child will not, therefore, progress beyond the initial jabbering stage, making the automatic experimental sounds without realizing what he is doing. Unfortu-nately, among those sounds there will inevitably be some which sound like 'da-da' and 'ma-ma' and other one- or two-syllable words, which proud parents will interpret as the beginnings of speech, thus delaying the diagnosis of the condition. The slightly deaf child, who hears reasonably clearly sometimes when people speak loudly to him, may well follow the normal early stages of development but at much less than the normal speed. The child with adequate hearing for the low frequencies but seriously im-paired hearing for the higher frequencies will hear the vowels without being able to distinguish the consonants (Chapter 14); his speech, too, will develop slowly and remain well behind the milestones for his age. Though he will try to put words together in short sentences the words themselves will be indistinct.

The mentally retarded child will hear sounds but in this, as in other things, he will be a slow learner. He will take longer to appreciate the significance of sounds, to understand the differences between them and to store in the bank of his memory the words which he hears, as well as being slower to use that bank in the production of meaningful sentences. It is quite possible for him, in the end, to develop reasonably good and intelligible speech without specialist help, thus doing rather better than the child with high-frequency deafness.

The commonest reasons, however, for the multitude of moderate developmental defects in speech lie outside the child himself. If a normal person is slow to learn there is likely to be some defect in the teaching and this is as true of speech as of every other activity. The natural speech teachers are the parents—especially the mother—and in a lesser degree the other members of the family. The child in good rapport with an intelligent mother is, as it were, bathed in the sound of the same simple words and phrases in the same surroundings, day after day, and associates sound, intonation, expression and meaning, gradually building up the potential and the actuality of speech and naturally extending his powers and his vocabulary as his experience and the range of his contacts with people increase. If circumstances deprive him of this close contact with mother and he is not given an adequate substitute or if, for any reason, the mother-child relationship is impaired, one can expect slower progress with speech.

In general, he must be taught the speech he is expected to have. He will easily acquire the mother's mispronunciations and accent and if there is too much 'baby-talk' carried on for too long, then the child will get the baby-talk habit. This is not to suggest that all adults should always talk pedantically to children or even that there is anything wrong with the way in which most children acquire and use for a time strange words of their own devising; it is rather to warn against the way in which some parents find their children's baby-talk 'cute' and appealing and either consciously or unconsciously try to preserve it.

Even learning to speak demands some effort and for effort there must be incentive. The home where the child's wants and needs are anticipated so that he need not do more than point or grunt, or where everyone is too busy to listen to him when he tries to communicate will delay progress. Other children at risk in their environment are children of a mixed marriage, where two languages are used in the home, the youngest children of large families and, not infrequently, twins.

The principles of care and treatment follow quite logically from the foregoing. The special needs of children with hearing disabilities or defects of intelligence are dealt with in the appropriate chapters. Where these factors are not present, advice to the parents on management and, in older children, admission to a nursery school or infant school and association with more accomplished talkers can achieve a great deal. Not infrequently the child may catch up with his peers without special treatment, but it often happens that faulty pronunciation habits and specific difficulty with certain sounds persist; if so, speech therapy can be expected to correct the trouble.

In the normal child in a good home, then, retardation of speech development is not a very grave matter and can probably be dealt with effectively. This makes it all the more important to end this section with a serious warning. While faulty or delayed talking is quite likely to be something which may come right spontaneously or quickly respond to treatment there is always the possibility that it may be the result of impaired hearing or intelligence, of early emotional disturbance, or of defective family relationships. No speech disability should be dismissed as trivial or transient until these possibilities have been carefully considered and eliminated.

## Stammering

On the live stage or the cinema screen, on television or on sound radio, the dramatist or script writer knows that he can usually count on some laughs if he introduces a character who stammers. The Great Stammer Joke is by no means new; Aristophanes used it in a play twenty-three hundred years ago and he was undoubtedly following a formula which had been tried and trusted by generations of writers before him. In real life, of course, a stammer is anything but a joke to the sufferer. Because stammer commonly begins early in life, the victim suffers more—and longer—from the laughter of others than does either the Short-sighted Professor or the Deaf Mother-in-Law, the two other handicapped people who are commonly found to be ludicrous. The fear or the fact of others' laughter does not make either short sight or deafness worse, but it well can and often does add to the severity of a stammer. It is thus hardly surprising that over the centuries a multitude of 'cures' for the condition and theories as to its cause have been sought, used and, alas!—discarded as failures.

Stammer, or stutter (the two words are virtually interchangeable) is essentially a disturbance of speech rhythm. It shows itself as repetition of sounds or syllables or as more or less prolonged complete blocks in utterance, often accompanied by grimaces or body movements. Most stammerers do not stammer all the time but may in some circumstances speak quite fluently for a longer or shorter period. The moderate or even the severe stammerer may on some occasions be quite fluent and on others be unable to utter a word. Whether the stammer be mild or severe there are often certain 'key' sounds which cause him trouble and when he comes to one of these—or even when he sees the obstacle half a sentence ahead—he will stumble over and repeat the syllable or even 'dry up' altogether.

In some degree it is a common disorder. It is estimated that one per cent of the general school population suffer from it as a more or less persistent condition and that as many as 4 per cent go through a phase of slight stammer but recover spontaneously. Some authorities regard a short stammering phase as a normal part of speech development, but others draw a distinction between the hesitancies of the pre-school child, which usually clear up without difficulty, and true stammer. It is commoner in boys than in girls, the ratio increasing as the child grows older. For a long time it was commonly believed that it was mainly associated with high intelligence but recent investigations suggest that the reverse is correct. Often there is also a history of stammer in the family.

The usual pattern is for the disability to start in the early school years and to grow worse between 11 and 14 as the child becomes more self-conscious. If untreated, it reaches its maximum in adolescence or early adult life, after which there may be a tendency for it to improve, probably because the victim learns to live with it. He may do this by acquiring more poise and learning to avoid the use of words which contain the key sounds, but it must be remembered that stammer can in itself delay the acquisition of poise and that the deliberate choice of easier words can produce tensions which actually cause bouts of stammering.

## Causation
Theories about the cause of stammer are still many and varied. The

presence of family histories of stammer suggests a possible genetic cause. It is sometimes associated with signs of 'minimal brain damage', which suggests that the cause might be defect of perception or mild mental subnormality. Many authorities regard it as probably the result of emotional disturbance or conflict and some suggest that it is at times due to learning difficulties. The association of stammer with a tendency to left-handedness has long been a subject for speculation; it gave rise to some ingenious theories about the possibility of some 'interference' between those neighbouring parts of the brain which deal with speech and with arm and hand movement, but current thought is rather on the lines that in these cases stammer is due to the child's being confused emotionally or perceptually by being forced to use his right hand when his natural tendency is to use the left.

As in so many other fields, there is plenty of scope for argument. If stammer and emotional disturbance are present together, may it not be that the embarrassment of the stammer is itself enough to cause emotional stress? Is it possible for a child unwittingly to imitate a stammering parent or relation, or may the inherited factor be simply a tendency to be emotionally unstable which sometimes shows itself in a stammer and sometimes in other ways? If learning difficulties can produce stammer, is it not equally possible that the possession of a stammer may impede a child's progress at school? It is probable that every theory I have mentioned, except the 'brain-interference' one, has some foundation and that any one of them, or several of them in combination, may account for stammer in any particular case.

## Treatment and Management

This uncertainty about causation makes it impossible to devise any standard treatment based on the removal of the cause. If there are other signs of emotional upset, then these should certainly be investigated, but psychiatric treatment is not often essential. The great majority of cases respond very well to speech therapy combined with the right management and counselling. Relaxation plays a large part in treatment, but there is no special magic in just lying down and relaxing on the floor of the speech clinic for half an hour twice a week. Relaxation is taught in the clinic in the hope that the child will learn how to find greater mental and physical ease when he is faced with the ordeal of speaking and reading, and it is important that both the home and the school should encourage and help him in this. In addition some special techniques are used by therapists in individual cases.

Most important is the 'feed-back' mechanism in stammer. The knowledge that one stammers makes for fear and hesitation and confusion; an actual paroxysm of stammer builds up tension. Fear, hesitation, confusion and tension all combine to make the stammer worse and so on ad infinitum. If the stammerer once begins to learn to live with his disability then the disability quickly starts to grow less. Should parent or teacher or the person he is talking to show anxiety and apprehension about the stammer, then the stammerer catches the anxiety and stammer is precipitated. In so far as there are any golden rules in management they are that the child and his stammer should be accepted in as matter of fact a way as possible and that those who look after him should try to keep any sort of stress and anxiety situations down to a minimum.

Should the pre-school child or the primary school child with the first signs of a stammer be referred to the speech therapist? If this is done clumsily, with much fuss and apprehension, then it may make things worse, but the answer to the question is undoubtedly 'Yes'. The stammer which is caught in its primary stage offers excellent prospects of quick success in treatment and, bearing in mind that entry to school is often a dramatic exposure of an immature child to social and emotional shock, the pre-school stammerer should have care in good time.

The apparently cured stammerer can relapse if he is subjected to sudden stress. This may be due to a crisis in the home, to happenings at school or to a combination of the two. School crises are usually those which involve a change of surroundings, for example a move up from the class of a well-loved teacher into the class of an unfamiliar teacher with a reputation for strictness, or the transfer from primary to secondary school. Two periods which are specially important are, rather obviously, the months before the 'eleven plus' examination and before the G.C.E. examination. Especially in the case of the two latter, reassurance is unlikely to make much difference to the type of boy or girl who gets anxious about these things and is unnecessary for the phlegmatic child. All that can be done is to watch for signs of trouble and then enlist the speech therapist's help quickly.

Relapse during the few months after leaving school is also not uncommon. This is not unexpected. Every adolescent at this period has to make considerable adjustments to a new type of environment and new responsibilities and the stammerer is, in addition, moving from an environment in which his stammer, when it occurred, was accepted with equanimity to one in which it is likely to be met with laughter or impatience or both. It is most important that there should be some follow-up facilities for speech therapy at this stage and most education authorities encourage this, either directly through their own clinics or by liaison with the hospital services. An arrangement which has much to commend it is for the local authority's speech therapist to carry out a weekly session of work in the hospital where, in addition to seeing general hospital cases, she can give this continuing care to her former clinic patients.

## Organic Speech Defects

Though organic speech defects may be uncommon it is desirable to make some brief reference to them in this chapter. The actual 'machinery' of speech involves a complicated chain of processes which may be roughly outlined, without using too much technical terminology, as follows.

Conversation—speech in response to hearing—begins with the reception of sound by the ear. Impulses pass to the brain by the auditory nerve and it is the task of the brain to interpret them and relay them to those brain areas where 'thought' takes place. The reply to the incoming message passes along a similar chain, via the areas of the brain which control the muscles of speech and along the nerves which activate the muscles so that in the end the respiratory muscles, the larynx, the tongue, the palate and the lips combine to produce the speech sound. Spontaneous speech— speech which is not prompted by something which has just been heard but which originates in the individual's own thoughts or wants—starts in the higher brain centres and is, of course, independent of the reception-interpretation process. Organic speech defect is essentially an interruption of this reception-interpretation- expression chain by damage or developmental failure in any of its parts.

Defects in the ear and the auditory nerve are forms of deafness and must be considered and dealt with as such. Defects which interrupt the chain between the reception of impulses in the brain and the sending out of impulses which will activate the speech organs are generally spoken of as 'aphasia' (absence of speech) and 'dysphasia' (difficulty with speech). A number of terms have been coined to describe various types of aphasia and dysphasia but since the whole matter is still the subject of intensive study and not all the technical terms are yet generally accepted as precise it may be best to think in terms of function.

One type of difficulty is failure to differentiate between and to recognize speech sounds, even though these may be perfectly received by the ear. This needs to be distinguished from the condition known as 'word-deafness' in which the sufferer cannot understand spoken language or repeat spoken sounds though, again, his hearing for sounds in general is not impaired. In both these groups spontaneous speech can be present, though it may be imperfect because the imitation of heard sounds depends, naturally, on the power to distinguish them as well as on the power to hear them.

Another difficulty, often called 'expressive aphasia', lies in the inability to distinguish between words when these are being formulated in the brain before they are used in speech. This may result in the use of a word which is vaguely similar to the one intended or in the use of one entirely different. 'Motor aphasia', a term which is undoubtedly quite valid, refers to a condition in which all goes well until the time has come for the speech muscles to be put into action but the action of those muscles is not properly co-ordinated.

One important and obvious consequence of any kind of aphasia or dysphasia is secondary emotional disturbance. Since one's relationships with other people depend very much on ability to communicate with them it is only to be expected that inability to communicate will prevent the formation of normal relationships and may promote the formation of abnormal ones. The child with these disabilities may, therefore, be in varying degrees withdrawn, hyperactive, over-dependent and unstable and show behaviour disorders. But these features are precisely those which we can expect to find in many psychotic or autistic children, and it is not surprising that a diagnosis of aphasia is provisionally made in some children who later turn out to be autistic! Again, lack of communication tends to slow down normal intellectual development, so that the dysphasic child who shows slow progress and some emotional upset may be classed as 'brain damaged'. As his dysphasia may indeed be due to brain damage it may be complicated by other and quite genuine evidence of such damage and the problem of sorting out which of his troubles are primary and which are secondary can be most puzzling.

So far as care, treatment and management are concerned, the first essential in the dysphasic child is to get expert help in the task of defining the elements of the trouble. Once this is done it may be possible to do quite a lot to reduce the disability by special training in either the comprehension of heard speech or the production of speech sounds, though in severe cases one must not expect too much in the way of results. Fortunately, even a moderate degree of improvement in response to training is likely to be followed by substantial emotional improvement and general developmental progress.

As regards organic speech defects due to faults in the actual speech mechanism, the commonest is deformity of the palate in the shape of cleft palate with or without hare lip. The upper jaw and palate begin to develop in two halves which normally join together, but in some cases the joining is imperfect or fails altogether. In the most severe cases there is a complete division running from the back of the soft palate right through to the front of the upper lip but one is more likely to find a lesser degree of defect ranging from a minor notch at the back of the soft palate to a substantial gap in both soft and hard palates.

Modern techniques of surgery are usually effective in producing a good functioning palate in all but the most severe cases. Specialist surgical advice must always be sought as soon as the defect is noticed and in fact surgery may have to begin in early infancy. Where surgery cannot effect complete closure the child may have to wear an obturator—a kind of upper dental plate—to close the gap mechanically. The 'good functioning palate', however, is not necessarily a perfect one and speech training and therapy will commonly be needed unless the defect is very minor indeed. There is a good case for enlisting the help of the speech therapist at an early stage and not waiting to see if the child develops 'cleft palate speech'.

There remain a miscellany of other defects which need not be considered at great length. 'Tongue tie'—a shortness of the fraenum or fold of membrane under the front of the tongue—looms larger in the popular imagination than it need. It worries many mothers without real cause for in fact a fraenum which looks short in a small baby is likely to stretch sufficiently to give perfectly normal speech. If it is long enough to allow the baby to suck his food there is every prospect that it will be long enough to enable him to talk; in the rare cases in which it is genuinely so short as to impede speech only a very minor surgical procedure is needed to put it right.

Paralysis of speech muscles in the larynx or palate is uncommon in childhood. Since such paralysis is due to nerve damage there is little chance of recovery even with surgical help and the most one can do is to give the child training and speech therapy.

What might be called 'resonance troubles'—the so-called 'catarrhal' or 'adenoidal' speech—cannot fairly be classed as speech disorders but may be briefly mentioned for the sake of completeness. Their essential cause is one or other type of chronic catarrh of the nose or sinuses and this can be cleared up satisfactorily by attention to general health or, if necessary, by the removal of adenoids. Quite often, if the catarrh has gone on for a long time, the bad speech habit will persist long after the organic trouble has been cleared up and speech therapy will be necessary to correct it. There is also some evidence that some persistent types of catarrhal speech trouble may be partly due to faulty voice production and in such cases speech training can be a useful step in improving the underlying condition.

### FURTHER READING

*Speech Defects*
Morley, M. E.   Development and Disorders of Speech in Childhood.

The College of Speech Therapists has published a number of useful booklets on the care and treatment of children with speech disabilities.

# CHAPTER 22

# Psychotic Children

During the past fifteen years or so, there has been increasing concern about 'non-communicating' children. These are, literally, children who fail to communicate with other people. They may have no speech, or speech which is largely unintelligible; they may make little or no attempt to communicate even by gesture. In extreme cases they may be virtually unable to make any relationship at all with other people. The obvious questions which one asks about them are, first, are they able to 'receive' communication from others (are they deaf or blind?), second, are they able to receive but unable to understand what they receive (are they grossly mentally handicapped?) or, third, can they receive and understand but are they unable to make any response?

There is no doubt that many of these children are, in fact, deaf or mentally handicapped. There is equally no doubt that many of them are intelligent and have little or no hearing defect but have been wrongly diagnosed as deaf or mentally handicapped. In fact, quite a number of factors may operate, separately or together, to produce communication failure. Recent research suggests that something approaching one-half of all non-communicating children are seriously mentally handicapped and that one-third of these are also deaf or emotionally disturbed. By contrast, deafness, with or without emotional disturbance, is the principal factor in only about one-tenth of the non-communicators. A few are aphasic and a few brain-damaged, but in some 25 per cent of the total the trouble is primarily due to emotional disturbance of greater or lesser degree.

The terms 'psychotic' and 'autistic' have come into use, somewhat loosely, to connote this particular group of unfortunates. 'Psychotic' is, in any event, a difficult term to define. In adult psychiatry it is generally used of people who have severe and lasting mental illness or disturbance of a kind or degree likely to require admission to and treatment or care in a hospital for the mentally ill. In childhood, the child guidance clinic is likely to call a child psychotic when he is considered to be too severely disturbed to be acceptable to a school for maladjusted children or to benefit by attending such a school. 'Autism' is most correctly used in referring to a special kind of manifestation of psychosis in which the child is 'withdrawn' in an extreme degree.

Perhaps the best introduction to the subject is to give a history of one case which vividly illustrates not only the problems of the child but the problems which face those who try to find out what is wrong with him and what they can do to help him.

Hugh was taken to the local hospital at the age of four and a half, with the story that his speech had been normal till he was four but had deteriorated and almost disappeared during the last six months. The hospital regarded him as very deaf and recommended him for special school education. His history, when we enquired into it, was rather peculiar. His home was not very stable and from infancy, though he lived with his parents, he was mainly cared for by a neighbour. About the time when his speech began to deteriorate the parents moved house and took him with them, thus separating him from the neighbour, but they went back to the old place after a couple of months and Hugh was again spending much of his time with the neighbour and seemed well and happy. Though the father said his speech had previously been normal, the mother and the neighbour were less sure about this and there was also some evidence that the boy had had an infectious illness of some kind shortly before the trouble began.

We suspected emotional disturbance as a cause, but on enquiry his behaviour and his relations with other children appeared to be quite normal. He seemed slightly mentally retarded, but this was probably not important. There remained the undoubted possibility that the illness had damaged his hearing and this, in act, would have been quite consistent with a history of previous normal speech which had progressively deteriorated. We sought the advice of most eminent experts in the field of deafness and their findings were quite definite; he was severely deaf, this was the cause of the speech trouble and he urgently needed special education. A place in a suitable special school was found for him but the parents refused to accept it. After fifteen months of vain attempts to persuade them to co-operate—fifteen months during which Hugh's speech had entirely disappeared—a compulsory school attendance order was made and he started at the special school.

His attendance was interrupted from time to time, the parents finding various excuses for keeping him at home. Nevertheless he seemed to settle down though he made little educational progress. All orthodox tests confirmed his serious hearing defect but the headmaster of the school suspected that there might be some other factor involved and used a variety of ingenious and unorthodox tests. By the end of a year there was convincing evidence that he had a substantial amount of hearing. In that time he had been heard to speak twice only, once to quarrel with another boy and once to swear at the school dentist, but both times he was quite intelligible!

Obviously there was a need for psychiatric investigation but the parents flatly refused to let him go to a psychiatrist. Only after a further six months of strategems and conspiracies with a friendly paediatric unit did we eventually get a psychiatric assessment, to the effect that Hugh had pretty certainly had an unusual but severe episode of mental illness. With the psychiatrist's concurrence we arranged for Hugh to go to an ordinary day school near his home, where the headmaster was particularly interested in and patient with disturbed children. After a rather difficult settling down phase he began to make some slow progress but new troubles beset him. The father was becoming seriously mentally disturbed himself, while the mother was a weak and rather unstable character. Things came to a head just as the boy was due for transfer from primary to secondary school and the parents separated, though the father stayed in the neighbourhood and continued to exercise some authority of a blustering and tactless kind over both boy and mother. Almost inevitably, it would seem, Hugh became difficult and aggressive in school, losing much of the ground he had gained, and found himself before the juvenile court after some petty thefts.

In the event, this worked to his good. We were able to use the court appearance as the occasion for another full investigation, which, incidentally, showed his I.Q. to be in the region of 90 and his hearing to be little below normal. The father was sufficiently awed by the court to cease interfering and the mother took a little strength from the help of a good probation officer. For the first time she began to show some understanding of her boy's problems and she agreed to his admission to a day special school for E.S.N. children. In fact, the slower pace of that school, the smaller classes and the insight and experience of the staff fitted Hugh's needs well. His speech improved rapidly and he soon began to make good progress in school work. He left school at the age of sixteen with an attainment level consistent with his intellectual potential, but the family left the district and it has not been possible to follow his later career.

This is not a pleasant story. The only people who come out of it with real credit are some of his teachers. But it is worth telling because it is the sort of tale that is still too often met with in these cases of psychotic and autistic children. It is easy to be wise after the event and to see which clues to the mystery were valid and which were merely red herrings but at the time the misleading ones appeared strong, the parents, partly by design and partly by accident, confused the issue repeatedly and the depth of their own emotional troubles, probably the most important factor of all, was deliberately hidden from us.

Hugh's autism—his contracting out of normal relationships, emphasized by the way in which his disturbed mind closed his ears and bound his tongue—was fairly typical but was not so severe or prolonged as in some cases. He certainly showed what one might call a tendency to 'positive but abnormal' relationships, as exemplified in his aggressiveness and his later delinquency. Nothing very special has been done for him in the way of treatment or management, but as long as a year ago the psychiatrists felt that he was beginning to pass out of his mental illness and recent happenings suggest that this was a correct assumption. Not every autistic or psychotic child is so fortunate.

Looking at psychotic children as a whole one finds two things which are almost invariably present, serious and prolonged impairment of emotional relationships with people, and serious retardation with learning difficulty, often with 'islands' of normal or even higher than average ability in some things. Because most normal learning comes from or through relationships with others, the retardation is probably largely the consequence of the emotional failure though—and this is important—the child may be basically mentally subnormal. Whatever his inherent capacity, however, the emotional disturbance prevents him from making full use of it.

The other things which may accompany psychosis are variable. Hearing and speech, the normal media of contact with other people, often fail. Some children, psychotic from early infancy, may not develop speech or show signs of hearing at all. Rather more often, the psychosis develops in the toddler years and speech and hearing regress, as in Hugh's case. Sometimes it is obvious from the child's response to music and other sounds that there is no serious hearing defect, but there is still no speech; this arouses suspicion of aphasia—organic speech failure—or 'word deafness'— a failure to perceive words. Sometimes he uses words and phrases and is obviously capable of speech but he is unable to use speech purposefully and to converse.

Outside the field of hearing and speech there may be poor response to vision, giving rise to suspicion of eye defects, or insensitivity to physical pain. Excessive anxiety and fear are quite common and these may be coupled with lack of fear of real and common dangers. There may be excessive or subnormal physical activity, bizarre movements and mannerisms or clumsiness. Anxiety is common and so is aggression. The child may be intensely attached to all manner of curious objects and yet have no interest in toys.

## Causation

In the sense that he is concentrated in himself and is the only part of his world that he is aware of, every child starts life by being autistic and normal development is a continuous process of growing out of this, punctuated by phases in which he briefly behaves autistically. We might, therefore, look for causes in factors or influences which will prevent or retard normal development. These may well be social or emotional—instability in the home, especially if the parents are emotionally unstable, or maternal deprivation can undoubtedly play a part. It seems, however, that there can also be organic causes, including such things as brain damage or brain tumour. Certainly this kind of trouble can occur in children who are mentally subnormal, blind or deaf. How these causes operate is uncertain, but it might well be argued that the brain damage, mental subnormality, blindness or deafness make it harder for the child to respond to the stimuli which normally awaken children to the world around them. This cannot be the whole story, since most children with these disabilities do not become psychotic or autistic; we can only assume that the organic factors combine with social and emotional factors to produce the end result, though which loads the gun and which pulls the trigger is as yet unknown and probably varies from child to child.

## Diagnosis and Assessment

There are no short cuts to diagnosis and assessment. The psychotic child can have a wide variety of symptoms and most of those symptoms could be due to a number of causes. In Hugh's case the apparent deafness was so obvious that he was referred to people who specialized in dealing with children who had hearing defects. They concentrated on this aspect and produced the expected answer. With the psychotic child whose chief symptom is slow development it is easy to make a diagnosis of mental subnormality and get expert confirmation. In other cases equally firm diagnoses of brain damage and various sensory defects can be made. A counsel of perfection might be that every child who appears dull, deaf or otherwise abnormal and has no obvious physical disability of sensation or movement should be considered as potentially psychotic and should have a careful and thorough team investigation to make sure whether this is the case, but obviously the skilled resources at our disposal are not enough to provide for this.

Experience shows that when psychotic tendencies are detected early it is usually because some shrewd person who has seen quite a lot of the child has found something which does not quite fit into the expected pattern. Hugh's headmaster in his special school did this. Where the obvious disability is retardation and intelligence tests in expert hands have appeared to confirm this, one finds that someone who is in close and regular contact with the child—a nursery matron or a teacher, for example,—may catch him at odd moments with his barriers down and see flashes of normal intellectual function. The interested and perceptive health visitor has proved quite a good case-finder in this field, for more than one reason. Not only may she have the chance of seeing the child in a variety of surroundings, but because of her contacts with the family and her knowledge of the neighbours and the neighbourhood she may be able to get clues to emotional tensions in the home which have been successfully concealed from the doctors and the other special investigators. Once there is reason to suspect emotional disturbance in the parents, in the child or in the parent-child relationship it is worth while to take a new look at the apparent basic disability.

Assessment is a prolonged task for a wide-ranging team. Non-verbal intelligence tests can certainly be useful, but the fact that they show a certain capacity to solve practical problems is no sure indication of capacity to respond to formal education. More than in any other form of disability, prolonged expert observation is the only method which is likely to produce results. We are not only looking for signs of ability or disability but for response and reactions to education, environment, stimuli and people. For the most severely disturbed children, and especially for those in whom autism is prominent, a special observation unit is likely to give the best results and more such units are urgently needed. But this must not obscure the very real value in the less severe cases of observation in a more normal environment—the home, the nursery and the school (including the special school).

## Treatment and Education

The obvious question to be asked is whether, since these children are showing the signs of mental illness, they might be helped by the methods of treatment which are used for mentally ill adults. Experience so far suggests that this has only limited scope. Some drugs may be of use in helping to reduce excitability and insomnia but they do not touch the underlying trouble. Shock therapy has little if any value. Psychotherapy offers help to a few, especially when the child has become psychotic or autistic after making a normal start in development in the early years of life, but it is not to be expected that there will be enough therapists to treat the majority even if treatment offers some slender hope for them.

The aim of treatment and care is essentially to crack the protective shell into which the child has withdrawn and this is first and foremost a problem of personal relationships. Up to now, it would appear that the good teacher in the school environment, given adequate expert support, is the likeliest person to succeed in this. In the right circumstances, indeed, the school can provide a 'therapeutic environment', giving the child a chance to express himself and his phantasies and, perhaps, through a relationship with things and pets to work through to a relationship with people.

What sort of school should he go to? There is no general answer to this. Some people advocate special schools for autistic children and, indeed, there are some successful special units. As yet, however, we do not know how many such children there are and it seems probable that the number will be so small as not to make it practicable to provide special units for the majority within reasonable distance of their homes. It can also be argued that since the first need of these children is for stimulation and most of them have no speech it is unwise to segregate them into small, isolated groups.

It has been suggested that, since they are emotionally disturbed, psychotic children might do well in schools for the maladjusted; experiment shows that this rarely works, probably because the child has already withdrawn so far from reality that he cannot begin to make contact with those who are much less disturbed.

Because treatment and education cannot be separated and because education is a part of the process of assessment, it seems reasonable that wherever a treatment or diagnostic unit is set up in association with a hospital there should also be a teaching unit and this idea is proving its worth in practice. But, looking generally at experience up to date, it would appear that the actual type of school is not important. Placement in special schools for E.S.N. children can and does work, probably because the school is geared to a slow speed of educational progress and because class groups are small. The Rudolf Steiner organization, whose work in special schools is characterized by infinite patience, has scored some successes.

Though it is impossible to be dogmatic, we may here have the basic answers. However and wherever psychotic children are educated, they must be in small groups, and there is a good case for mixing the autistic with those who have some communication by speech. The staff must be chosen with special care, no less for their personality than for their training and experience, and the children must have a judicious mixture of group and individual care. There must be psychiatric supervision and help readily available in the school. And, finally, school and home must work together, an argument against residential units for most cases, The home has a cardinal part to play and the parents must be given guidance in the care and management of the child with, in some cases, more material help through the social services. Theoretical guidance and material help must, however, be translated into practice and the best way of achieving this is by a genuine partnership between teachers and parents in which each may well learn something from the other.

## The Outlook for Psychotic Children

Under this heading there is, unfortunately, little to be said with authority. Our understanding of childhood psychosis is limited, largely because its nature has been recognized only very recently. Some children seem to improve spontaneously and one must, when looking at the results which present care seems to produce, wonder whether some of its apparent successes are really due largely to chance. It is likely that the severely psychotic child, if left alone, will have a somewhat bleak future in which he may be severely mentally ill in the adult sense or at best will lead a life in which he is functioning at much less than his potential.

With early recognition of his disability and the right sort of care he may, by adolescence, come to something approaching normality in both intellectual function and social behaviour. How far, from this point on, he is still psychological vulnerable and exposed to serious risk of relapse into mental illness we do not know, though it would seem likely that he may need a good deal of support from time to time if this is not to happen. Only in ten or fifteen years' time, when some of our apparent successes have been watched during the years of exposure to the stress of living, shall we be able to assess our results. Meanwhile, the knowledge that already some successes are being achieved and that we are learning more about the subject with every year that passes justifies at any rate qualified optimism.

### FURTHER READING

*Psychotic Children*
Rutter, M. Infantile Autism. Churchill/Livingstone.

# CHAPTER 23

# Specific Learning Disabilities

In Chapter 18 it has been pointed out that substantial disability of any kind, by delaying the start of a child's education or by interrupting or impeding his attendance at school may slow down the rate at which he learns, so that his attainments at any stage are below the average for children of his age. Obviously children with mental handicap will learn more slowly than the average, while children with marked visual or auditory handicap will have difficulty in learning at the normal speed.

Over the years, however, it has been found that a number of children with no apparent substantial disability make slow progress in school, often in reading and writing, rather less often in arithmetic and sometimes in all of these. This has naturally caused a good deal of speculation as to whether, apart from the conditions which are usually recognized as 'handicapping disabilities', there can exist less obvious disabilities which directly and specifically affect a child's learning without otherwise interfering with his daily life.

In particular, there has been much reference to a condition sometimes called 'word-blindness' and sometimes 'dyslexia' or 'specific dyslexia'. This subject has produced much heated argument and the fact that some people have chosen to adopt doctrinaire attitudes has not helped progress toward understanding. One school of thought has taken the line that there is no such thing as word-blindness or dyslexia. Another insists that there is actually some highly specific organic condition which essentially affects reading ability, uses the term 'specific dyslexia' for this condition, and strongly objects to the word 'dyslexia' being used to describe any other form of reading difficulty.

There is still a great deal of ignorance and uncertainty in the matter, but in recent years discussion has become much more reasonable and open-minded. In any book of this kind it is important that some reference should be made to the subject and this chapter attempts to set out the situation as it stands at the moment.

Any incompetence in reading and writing is bound to handicap a person substantially or even severely. Inevitably, much education in any school subject is obtained through books, so that the non-reader or the child who has difficulty in reading is, consequently, a slow learner generally. Writing is, perhaps, a subordinate skill, but in the educational process it is difficult to separate the two and the child who cannot write will have problems in the expressive aspects of communication and the acquisition of language skills and facility.

Outside school and after school life, the acquisition of informal education from books and newspapers is greatly impeded by reading difficulties though at the present time radio and television are a considerable help to discovering something about the affairs of the community and of the world at large. Much of the ordinary traffic of daily life is based on the assumption that everybody can read and write and the majority of employments also postulate a certain level of literacy; anyone whose attainments fall below that level is socially disadvantaged. No less important, in the long run, is the popular belief that since the intellectually handicapped tend to be illiterate the fact that a person has trouble with reading and writing is a sign of deficient intelligence; the poor reader consequently may find himself looked down upon by his fellows, and has to face a considerable amount of emotional stress and even stigma.

There is no doubt that reading difficulty can be a severe handicap in every sense of the term and that those who suffer from it need sympathy and active help just as much as, say, the hard of hearing and the speech handicapped. General lack of accurate knowledge on the subject has made it hard to get any practise estimate of the number of sufferers but it seems quite possible that 2 per cent or more of children of average or higher intelligence have substantial difficulty in learning to read and some authorities would suggest that this is an under-estimate.

## Causation.

The current view is that the majority of cases of reading difficulty are caused by a number of factors acting in combination. A small proportion cannot be adequately accounted for except on the assumption that the child involved has some specific neurological disability, which is constitutional in character and may be congenital (due to developmental anomaly or injury before or during birth) or the result of brain injury by disease or accident after birth. No-one knows the nature of the disability. In some cases reading difficulties appear to run in families but it is not possible to say with any assurance that this points to the probability of a specific genetic cause. In cases of this kind it seems correct to use the term 'specific dyslexia'. However, while sometimes the whole of the individual's reading disability can be ascribed to this cause, it is probable that in many instances the specific disability may be reinforced by other causal factors.

It is certainly convenient to use the term 'dyslexia' (its literal meaning is 'difficulty with words') to cover a condition which may be roughly defined as 'marked difficulty in acquiring reading skills in a child who has normal intelligence and has had normal educational opportunities' and a definition along these lines is now being accepted by many people working in the field.

As regards the many causal factors which may operate in dyslexia, it is not possible in this chapter to give more than a somewhat superficial survey of the most probable ones.

In the first place, the written and printed word is an arbitrary and highly sophisticated way of expressing language. To develop reading skills requires in any event a good deal of hard work and anything which reduces the child's capacity for work may in itself impede reading development. It may well be, therefore, that any child with any substantial handicap may find the acquisition of reading specially difficult. Moreover, this hard work is not immediately rewarding; it is not uncommon for highly intelligent normal children to make slow initial progress, often for a matter of years, but to begin to forge ahead rapidly on making the discovery that the ability to read literally opens a new world to them. Lack of motivation and lack of cultural opportunity in the home can be important factors. Often the parent of a slow reader may say 'Me and his father weren't no scholars neither' or something to that effect.

Much remains to be discovered about learning mechanisms. There is no doubt that people have what might be called 'preferred memory patterns'. Some remember and learn—these are the largest group—mainly visually; they remember mainly by 'seeing things in the mind's eye'. Others work mainly by an auditory mechanism, 'hearing things in the mind's ear' as it were.

Yet others learn and remember mainly by association. We do not know whether these preferences are inborn or acquired, but it would seem likely that the 'auditory' and 'associative' groups will have inherent difficulty in learning something like reading, which is essentially a visual matter; most written language is not phonetic and commonly lacks any really rational pattern.

If reading and writing involve understanding of the expression of language in symbols—which, of course, they do—then anything which impedes the child in distinguishing language sounds and symbols will hamper him in this field. It is certain that defects of vision and hearing, probably quite minor defects which cause him no trouble in other activities, will contribute to his learning difficulty in this sphere. There is, however, more to be taken into account than shapes and sounds in themselves. The significance of reading symbols depends not only on their actual shapes but on their relationship to one another.

Before he reaches school age the child is accustomed to deal with concrete objects which have a fixed and constant shape. A spoon is a spoon, a plate is a plate, a bus is a bus; though their shapes and colours vary one plate differs from another considerably less than a capital A from a small a or a printed z from a written z. And at least spoons, plates and buses keep their identity whether they are right side up or upside down. To the logical mind of a child it must seem quite irrational that one simple symbol has four different meanings according to whether it appears as b, d, p or q. If the child has some disability which makes it hard for him to discriminate between shapes or between the position of shapes, then he will obviously find it hard to learn to read. In fact, we do find that defects in discrimination and in recognition of orientation are quite commonly met with in dyslexic children. How these defects arise is uncertain. Sometimes they are genetic and sometimes they may be due to minor brain damage. But whatever their origin, they certainly do play a part in the production of dyslexia.

Quite often, inco-ordination and clumsiness are also associated with dyslexia. Obviously they will impede writing, probably they will interfere with the child's learning about shapes and relationships in the early years and may so lead on to reading difficulties. However they are commonly due to brain damage and it is thus possible that the child may also have independent perceptual difficulties.

Some authorities believe that dyslexia may be produced by

purely emotional causes. It is reasonable to expect that a child who is emotionally disturbed may have a 'learning block' and that this should show itself particularly in an inherently difficult subject. We know that the relationship between a child and a teacher or between a child and his school as a whole may produce a situation in which the child will not learn from that teacher or in that school. We know that many dyslexic children have emotional difficulties. What we do not know is whether the chicken or the egg came first. For it is only likely that if a child has difficulty in making progress in a key subject at school and, for reasons which he cannot understand, finds himself in consequence much inferior to his peers, he will develop emotional problems. If a teacher finds that an obviously able child is getting nowhere in reading and writing, in spite of her best efforts, it is not unnatural that she should begin to label the child lazy, stupid or just plain 'awkward' and thus produce a teacher-child relationship which conduces to behaviour disorders and maladjustment.

Just how these many kinds of factor relate to each other it is hard to say. Possibly the best way to sum up the situation is to say that a very few children have a specific disability which, even if they are otherwise quite normal, will make it exceedingly difficult or even impossible for them to learn to read. Some of these few, and a considerably larger number without such specific disability, will have other disabilities which will make reading difficult or demand of them, if they are to learn to read, much more effort than a normal child would have to expend. And any of these may have further disabilities which will restrict the amount of effort they are going to be able to put into the task.

## Diagnosis and Assessment

Dyslexia, from whatever cause or causes, too often goes undetected or is detected only after the first few years in school. It would be helpful if there were some means of predicting, from signs in the early years of life, those children who would be likely to have reading difficulties, but progress in identifying such signs has not as yet gone very far. The most that can be said at present is that children with any evidence of even slight defects of vision and hearing and with any signs suggestive of even minor brain damage should be regarded as potential dyslexics. Of course, 'signs suggestive of even minor brain damage' is a rather indefinite term. There are a few such signs, but in Chapter 20 it is pointed out that many children with disabilities which might be due to minor brain damage do not show any specific signs. Where there is something specific, the hint which this gives of risk of dyslexia is most useful. However, in a field of work so little explored and understood, there is a good deal in favour of following a more general rule—that any child who has been a 'slow developer' in the pre-school years should have some special attention during the first year or two of school life. Whatever the causes of that slow development he is certain to have some difficulties in settling into school and will benefit by timely help of some kind.

For reasons suggested above, many children who cannot fairly be termed dyslexic are going to have difficulty in getting started on reading. The child whose early history suggests that he is a potential dyslexic should be watched with particular care and referred for special investigation if he seems to be finding any appreciable difficulty in reading during the first two school years. Otherwise it is a good working rule to refer a child for investigation if he is making outstanding progress in other school activities but has not made a fair start on reading by the end of his first year in school or if by the age of seven or eight he is two years behind the average in reading attainment whatever his achievements in other activities may be. Such a child, whether dyslexic or not in the stricter sense of the term, is certainly going to need some special help with reading or, quite possibly, some special arrangements for his education as a whole.

What sort of special investigation should these children have? It is probably unnecessary to arrange for a complete neurological examination in the majority of cases and in any event there are not enough paediatric neurologists to provide this for all such children. The school health service, in collaboration with the educational psychologist (who is in any event an important member of the school health team) will be able to check his hearing and his visual acuity and find any substantial clumsiness, defects in co-ordination and 'handedness' disability and, also, make some assessment of his intelligence. Emotional difficulties and cultural deprivation in the home should also be looked for.

### Treatment

Any defect of vision or hearing should be dealt with and any physical illness treated. Substantial maladjustment will justify referral to the child guidance clinic; minor maladjustment is as likely as not to be a result of the learning disability as its cause and would not justify child guidance referral.

Whether or not any physical or emotional defect is discovered, remedial teaching should be started. There is no particular system of remedial teaching which can be advised for any of these children. Some teachers have claimed specially good results from the use of some systems, but it is probable that what really matters is the amount of attention given to the child and, perhaps even more, the personality of the teacher and the rapport she achieves with the child. How the teaching is organized depends much on circumstances. A large school may be able to provide its own remedial class; a smaller school may make do quite well with a visiting special teacher or with a member of the regular staff who has had special training in remedial work and who is allowed adequate time to do the job. Some education authorities have provided remedial education centres which serve a group of schools and which the children attend part-time.

This last has advantages and disadvantages. It is a convenient way of making use of specially trained staff with economy of time. It does, however, interfere with the child's ordinary school attendance and carries the risk that the child's school may feel that it need take no responsibility. This can be really dangerous. Reading is certainly a basic part of education but it is only a part. The child's general management in school must fit in with whatever special teaching he is receiving and his ordinary class teacher be an understanding partner of the remedial teacher. It would, indeed, be much to the good if all teachers had some training in the elements of the problems presented by special learning difficulties.

## The Outlook in Dyslexia

Because the ability to read and write is basic to all education, the dyslexic child will be permanently educationally disadvantaged all round. However, experience shows that if the right sort of special help is given early enough the majority of these children will become reasonably competent readers. If the special help is delayed beyond the age of ten the prospects of success are considerable reduced.

Some, however, will not achieve average standards however good the remedial teaching and however early it is begun. Very few of these will be in the end completely unable to read. Their problem is rather that they will be able to read only very slowly, that they will stumble over or misread even slightly unfamiliar words and that their spelling will be not merely somewhat bizarre but sometimes incomprehensible.

So far as career prospects are concerned, it is obvious that life will be made easier for them if they can be groomed for a kind of occupation which is not too demanding on the slow reader. The trouble is that too often the process of education for a career requires that they should have some knowledge of subjects which are difficult to learn if one cannot read and that very often, before one can actually start on a career, one has to get over the hurdle of examinations. Slowly, the understanding of the dyslexics' problems is spreading and an encouraging number of examining bodies are making allowances for them in the actual conduct of examinations. Individual coaching in special subjects, making minimum use of reading, and the new examination policy are making the career outlook considerably better.

But, as for people with other handicaps, there may be conflict between the career one wants and the career which seems 'sensible' in theory. There are few better examples of the way in which achievement for a handicapped person is related to the price he is prepared to pay. The case of a certain eminent actor is worth quoting. A basic skill in his profession is the study and memorising of parts. For him, reading is a task which takes many times as long as it does for other people and he cannot guarantee accuracy. However, his wife and friends are prepared to help with the words about which he is uncertain and he finds that with this help he can learn parts provided that he is prepared to give all his reading time to this study. He has willingly abandoned not only 'leisure' reading—books and the weekly reviews, for instance— and even the attempt to keep up with current news through the daily papers for the sake of his profession. That this should disadvantage him socially in a profession in which social contacts can be extremely important is to him an acceptable, though by no means a minor, penalty.

To be dyslexic in a world of readers produces stresses long after school age has passed. A source of 'inferiority' which cannot be accounted for is considerably more difficult to put up with than one which can be understood by oneself and others. Some dyslexics are specially discomfited by the knowledge that they are handicapped by something which can never be cured, though against this one must set the occasional case in which a person who has stumbled and faltered through a school career which has convinced him that he must be stupid has been helped to come to terms with life by the final realization that his slow progress has been the result of an irremediable disability which has nothing whatever to do with stupidity.

The realistic dyslexic, like so many other handicapped people, can, give understanding help, develop various techniques which help him to by-pass his disability, sometimes by using a private code of symbols or by anticipating situations in which he might be required to read or write. But he is constantly confronted with a disturbing dilemma. Is he to risk displaying himself in public as illiterate or substantially so—with the loss of esteem which this involves—or is he to restrict his social contacts to the small circle of friends and the limited number of activities within which embarrassment will be tempered with sympathy? What the dyslexic probably needs most of all is for his disability to be better understood and his difficulties to be better appreciated by the public at large.

## Other Learning Difficulties

Are there in fact many people who suffer from other special learning disabilities? It is difficult to say. Certainly many dyslexics have trouble with figures—arithmetic and the more advanced branches of mathematics. Possibly their number disability may be secondary to their dyslexia and the basic learning retardation which it produces, but there are some non-dyslexics who appear to be what might be called 'dysnumerate', so the existence of such a special disability may be assumed as probable. Fortunately, or unfortunately few people are afraid of confessing that they are no good at mathematics; fortunately in that they get ready sympathy but unfortunately in that their disability does not attract special study.

Number symbols are fewer than letters and easier to cope with in that there is none of the confusion between sound and symbol that bedevils reading. Some people have inherent difficulty in 'sequencing'—appreciating the relationship between a series of symbols. This certainly contributes to dyslexia and can clearly be a fundamental obstacle to dealing with number. However, much remains to be discovered in this field.

Other 'special subject difficulties' are still a matter for speculation. Probably some of them are due to the operation of preferred memory patterns. Particularly a person with a poor visual memory will have trouble with subjects which are primarily visual. Arthur, a highly intelligent lad, did outstandingly well at school and met with no difficulties of any importance until he became a medical student, when he failed abysmally to make progress with anatomy. His career might have ended prematurely had he not been lucky enough to meet a teacher who taught the subject functionally; when he realized that if a muscle was to do its job it must be attached to a particular spot on a particular bone and that a joint would not operate as it should unless its ligaments and its internal surfaces were in particular places and had particular shapes the subject began to make sense and lost its worst terrors.

Fortunately, most school subjects can be taught both visually and auditorily, and there is usually a sufficient mixture of the two techniques in the teaching methods of most schools for the majority of children to learn the fundamentals of the important subjects. However, if this matter of memory mechanisms were more deeply studied and teaching of children who experience difficulties were appropriately oriented it is probable that more than a few children would learn with less pain and, perhaps, some would be compelled to waste less time on unnecessary school subjects in which they can never be expected to attain competence.

# CHAPTER 24

# Unusual and Multiple Handicaps

It has been said that no handicapped child has a single disability. There is some literal truth in this. To have one disability puts one at risk of developing others, whether the speech disability which so commonly follows hearing impairment or the emotional or social disability which can further hinder the child with substantial motor, sensory or mental handicap. But there are some children who have two or more primary disabilities and these need special consideration.

The second commonest combination, much less frequent than the first but still quite often found, is that of maladjustment with some physical handicap. I have tried to show in various chapters of this book how every physically handicapped child has special emotional problems to face and though most, with skilled help, solve their problems there remain some who do not achieve emotional adjustment. 'Chestiness', which includes asthma, has, as we have seen, an emotional aspect. All schools for delicate children contain some who are emotionally disturbed and all schools for maladjusted children have some pupils who suffer from asthma, eczema or other partly allergic disorders.

Much less frequently one meets children with combined physical and sensory or two sensory handicaps. A blind or deaf child may be crippled by illness or accident, or a crippled child may develop a disease of the eyes or ears. We have seen that infections and other factors still imperfectly understood may affect the proper development of the mechanism of sight or hearing, cripple a child or produce a congenital defect of the heart. It is hardly surprising that these causes should sometimes produce two defects simultaneously—indeed the marvel is that they do not do so more often.

## Assessment
The greatest risk in all cases of multiple handicap is, as in this case, that of underestimating intelligence. Since intelligence can be

measured only by the way in which the child uses it, virtually any physical disability in the early years of life may produce some suggestion of mental subnormality. Defects of sight and hearing make verbal intelligence tests useless, while performance tests in general are by no means accurate and many of them are impossible to a child with severe visual disability.

Mental subnormality has its physical repercussions. It is not possible to assess the hearing of a young child without intelligent co-operation and while total or gross general deafness can be diagnosed fairly easily in the mentally subnormal, partial hearing loss and especially hearing loss over part of the frequency range cannot be accurately measured until the child has reached a mental age of four or five, which may not be till his chronological age is much greater. Manual dexterity has definite association with intelligence and, as already mentioned in the case of cerebral palsy, it is often hard to say whether impairment is primarily physical or mental.

In all cases of multiple disability assessment, therefore, demands prolonged observation. This may be possible in the home, but it is probably best done in a special centre or school at least in the beginning. The clues are often subtle and variable and the child's response to management by experienced people in the centre is at least as important as the results of specific tests.

Not only assessment but even actual diagnosis of disability may be seriously complicated when two handicaps exist at once. This is well illustrated by the case of Alice, who was referred to me at the age of three because she had virtually no speech and showed other signs of mental subnormality. She was referred somewhat late because she had a congenital cardiac defect which had received first consideration and had just been repaired by surgery. Her general history was quite consistent with gross subnormality. She did not begin to sit up till she was over two and she was not yet walking, while she had made virtually no response to toilet training. Standard intelligence tests produced no worth-while results and it would have been excusable to estimate her I.Q. as probably between 30 and 40. She was, however, interested in toys and her use of her hands was certainly developed beyond her apparent general level.

Simple tests of hearing gave doubtful results, but if she were deaf the lack of speech development would be accounted for. Was it possible that her failure to walk had been due to the heart defect?

Alice answered this question for us—within a month she was walking with support. She also responded quickly to pot training; with her heart handicap she had not been strong enough to sit on the pot for long enough to use it! Within six months she was walking and running as freely as a normal child. In the meantime audiometry had demonstrated substantial hearing loss. A hearing aid had been provided and she quickly began to make skilful use of it. A period as a weekly boarder at a nursery school for hearing-handicapped children showed that she was certainly intelligent and that she was probably likely to do well in a school for partially hearing children. This promise was fulfilled and as she approaches school leaving age she bids fair to become a useful, well-adjusted —and, indeed, a charming—young woman.

Unfortunately, special centres and schools for doubly handicapped children are not to be found in every street. Centres for spastic children have been mentioned in the appropriate chapter and are making good provision for children whose multiple handicap is due to cerebral palsy, but for the remainder the situation is complicated by the tendency of schools to specialize. I recall the case of a child who, normal up to the age of five, contracted measles and developed encephalitis. He survived, but was grossly mentally subnormal and substantially physically handicapped and showed also a good deal of behaviour disorder. His home was quite incapable of providing what he needed but no special school for any of the three classes of handicap from which he suffered was prepared to admit him. He could have been classed as ineducable and admitted to a hospital for mental defectives, but I resisted this drastic step because I felt that he was capable of some improvement in all three respects if he were given good general care and management. Eventually, admission to a Rudolf Steiner centre gave him his chance and in the course of a few years he settled down to a state in which he was slightly physically handicapped, mentally retarded but educable in a special school and virtually normal— for his category—in behaviour. If the story of Alice emphasizes the need for early definite action in some cases of multiple handicap, this second story demonstrates that more Fabian tactics are sometimes justified.

## Treatment

The treatment of multiple handicaps is, from the strictly medical or surgical point of view, the sum total of the treatment of the

L

single handicaps. It is in the working out of a treatment programme that trouble begins. It may be that the treatment of one involves a regime which conflicts with the treatment of another, or that to admit the child to a hospital which deals with one may interrupt the treatment of another. Certainly if more than one of the handicapping conditions is likely to respond to treatment there is a risk that the total treatment programme may grossly disrupt the child's education.

Sometimes, as in the case of Alice, it is obvious that one disability which is fundamental is likely to respond well to early treatment. Even had the full range of her hearing disability been understood early it would still have been worth while to postpone or seriously interrupt her early auditory training while the cardiac disability was being treated. As it was, not only training and education but general assessment were impossible while her deformed heart disabled her.

While I dislike generalizations in any field of work for the handicapped, I am ready to say that if one disability in a child with multiple handicap is likely to respond to *early* treatment, then it is usually sound to give treatment of that disability priority, even if care of the others has to be temporarily neglected. Where treatment offers hope of curing or alleviating more than one of the disabling conditions, first choice should go to whichever treatment is likely to be most successful in producing a cure; if a doubly handicapped child can thus be changed into a child with a single handicap the advantage is obvious. The most invidious choices occur when treatment of a defect, though holding out good prospects of improvement, may be prolonged and conflict with other forms of long-term treatment. If a child is substantially but not totally deaf and also crippled, auditory training and speech training during the first few years of life are of vital importance. They cannot be given in an orthopaedic hospital, so that a long stay in such a hospital would have deplorable effects on the child's prospect of ultimately hearing and speaking. Even if delay in starting orthopaedic treatment would reduce the prospect of first-class results, such delay is the lesser evil.

Because the education of the child with multiple handicaps is more difficult than that of the singly handicapped child, the balance between the educational need and the medical and surgical need has to be very carefully struck. It is sometimes possible to get through the major part of the treatment programme before the child is seven or eight; if so, this should be considered because an uninterrupted educational programme from seven or eight to sixteen is better than one from five to sixteen with interruptions. If, however, the best results from treatment demand a series of spells of treatment at intervals, then they must be timed so that they do not interrupt or disrupt education at critical stages. And what I have said above of orthopaedic surgery can apply also to other forms of treatment; it may be necessary to accept less than the best in one field so that the best can be obtained in another.

## General Care and Education

In the child with multiple handicaps the first principle still applies: one must find out what the child has on the credit side of the balance sheet and build up on that. The highly intelligent child, though crippled and deaf or crippled and blind, must found his life upon his intellectual ability. The dull child, whatever his other disabilities, needs full concentration on his physical powers and treatment, management and education must all be oriented in that direction. In respect of each individual handicap the child needs the care and education appropriate to that handicap, but it is obvious that it will be more difficult to give him the specific care which is needed and the home, however good, will have a harder task so that help from outside and education in a special school will be more likely to be necessary.

As I have said, the incidence of two or more simultaneous severe handicaps is comparatively uncommon, so that the demand for and the supply of special schools for the severely multiple handicapped is not very great. Most special schools, however, can tolerate and accept children who in addition to the appropriate principal handicap have a minor or moderate additional handicap and some little general guidance can be given on certain combinations.

*Crippling and mental handicap.* Most schools for the physically handicapped have small classes and many of their pupils are already educationally retarded because of interrupted schooling. They are, therefore, likely to be able to accept children with an I.Q. down to 75 or even 70 and to give them some education with children who are their equals in attainments though their superiors in intellect. A school for the educable mentally subnormal will provide for children with I.Q's. down to the 60 or even 55 mark and can accept a few children who are moderately physically handicapped;

the severely physically handicapped may lose much from being unable to participate in the considerable and important physical activities of the school. The majority of those children who are markedly handicapped both mentally and physically are victims of cerebral palsy and special schools for spastic children are beginning to do promising work with them.

*Epilepsy and physical handicap.* As I have indicated elsewhere, ordinary schools are reluctant to take epileptic children and this reluctance is more marked in special schools, some of which insist that any history of 'fits' shall be an absolute bar to admission, even if the fits are being or have been brought under control. Enlightened schools for the physically handicapped are beginning to take some well-controlled epileptics, but the best prospect of acceptance is in a special school for epileptic children.

*Epilepsy and mental handicap.* Much the same applies in this combination, perhaps with the greater justification that mentally handicapped children will be more disturbed by the fits of an epileptic schoolfellow than mentally normal children. (It must also be conceded that a boarding school for children with other handicaps which accepts an epileptic child has to face the grave responsibility of looking after him outside school hours.) Since mental deterioration is not uncommon in epilepsy, the special school for epileptics already has some pupils who are mentally retarded and not only is the combination familiar to the school but the child has some of his equals to associate with.

*Maladjustment and Physical Handicap.* In this combination, the maladjustment is often in a large degree the consequence of the physical disability. If it is not gross, understanding care in a school for the physically handicapped may produce substantial improvement. The association between maladjustment and 'chestiness' has already been referred to and schools which cater for chesty children expect to receive a certain number of maladjusted pupils as a matter of course. Provided there are not too many and provided that the necessary psychiatric supervision and advice is available, things seem to go well. The maladjusted child with a physical handicap does not fit well into a school for maladjusted children unless the physical disability is very slight; the contrast with physical normality is usually so emphatic and painful that the maladjustment is worsened.

*Maladjustment and epilepsy.* Instability of personality, like intellectual deterioration, is not uncommon in epilepsy. Schools for the maladjusted prefer not to take epileptics unless the fits are well controlled. Some experts believe that the combination is sufficiently common and sufficiently difficult to deal with to justify special school provision, at any rate on an experimental scale, for maladjusted epileptics, but this has not yet been tried. In the meantime, the special school for epileptics is probably the best choice when the fits are severe or frequent.

*Blindness or deafness and mental handicap.* The child who is blind or deaf needs full normal intelligence to do himself justice; if he is mentally below standard his problem is naturally more difficult. Because he needs teaching by special techniques the ordinary special school for mentally handicapped children cannot even begin to help him. He must, therefore go to a special school for the blind or the deaf. The association of blindness with mental handicap is particularly difficult to deal with and requires a special school for the blind which includes a unit for those who are also mentally handicapped.

*Blindness or deafness and maladjustment.* Early adequate training, in the home and at school, usually does much to make the deaf or blind child adjust satisfactorily. The child who acquires deafness or blindness is certain to have difficulty in readjusting to his new life, but since the sense defect is the dominant one, admission to a school for the blind or the deaf is imperative and the school will be prepared to deal with his emotional problems.

*Blindness or deafness and physical handicap.* Here again, the sensory handicap is the more urgent. For the blind, physically handicapped child a special school for the blind will be necessary throughout his school life and if the physical disability is severe a special unit for children with the combined disability is best. The intelligent deaf child, if his deafness is not total, has, as we have seen, a prospect of finding his way in the end to an ordinary school and there are deaf and physically handicapped children who, equipped with a hearing aid and given auditory and speech training, transfer to and make good in a school for the physically handicapped.

*Blindness and deafness.* The blind-deaf present the most difficult of all problems. Helen Keller has been a superb example of what can be achieved when a person of high intelligence suffering from this dual disability receives skilled individual teaching, but her type of exceptional success demands exceptional qualities of intelligence and personality; it is not within the powers of the majority of blind-deaf children. The fact that the gateways of both sight and sound are closed makes it quite impossible to use the methods practised in schools for the ordinary deaf or blind child, though if the deafness is moderate and if a hearing aid is provided early and auditory training is given the child may make some progress in a school for the blind. Teaching techniques for this combination of handicap are not yet fully worked out; the future probably lies in special units for the deaf-blind.

## The 'Thalidomide' Children

As far back as records go, a small number of children have been born with limb deformities or limbs missing. It is estimated that in Britain the annual number of babies with severe defects of this kind is in the region of 200. But in 1960–61 it seemed that the number was suddenly increasing. Two hundred is, of course, only one in every 4,000 births and even if the number were going to double—which is just what happened—no individual doctor would see more than the occasional one and it would necessarily take some time before obstetricians, paediatricians and orthopaedic surgeons getting together to compare notes would be in a position to find out what was happening and look for a cause. Helped by clues from Germany, British investigators came to the conclusion that many of these cases were occurring in children born to women who had, during pregnancy, been given the new sedative 'Thalidomide', which had been on the market in Germany for some years. On the assumption that the drug was poisoning the unborn child and producing faults in development it was withdrawn from use and its withdrawl was followed by the passing of this increased incidence of limb deformities.

Just how the drug acted is still not completely understood. The first assumption that it 'poisoned' the child is not fully proved and there is a new theory of its action which may turn out to be the right one. This is that many children with deformities of this kind are born too prematurely to live (Nature, as it were, discarding imperfect handiwork) and that the effect of thalidomide was in fact to enable the mother to carry a deformed child to full term rather than to have a spontaneous abortion. Such an explanation is by no means impossible and if it is true we have to face the possibility that the same kind of thing may happen again when other new and successful sedatives are put on to the market. Meanwhile, two things have happened. Though some of the limbless children have died, quite a number of them are now in or about to enter school and they present the community with a problem which has to be solved. But on the credit side the sudden arrival on the scene in such dramatic and distressing circumstances, of about three hundred children with severe limb disabilities has stimulated research into ways of helping them and those children who in later years form the 'normal quota' of the limbless will have a better outlook as a result.

The actual deformities vary widely. Some of the children lack all four limbs or, at least, have all four so severely deformed as to be of little use. Some have useful arms but absent or grossly deformed legs, some have normal legs and feet but have no arms or only short 'flippers'. There may also be other defects. Very few have impairment of intelligence—not more than would be expected among a random group of physically normal children—but it is not very uncommon for them to have congenital heart deformities or defects of sight or hearing.

Parental rejection, as might well have been expected, was very common at first, but so far as one can tell the realization that other parents were facing the same difficulties and the immense wave of public sympathy which was produced by the dramatic circumstances seem to have radically altered the picture. The public conscience felt strongly that something must be done and there has, in fact, been a quite unique professional effort, individual and collective, to see that something is done. It is too early to say whether and to what extent the effort will produce satisfactory long-term results, but a brief account of what is happening can be given.

I have repeatedly referred to the importance of experience and stimuli in early life in enabling children to learn how to do things. This has been fully taken into account in attempts to enable these deformed children to get some kind of sitting, toddling and reaching at the ages at which they would normally begin to do such things. For the child with no legs, who cannot sit up, a moulded plaster cast—the 'flower-pot'—is made, so that he can spend some of his time in an upright position. Short calipers with 'rockers' at the ends are fitted to the leg stumps so that balancing and some kind of movement can begin during the second year of life. The child with feet but no arms is encouraged to use his feet for 'hand' purposes in the beginning, but artificial arms of a simple type can be fitted at, or soon after, a year old. Both artificial arms and artificial legs are, of course lengthened and made more elaborate as the child gets older and grows in size. (The chief virtue of using the feet at first is, of course, that it helps to develop the idea of a sense of touch, which cannot be done through an artificial arm.)

Most past experience with artificial limbs has been with adults or with children who had lost a limb through an accident. Such patients are conscious of their loss and have the task of unlearning their old way of doing things before they can start on the new. The limbless babies start with a clean sheet and take to their artificial limbs quickly and successfully. Since young children tend to be more interested in what they themselves can do than in the achievements of other children, they tend to prefer the artificial arm which is useful to the one that 'looks normal' and much use is being made of the split hook type of arm and the arm to which practical attachments can be fitted rather than the 'cosmetic' arm and hand which look more like ordinary limbs but are less practically effective. Because of the smallness of the limb-stump it is often difficult to make use of the type of arm which is controlled by the wearer's own muscles and light-weight arms powered by cylinders of compressed gas are being produced and seem to be very effective.

Assessment of these children needs to be just as complete and careful as that of children with any other type of handicap. Among points to be considered in their special disabilities are the possible need for surgery, which can sometimes make a deformed limb usable or a stump more suitable for the fitting of a prosthesis, and the potential usefulness of a short arm or of a hand with some of the fingers missing. Because of the possibility of other defects, assessment must take special account of vision and hearing and though the child's intelligence is likely to be normal it should nevertheless be estimated; the occasional mentally subnormal child and, of course, the one with unusually high intelligence, will need appropriate special care and management.

What kind of care is given in the pre-school years will depend on circumstances. Mixing with other children is important but so is the provision of whatever artificial limbs may be necessary and training in their use. Ideally one would think in terms of living at home, going to a day nursery and attending a day centre for limb-fitting and training, but there are comparatively few limbless children and it is obviously impossible to have a day centre within easy reach of all of them. If the question of limb-fitting is the most urgent, then a residential centre for limbless children is the most practical answer for the majority, but always the desirability of getting the child into a more normal environment must be borne in mind. If the deformity is not very severe or is confined to one limb it may be better to put the emphasis on normal environment right from the start.

If there is a hearing defect it is important that the child should have auditory training in the early years; the risk of adding communication difficulties to deformity might justify giving first priority to this and accepting rather less successful limb-fitting. Similar considerations might apply in the case of blind limbless children. It might, however, be possible to combine attendance at a day centre for the limbless with special sensory training in the home.

So few of these children have completed schooling that their educational problems are still rather a matter of theory than of practical experience. As always, attendance at an ordinary school should be the ideal and in fact something like half of those who have started schooling are making the grade in such schools. Both physically and temperamentally some limbless children are not ready, at the age of five, to cope with the rough and tumble of large classes. It is important that they should learn to stand on their own feet, both literally and metaphorically, but this means that the class teacher will have extra labour in looking after them; it may be easier for the school to let them stay in their wheel-chairs but it is not good for the children themselves, and their management may demand more of the teacher than is compatible with the present size of classes in many schools. A start in a school for the physically handicapped, with the intention of later transfer to a normal school, may be the best thing for many.

Their later school years are still a matter for conjecture. Will they run up against the problems of social adjustment which I have mentioned as difficult for many senior physically handicapped children, or will they by the time they are eleven or twelve have found their own way of life for themselves? One hopes that the latter may happen. Their prospects after leaving school, in employment and in living generally, need not be too bad for limbless people can, we know, lead useful and happy adult lives. Much will depend upon the possibility of developing more and better aids for them and current work in this direction is certainly promising well.

## Spina Bifida and Hydrocephalus

Spina bifida is a developmental defect of the lower vertebrae accompanied by protrusion of and damage to the spinal cord. It produces complete paralysis of the legs. It is very often accompanied by a blockage in the circulation of the cerebro-spinal fluid which causes enlargement of the skull and severe damage to the brain; without treatment the child is doomed to be a crippled mental defective whose only hope is that in increased liability to dangerous infections may produce early death.

The surgeons' dilemma was a cruel one. An operation might or might not avert the paralysis, but was it reasonable to take, say a one in four chance of lessening the crippling defect if there was still the probability of gross mental defect? There were times when the operation was undertaken with the feeling that perhaps an operative failure bringing more speedy death might be the better result; certainly the situation was not one which would encourage research into operative techniques. But the prospect changed radically when, in the late nineteen-fifties, successful experiments were made in inserting an artificial valve (the Spitz-Holter valve) into the base of the skull so that the fluid might drain away into the blood-vessels instead of accumulating within the brain. The technique is now safe and successful, so that the risk of hydrocephalus developing has been dramatically reduced and during the past six years there has been considerable progress in the surgery of spina bifida. The more severe cases are still beyond operation but in the less marked cases—which still, if untreated, will produce complete leg paralysis—operation undertaken within the first forty-eight hours of life gives a prospect of preserving virtually normal function in fifty per cent of cases and of keeping some worth-while function in many of the remainder.

We still do not know what the long-term consequences of these will be, but it seems likely that in total several hundred children in Britain whose prospects would formerly have been hopeless will now have a chance of worth-while life. When the spina bifida operation is completely successful and either the brain is normal or hydrocephalus has been prevented by a Spitz-Holter valve the child will be to all intents and purposes normal, though there may be some risk of the valve breaking down or becoming ineffective as time goes one. There must, however, be some children whose spina bifida is inoperable or in whom the operation has failed or been only partly successful. Assuming successful valve treatment or the absence of a block to the cerebro-spinal fluid, these will be for all practical purposes physically handicapped children of normal intelligence.

There is no prospect of later surgery reducing the leg disability, so that most of them will be permanent wheel-chair cases. Often, though by no means invariably, they are incontinent of urine, faeces or both. Apart from the fact that the paralysis of the bladder which produces the incontinence also predisposes to urinary infections, which can ascend to the kidney and be dangerous to life, there are considerable problems of management arising from the incontinence and one has to face the possibility that they may for these reasons be beyond the scope of an ordinary school. If the home is a good one and close to the school or transport can be provided and if the school staff are not too overloaded to be able to deal with the incontinence, a trial in an ordinary school is worth while, though school attendance may be interrupted by infections. So far as one can tell, in most cases the smoother and more flexible routine and the more generous staffing ratio of a boarding special school are likely to be best suited to the needs of most spina bifida children, at any rate during the greater part of school life, though the possibility of transferring them to an ordinary school should be considered for the last year or two of schooling. But much more remains to be discovered about these children; even now, operative treatment offers little better than an even chance of survival with good intelligence and useful limb function and in all cases it is necessary to be cautious in making long-term forecasts.

## Haemophilia

This is a very rare condition, occurring perhaps in about one child in 35,000. It is an inherited disability, which appears in males only and is transmitted through the female line. (A very few cases have been reported in females and occasionally a case is found without any family history. The absence of family history could be due to genetic mutation but could also be due simply to the fact that there had been no male children in the family for the last two or three generations.)

The essential feature of haemophilia is that the blood of the person affected takes a long time to clot; the amount of clotting delay can vary considerably and is sometimes not very great, but as a rule the haemophilic is likely to have prolonged bleeding after even minor injury. Not very many years ago there was a strong probability that most haemophilics would suffer injuries which caused fatal bleeding before reaching adult life—often, indeed, in childhood—and the approach to their care was pessimistic in that all that could be suggested was a severely restricted life, with maximum shelter from even minor hazards, until the inevitable happened. However, with increasing knowledge of the disease it is becoming possible to exercise a substantial degree of control over the bleeding and provided that the right care is available a haemophilic has a good prospect of not merely surviving but of leading as complete and satisfactory a life as do most substantially handicapped people. In fact, experience is coming to suggest that if the child survives to adolescence there is good prospect of the condition improving.

The most obvious physical risk is, of course, that of fatal haemorrhage. However, there are risks short of this which are important and the one which is most damaging is that of a minor blow, fall or twist causing haemorrhage into a joint. The haemorrhage in this case is concealed, action may not be taken in time and the re-absorption of the blood may be slow so that permanent stiffening and deformity of the joint may follow. Even if things do not progress so far, joint haemorrages and other injuries may lead to a substantial period of temporary disability, with interruption of schooling or, later, employment. It must also be remembered that because of the risks of excessive bleeding at operation the possibility of correcting deformities by surgery are severely limited.

The general picture, therefore, is one of an apparently normal boy who wants to do all the things that a normal boy should do. But if he is to survive with minimal damage and maximum function he must be sheltered from risks of any kind of injury as far as is reasonably possible, which means that he must forego many of the things that go to make up a normal boy's life. The emotional risks, therefore, are exceedingly important. Things are made worse by the fact that frequent minor haemorrhages tend to make him constantly anaemic and generally below par, so that he has less strength to do what he can do and less overall energy to face the business of living.

Many haemophilics can and do make a success of normal

schooling, but some need a sheltered and 'gentle' environment which cannot be provided in an ordinary school. This need is by no means always due to purely physical reasons but rather to a natural reluctance to being shut out from so many of the activities which are an essential part of the life of his school and his schoolfellows. Otherwise, the indications for a special environment would be usual severity of the condition or the fact that his home or school were situated in a place where special treatment facilities in an emergency could not be easily available; fortunately this is now not often the case.

It is manifestly impossible to put any haemophilic in an environment in which all risks of injury are eliminated. The most innocuous commonplace things in the home and its surroundings can be dangerous in certain circumstances. Sharp instruments can, of course, be proscribed, but all parents know only too well that all young children can break their skin quite bloodily by a fall against a comparatively blunt step or a piece of furniture and that a nose bumped against a flat surface will bleed more than many cuts. This means, in effect, that the young haemophilic cannot be left alone until he has learned to move about with more than common prudence and to watch more carefully than the average child of his age for possible hazards. And it is not enough for him to be accompanied by other children; he needs the company of a cool-headed adult long after other children have reached the age at which they can be allowed to play with their peers.

Learning to be careful is a slow business but not too difficult. The worst part of the haemophilic's learning to live is the acceptance of a restricted life. Almost all other handicapped children learn to restrict their activities as a matter of immediate and obvious necessity; there are some things which they physically cannot do and others which are too tiring or painful for them to do often or regularly. The haemophilic is physically able to do everything which the normal child can do and to do it without pain and, usually, without undue fatigue. There is no certainty of untoward consequences if he does them; in some activities there is a probability of damage if he does them repeatedly, in many there is only a possibility of damage. He may, given wise counselling and, probably, some unhappy experience, overcome the urge to do potentially hazardous things—indeed he must do so if he is to survive—but he may never be able to conquer the wish to do them, knowing full well that he can.

So it is a special and essential part of his education in living that he should be given all possible encouragement, help and opportunity to find fulfilment in non-physical activities, and to acquire a taste for the less robust and non-competitive physical activities so that he may get essential physical exercise in the least hazardous ways. This demands an early start and the prime responsibility will lie with the home. If, before he comes to school age, his life can be biased toward the quieter things it will help him enormously to face the more frustrating aspects of school life and make the inevitable emotional stresses at least a little easier to cope with.

## Multiple Minor Disabilities

It is impossible to deal with all the possible permutations and combinations of all degrees of all handicaps. Probably the best general line to follow if in doubt is to concentrate on the child's general education in whatever school offers the best prospects.

There remains, however, one class of multiple-handicapped child who has not yet received the special attention he deserves. This is the child who has no obvious major handicap but several minor ones. His lack of major handicap may make him at first sight unsuitable for a special school where the other children are more disabled than he is, but in any ordinary school he is at the disadvantage of being unable to come up to average standards in any activities, mental or physical, scholastic or recreational. He therefore faces all-round frustration and the prospect of becoming a maladjusted failure in school and in life. Despite the moderate degree of any one of his disabilities, there is a good case for putting him in a special school environment where in some one way he will have the satisfaction of knowing that he is as good as or better than his fellows.

## The Prospect in Multiple Handicap

Obviously, multiple handicap will be more disabling in the long run than single handicap. The effect is not one of simple arithmetic. Certain employments are open to the blind and certain employments are open to the deaf but it must not be assumed that those employments which are common to the two lists are open to the deaf-blind. In theory they may be, but the combination of deafness and blindness will have so restricted the education of its victim that he is quite unprepared to attempt some of them. The same principle applies to other combinations of disability. The handicapped person has to live as well as work and the more of his available energy which is taken up by the essential business of living the less he will have to give to his employment; the victim of multiple handicap may be so involved in and exhausted by the effort of living that his capacity for employment is greatly diminished.

Because some common combinations of handicap specially impede or delay education, education substantially after the age of sixteen may be needed to bring a doubly- or trebly-handicapped young person to any moderately adequate standard of attainment. This can apply not only to general or vocational education but to education for life as a whole. Prolonged education, whole-time or part-time, should always be considered. Even so, the sheltered workshop is more likely to provide a suitable environment than is open industry. Independence in living is difficult and may be reached only by degrees. A spell of hostel life with an atmosphere of adult semi-independence can provide a useful bridge between the full shelter of a special school and the rigorous life of the world at large.

What I have said of the long-term outlook for the spastic applies in other types of multiple handicap. Confidence tempered by realism is the guiding thread, encouragement within the patient's inevitable limitations but never beyond them. Shelter in work or in life outside work, or at any rate some substantial measure of help from others is almost certain to be permanently necessary, but the environment of help and shelter can be used as a base for modestly satisfying adventure into some of the things that go to make up normal life.

## CHAPTER 25

# The Role of the Voluntary Organisations

Were it not for the past work of voluntary organisations, work for handicapped children would be far less advanced than it is. Were it not for their present activities, the shortage of facilities for handicapped children would be grave rather than merely disturbing. Unfortunately, their part in the total of work for the handicapped is not always played as successfully as it might be and, especially in a time of rapid change and development, it is worth while to take a look at their activities and see whether they might be more effectively deployed.

In any but the most totalitarian kind of social organisation, whether in the advanced countries or the less-developed ones, there is a consistent pattern. It is part of the essential nature of any community, local or national, that it will be slow to spend public money until it not only sees a definite need but has some idea of how that need might be most effectively met. It therefore falls to private individuals, first singly and then in groups, to make initial provision to meet the needs which they see and, in doing so, to explore the extent and nature of that need and to experiment with methods of meeting it. This awakens public interest and brings nearer the time when the community makes the meeting of the need a matter of formal social organisation. In a sense, it follows that all voluntary organisations are working toward their own extinction, but this is by no means true of most organisations which work for the handicapped. So varied and so constantly changing are the needs of the handicapped that it is virtually impossible that a state-organised system can provide all the necessary help which any individual needs all the time, and there is continuing scope for the voluntary organisations to find a means of working in partnership.

Most voluntary work began as little more than organised almsgiving. This is obviously a function which must decline as the concept of the Welfare State is increasingly accepted and put into practice. Anyone experienced in work for the handicapped, however, realises that it is unlikely that any state scheme will ever meet all needs and that there must always be cases in which cash assistance 'outside the rules' may avert or tide over a crisis. The trend, however, is that as state schemes become more comprehensive the 'personal' help given by voluntary organisations will be given in kind, perhaps to provide the handicapped person with some instrument, appliance or other article which will make life easier or more pleasant for him.

Where handicapped children were concerned, however, the need for direct almsgiving has always seemed less. It may well have really been less, but one cannot discount the assumption which has been common until recently—and is not yet dead— that to give money to the family of even a handicapped child is in some way to 'take away the parents' responsibility' and to encourage parental improvidence. However this may be, the voluntary organisations have in this field tended to channel their generosity into providing 'homes' and special schools for handicapped children. The early pioneer work in special education was initiated by voluntary organisations and even when the community began to make provision through the state educational system the voluntary schools had a continuing part to play in supplementing state provision.

One must pay tribute to the way in which the Board of Education and its successors have realised the potentialities of partnership between the state and the voluntary bodies in this field. If an institution—educational or otherwise—is provided and maintained out of state funds there is an inevitable tendency for it to have to work on lines which have already proved their worth. But in a field which is constantly changing there is an imperative need for flexibility and the trial of new ideas. It would be quite wrong to suggest that the public authorities have discouraged experiment but there is no doubt that an institution which relies substantially on 'voluntary' money has greater freedom to be unorthodox if it wishes. This important consideration apart, local education authorities will provide special schools in their own areas primarily for their own pupils; if there are vacancies they will admit children from other areas but their own pupils have priority. Since many authorities do not have enough children with the less common handicaps within their own boundaries to justify providing special schools for them, there is obviously plenty of scope for voluntary organisations to set up schools for these children with wide regional, or even national, catchment areas.

These numerous independent special schools for handicapped children are sometimes local foundations in origin and maintain a strong local identity, even though their nets are widely cast. Others have been set up by national organisations and work under the aegis of the national bodies though they usually have local management committees with a reasonable amount of autonomy. Whichever type they may be, their relationship with the Department of Education follows the same general pattern. Once the Department has 'recognised them as efficient' it will discuss with the school's managers the amount of the annual fee which would meet running costs and will authorise any local education authority to send pupils from its area to the school and pay that fee. In addition to this indirect subsidy, the Department may also make grants to a school for necessary capital development, the more readily if the school will itself raise the funds for part of that development. The schools are, of course, regularly inspected by the Department's specialist inspectors. Their special duty is to see that the school maintains its standards, which they do firmly but with understanding. From time to time the Department does withdraw its approval, which may well be the kiss of death for that school, but the inspectors are usually welcomed as sympathetic guest experts who are only too ready to guide and advise the school which is having difficulties so that in due course it will solve its problems and fulfil itself.

So extensive and important has been the past work of voluntary organisations in providing special education that it forms a theme in itself. However, there have been new developments in the past fifteen years and both the nature and the job of the organisations are taking on a new shape. The rise in building costs alone has made it difficult, if not impossible, for purely local philanthropic groups to set up from the beginning new special schools or other substantial institutions. Though those at present recognised by the Department of Education will doubtless continue in being, some of them may have to change their character as the prevalence of the disability which is their main concern becomes less. For the increasing number of children with multiple disabilities, more elaborate and costly provision is going to be needed. The comparatively moderate numbers of children suffering from some of the newly-recognised disabilities makes it improbable that any areas will have enough of them to demand special local provision or to make local need sufficiently clamant to stimulate local giving on the scale needed to set up local schools for them.

The pattern of organisation which is emerging is that of the national organisation with local branches which concerns itself with the needs of children suffering from particular disabilities. Their fund-raising is nationally organised and in this respect the work of the local branches is largely to help with the national fund-raising to finance major projects though they may also help by raising local money to give incidental help to meet specifically local needs.

Their work, nationally and locally, is coming to fall under four main heads—the pressure group, whose job is to awaken collective public interest and persuade the state and the local authorities to make better provision, the provider of services to supplement 'official' provision, the enlightener, in which they seek to change public attitudes and thus make people at large more ready to accept the handicapped and give them the right kind of personal help, and the patron of research, which is becoming steadily more important, complex and costly.

## The Pressure Group

It is obvious that as a new kind of disability is recognised there will be many children suffering from that disability whose special needs are being met inadequately, or perhaps not at all, within the existing system. It is also obvious that the system will bring its provision into action unevenly and somewhat slowly, waiting, before committing itself, until there is more information available about the actual need and the ways in which they can best be met.

The consequence is that there is a coming together of parents of children suffering from that disability who are anxious, frustrated and convinced that their children are getting a raw deal. They know little of the complexities of the problem but they do know that *their* children need help *now*. It is clear that in a democracy provision will not be made until a sufficient number of members of parliament, town and county councillors and local officials are aware that something needs to be done. There is a general, and not unfounded, belief that he who shouts the loudest gets the most—and most quickly. It follows that the newly-formed pressure group shouts loudly and usually shouts angrily, giving the impression that it regards itself as the victim of a conspiracy between the wicked or unfeeling legislators and the lazy or callous professional workers.

It is only too easy to antagonise public opinion by excessive clamour, especially if that clamour is uninformed. Legislators are certainly sensitive to loud shouts, but they may well show that sensitivity by wearing metaphorical ear-plugs. Administrators, at local or national level, have to balance claims on a limited budget and realise only too well that unless they move cautiously and diplomatically they can help a new group of the handicapped, however deserving, only by cutting down what is already provided for other groups. But perhaps the greatest risk is that if a pressure group gives the impression of criticising the professional workers, doctors, social workers, teachers, psychologists and the rest, too severely it may alienate its most important potential allies.

Of course, not all the professional workers are equally enlightened and dedicated, but they are basically on the same side as the anxious parents. What is more, their sympathy is invaluable. It is they, because of their professional knowledge, who may carry most weight with the administrators and the elected members of the local authorities and thus be invaluable in getting work started. Even more important, when that work does get started it is they who will have to do much of it and they would be less than human if they were able to start at a moment's notice an intimate partnership in the care of a particular child with parents who had been blackguarding them in public for months or years.

In counselling patience to parents, one must also commend it to the professionals. Few of them know at first hand just what the parent of a handicapped child has to put up with in day to day family life. Because they have the knowledge and are, or ought to be, reasonably articulate, it is for them to swallow criticism and insult, however much those may stick in the gullet, and to get together with the more understanding members of the pressure groups. One of the greatest services which they can do to themselves and the pressure groups is to help the groups to press to the best advantage.

But talk plus action counts far more than talk alone. If the professional can channel the energy and enthusiasm of the local voluntary organisation into doing something constructive, however simple and limited, not only is something accomplished to meet the children's need but the group's pressure is the more effective because it becomes clear that its members are realistically and sincerely doing something to help themselves.

I have stressed local relationships and local action deliberately. Of course there must be pressure activity at national levels, but at those levels there is a tendency for negotiators to regard themselves as committed to particular lines of action or inaction and for organisations to put forward their more intransigent members and officers to represent them in argument. Experience shows that pressure groups in this field become more effective as they grow more mature and the genuine understanding which marks that maturity is something which percolates upwards from those who are actually working on the job.

## The Provider

As already indicated, the provision of special schools or institutions for many of the children who suffer from the 'new' or more complex disabilities is such a costly business that it requires the sort of money which can be raised only on a national scale. In the case of some disabilities, irrespective of actual questions of cost, the number of children recognised as suffering from those disabilities is, at least initially, so small that few localities have a sufficient number of children to make a local special school economically viable and something much larger than a local group is needed to set up a satisfactory unit.

This gives the national organisation the very important task of being a fund-raiser and indeed this role is usually given at least as much prominence as that of pressure group. It is, however, being realised that the voluntary organisation has at its disposal, if it sets about its work realistically, not only the money of well-disposed people but the time and the energy of men and women who are better able to give those than to give money or who deliberately choose to offer service rather than cash. It follows that the local branches can, if they wish, be a great deal more than fund-raisers for the parent body and can, in their own localities, make various kinds of local provision to supplement whatever the public authorities may be doing.

The kind of help which can be given in this way varies with local need, with the availability of resources and with the ingenuity of local organisers. It is inevitable that the local branch will begin as a pressure group but it is important that it should graduate from that to becoming a self-help body. Indeed its success as a pressure group will be considerably enhanced if it shows that it can act as well as clamour. There is no more effective way of bringing to light handicapped children who have been hitherto unnoticed than to make some provision, however primitive, toward meeting their needs. Moreover, the much-abused local authorities have at least one quality attributed to God; an inclination to help those who help themselves.

Most local branches of the voluntary organisations perform one useful function by merely existing, in that they bring together the parents of children suffering from similar disabilities. For the parents of a handicapped child to meet others in a similar situation and to know that they are not alone gives a considerable lift to morale. To discuss one's problems with others facing the same problems and with those who have either solved or at least come to terms with those problems helps enormously to understand the nature of one's own difficulties.

It is not necessary to attempt to set out in detail what a local organisation can do as a self-help body; it is sufficient to mention a few of the things which have been done in many places. Good 'neighbourly help' by which one parent of a handicapped child may take in another such child for a while so as to give his mother and father a chance to have an evening out may point the way to co-operating in running a short-time creche for shopping mothers on one or two days a week and the creche may grow into a play-group, especially if, as often happens, there are one or two retired teachers who are prepared to help free of charge or for a token fee. Parents who have cars may help solve some of the transport problems of those less fortunate. A father— or a well-wisher from outside the group—who is good with his hands can be invaluable in the making of simple gadgets which are useful to a physically handicapped child in matters of daily living.

For the local group which is successful in fund-raising, to have a little money at its disposal for local purposes is invaluable. Local authorities have the power to help the activities of voluntary bodies in a number of ways, direct and indirect. They can provide training for play-group staff, make grants toward the provision of play-group equipment or pay any necessary fees for a handicapped child who is attending a voluntary play-group. However, the fact that they have the legal power does not guarantee that they have money available in the relevant part of the current year's budget and the willingness and ability of the voluntary body to bear some of its costs itself can certainly encourage the authority to match that willingness. There have indeed been cases in which a local authority has been hesitant about making its own provision for some type of handicapped child because of the high initial cost of equipment and the scales have been tipped by the offer of a local voluntary body to provide one of the more expensive items.

It is of the utmost importance that the professional staff should take a constructive interest in the self-help activities of a voluntary organisation in their locality. It helps them in their own work, by bringing them into a closer understanding with the individual parents of individual children. It also helps the voluntary organisation by making professional help and guidance available and so preventing or minimising the waste of the organisation's resources, whether of money or man-power. It is, however, most important that the help and guidance shall be given diplomatically. The organisation particularly which is just growing out of the pressure-group phase will tend to be a little shy of public bodies and their officers and may easily misinterpret the too-ready offer of help from those officers as an attempt at a take-over bid. The prudent professional will begin by letting it be known that he is interested and will be available to help if he is needed. If the organisation comes to him and asks 'What do you think we could usefully do?' he will, before he makes any suggestions, try to assess the willingness and ability of the organisation to put such suggestions into practice.

His position can, however, be awkward if the organisation comes to him saying 'We have decided to do so-and-so and would like you to help us.' If the proposal is reasonable and practicable, well and good. But it may be unrealistic, out of accord with the manifest priorities of the area or even carry the risk of doing positive harm in local circumstances. To veto the proposal may kill the energy and goodwill which have prompted it. It is axiomatic that voluntary work is done best if it is not merely what the volunteers should do but also what they want to do. In this sort of case, it is probably best to seek a compromise, which modifies the proposal or reduces it to something less ambitious in the same direction so that if it is tried and fails not too much is lost. If no compromise is possible, then the answer of the professional must be 'I believe you are wrong and I can therefore give you little help, but what help I can give I will give.'

Ideally, this situation should not and need not arise. If the professional workers have shown sympathy with and patience toward the voluntary organisation in its early pressure group stage it is virtually certain that they will have earned its respect before it comes to the point at which self-help schemes begin to form. There must be occasions when the dominant person in the organisation is so intolerant of the professionals that no working relationship can be achieved but experience suggests that if open hostility can be avoided the organisation itself is likely in due course to extrude its dictator and find a better leader.

## The Educator

It is plainly in the interests of the handicapped that more people should know more and understand more about them. There is work in this field for the voluntary organisations to do and most of them become substantially involved in it. It comes under three main headings—education of the public, education of the families of handicapped children and professional education of those who work with the handicapped.

The education of the public is basic; the more people in general understand about the handicapped and their problems the more one would expect the necessary help to be forthcoming both from individuals and from public bodies. Unfortunately, it is only too easy for this kind of education to take the wrong turning and to end by doing harm as well as good. For there are different kinds of help, all equally necessary. Some of these consist of the provision of services but others involve the giving of personal assistance.

It is natural for a newly-formed organisation to begin by trying to demonstrate need and to get provision made to meet that need. Whether it is seeking to persuade a local authority to set up special units, educational or other, or to persuade people to give to its funds so that it may itself set up special units, it is in competition with a large number of interests, all of which have claims of their own. In this situation a case must be made out for urgency and this is most easily done by publicising the desperate plight of whatever group of the handicapped the organisation is working for. The temptation into which it is easy to fall is to paint dramatic pictures of handicapped children as pathetic creatures whom the community is neglecting. This is not very difficult to do and the appeal to the heart goes a very long way toward loosening the strings of both public and private purses.

However, this approach carries the considerable risk of having precisely the wrong effect upon public attitudes to bring about the right kind of long-term success. Special treatment and special educational facilities are necessary to prepare the handicapped child for living in the community, but they are liable to be wasted unless, when the child becomes an adolescent, the community is ready to accept him. He must be acknowledged as an acceptable friend or house-guest and also as an acceptable employee or work-mate. True, the special care and education will have gone some way toward making him in theory more acceptable, but the more effort which has gone into arousing pity the greater is the probability that damage has been done to the sympathy which depends essentially on realising that he is a person in his own right and consequently in many ways a potential, if not an obviously actual, equal.

This danger is now being increasingly realised by the major organisations, which are trying to re-orient their approach, but it is not, perhaps, being sufficiently appreciated at working level in the branches of the organisations. It is at this level that contacts between the handicapped and their families and the members of the public are most close and it is vital for the members of the branches to realise that, however vital fund-raising may be, the basic job before them is one of public relations.

As educators of parents of handicapped children the voluntary organisations have a role which no statutory organisations can equal. The value of the parents' group as a mutual self-help educator has already been mentioned. The organisation as a whole is specially well placed to do something more formal, in the way of producing leaflets and booklets dealing with the day to day practicalities of the bringing up of a handicapped child and in fact most of the really down-to-earth literature available for the use of parents is at present coming from these bodies.

This is a very proper and important task for the organisations. Specialised booklets of this kind simply do not fit into the ordinary production and distribution mechanism of the publishing and book-selling trade. For obvious reasons it is important to keep down the cost and the leaflets must get into the hands of those who need them. An organisation which is not out to make a profit—which may, in fact, be prepared to subsidise production—and which has contacts with those who are likely to benefit by having the leaflets is the only body which can put them out effectively.

Some organisations are moving into the field of education of professional workers. Doctors receive little or no education in the problems of handicapped children as part of their basic under-graduate training and even medical post-graduate training in the relevant specialties, like orthopaedics, otology, neurology and physical medicine is oriented mainly toward the care of adult patients. Much the same is true of some of the medical auxiliaries and social workers. There are too few specialist teachers in special schools and the general training of teachers in ordinary schools includes very little indeed on the special needs of handicapped children, in spite of the current trend for more of the moderately handicapped to be placed in ordinary schools.

One of the pressure-group functions of the organisations is to strive after better and more appropriate formal training for members of the professional team, but one must be realistic and accept that such changes can come only slowly. However, voluntary organisations can stimulate the development of in-service courses locally and sponsor and even subsidise 'study days' and seminars. The wealthier organisations are even able to provide their own short courses. It is probable that in present circumstances it is more realistic and effective for them to spend their funds in this way than in setting up independent special schools.

### Research

One role which is increasingly being taken by voluntary organisa-tions is that of the patron of research. There is no disputing the need for more research into all aspects of work with the handicapped—causation, prevention, treatment, education and management—and there is no doubt that greater resources are needed for the purpose. It is still, and always will be, possible for the individual working in any part of the field to intelligently exercise his curiosity in his ordinary job and contribute sub-stantially to the total body of knowledge. However, the unaided individual's potentialities are restricted and even he will make a greater contribution if he can have such assistance as secretarial help or the services of a statistician or a social worker for a period. Apart from staffing assistance, it may well be that, especially in the clinical field, a grant of a few hundred pounds for a piece of apparatus may make possible a piece of work which he could not otherwise do.

The more elaborate research projects, of course, will be impossible for the individual who is engaged whole-time in the field; these demand whole-time expert workers with access to the staff and physical resources of research departments. There is no research organisation in the country which could not do more work if it had the resources and it follows that some patronage is necessary if all that needs to be done is in fact undertaken.

There is much controversy at present about the relative values of basic research and specific research projects. In the sphere of work for the handicapped, argument of this nature has little more virtue than argument about whether a strawberry is better than a raspberry. Any advances in, for instance, physiology, genetics or educational methods may help in some aspect of making better provision for some types of handicapped children. With the increasing number of multiple-handicapped children, any specific increase in the understanding of any disability may have benefits which will be widely diffused.

It has, therefore, been unfortunate that so many of the voluntary organisations have grown up with somewhat specialised objectives. This is understandable. If an organisation has put a considerable amount of labour into collecting money for sufferers from a particular disability, if its members, as so often happens, are parents of children suffering from that disability, if generous donors of large sums have given their money because they have a special interest in the disability, the organisation will feel itself under some moral obligation to see that its funds are used for purposes which are manifestly and directly concerned with that disability and those who suffer from it. But the inevitable consequence of this is that the funds available for the sponsoring of research into some fields of disability have been restricted because the body most directly concerned with that disability has not been able to mount as wide and attractive an appeal for funds as have some of its competitors for the money of the benevolent.

## The Future of the Voluntary Organisations

It is obvious that whatever may be the shape and extent of formal community provision for the handicapped there will continue to be a need for voluntary work and for organisations to do that work. It is improbable that the specific objective of any substantial national organisation in the field will become redundant, though perhaps the work now done by some of them will materially decrease.

Their role as provider certainly promises to become less important in extent, though certainly not in quality. Developments in the social services are likely to increase the amount of community care facilities and thus reduce the need for institutional places, but this will be a slow process and there will always be some who need institutional care. It is to be expected that more handicapped children will be accepted into ordinary schools and that for children who really need special school care there will be a trend toward the multi-handicapped rather than the single-handicapped school, with a lessened demand on the organisations which specialise in particular disabilities. But there are notable gaps to be filled, especially in provision of hostel and training accommodation for adolescents, and it is important that in this part of the field, as well as in provision for the multiple-handicapped, there should be scope for experiment and flexibility. The special usefulness of partnership between voluntary organisations and the State must not be overlooked from this point of view.

The extension of community care will, one hopes, be accompanied by the provision of more trained workers by the local authorities, but however much the staff of the Social Services Departments may be increased it is impossible for community care to be effective unless there is a substantial increase in informed public goodwill. This means that the role of the voluntary organisations in public education will become even more important than it has been in the past. How is this role to be developed? Certainly there must be a better public information service, constructively oriented, but the purveying of information is not enough. What is particularly important is the bringing of the public into the right sort of contact with the handicapped and this is best effected by public participation. Here one foresees scope for the local organisations, perhaps by taking the initiative in providing such things as play-groups and clubs and in enrolling voluntary workers to help in the 'outside'—and even the inside—activities of centres and schools for the handicapped provided by local authorities. Certainly genuine partnership between voluntary and state or local authority services will be more important than ever before.

The field of inter-disciplinary professional training has already been explored by some voluntary organisations; indeed, in many instances the voluntary organisations have been more active than the 'official' ones. Local authorities are now moving into this field and probably the larger local authorities envisaged under local government reform will be able to do it more effectively. However the separation of the 'health disciplines' from the local authority workers will not make things easier and while it is very much to the good for a variety of workers in the same area to be brought together in week-end schools and seminars and in day release courses, it is essential to have the cross-fertilisation of ideas which can only come by mixing workers from different areas. This is outside the scope of the local authority and, while local authority and state funds may be able to contribute to the fees and expenses of their attending courses outside their own areas, the actual organisation of many such courses will have to be undertaken by a variety of voluntary bodies. It would be good to see every major national voluntary organisation setting up 'education and information' units for this purpose on the lines on which some have already done.

Obviously research into all matters that touch upon handicap must expand. This is going to demand more research workers and also more sophisticated—and, consequently, often more expensive—techniques and apparatus. The demand for funds will consistently exceed the amounts available, which means that voluntary organisations, as patrons of research, must be discriminating as well as generous; research advisory bodies with really knowledgeable members would seem to be essential for all organisations which intend to spend money in this direction. But if there is to be a better balance of research activities over the whole field, then some of the voluntary organisations must learn to think more widely and be prepared to subsidise basic research which is not restricted to their specialised field or, in the case of the wealthier ones—there are precedents for this—contribute to the endowment of research departments which have very broad terms of reference.

One question which has not infrequently been asked in the past and which is being quite often put at the moment is whether there should be a fusing of voluntary organisations. The case for amalgamation of kindred special organisations is overwhelming. The current argument is rather whether instead of one organisation for epilepsy, one for cerebral palsy, one for autism there should be a move toward amalgamation of organisations with specialised objectives into a smaller number with more general objectives. Is it a good thing that if a child has three or four disabilities there should be three or four different organisations interested in his care? Would not amalgamation make administration easier by reducing duplication and thus cutting down overhead costs? Where fund-raising is concerned—as it must be for some time to come—would the public not contribute more readily to one major appeal than to several minor ones?

All these furnish strong arguments in theory for amalgamation. In practice they are weakened by the fact that all these organisations depend for all their activities on a good deal of unpaid labour and that people give their services without reward only for causes in which they have a direct personal interest. Amalgamation on a large scale might well cause a loss of voluntary labour which would counterbalance theoretical gains in income and effectiveness.

There are, however, a number of reforms which are well worth consideration. The first and most obvious is the setting up of a really effective 'Standing Conference' of voluntary organisations for handicapped children in which the organisations would retain their identity but would collaborate in their activities. This could lead to better understanding between organisations, cut down direct competition and, probably, make more effective the distribution of authoritative information to the public.

A second could be the organisation of joint fund-raising activities by groups of those smaller organisations which do not have the mechanism or the popular appeal to launch effective appeals by themselves. This, unfortunately, is somewhat hampered by present charities legislation and even more by the attitude of the Inland Revenue Authorities, who look more kindly on a body which raises money for direct beneficiaries than on one which raises money on behalf of other bodies. The idea seems worth consideration because there is some evidence that members of the public would rather make one donation of fifty pence to be divided between a group of charities than give five separate florins—especially if the appeals are made by post.

At local level, where the voluntary organisations are so often concerned with the giving of individual personal service, then even if the branches of national organisations maintain their formal identity there is no doubt whatever that it is in the best interests of all parties that the members should work out some practical unity. It may be uneconomically impossible in a locality to organise, say, one play-group for the mentally handicapped one for the children with cerebral palsy but quite possible with local resources to have a joint one. Tommy Jones may have a paralysed limb and Mary Brown suffer from epilepsy, but that does not mean that the Jones family and the Brown family have no common ground or that they may not both benefit from getting together. Mrs. Jones's interest in the handicapped may have been first aroused because her niece is deaf but she may well be the sort of person who would be an invaluable voluntary worker in the service of the handicapped generally. Nothing is so likely as local joint activities to break down the 'caste system' which makes some disabilities respectable and others unmentionable. Even in the work of local organisations as pressure groups and fund raisers, a common cause can be a stronger cause.

# Epilogue

'Rehabilitation isn't just a job—it's a religion.' This was the casual comment of a colleague in the Rehabilitation Unit of the Secretariat of the United Nations. It expresses the devotion and the fervour with which the great majority of those engaged in work for the handicapped set about their various tasks. The slow, laborious, day by day grind of the therapist or teacher with little to show in the way of progress after weeks or months could not be undertaken without devotion. Devotion, too, inspires the patience of the parent who constantly sustains and guides the child and the doctor or lay administrator who strives to build up services on slender resources. Fervour kindles the enthusiasm of those who are weary in the work and those who, as yet outside it, need to be brought fully into it.

But the theoretical harmony which religion should bring is riven by sectarian differences and in rehabilitation all is not always sweetness, light and peace. Enthusiasts necessarily tend to be individualists; indeed if they ceased to believe that their part in the total work was fundamentally important their best qualities of personality would be impaired. It follows that they show the normal human failings and are acutely aware of those failings in others. Any member of the team of workers for the handicapped child may sometimes be jealous of others, may feel that his particular specialty is not being given sufficient importance, may resent suggestions from workers in other specialties or may develop a possessiveness over child patients which is no less harmful than the possessiveness of parents! Eager advocates of new ideas arouse the conservatives to the defence of last ditches and suffer flank attacks from their fellow-innovators. The concept of a team evokes the concept of a captain of the team and many are those who assert their divine right to the captaincy.

In the end, if not in the beginning, community of purpose and zeal in a cause reconcile the conflicts. The commonest reason for the failure of any individual to accept the team idea is simply ignorance—ignorance of the overall picture and ignorance of the parts which others play in making up the picture. If anyone who reads this book should at any time feel that someone who should be a collaborator is not joining in the task I would suggest that he—or she—asks himself or herself this simple question—'Have I explained to so-and-so exactly what I am trying to do?' I would also add the suggestion that when one is trying to enlist the aid of the unconvinced it is better to give explanation before rather than after one starts to do one's own part.

Should there be a captain of the team? Because every aspect of the care of the handicapped child has some health connotation it is necessary that the work as a whole should be medically informed and that medical guidance should be readily available and should be sought frequently by the lay as well as the medical auxiliary workers. But this does not give doctors in general or any specific doctors automatic charge of the whole. The membership of the team varies from child to child and from time to time in the progress of any individual child. Now one and now another of the members comes into prominence and speaks with special authority.

Perhaps the team analogy is not, in this respect, the best. It may be closer to the true spirit to think of the string quartet in which each instrumentalist in turn comes to the fore with the theme and then has the role of joint accompanist to one of his fellows, with the interpretation of the composer's work serving as the common guide.

M

## APPENDIX I

# Handicapped Children in the
# Developing Countries

This book has dealt mainly with work for the handicapped child in countries in which the social services are highly developed. A large part of the world's population lives in countries which are less fortunate. In Africa as a whole, for instance, there is an average of one doctor to every 9,000 inhabitants, in Western Asia one to every 5,000 and in South America one to every 2,000 as compared with the European average of one to every 1,000. These broad averages do not tell the whole story. In every region or continent there are some places where development has gone on comparatively rapidly and where doctors are concentrated. Though Africa averages one doctor to 9,000 people there are some African countries where the ratio is as low as one to 30,000 or 40,000 people. What is true of lack of doctors applies equally to lack of nurses, while such important auxiliaries as physiotherapists may be virtually non-existent. Where the *normal* educational system provides an average of four years of schooling for half the child population, how does one start a system of special schools? Where people live in isolated small communities and public transport is virtually non-existent, how does one make and keep contact between the child and those who are trying to help him?

It is natural for eager workers in a young country conscious of its need to develop to see what the highly-developed countries provide and to seek to make the same provision in their own lands. It is natural—but dangerous. I trust that this book has made it clear that whatever is done for a handicapped child anywhere is done with the idea of making him as fully able as possible to live in the social conditions of his own country and that work for the handicapped must be constantly related to social background. The basic principles set out in my earlier chapters have some universal validity, but their practice must be considered in its social context. I hope that this appendix will give some useful hints on how this should be done.

344

Both the nature and the extent of the problem vary from country to country and even between different parts of the same country. To some extent, climate and other physical conditions may determine the pattern of disease in childhood and thus the relative prevalence of handicaps arising from disease. Thus, respiratory problems may be more prevalent in a cold climate while parasitic diseases are commoner in a hot one. Natural soil fertility may affect the prevalence of defects due to nutritional faults. But in general the stage of social development which has been reached in a country is the deciding factor in both the apparent and the actual prevalence of various disabilities.

There are still countries which are beginners in development, whose medical and social services are rudimentary and whose basic social organisation has not progressed far. Such a country will say that it has virtually no handicapped children. It may well know of few, because it lacks the means of finding them, of collecting and collating the information about their very existence. But such a country is certain to have many serious hazards not only to child health but to child life, with possibly one-third of all its children dying in the first year of life and one-half before the age of five. Handicapped children are almost invariably specially vulnerable to those hazards, and while some undoubtedly survive it is probable that the great majority of the handicapped just die. Some handicapped survivors are not brought to the notice of such medical services as exist for the very practical reason that since there are no services to help them there is nothing to gain by bringing them forward. But it does happen that if some philanthropic individual or organisation is moved to start some voluntary work for, say, the blind or the deaf, the children do emerge from concealment.

There are, happily, comparatively few countries where this situation exists on a country-wide scale. It is more likely to be met with in the remoter rural areas of countries which have moved on to a higher stage of development and in which social organisation and the provision of child health services have made some beginning. At this level the children with severe congenital disabilities are still unlikely to survive the first years of childhood and the pattern is usually one of acquired handicap. It is there one finds children suffering from blindness caused by smallpox, trachoma or malnutrition, from deafness due to neglected infections or from crippling which has followed bone or joint tuberculosis or accidental injury. Poliomyelitis, a disease which does not become epidemic until a certain level of social development has been reached, may or may not have stricken these countries on a substantial scale.

As health services develop, the pattern changes again. Smallpox and trachoma come under control, ear infections have some likelihood of being treated, tuberculosis diminishes, but more slowly because the predisposing factor remain. Poliomyelitis may become a scourge though there is the hope that an intensive vaccination campaign may conquer it in the course of a few years. But this is the point at which the developing country is likely to follow the experience of the highly developed; better obstetrics and paediatrics make for increased survival prospects of the congenitally handicapped and brain-damaged and multiple-handicapped children fill the gaps in the ranks.

Obviously, the significance of different types of disability varies with the social setting. In a country which depends upon unskilled and semi-skilled labour for most of its productive activities, physical fitness is at a premium and physical handicap is specially disabling; the chance of making the cripple self-supporting in skilled sedentary work is much reduced. The moderately mentally handicapped who are physically sound have little difficulty in finding useful employment. Deafness in any setting impedes communication and tends to isolate the individual but need not seriously impair employment prospects. The blind are obviously disadvantaged so far as general employment is concerned, but in countries on this level of development mass production has not yet come to replace individual handwork and there are good opportunities for making a living in craft work which can be done in the individual's home, in his own village community. However, with the progress of urbanisation and increasing mechanisation, the problems of the handicapped are steadily moving toward the pattern which obtains in the developed countries.

Effective case-finding demands well-organised child health services and provision for general medical care. As in all countries, the sooner the disability is detected the better is the prospect of cure or at least some alleviation of the handicap or its effects. The less-developed countries are precisely the ones in which these services are the most deficient. It must be emphasised again that until it is known among the people that something can be done for the handicapped, parents will not spontaneously bring their handicapped children forward. Too often a child is not found to be handicapped until he starts school, and where schooling is available only for one-half of all children even this late detection is only of limited use, the more so since quite a number of children are, because of their disability, not presented for school admission. Indeed, in many countries, the only children who have much chance of coming under early care are those whose disabilities are due to accident or acute illness, who are brought to the doctor for urgent care at the time of the accident or illness.

## Prevention

The scope for the prevention of handicap is enormous in these countries and it must have high priority. Much of this work will be initially social rather than medical. Better housing, better milk supplies, better feeding and better standards of general living will play a part. Specific preventive measures on the medical side— vaccination and immunization against the diseases which cause disability—are needed. Encouraging news comes from some countries where mass early treatment of crippling or disabling diseases is being undertaken in the hope of curing the condition before disability develops; campaigns for the treatment of trachoma, for instance, are substantially reducing the incidence of blindness. Better maternity services will certainly reduce the risk of birth injury and certain defects of development. On the other hand, everything which is done to improve medical and social services will increase the number of children who, instead of dying young grow up with a disability.

## Treatment

It is clear from the foregoing that the immediate problem in the less-developed countries is one of dealing with physical rather than mental handicap. Probably the most urgent question is that of providing orthopaedic hospitals and ancillary services. These depend on the availability of buildings, materials and equipment but even more on the availability of staff. There is no substitute for a well-trained orthopaedic surgeon, but if the dire shortage of nurses and physiotherapists is to be met it will be necessary to accept for the time being some lower standards of training than are required in the highly-developed countries. Because of shortage of schools, the number of young women and men with a good basic education is limited and this in itself limits the capacity of the student to receive higher training. This is being fully realized and a number of countries are embarking on short, simple, intensive training courses in order to meet short-term needs. It must, however, be realized that such partly-trained staff will not always achieve results in treatment equal to those of the highly-trained workers in the fortunate countries, so that when treatment is ended the amount of residual disability may still be more than one would ideally like.

### Case-finding and Assessment

The only way of finding cases in time is to have plenty of people looking for them. If there is a shortage of doctors, health visitors and other skilled workers, then case-finding will have to rely on the observation of auxiliary medical, nursing and hygiene staff. The school-teacher, especially in the villages, will not only have a chance to observe children who come to school but will know something about the other members of her pupils' families and even about families whose children do not go to school.

All these can be taught to do some elementary screening of children who seem to be handicapped, but the less skilled and experienced the person who first sees the child the greater is the need for expert assessment after screening. The shortage of expert staff is complicated by transport difficulties, but two lines of approach have been tried in various places. The first of these is the permanent assessment centre, which can sometimes be combined with a treatment centre or a special school. Children who are found or suspected to have a disability can be taken to the centre, where, according to the type of handicap, they may spend a shorter or a longer time undergoing full clinical investigation as well as educational and vocational assessment. The second type of scheme is the mobile assessment team. A team consisting of whatever medical and other experts may be appropriate tours the country, visiting provincial centres in turn at regular intervals. Both have their advantages, but it is plain that in a country with very limited resources it may at first be difficult to provide all the necessary equipment at provincial centres and where assessment needs a substantial period of observation the team's short stay in a provincial centre will not be adequate. Probably a combination of the two will be the most effective. Even so, circumstances will certainly prevent many children from receiving the detailed assessment which is the rule in highly-developed countries. It is, therefore, necessary to be much more elastic in the use of hospitals and special schools and to allow children to have periods of observation and assessment there.

## Education

The question is sometimes asked whether a country which cannot afford more than four or five years of general education for fewer than two-thirds of its normal children should spend money on special schools for the handicapped. The answer is, in most cases that in such a country there is a shortage of literate people and that anyone who is intelligent and can read and write is certain to find and keep employment; to give education to an intelligent physically handicapped child is to make sure of at any rate his material prospects for life.

If the disability is not severe, an ordinary school may meet his needs. Not all the less-developed countries yet have a free education system and parents may be unable and unwilling to pay fees for the education of a cripple; social enlightenment may not have reached a point at which the value of education is generally appreciated. Short-term policy would be to remit school fees for the handicapped, but in the long run education of parents is obviously required.

Where transport is limited and distances are long, the boarding special school will be the solution. If it is hard to justify the use of money and skilled teachers for such work in a country where there are still too few schools for ordinary children, a beginning can be made by introducing education into the long-stay wards of orthopaedic hospitals. Indeed, no orthopaedic hospital in any country which takes in children for long periods of care and treatment should be without one or more teachers. It has happened and will happen again that from such a beginning the idea of special educational provision has spread considerably.

A word of caution is necessary on the risks of early specialization. Enthusiasts who have been inspired by what they have seen in advanced countries may think in terms of separate schools for children with specific disabilities. Everything which I have said in regard to the shortage of medical and other staff, assessment difficulties and problems of transport favours a beginning with limited facilities which are within the possibilities of the country's limited resources of money, material and man-power. Three main types of school—for the blind, for the deaf, for the physically handicapped—are quite enough to begin with. In the early stages, all types of physical handicap can be brought together in a single school; separate establishments for spastics and paraplegics can wait for later developments. In spite of various disadvantages it is possible at this stage of development to combine a school for the deaf with one for the partially deaf. For the reasons already mentioned, schools for the mentally handicapped can reasonably be left to a later part of a development programme and will then most usefully begin in the larger cities.

Perhaps the necessary compromise between the ideal and the realistic points of view can be best illustrated by commenting on the major types of disability separately.

## 1. Blindness

The rural areas of the less-developed countries accept and absorb blind persons fairly well. The blind man in an African village has no need to travel far and can quickly learn to move about his immediate neighbourhood with confidence. If his neighbours are illiterate his inability to read places him at no disadvantage. To take a blind child away from his village and family to teach him skills which he does not need and which he is unlikely to practice is wasteful and even cruel. Recent experiments in Uganda have shown that it is a good idea to keep the blind in their own rural areas and train them for work on the land, in which they can become self-supporting. It is the blind child who lives in the town where industry is developing who is likely to need special education and the logical beginning is to make provision for him first.

Premises and equipment can be very modest in the beginning; in fact the simpler they are the better. The aim of education while resources are limited should be as practical as possible, concentrating on essentials. The objection to traditional craft training which I have mentioned in the main chapter on blindness is less valid here because in a country in an early stage of development it is possible for a person to earn a fair living by the practice of a craft. In the less-developed countries, too, competent craft instructors will be much more easy to find than skilled teachers of the blind in academic subjects and the more complicated types of work. Logically, then, the start should be with general education and craft training but those responsible must be on the watch for every opportunity to expand and develop as time goes on and opportunities arise.

## 2. Deafness

Here the difficulties are greater. The modern care and education of the deaf depends very largely upon the use of elaborate and expensive equipment under the guidance of skilled people. Initial assessment depends on audiometry and the use of group and individual hearing aids. I have seen this spectacularly demonstrated in one developing country in a large school which held some four hundred deaf mute children. It was possible to arrange for the provision of audiometers and hearing aids through one of the international organizations and for visiting experts to give guidance in their use. A year later, when I next went to the school, the head master, with justifiable pride, insisted that before I did anything else I should hear the school choir singing! In even that short time, three-fourths of the children had been shown to have useful remnants of hearing and had begun to use them.

Though international funds can be used to supplement national ones, it is obvious that the education of deaf children in any country must begin on a small scale and develop as equipment and staff become available. Speech training will need time to develop and the value of 'guest experts' is strictly limited. The most capable of French, English or German teachers of the deaf will not be able to use her techniques effectively in a country whose language is unfamiliar to her. Indeed, adequate speech training and speech therapy demand that there should have been some phonetic analysis of the language of the country; in the case just mentioned I was delighted to find that the school concerned had spontaneously made an excellent contact with the department of phonetics of the neighbouring university.

It seems inevitable that in the beginning more emphasis will have to be placed on lip-reading and sign language than is at present fashionable in the highly-developed countries and, even so, since sign language is not yet international, local sign language will have to be evolved.

## 3. Physical Handicap

It is fortunate that in this field, the commonest and the most significant in the less-developed countries, elaborate apparatus is not needed. Physiotherapy, as I have indicated, can be provided on a reasonable scale by persons with shortened, simple training and the teachers need only teaching ability and experience coupled with patience. The essential guiding principle is, of course, that the child should be prepared for a career in which his normal or high intelligence will enable him to earn the livelihood which his impaired physique will not provide for him. His opportunities will be limited, for the economy of the country will not yet be able to offer much in the way of skilled work in light industry.

His mobility may be restricted. Wheel chairs, hand or mechanically propelled, and invalid cars are not easy to provide, require skilled maintenance and are, in any event, of little use where roads are bad or non-existent. As in the case of the blind, the fact that handcrafts of various kinds are still of economic value must be turned to advantage.

### 4. Mental Handicap

Schools for the mentally handicapped are probably only a second priority in the less-developed countries so long as physical work remains the main basis of employment and literacy is not an essential for daily living. When they are needed it will be in the towns, where they can be most easily provided. Mental handicap combined with physical disability will present at first an almost insoluble problem, and since it is necessary to make the most economic use of skilled staff and special equipment the less-developed countries will have to take the harsh but practical decision that they can do little in the early stages to help the spastic child.

What I have said of the rural areas of the highly-developed countries does, however, hold good over large areas of the less-developed ones. Urbanization and civilization may have their merits but they tend to destroy neighbourliness and the community spirit; the village community in any land is always ready to be sympathetic to the simpleton and it is probably wisest and kindest to leave him in his community to grow up as part of it.

I have said that the basic principles of work for the handicapped have some validity in all countries, whatever their stage of development. In concluding this appendix, it may be worth while to comment on some general aspects of practice, as I have seen them in operation. The most important thing to be remembered is that in the less-developed countries there are many pressing claims on limited resources of money and material. The pioneer will be asked how it is possible to spend public money on helping the handicapped when for lack of that public money men, women and children are daily dying by hundreds or even thousands. The argument that by turning people who are a burden on the community's resources into useful contributors to those resources it will more than repay its cost is valid, but that repayment of costs will be a long-term matter. It is inevitable that the beginning must be made by mobilisation of charitable funds and that even after the beginning there must be a period when private charity works in partnership with public resources.

The highly-developed countries are the places where services are to be seen at their best. It is after seeing them in those countries that the enthusiast comes back to his own country full of ambition and it is easy for ambition to be quenched by the manifest impossibility of reproducing what he has seen  He must learn to reconcile the opposites, to work for his hopes as if he wants to fulfil them immediately and yet to feel satisfied if he achieves a tenth of what he would like over the course of a couple of decades. I have seen ambitious schemes abandoned because their originator despaired of their fulfilment and would not be content with less. I have seen the generous help offered by wealthier countries end with thousands of pounds worth of valuable and sophisticated apparatus standing idle and deteriorating because the people with the skill required to make use of them were not available and, indeed, would not be available for years.

Every success story in work for the handicapped child in the less-developed countries has begun with one dedicated worker starting with the limited means available and improvising as best he could. I would mention only three of many examples— the Buddhist teacher, touched by the plight of the neglected mentally handicapped children, collecting a small group of them in his own house, finding as the numbers grew that many of them were in fact physically handicapped and enlisting the spare-time help of surgeons and therapists from a neighbouring hospital—the orthopaedic surgeon who discovered that one of his physiotherapists had been a teacher before she became a therapist, who begged the use of a small derelict building from the community and founded the first school for the physically handicapped in his province—the otologist whose wife had been a speech therapist before she married and who, jointly with her, started the country's first rudimentary audiology centre.

There are positive advantages in small beginnings. No two

countries have identical needs. To begin with firm plans is to run the risk of becoming prematurely committed to policies and practices which may not, in the event, be the best ones in a country's social context. To start from first principles is the only way to explore needs and their appropriate satisfaction and to have the opportunity of modifying one's plans as the realistic picture emerges. I have been critical in this book of the way in which some of the highly developed countries have become so firmly set in their patterns of provision that they have been unable to adapt to changing needs or to changing understanding of the problems of the handicapped. I have seen less-developed countries, precisely because of their lack of trained staff—for all staff training will inevitably have an element of the traditional and even the doctrinaire—working out new and original solutions to the problems of the handicapped which the advanced countries might study with considerable profit.

This is not to say that these advanced countries have nothing to teach the developing ones. They have indeed and it is good to see that both individual advanced countries and the international organisations, inter-governmental and non-governmental, are accepting a moral obligation to share knowledge and material resources with the less fortunate lands. But it is important to realise that more can come from this than international goodwill; if they are willing to learn as well as teach, the cause of the handicapped will be advanced the world over.

## APPENDIX 2

# The Handicapped Child and the Law

This book would be incomplete without some brief notes on the law as it exists to help and protect the handicapped child. Legislation varies from country to country and I propose here to deal mainly with the law as it stands in Britain.

The Education Act of 1944, which governs education in Britain, makes it the duty of every parent to provide education for his child suited to the child's age, ability and aptitude. If the child is attending a school provided by the local education authority or recognized by the Ministry of Education it is assumed that the duty is being fulfilled. If the child is not attending such a school, public or private, the parent must be able to prove, if necessary to the satisfaction of a court of law, that he is receiving proper education at home or elsewhere. This duty does not normally apply when the child is under five or over fifteen; its effect in practice is to make school attendance compulsory between those ages unless the circumstances are very exceptional.

The Act also requires the Education Authority to seek out children who, by reason of handicap, are not suitable for education in ordinary schools and to take steps to see that they receive appropriate education in school or elsewhere. It may do this by providing its own special schools, by sending children to schools provided by other Authorities, by sending them to schools provided by independent bodies or by arranging home tuition.

Education in public day schools is free. When an Education Authority provides boarding schools for normal children, tuition is free but a charge for residence may be made according to the parents' means. Independent boarding schools for normal children charge fees for both tuition and residence; in certain circumstances the Education Authority may pay part or all of the tuition or boarding fee, according to the parents' means. Independent day schools charge fees for tuition and, again, an Education Authority may in certain circumstances pay part or all of the fee.

The handicapped child, however, is entitled to receive suitable education without cost to the parents. If, therefore, it is considered necessary on grounds of handicap for a child to attend an independent special day or boarding school, or a local authority special boarding school, the Education Authority pays the whole of both the tuition and boarding fees. This provision also applies when, as sometimes happens, it is considered necessary, because of handicap or other medical grounds, for a child to attend an ordinary boarding school.

Technically, before a handicapped child can be admitted to a special school he should be formally 'ascertained' as handicapped, a procedure particularly required in respect of mentally handicapped children, whose ascertainment must be carried out by a medical officer specially trained in the examination of mentally handicapped children. In practice more and more children are being admitted to special schools informally and the examination is becoming much more of a general assessment. Though the examination must be done by a medical officer of the authority, he is expected to take into account any pertinent information from any source, including reports from hospitals and other doctors, reports from special clinics and reports from the child's teachers (if he has been attending school). The prudent medical officer is usually at pains to seek out such information and, where necessary, to refer the child for specialist examination and investigation of various kinds.

Though the medical officer examines the child and makes recommendations for his special education, he is, in the eyes of the law, only the adviser to the Education Authority, whose lay officers and members are not compelled to take his advice. It is, therefore, important that his advice should be soundly based, detailed and explicit. It is no less important that he should be at pains to cultivate a relationship of confidence with his lay colleagues, so that his advice is respected and they are ready to discuss with him any points of doubt. This is of particular value in the selection of the right special school for the child.

The Department of Education and Science has so far retained the categorization of special schools and of disabilities, but this has been done for administrative convenience only. The increased prevalence of multiple disabilities has been taken fully into account in practice and the number of schools which restrict admissions to children suffering from only one disability is very small indeed.

Classification of schools is on the basis of the principal type of disability for which provision is made and the classification of children at ascertainment takes into account the dominant disability or the disability which requires the most urgent or specialized care. The selection of the most appropriate school within a particular category for any given child requires current knowledge of the provision which individual schools are making. It follows that both the medical officer and the non-medical members of the team must be at pains to know the characteristics of schools. In cases presenting doubt or difficulty, direct consultation with the school and, desirably, an 'assessment visit' by the child to the school, should be part of the ascertainment process. It is also worth emphasizing again that when an approach is made to a school for the admission of a child the school should be provided with the fullest possible information on the child's history, present condition and family and social background.

Compulsory school age for the normal child is at present, as I have said, from five years to fifteen. For the handicapped child the age of compulsory education is from two to sixteen. This is not interpreted as requiring that all handicapped children should stay at school from two to sixteen; its effect is that *where it is considered necessary* compulsion can be exercised between those ages.

The compulsory powers, however, apply only in respect of special schools and cannot be used to compel the attendance of a handicapped child at an ordinary school while he is under the age of five or over the age of fifteen. (For this purpose a special unit for handicapped children which happens to be in the premises of an ordinary school is regarded as a special school.)

In practice these powers are not often used. Provided that parents are taken into the medical officer's confidence from the start and are progressively prepared for their child's admission to a special school they usually accept it as a matter of course. Occasional refusals are, however met with, most commonly in the case of mentally handicapped children but sometimes in parents whose children are deaf, epileptic or crippled. It is always best that the parents should acquiesce in the child's special education; if they do not, then the tug-of-war between the opposing influences of home and school may do the child considerable emotional, social and even physical harm. In the vast majority of cases admission to a special school is not a matter of such urgency that weeks, months or even a year of persuasion cannot be tried. Often an experimental period in an ordinary school may convince the parent that something more is needed.

The need for compulsion will most often arise with mentally handicapped children. The reasons for this may be easily inferred from what I have said in the appropriate chapter; the critical points are usually that the child cannot hope for any worth-while education in an ordinary school and that the parents are too dull to understand the problem or to give the child the right home environment. Sometimes the intelligent parent who is worried about the 'disgrace' of his child's attending a special school for the mentally handicapped may be quite intransigeant and in the end send the child to a private school where he may or may not—most often not—receive the special education he needs, but it is difficult to convince a court of law that compulsory admission to a special school should be pressed in such a case.

Genuine urgency is most likely to arise in the case of deaf children, where a delay of a year can be disastrous in its effects. For some reason the parents of deaf children tend to be more 'difficult' than parents of some other groups of handicapped children. Persuasion is still worth trying, but if it seems unlikely to work quickly there should be no hesitation in invoking the law.

It is not very common for parents to oppose their handicapped child's remaining at school after the age of fifteen; by that time they are usually convinced that school is giving him something worth while. Occasionally the parents of a mentally handicapped child may wish to make use of his earning power when he is fifteen—this is usually unfortunate, as he is in need of the extra year to acquire a little more social maturity. It may, of course, happen in the case of any handicapped child that a particularly suitable chance of employment arises a few months before his sixteenth birthday. In such exceptional circumstances the school medical officer may re-examine the child and certify him as no longer in need of special education.

As mentioned in Chapter 18, the former legal necessity for a child to be categorised as 'unsuitable for education' before he can be admitted to a Training Centre has been eliminated, in the sense that the Education Authority is responsible for his education, whatever his need or ability, so that there is considerably more flexibility in administration. It is implicit that the educational needs of all handicapped children will be kept under continual review and that provision be changed to meet changing need.

It is also open to parents to ask for reconsideration of categorisation if they feel that there should be a review.

On reaching school leaving age, the handicapped young person may register as a disabled person under the Disabled Persons (Employment) Act of 1944. A person is eligible for registration if, on account of injury, disease or congenital deformity he is substantially handicapped in obtaining or keeping employment, or in undertaking work on his own account. Registration offers one concrete benefit. Every employer with more than twenty employees is obliged to employ a certain percentage of registered disabled people. If he has fewer than his quota he is under an obligation to fill his next vacancies with disabled persons unless he is granted a specific exemption on the grounds that no suitable disabled person is available. It follows that someone who is registered has an appreciably greater chance of entering normal industrial employment than someone who is not. Furthermore, many concerns which operate pension and similar welfare schemes and require that all entrants to their employment shall be physically sound are prepared to relax that requirement in favour of a registered disabled person.

The qualification for registration is generously interpreted and can include emotional as well as physical illness and disability. In practice, a substantial number of young people who could register do not do so. This may be due to a reluctance to admit 'in public' that they are disabled, probably combined with ignorance of what the Act means and the possible advantages of registration. It would seem desirable that those responsible for the education and the introduction to employment of the handicapped adolescent should discuss the subject fully with him and his parents, advising, on balance, in favour of registration.

Local Authorities have, under Section 29 of the National Assistance Act of 1948, enjoyed wide powers to provide help for the handicapped through their Welfare Services, though not all of them have exercised those powers with equal generosity. Under the new 'Chronic Sick and Disabled Persons Act' the powers have been extended and, indeed, the duty has been imposed on Authorities of seeking out the handicapped and making appropriate provision. The local responsibility lies with the Social Services Department, which includes the former 'Welfare' and 'Children's' Departments and has taken over some former Health Department responsibilities including mental welfare, the home help service and the provision and management of day nurseries. In addition to such wide-ranging provision for the handicapped as the organisation of home employment, the maintaining of hostels, centres and sheltered workshops, the payment of charges in homes and hostels maintained by voluntary bodies, the supply of aids for use in the home and the making of structural alterations in the homes of the handicapped, a cash allowance can now be paid for 'attendance' in the home of a child or adult whose disability makes it impossible for the family to give him the constant care he needs.

Obviously, provision of this kind will be of greater benefit to the adult disabled than to the handicapped child. At school leaving age it can offer the kind of support and supervision which has previously been given by the education and school health services and it is essential that the child's future needs should be assessed and provision planned jointly by those services and the social services department, well before he is due to leave school, so that the take-over of responsibility can go smoothly. This is specially important in the case of the child who has been in a boarding special school; the home which has been able to look after him without undue strain during comparatively short school holidays will have to face much greater stresses when he comes to live there permanently and unless the difficulties are foreseen and anticipated these stresses may be disastrous for child and family.

It has not, however, been sufficiently realised in the past that in a substantial minority of cases the 'welfare' services have something useful to offer to a child during his school years—or even in the pre-school years.

The widening of doorways and the fixing of ramps so that a wheel chair can be used in the house, the provision of handrails, the supply of adapted cutlery, specially made stools and hoists are examples of what can be done. This kind of provision can sometimes make the critical difference which enables a severely handicapped child to stay at home instead of going away to a residential school and certainly makes it easier for the parents to look after the child during holidays from a residential school. The possibilities of providing such help should certainly be explored early in all appropriate cases.

## APPENDIX 3

# Functional Assessment of Handicapped School Leavers

A system of functional assessment of handicapped school leavers is in general operation in the School Health Service in Britain. Its aim is to provide a simple means of communication by which the school medical officer may inform the appropriate persons and agencies of the principal defects of function which might impair a young person's suitability for employment or restrict the range of employments which he might attempt. It is obviously impossible for the School M.O. to have extensive knowledge of the particular requirements of employments which might be open to school leavers—though the good School M.O. will take trouble to familiarise himself with those types of work which are common in his area. It is equally impossible for the careers adviser to have more than a basic knowledge of medical terminology and its meaning. Form Y9 summarises in very general terms the School M.O.'s view on whether the school leaver has any defects or disabilities which would make it *prima facie* undesirable that he should undertake certain types of employment. Form Y10, which is used only in the case of school leavers who have substantial disability, indicates the disabilities which may be present and also indicates the extent to which these might affect function, in sufficient detail to help the careers adviser to advise on suitable employment and make a selection of jobs which might be suggested to the school leaver.

As I have emphasised more than once in the body of this book, there are many factors which cannot be precisely expressed on forms which may influence the suitability of a specific job for any given adolescent. The introductory paragraph of the 'Notes for Guidance' for School M.O.'s takes this into account and stresses that the form is by no means a substitute for detailed discussion between School M.O. and careers adviser; it is rather, if the youngster's disability is at all severe, an invitation to and a

361

basis for such a discussion. It should be noted that the date of 'nine months before the pupil leaves school' is given as the *latest* date by which Y9 should be completed. If the school health service and the employment-finding service are working to the best advantage, they will have been in consultation long before that date.

Youth Employment Service-Certificate of School Health Service

| Surname | Forenames |
|---|---|
| | |

| Address |
|---|
| |

| Date of birth | School |
|---|---|
| | |

In my opinion this pupil is NOT suitable for:-

(a)  Heavy manual work or heavy lifting ☐

(b)  work involving exposure to dust and fumes ☐

(c)  work demanding continual exposure to weather ☐

(d)  work at heights or near vehicles in action ☐

(e)  work requiring fine or accurate vision ☐

(f)  work requiring normal colour vision ☐

(g)  work with a high dermatitis hazard ☐

(h)  work requiring normal hearing ☐

(i)  work involving handling or preparation of food ☐

In my opinion this pupil is advised to wear at work:-       (a)  spectacles ☐

(b)  hearing aid ☐

Other remarks:-

Signature of School Medical Officer................................................................................

Address ............................................................................................................................

Date of examination...................................................................

4468 OM714309 150m 6/70 R.P. Ltd Gp 791

*Boy/Girl

## Medical Report on Severely Handicapped School Leaver

*This report should be completed for severely handicapped school leavers only—in other cases Form Y9 should be used.
It should be sent to the Youth Employment Officer not later than nine months before the pupil **leaves** school.*

School............................................................Local Authority.........................................................

Surname...........................................Christian or other name(s)..............................................

Address....................................................................................................................................

.................................................................................................................................................

Date of birth.....................................................................................

Diagnosis    (Main disability first)

SPEECH — *Intelligible/Intelligible with difficulty/Unintelligible

HEARING — *Normal/Partial/Deaf

HEARING AID WORN — *Yes/No

| VISION — Snellen System | | R | L |
|---|---|---|---|
| | Without glasses | | |
| | With glasses | | |

COLOUR VISION Impaired — *Yes/No

INTELLIGENCE Impaired — *Yes/No

EMOTIONAL STABILITY Impaired — *Yes/No

| SPHINCTER CONTROL — *Yes/No | | Day | Night |
|---|---|---|---|
| | Bladder | | |
| | Bowel | | |

WEARING URINAL — *Yes/No

EPILEPSY — *Major/Minor
Seizures — Frequency ...................................................................................
          *With/without warning
          *Times of occurrence — Day/Night
          *Taking anticonvulsants — Regularly/Intermittently/No

HEART Defects or disease — *Yes/No

LUNGS Defects or disease — *Yes/No

Other Defects or disease   (state)

NOTE:   Detailed information about defects or disabilities may be given under General Remarks.
*Delete as necessary
Y10

## USE OF LIMBS

Figure  1  function full or slightly impaired
        2  function substantially impaired
        3  function grossly impaired or absent

| Arms | | Hands and fingers | | Touch | Legs | |
|---|---|---|---|---|---|---|
| Range of movement | Muscle power | Co ordination | Muscle power | | Range of movement | Muscle power |
| R | | | | | | |
| L | | | | | | |

### ABILITY TO

| Walk | | Stand | Sit only | Hurry | Balance | |
|---|---|---|---|---|---|---|
| With load | Without load | | | | Static | In movement |
| | | | | | | |

| Kneel | Stoop or bend | | Push and pull | Lift and carry | Climb | |
|---|---|---|---|---|---|---|
| | Occasional | Prolonged | | | Stairs | Ladders |
| | | | | | | |

USES — *Wheelchair/walking stick/other aid

WEARS — *Calipers/Spinal jacket

FIT TO WORK — *Full-time/Part-time/Regularly

FIT TO TRAVEL TO WORK — *Yes/No

GENERAL REMARKS

Signature of School Doctor.................................................................................................... Date

---

### Statement by Parent or Guardian

I agree that this report may be sent to the Youth Employment Service. I understand that the report will be treated as confidential but that it may be disclosed to the members of a Disablement Advisory Committee, or Panel, if application is made for registration under the Disabled Persons (Employment) Acts, 1944 and 1958.

Signature.................................................... (Parent/Guardian) ............................................ Date ....

Signature.................................................... (Witness)

Address..............................................................................................................................

*Delete as necessary

581960-R88409 15M 8/68 C.P.

# FORM Y10 — NOTES FOR GUIDANCE

The precise functional assessment of a handicapped school leaver depends not only on the nature and degree of the disability but also on such factors as total personality, home background and the range of employments available. The purpose of the report form is not to make a specific assessment of fitness or otherwise for any given employment but to indicate to the Youth Employment Officer the degree and nature of functional impairment which might affect choice of employment. Direct and full consultation between the Youth Employment Officer and School Medical Officer will of course be desirable or necessary in many cases—the form should enable the Youth Employment Officer to judge when and on what points further information is needed.

**HEARING** The standard of normality is ability to hear ordinary conversation in the presence of background noise corresponding to that of an average office (including outside street noises) without the use of a hearing aid.

**VISION** Substantial defect of near vision should be noted under 'General Remarks'.

**INTELLIGENCE** 'Impaired' means the child has been classified as educationally subnormal even where there has been no formal ascertainment.

**EMOTIONAL STABILITY** 'Impaired' means the child was emotionally unstable or maladjusted on leaving school or that his history gives grounds to expect a period of instability on leaving the school environment. Marked behaviour problems should be noted under 'General Remarks'.

**ARM MOVEMENT** Relates to the total range of the movement of the limb as a whole.

**ARM MUSCLE POWER** Probably best assessed in terms of ability to lift and hold ordinary heavy objects (e.g. suit-cases or buckets of water), light objects only (e.g. books or cups) or inability to handle light objects effectively.

**HANDS AND FINGERS**

    **COORDINATION** Relates to ability to make skilled use of hands irrespective of muscle power and without regard to whether the incoordination is of nervous or muscular origin.

    **MUSCLE POWER** Relates mainly to grip and ability to exert pressure on object being handled.

**WALK WITH LOAD** Includes ability to maintain balance of load and person.

**WALK WITHOUT LOAD** Such factors as pain on walking should be taken into account.

**STANDING** Normality should be regarded as the ability to carry out work which involves substantial periods of standing.

**SIT ONLY** Relates to sedentary occupation. Details of disability should be noted under 'General Remarks'.

**BALANCE-STATIC** Relates to ability to retain position in the working attitude, whether sitting, standing or bending.

**BALANCE IN MOVEMENT** Relates to unsteadiness or clumsiness in walking and should take account of any disability which may cause difficulties in walking over an uneven floor or along a narrow gangway.

**STOOP OR BEND OCCASIONAL** Should include defects of balance which make any stooping difficult or undesirable.

**STOOP OR BEND PROLONGED** The effects of stooping or high myopia should be considered.

**PUSH AND PULL** Should be considered in terms of ability to manoeuvre such mobile objects as a truck or trolley.

**LIFT AND CARRY** Relates to ability to lift a moderately heavy object, such as a small packing case or suitcases, from the ground to a table or bench.

**CLIMB STAIRS** Normality is ability to go up and down a flight of 15 ordinary stairs at normal speed without using a handrail.

**FIT TO WORK** If part-time indicate number of hours a day.

**FIT TO TRAVEL TO WORK** If 'yes' indicate whether by public transport in rush hours or whether special transport required.

'General Remarks' should be used to indicate if regular or periodic medical treatment is required during working hours or if a prolonged course of treatment involving absence from work is planned.

581960/888409 7,500 8/68 C.P.

# Index